THE SELECTED LETTERS OF
JOHN CIARDI

THE SELECTED LETTERS OF

JOHN CIARDI

EDITED BY

EDWARD M. CIFELLI

The University of Arkansas Press
Fayetteville • London • • 1991

Manufactured in the United States of America
95 94 93 92 91 5 4 3 2 1

The paper used in this publication meets the minimum requirements of the American National Standard for Permanence of Paper for Printed Library Materials Z39.48-1984. ∞

This book was designed by Chiquita Babb using the Garamond typeface.

Library of Congress Cataloging-in-Publication Data

Ciardi, John, 1916–1986
[Correspondence. Selections]
The selected letters of John Ciardi / edited by Edward M. Cifelli.
p. cm.
Includes index.
ISBN 1-55728-171-8 (alk. paper).
1. Ciardi, John, 1916–1986 —Correspondence. 2. Poets, American—20th century—Correspondence. I. Cifelli, Edward M. II. Title.
PS3505.I27Z48 1991
811'.52—dc20
[B] 90-36333
CIP

This book is for the people
who made it possible,
the friends of John Ciardi:
*"Until our next ramble, goodbye—
and good words to you."*

Acknowledgments

It is always a great pleasure to say thank you. And for a book like this, which has depended on so many people, it is a double pleasure. First, I am especially grateful to all those who sent me copies of their John Ciardi letters, only a small portion of which, unfortunately, could be printed. I am sorry I could not include at least one letter from each one of John Ciardi's correspondents, but that proved to be impossible. However, without the cooperation of all those who sent letters, this book could not have been completed.

I am equally indebted to the Library of Congress as well as to various university libraries and historical associations which have either sent photocopies of Ciardi material in their collections or made them available to me when I visited. All of the professional staffs of the institutions given in the abbreviations list have been unfailingly able, kind, and cooperative.

I would like to acknowledge the following libraries for their contributions:

John Malcolm Brinnin papers, University of Delaware Library, Newark, DE 19717-5267.

KC: 1/3/1, President's papers, University of Missouri-Kansas City Archives.

Abernethy Library, Middlebury College.

Harry Ransom Humanities Research Center, The University of Texas at Austin.

George Dillon, Peter De Vries, Marion Strobel, and Karl Shapiro, 1936–53, and Henry Rago, 1954–61, *Poetry* Magazine papers, University of Chicago Library.

It is a pleasure, too, to thank funding agencies that have helped make this collection possible: the New Jersey Historical Commission, the National Endowment for the Humanities, and the County College of Morris Foundation.

No one has been more helpful on several levels than Miller Williams, one of John Ciardi's truest and staunchest friends and undoubtedly his most trusted poetic counselor. Williams, in fact, served as Ciardi's literary executor, and in that capacity he spent countless hours organizing the papers Ciardi left behind and preparing several posthumous books for publication. Williams' affection for John Ciardi as a man and his high regard for John Ciardi as a literary figure in mid-century America are everywhere evident. It has been the greatest of pleasures to work with him on this book.

Far and away, however, my greatest debt and thanks go to Judith Ciardi, John's capable, charming, and life-celebrating wife. She has given me open access to the papers John Ciardi left behind—and has, as a result, had me tramping about her house and John's home office more often than she bargained for. For this act of forbearance, which she somehow managed with a full display of warmth and graciousness, I shall be forever, and happily, in her debt.

There are many others to thank as well, including John Ciardi's children—John L. (and his wife, Valerie), Myra, and Benn. Also of considerable assistance has been John's sister, Ella Rubero. I am also extremely grateful for special kinds of assistance provided by many, many people, among them: X. J. Kennedy, John Bauer, Carl Prince, Kenneth Silverman, Warren Walker, Cliff Wood, Rita Licciardolo, Janett Eber, John and Nancy Williams, James Whitehead, Gil Gallagher, Irma and Nika Kachadoorian, Vince Clemente, Richard and Charlee Wilbur, Robin Rogers, John Keeler, and Kyle Poyer—who is always my right arm. Special thanks, too, go to my very able research assistants, Ray Chambers and Charlie Rubin. I would also like to thank the scores of people whom I have met and interviewed over the past two years, many of whom are represented in this book, but many others as well who are not.

Finally, I take the greatest joy in thanking my family—my patient and generous mother; my two budding scholars, Lisa Louise Cifelli and Laura Ann Cifelli, both of whom performed various and sundry services in the preparation of this book; and Bobbi, the lovely Roberta Louise, who as always has my love and thanks, not only for the word counting and proofreading and patient listening, but, what is more important, for the light-footed tap dancing that has always made coming home a pleasure.

Contents

Introduction

John Ciardi occupies an important position in the literary life of mid-century America. His reputation today is rather a complex issue largely because it is so diverse; he is known as a poet, as one of this century's premier translators of Dante's *Divine Comedy,* as poetry editor of *Saturday Review* from 1956 to 1977, as the director of the Bread Loaf Writers Conference for seventeen years, as a popular lecturer on what he liked to call the "lecher circus," as a poet for children, as an amateur etymologist with three books on the subject, even as a radio and television personality.

Further complicating the question of Ciardi's reputation today is his record of outspokenness, principally about poetry, but about other things as well. For example, as a result of a Maryland speech he made in 1949, he was accused of being a Communist in a scandal that made headlines throughout the country and tested the liberal underpinnings of Harvard, where he was then teaching. (Ciardi never knew it, but the Federal Bureau of Investigation had actually begun keeping a file on him, number 100–17136, in 1941, and continued updating it until 1969.) John Ciardi's measured defense of himself at that time appears in this book in an open letter to his accuser, Frank B. Ober (see June 1, 1949).

As John Ciardi's literary career gradually took shape, however, he drifted further and further from the sort of ideological principle that had prompted him to make political speeches in the late 1940s. As early as election day 1948, for example, he had come to regret his active campaign role in support of Henry Wallace's Progressive party bid for the White House, and in the privacy of the voting booth, he acknowledged his error and cast his ballot for Harry Truman. By the time of his Maryland speech in 1949, Ciardi had already begun to maintain a distinctly lower political profile, which, despite an occasional flare-up, he continued for the rest of his life. Of course, he could be moved now and then to heated argument over specific politicians and issues, for he was always a man of strong feelings and convictions. He opposed the American involvement in Vietnam, for example, voted loudly against Ronald Reagan, and generally supported Democratic candidates—although frequently without much enthusiasm (see February 12, 1984, and April 9, 1985). He did maintain a more or less liberal political position and occasionally spoke out in his column and elsewhere for the protection of individual freedoms, but that leaning notwithstanding, it is most accurate to say that by the last years of his life, John Ciardi had become steadfastly apolitical.

As early as 1962, Ciardi was able to articulate the reasons for his withdrawal from political forums. At that time he had been invited by Corliss Lamont to speak at a meeting of the Emergency Civil Liberties Committee in New York. He was sympathetic but determined in his new direction: "Some time ago, after a number of years of chasing around after good causes, I came to a decision in which I have by now grown confirmed: I am a writer, my work is what I do, and once I have survived the distractions of making a living, my writing gets my energy. My sympathies are with you, but to put it bluntly, they are even more with my workbook" (see September 22, 1962).

As far as poetry is concerned, however, John Ciardi's outspokenness has become almost legendary, a lifelong commitment—perhaps even a crusade—on behalf of excellence, and a simultaneous refusal to tolerate incompetent foolishness posturing as poetry. If his politics were liberal, his poetics were conservative. He was a great admirer of the free verse of William Carlos Williams, but his admiration of the traditional forms found in Robert Frost was even greater. And so he preferred Emily Dickinson to Walt Whitman—and almost anyone to the loose-limbed Beat poets.

As a young poet in the 1940s and 1950s, Ciardi had stood against the sort of esoteric erudition that had taken poetry away from the people. His sense of poetry had been formed at Tufts and at the University of Michigan, then reinforced at the Bread Loaf Writers

Conference (sponsored by Middlebury College in Vermont), which he attended for the first time in 1940. He became director in 1955 and felt himself the inheritor of a tradition that stretched back to the 1920s, a tradition that brought professional writers and editors together to help novice writers learn their craft. Increasingly in the 1960s, however, there was pressure from Middlebury College to make the conference more academic, to make it more relevant to student needs, and, in the spirit of the time, more sensitive to student feelings. John Ciardi never wanted to be irrelevant or insensitive, but he firmly believed in urging young writers to be better by maintaining high standards and demanding hard work. So John Ciardi resisted the appeals of the 1960s, out loud and with dignity, and he was consequently cornered into turning in his resignation in August 1972, effective the following year. His final letter to President James Armstrong, bitter at the politics that had hurt the conference (see August 2, 1972), is published here for the first time.

John Ciardi had set himself in the Bread Loaf debate against the self-indulgent aspects of the new wave of 1960s "relevance," at least as far as poetry was concerned, and he was branded by the students and some of their teachers as a hopelessly dated poet-teacher—an outspoken reactionary. However, with a devil-take-the-consequences attitude, Ciardi stuck by his principles and continued scolding young writers till the end (see September 26, 1985), insisting on being obsolete, as he often said, and thus he was partly but determinedly responsible for digging the hole he put his own reputation into.

Although he was a fairly well known young poet in the early 1950s, it was not until he became poetry editor of the *Saturday Review* that he became famous and infamous at the same instant. His long review of Anne Morrow Lindbergh's *The Unicorn and Other Poems* (January 12, 1957) provoked a national storm of protest against this brash poetry editor who thought more about poetry than about a lovely woman's sensibilities. The controversy was enlivened when Ciardi was taken to task by *SR*'s editor, Norman Cousins, in an editorial (February 16) that sparked further letters of denunciation as well as letters of support. Suddenly poetry was news, a fact not lost on either John Ciardi or Norman Cousins' subscription department. Published here for the first time are John Ciardi's long and measured letters of angry protest written to Norman Cousins from Italy (where Ciardi was spending a year translating Dante at the American Academy in Rome), letters that established the uneasy terms of the delicate truce they lived by for some twenty years thereafter.

There are other particular letters with a documentary significance for those who are piecing together a literary history of the twentieth century, but Ciardi's letters are also illuminating and important for two other reasons. First, they constitute a running and colorful record of the poet's life from age nineteen till his death at age sixty-nine. Second, they provide a new format for us to experience the words and wit of John Ciardi. Clearly ours is not an age of great letters, so it is especially satisfying to be with a master writer, at ease with ideas and words and people, over some fifty years of personal correspondence.

To show John Ciardi's growth and development as a man and poet, I have organized this book into three parts. Part One, "Footholds," shows Ciardi as a young poet making his place in the world. In one of his earliest surviving letters, the second one in the book (October 27, 1937), for example, he writes to Theodore Roethke for help with some poems he was working on. In this section we see John Ciardi in graduate school at the University of Michigan and in correspondence with one of his oldest friends, John Malcolm Brinnin; we see him as poetry editor of the University of Kansas City *Review* and as the young author of *Homeward to America,* which he published in 1940 and disowned in 1942 (see June 4, 1942). We see him in regular correspondence with the editors of *Poetry* throughout the war years and with Clarence Decker, president of the University of Kansas City, who had given Ciardi his first job as a teacher. Throughout this period he was earning his credentials as a poet, as a translator, as a professor, as an editor, and as an executive with Twayne Publishers.

Part Two, "Eye of the Storm," begins with Ciardi's appointment at Rutgers University and is framed by the two greatest controversies of his life, over Anne Morrow Lindbergh at the outset and over Bread Loaf at the end. It is during this period that John Ciardi became a celebrity—partly through his own books of course, but largely as well through his work at *Saturday Review,* at Bread Loaf, on lecture platforms all over the country, and on network television. He resigned his professorship at Rutgers University (see November 4, 1959) two years short of being vested in the pension plan and followed poetry to fame and considerable fortune.

By 1972 the storms had passed. Bread Loaf was over, and *Saturday Review* was winding down to a quiet conclusion. Without his national platforms Ciardi found his call to local platforms to be diminishing. Very gradually he slipped into the security of his own study, speaking often enough to keep body and soul and his home in Metuchen, New Jersey, together, but less frequently than he had during his heyday. He may have felt deflated by a sense of having been defeated at Bread Loaf; it may simply have been that he preferred to live now in the measured boundaries of his work and memories—being "insistently obsolete." For whatever reason, he drifted into a world he would never have earlier predicted for himself, the world of etymologies.

Part Three of this book contains letters from his last fourteen years, a time largely taken up with what he came to call "felonious footnotery." This was not an altogether happy time for John Ciardi. His health was failing, his reputation as a poet was in decline, and toward the end his familiar refrain was a not-very-convincing, "I have no complaints" (see May 23, 1984, and *passim*). But although the time may have been out of joint for him, the letters from this period are among his best—warmly personal, surprisingly diverse, frequently humorous, and deeply moving. Increasingly, we hear the voice of a tired man, older than his actual years, a man who was consciously getting ready to die.

A Note on the Text

Most of John Ciardi's letters represented here are complete, but others have been edited down for particular reasons. Some, for example, repeat the same information (sometimes in the same exact language) as another letter in the book. A great many have detailed paragraphs tracking his long-range itinerary from lecture date to lecture date around the country, information hardly worth reproducing. And many letters quite naturally contain unclear references to earlier correspondence that is not included here and that therefore required either a great deal of interlinear commentary by me, or pruning. I selected pruning in order to keep my own voice out of the narrative as much as possible. My main editorial principle, in fact, was to keep out of the way and let John Ciardi tell his own story in his own way, which also explains the scarcity of footnotes and most other types of scholarly intrusion.

To indicate material missing from the letters, I use a system of ellipsis points: three to signify missing words, four to show missing sentences or a single paragraph, and five to indicate the omission of two or more paragraphs. When the missing material appears at the beginning of a letter, the ellipsis points appear before the first word of the first sentence. Any postscript that deals with the letter proper has been included as written; irrelevant additions have been silently dropped.

Careless misspellings and obvious typographical errors have been corrected—"know" for "now" or "hear" for "here." Ciardi rarely made errors in punctuation, but what few there are have been silently corrected in the interest of smooth reading. One of my aims has been to edit the letters without losing any of John Ciardi's rhythms, but I'm afraid that proved to be more of a job than I could wholly accomplish, and there may be an occasional ungainly shift in pace or tone.

Despite my occasional editorial presence, however, silent or otherwise, the letters appear here as they were written, with a full measure of the exuberance and passion and humor and incisiveness of John Ciardi.

In order to save space and simplify procedures, letter openings have been made uniform. Thus each letter is preceded by information that identifies the person receiving the letter, where Ciardi was when he wrote it, the date when it was written, and a bracketed abbreviation to show where the letter is now. Most often the initials of the person receiving the letter appear in the brackets, but when libraries now own the letters, they are identified according to a system of abbreviations listed at the end of this note. Inside addresses (when Ciardi used them) have been left out unless they contribute something to a reader's understanding of a particular letter. Similarly, Ciardi's various letterheads are not noted: for the most part he used whatever paper was handy, sometimes from a spiral notebook, sometimes from Twayne Publishers, sometimes from *Saturday Review,* sometimes from Bread Loaf, sometimes from a hotel on his travels, and so on. Occasionally, when it was not entirely clear where Ciardi was when he wrote a particular letter, I have put the city in brackets.

It should be noted that I worked mostly from photocopies of letters supplied by the various correspondents themselves, and that while Ciardi enjoyed writing with a pen and paper, the letters are about evenly distributed between those handwritten and those typewritten. Most libraries sent copies of the letters kept in their archives, but for various reasons I found it necessary to see for myself the material housed at the Library of Congress, Boston University, and Middlebury College. Many of the letters are from Ciardi's own file copies, stored for years in file cabinets, in desk drawers, and in cardboard boxes stuck under the attic eaves of his home office in Metuchen, New Jersey.

Altogether, I examined some ten thousand letters by and to John Ciardi in the process of putting this book together, but still there are unfortunate omissions. Ciardi's letters to John Holmes and Bill Sloan and Fletcher Pratt have not surfaced in any great numbers. His letters to Virginia Johnson before and during World War II are in the hands of her family and may not be read at this time under terms of her will.

And despite my greatest efforts to locate correspondents, many are no doubt unaware that this search has been going on and that this book has been published. I must assume as well that some correspondents preferred to keep silent. Unfortunately, too, there are very few letters from Ciardi to his mother and sisters, although a few of these are scattered through the book. Most unfortunate, from one point of view, is that Ciardi wrote very rarely to his wife and children, preferring instead to telephone from his various stops along the lecture circuit.

Identifications of the ninety-five correspondents represented in this book appear alphabetically at the end, a system that will simplify matters for most readers and keep the text from being thickened with explanatory footnotes.

Abbreviations

BU	Boston University
DC	Dartmouth College
FC	John Ciardi's File Copy
IU	Indiana University
KSU	Kansas State University
LC	Library of Congress
MC	Middlebury College
MHC	Historical Library, University of Michigan
SU	Syracuse University
TU	Tufts University
UC	University of Chicago
UD	University of Delaware
UMA	University of Massachusetts-Amherst
UMKC	University of Missouri-Kansas City
UML	University of Michigan Library
UNH	University of New Hampshire
UT	University of Texas
UW	University of Washington

PART ONE

Footholds

May 25, 1935, to December 23, 1953

"My special concern is for the reader of poetry: I cannot escape a feeling that the poets must face the responsibility of providing themselves with a wider audience."

To Karl Shapiro, April 29, 1949

1916. Born John Anthony Ciardi, Boston.

1919. Father died in an automobile accident.

1921. Family moved to Medford, seven miles from Boston.

1933. Graduated Medford High School.

1934. Entered Bates College.

1936. Transferred to Tufts.

1938. Graduated Tufts, B.A., magna cum laude and Phi Beta Kappa.

1939. University of Michigan, M.A., winner of Avery Hopwood Award in poetry, $1200.

1940. *Homeward to America,* first book of poems.

Invited to Bread Loaf Writers Conference.

Began at University of Kansas City as instructor of English.

1942–45. Entered Army Air Corps and became a B-29 gunner on Saipan. Received Air Medal and Oak Leaf Cluster.

1943. Oscar Blumenthal Prize, *Poetry.*

1944. Eunice Tietjens Memorial Prize, *Poetry.*

1946. Returned to the University of Kansas City, spring semester.

Married Myra Judith Hostetter, July 28.

Levinson Prize, *Poetry.*

Began a seven-year association at Harvard as a Briggs-Copeland Instructor of English.

1947. *Other Skies,* poems.

Joined staff of Bread Loaf Writers Conference and returned every year through 1972.

1948. Campaigned for the Progressive party presidential candidacy of Henry Wallace.

1949. *Live Another Day,* poems.

Became poetry editor at Twayne Publishers.

1950. *Mid-Century American Poets,* editor.

1950–51. On leave from Harvard.

Lectured on poetry at Salzburg seminar on American Studies.

1952. Daughter, Myra Judith, born, March 19.

1953. Son John Lyle Pritchett born, May 2.

Began teaching at Rutgers University.

TO ELLA (CIARDI) RUBERO*

Lewiston, Maine
May 25, 1935 [postmark]
[ER]

Dear Ella[,]

Just a brief few lines in answer to your letter. I won't be able to say very much because at the present time the campaign is going on for the mayorality of Bates College and within an hour I must have written a speech for hizzoner Willard W. Whitcomb candidate from the Freshman Class for the highly coveted position of Mayor of BATES.

This business of electing a mayor is considered the biggest joke of the school year. Invariably the most farcical boobs hereabouts are chosen to run for Mayor. Then follows a week of furious campaigning wherein everything and everybody in school is raked over the coals. After that the mayor is elected, throws in the first ball at a baseball game, fires the starting shot at some track meet and goes out of office—a grand time being had by all.

That does not alter for one moment the fact that I still have to write that blessed speech. So to business. My last examination comes Saturday afternoon June 9 so if you come up for the 9–10 everything will be hunky-dory and you will have the honor of taking me home.

Tell Sonny to go ahead with his plans for the store. I'll be there with bells on. Anything that spells money goes. Tell him that as long as there are a couple of bucks in it he doesn't have to ask questions—just tell me what to do and when I can see the green of the dollar I'm off. (Don't tell anybody I'm off though, will you? I want to keep it a secret.)

Thank you for your clipping. I take it you know what I mean now. As a matter of fact if I did take up writing I would stick more or less consistently to poetry. There is more money there, but still I don't see where sables and diamonds for baby are coming from even there. It's a fine hobby though and I hope to keep it up this summer etc.

"Arrowsmith" will be sent down to you as soon as I get enough ambition to send the laundry home. Don't you think something might be done about a job at the cemetery? There's a fine chance to make a little dough there. Has Sonny any definite plans for the summer? I've got to have darn close to $300 you know. In fact I think I'll need more than $300.

And by the way, when you come up don't forget that the trunk will fill the rumbler on the return trip—know what I mean? Why don't you get another car and make it a family excursion.

So with lots of love I close with a slightly different sentiment than you expressed in your quotation.

"You know my friends how long since in my House
For a new marriage I did make carouse
Divorced old barren reason my bed
And took the daughter of the vine to Spouse."

Love to all—John

P.S. Got mother's letter too.

*For a brief identification of each correspondent, see Correspondents at the end of the text.

TO THEODORE ROETHKE

Medford
October 27, 1937
[UW]

Dear Ted,

If you'll pardon the glaring ink (which I'm forced to borrow) and the stationary (which is probably misspelled but is all I have in any case) I'd like to write you a letter.

God knows how it (the letter) will end up but more than anything else I'd like to get your slant on one thing & another. What I'm thinking at this point is that your stuff as I see it puts you in entirely another tradition, school, predicament or what have you from mine. For that reason I'd like very much to get your point of view since it's bound to be different from my own. John Holmes is a swell incentive to me but I'm afraid he's too kind to say "putrid" once in a while. I suspect that fundamentally we lean in the same direction anyhow (though I admit I'm too blatant to fall entirely into the N[ew] E[ngland] scene) and that leaning into the same pool we're apt to get the same reflections. Do you think you could consult your particular oracle and tell me in so many words what the hell is the matter with the stuff I enclose? (Just so you needn't feel alone in hanging the crepe, I've already collected a couple of rejection slips on it within two weeks—The *N.Y.'er* sent it back in three days and the *Atlantic* in 5 and that I claim is fast.)

Anyhow, please don't be "kind." If you'd like to drop me a line about them, I'd really appreciate as much harshness as they deserve—I mean it. Drop me a line anyhow. I'll be glad to hear from you.

Incidentally have you seen John Gould Fletcher's latest kennel assortment in the *New Republic*? You probably have, but I'd like to have it down in black & white (or green and yellow) that if that's poetry I'm going to take up something else—something with a lot of dynamite in it, like judging beauty contests, or cooking school management.

I might as well confess here that the only reason I cite Mr. Fletcher is that I want it as straight as that about the stuff I'm sending.

Frankly I can't think of much else to say except that exams start for me tomorrow (and with a bang). That I hope speaks for itself.

Thanks for inviting me to write this letter. You've got to admit you brought it on yourself.

John Ciardi

TO THEODORE ROETHKE

Medford
August 26, 1938
[UW]

Dear Roethke,

Your letter, which I was very glad to receive, was forwarded to me yesterday morning. Thanks tremendously for your criticisms of "Humphrey"; they are wise, tactful and just what I need. I certainly would like to talk it over with you sometime. Perhaps an opportunity *will* come for you to let me bore you with it.

I suppose the wisest thing for me to do would be to put "Humphrey" definitely aside, but I can't bring myself to it. I've rewritten it a couple of times since the draft of it you saw but it isn't much improved and only a couple of dozen lines shorter. I want eventually to cut it to at least half its present length, or nearly that.

I'm afraid I've got to disagree with you about the name. This is sheer mysticism but it was the name that brought on the poem. Humphrey—it seems to have a rumbling, bewildered clumsiness in itself—yet to be something large—hulking, I guess, is the word I want. As I said, that's sheer mysticism.

If ever I get it rewritten to something approaching what I want, will you let me inflict it on you again? I'm delighted to have your comments at hand before tackling another revision.

You surprise me by what you say of taking myself too seriously. Well, I suppose I do take some things a bit too seriously, but actually I think the impression is due to the poems you've happened to see. Hell, we get to know so little about ourselves and what we are that an outside eye quite possibly registers more truly than our own. I assure you though that whatever I do take seriously it isn't myself. How can a man get up in the morning needing a shave and a half ton of food and take himself to be Prometheus? (And later Prometheus Unbound.)

I'm just playing around with this because it interests me. I know I'm considerable of an introvert and I enjoy mulling over things like this. Which may be proof that I do take myself too seriously. Well.

I'm sending along a few short poems out of this month's work book that you may (or may not) consider worth reading. They're all experimental, or practically all. I have a fundamental conviction that a poem should dictate its own pattern, which is not a great discovery, but I've been fooling around trying to let each poem make its own form.

It's probably too early to count results. (I've only been trying it consciously for a couple of months). The disadvantages of carrying the idea out, I suppose, would concentrate on about one point: the poems might become so widely diverse that they might grow unified. Certain things I'm trying for within the form, however (mostly variation of line & conversational stress in some cases, maximum compression in others), I think will, if done correctly & wisely, serve that purpose.

I dislike this technical jargon. It smells of leprosy. Please forgive it.

I'm leaving for Ann Arbor the 12th of Sept. Let me take it upon myself to write you again from there (to Pennsylvania I assume) and send you my address. I'd like very much to hear from you again.

Thanks a lot for suggesting people to know at Michigan. I certainly will look them up.

John Ciardi

TO THEODORE ROETHKE

Ann Arbor

January 25, 1939

[UW]

Dear Roethke,

It was good to hear from you again. I'm sorry you weren't able to stop off in Ann Arbor, but as a matter of fact I suspected at the time of writing that my note would be too late to interrupt your hegira from Saginaw.

An ex-room-mate of mine, Roger Fredland, is on the teaching staff of the English Dept. there at Penn. State. Have you met him? I think you'd enjoy looking him up if you haven't: he has a good head and is damn good company.

Your issue of *Poetry* arrived yesterday and I've re-read the poems several times. Damn nice work I think on the first six, but I think too the seventh lets you down. I suppose I'm about to stick my head into the noose and start criticking. Forgive me—I'm a critic-aster at heart.

Actually I've nothing very intelligent to say, I'm afraid. The poems are good, damn good. Mr. Dillon and I (and you of course) are 6/7ths. agreed. The other 1/7th. however could be reconsidered, I think. "The lips that never move" is the only specific touch I can discover in it, and that a *very* swell image. Why don't you do more of that in the poem? Love—old—young—waste—wrong—human—brute—mimic—gross—slow degrees—loss—small wit—belief —simple act—heritage of life—secrecy—heart—("fervency of eye" is not bad)—impulse—hatred—pride—love—summon—force—breadth to length—human strength—all are less vivid than they could be I think. [Especially] when put up alongside such marvelous lines as:

Though the devouring mother cry, "Escape me? Never—"
And the honeymoon be spoiled by a father's ghost,
Chill depths of the spirit are flushed to a fever,
The nightmare silence is broken, and we are not lost.

Against those (Somehow the echo of Browning is just perfect there—it just doubles the value of "devouring") I think the last four lines of the *Summons* (z.B. for a typical piece of the poem) fall flat.

Now we must summon all
Our force from breadth to length,
And walk, more vertical,
Secure in human strength.

Forgive me for saying so in that many words but I think those are bad lines: too flatly moralistic and naif I think. Certainly undramatic. Reminiscent even of (forgive me) Wordsworth.

Which I never would have dared say if you hadn't written six damn good poems before that one.

That of course is only personal opinion, and you have George Dillon on your side, and who am I? Dramatic detail is essential to good poetry though. Your other poems have it: this one I think misses it. Maybe I'm wrong.

Aside from that piece I have only praise. I like your epigrammatic quality, especially since it does not become too perfect. A hard and finished poem is a joy forever, an over finished poem buckles with time. "The Pause," with its definite end-stop in every line threatens to grow over-finished but I think it saves itself. I can't really tell until I've re-read the poem several times, at intervals, but it stands well now under fourth or fifth reading. None of the others leave any doubts: they seem sure and delicate. You have a nice (not slang this time) lyric sense in a form that is thoroughly closed. I mean you seem to like the discipline of a tight, strict form. Why don't you experiment a bit with less firmly shut cadences? You seem to have done everything that one possibly can with those you use: there don't seem to be many fields left to conquer here. Well . . .

Mid-years are coming up and I, I fear, am going down. Do you know Reinhard? He's a bastard. Do you know Rice? He knows too much. And I have courses under both of them and will have next semester. Thank god for Cowden, he's sometimes unexciting but he has enough good faults to at least keep me awake. How the hell is a man expected to stay interested in what a prof. says if he never makes a mistake? It's bad for the ego. Once and once only in the whole semester has Reinhard come through with an atom of misinformation. Rice never will. Oh well, I may get a degree for it. I certainly acquire no education. (In class.) Do you know any one who wants to hire a rising (?) young poet to instruct kids in things next year? Said poet will have an M.A. from Michigan he hopes and hasn't yet given up the fond fancy that father Hopwood* will be kind. Best of recommendations available. Warm personality. Loves children—at a distance.

I'm really beginning to worry about what will go on after I get through this place. Cowden is very kind and is doing all he can, but

Rice tells me I'll have to get a Ph.D. before Michigan will get me a college-job, and I *won't* get a Ph.D., and I *won't* teach high school, so it seems I have to find a job for myself. John [Holmes] suggests you might know of something somewhere. Any suggestions you can make will be more than valuable: they'll be life lines.

I'm enclosing a half-dozen recent poems. I'd like very much to know what you think of them. Forgive the rambling lollop of this letter—I've never learned to think into a typewriter—my fingers take all my energy and my mind goes blank.

Cordially—
John Ciardi

*A reference to the annual Hopwood prize in poetry at the University of Michigan, which carries a cash award. Ciardi did indeed win the competition in 1939, worth $1,200.

TO THE CIARDI FAMILY

Ann Arbor
March 8, 1939
[Ella (Ciardi) Rubero]

Dear Family:

Your "stationery" arrived in good condition. If this letter has grease stains on it you can blame your self: my fingers are still sticky from it.

And my mouth is full of chicken, tonacelle, cookies and coffee all at once. I've just gotten through giving a party and everybody in the house is patting his stomach. (But there's no chicken in it—I held out on that.)

Thanks a million Mum even though I expect to have a stomach ache for the next week!

I've just found out the date of the radio program: Tues. March 14, at 2:30 over WJR, Detroit. If you can pick it up it will be swell, but don't go to much bother because it will probably be a flop: the prof.

who's conducting is an antique moron and I expect him to gum up the works. Well.

I had lunch with one of my profs. yesterday (Prof. Norman Nelson who once taught John Holmes back at Tufts). He's a swell guy and I've gotten to know him rather well and to like him a lot.

Well we had lunch yesterday (rather the day before yesterday) and I asked him how chances were of my getting a teaching fellowship here at the U. of M. if I decided to go after my Ph.D. after all. (Ph.D.—Doctor of Philosophy, the degree above Master's and the highest degree given.) He tells me I stand an almost sure chance: as sure that is as anything can be.

So if nothing else turns up I can be assured of something next year. No great thing as far as salary goes: they range from $300 to $1000 a year depending on how many classes you teach, but it's good experience and I can probably get my Ph.D. in about three years.

I really don't want to spend that much time here, but if you want really to do anything in the academic world you've got to have a Ph.D. to start with it seems. It's anyway a last resort.

Well, then I asked him what else I could do, and he suggested I apply for an international exchange scholarship to the Sorbonne in Paris. He thinks chances are pretty good there, and he's investigating it for me now.

In the meantime I have applications out for teaching jobs and eventually will begin to hear from them. All in all things look pretty good and I'm especially hoping that Paris business comes through. La belle France!!! tra-la.

One of my ex-roommates at Bates—Lew Revey—has turned up in the mail. He's now at the University of Budapest studying history. Fredland is teaching at the University of Pennsylvania, and the other one (there were four you remember) is, as I understand it, a professor of the dance at Arthur Murray's Academy in New York. That makes the count complete: one Hungarian historian, one Quaker instructor, one jitter-bug, and one unclassified radical.

The first papers have come in for me to correct in this modern novel course, and I'm up to my ears in bad attempts to explain Zola's novel, *Germinal,* so forgive me if I sign off here and get some of this accumulated drivel out of the way.

Thanks a million more for the materials for this stomach ache I have coming up: if it does come I look forward to the most enjoyable good old fashioned belly-ache I've ever had.

Love and greasy kisses from me and the chicken to one and all.

And more love and more greasy kisses to Mom.

And love to the gang. I'll be seeing you in April, but I want a lot of letters between now and then so get busy.

Love
John

TO THEODORE ROETHKE

Ann Arbor
July 5, 1939
[UW]

Dear Roethke,

Thanks for your letter of June 24, which incidentally was one of my birthdays—they come pretty regularly. I left home the 23rd, however, and forwarding took a lot of time so that I just got it today.

I'm back in Ann Arbor for the summer session: I'll take my M.A. in August and then begin to worry about what then. Sorry as hell I didn't see you when you were in AA. How far is it from here to Saginaw? I bought myself a somewhat battered model A which took me to Boston and back: maybe I could cut up to Saginaw some morning and waste one of your afternoons.

Thanks for congratulations, though I'm not sure there's a whole lot to congratulate about. The money of course was most welcome, among other things lifting me clean out of debt for the first time in many years—but I'm not at all sure that I've done more than raise a golden splash in a very small puddle. I'm working nights now—or have delayed working—on revision & retyping etc. Holt's wants to see the thing & I've promised a ms. by the end of July. When & if it gets published it will have a clean chance to stand or fall outside of the closed circle of Hopwood competition. The results will anyhow be interesting to watch.

Any interest you take in its fate—proprietary or otherwise—is nothing if not O.K. by me (litotes). I'd like to send you the ms. later in the summer, when it's more or less revised and get your reaction. Do you think you could stand it? . . . . .

Cordially
John Ciardi

TO HIS MOTHER AND SISTERS

Ann Arbor
July 20, 1939
[Ella (Ciardi) Rubero]

Dearly beloved:

What's a matter—long time you no write? Am I being double crossed for some other guy? Such is life. Absence makes the heart grow fonder—for somebody else.

I warn you dearly beloved that hereafter I shall speak only when spoken to as all good children are supposed to be expected to do.

I've been snowed under a heap of work since I got to Ann Arbor, but little by bit it unravels. I finished the manuscript of the book today and will send it to the publishers tomorrow. If they take it as I hope they will it should appear off the presses in January or February. Right now I've got to buckle down to work and get past due work cleaned up and keep abreast of what comes up. Among other things I have papers to write and will need another book from home. Will you dig my copy of the *Divina Commedia* out of the closet and send it to me? Poor Dante should not be kept on closet shelves. It's a very fat green book and I don't know on which part of the shelf you'll find it but it's in there somewhere. I hope it's not on the back row and on the bottom.

How is Silver Lake? Are you still seriously considering a cottage in Wilmington? Keep thinking about it a long time before you do anything will you? There may be unforeseen undesirables involved. If I remember rightly there's a swamp nearby—investigate the mosquitoes before you spend any money. Also what are you going to do for water, both to drink and to swim in?—You'll probably find neither one available. Well.

Above all find out how much of a vacation you're likely to get out of a cottage in Wilmington. If you go off and build a shack which only means more work and no comfort and all in the name of having a place to take a vacation you're nuts. One of the things people are supposed to get on vacations is a rest. Keeping a shack out in the woods in order and fighting for your life with mosquitoes is no way to get rested.

Gee what a long letter I find myself writing! I don't really think you deserve it, but then I've got to do something to cover the fact that I wouldn't have started it if it wasn't for the book I wanted.

Book or no book however I want to say Happy Birthday again to Edith [his sister]. I grow old, I grow old, I shall wear the bottoms of my trousers rolled, for Mrs. Ciardi and her daughter wash their feet in soda water, they grow old they grow old, they shall wear the bottoms of their petticoats rolled. Another year another wrinkle. Ain't it hell to feel age creeping up your back, kid? One less year to live. Horrible ain't it? Just think—pretty soon we'll all be dead. I certainly don't want to be morbid about all this but how do you think it will feel when the worms start biting? Just think, one year less to wait before you find out. Well, anyhow kid, Happy Birthday and you don't look a day over 42, and I'll bet you've got another good ten years in you, I bet. Well, maybe less than that, but five anyhow. And anyhow, Happy Birthday.

I just thought I'd throw that in to cheer you up, because I want you to be very happy on your birthday. You know I can just imagine how you feel: as I write this letter you're only 39 years old and by the time you get it you will have crossed the fatal forties. What a step that must be in your life: never again the bloom of youth, rheumatism in your shin bones, wrinkles on your forehead, gray hairs, white hairs, no hair and pretty soon clunk, clunk, clunk up the back stairs comes the old man with the white beard and—BOOM! Well, anyhow, Happy Birthday, kid.

And to the incidental sisters—Cora and Ella, my love.

And to those two stinky old smelly good for nothing spoiled (pew!) brats—phooey.

And to my dear Mother, Mrs. Concetta Ciardi, née DeBenedictus, my love, my affection, my esteem, my kisses and best wishes.

And to one and all—Good night, and please get Mr. Dante Alighieri into Mr. Farley's hands for me.

Love and kisses children and Pax vobiscum, in saecula saeculorum carbarundum tuxedo encyclopedia brittanica amen.

John

Don't send it Special Delivery—just regular and ask for a *book rate* when mailing.

TO GEORGE DILLON

Ann Arbor

July 27, 1939

[UC]

Mr. George Dillon
Poetry, A Magazine of Verse
232 East Erie Street
Chicago, Illinois

Dear Mr. Dillon,

Thank you for your letter of July 25. I am very happy of course to have a poem accepted by *Poetry.*

My "autobiography," such as it is, follows:

Born in Boston, June 1916. Family moved to
Medford, Massachusetts, shortly thereafter.
Graduated Medford High School in 1933
and went to Bates College, Lewiston, Me.,
after staying out of school a year. Transferred

from Bates to Tufts College in the middle
of my sophomore year. Graduated in June 1938
and came to the University of Michigan
where I now am. I am taking an M.A. in
English next month. Won $1200 in the
Avery Hopwood and Jules Hopwood Awards with
a volume of poems. The poem which you have
accepted is the first any magazine outside
of college journals has accepted.

I hope that will meet all specifications, but if there are any further questions I shall be very happy to answer them.

Sincerely
John Ciardi

TO THEODORE ROETHKE

Ann Arbor
August 4, 1939
[UW]

Dear Roethke,

Forgive me for not answering sooner than this. I've been trying to figure out a free weekend ahead and see lots of difficulty in finding one. Three courses and an assistantship for one summer session keep me pretty close to Ann Arbor, nose to whetstone and so forth.

Sorry to hear your mother has been ill. I truly hope this finds her better. It's much too nice a summer to spend in bed.

I want very much to run up some time before the end of school. Right now I'm in the midst of two papers anent the lower drippings of American Lit.: one on Michael Wigglesworth and one on John Pendleton Kennedy both of whom should have died young. Somehow or other I'll find time however and call you a day or so before. My phone number is 2–1152 but it's practically useless to call me: I'm home from 12:30 A.M. to 8:00 A.M. usually and not always then and very rarely at any other time. I've got the manuscript for Holt ready and sent away and am now waiting for word (Yes or No).

At the moment I'm celebrating my first acceptance: *Poetry* took a middle-sized poem which I'm enclosing with this. It wasn't in the Hopwood ms. I wrote it a month or so after the contest closed.

Forgive me for this letter which is banged out in frenzy and tumult between a dozen other things and write soon. Hope to see you by the end of the month, for if not then it will probably be a long time.

Yours,
Ciardi

TO JOHN MALCOLM BRINNIN

Medford
October 24, 1939
[UD]

Dear John,

I've owed you a letter for so long that it's too late for apologies even, so forgive me for not rendering any.

I've been having a pretty busy and pretty productive three weeks or so since I came home: a number of new poems, a lot of reading, and a lot of necessary general organizing and reorganizing.

I have just read [and re]turned the galley sheets of the book to Holt's along with a proof of the poem *Poetry* took. Obviously they intend to run it soon or fairly soon to get it out before the book which is due January 17.

I've placed yours and Kimon's names on the list for advance copies which Sloane (Holt's trade manager) asked for. Do you think Kimon [Friar] will receive his? All the address I could give was Eng. Grad. School, Univ. of Iowa, Iowa City.

That about includes all the news except a lot of good, interesting and amusing letters for Holt about one thing and another. Have you seen Holmes' new book of light verse? It's really something. Whatever deficiencies he has as a serious poet, he very definitely has the touch for light verse.

Sloane sent me a copy from New York as a sort of gratuity and I presented it to Holmes for autographing asking for something "very intimate, and very witty please, Mr. Holmes," and by god he rose to the occasion like a professional master of ceremonies. Plucked out his fountain pen and wrote:

John from John
this uninhibited antidote
from one pote to another pote
all of which I really wrote.

. . . In a way I'm definitely sorry the book is so good of its kind, because the ability to do it seems to stem out of the weaknesses of his serious stuff or vice versa. But it's not as simple as that: he sometimes surprises me with something that really lifts such as the one that appeared in last month's *Atlantic* (or was it the month before) viz. "Evening Meal in the Twentieth Century," which is really a good poem from any angle. I'm afraid it's the farthest limit he can break out to however and it's not exactly a stopping place. Well. . . .

Has there been any reaction to [Socialist Earl] Browder's arrest in Ann Arbor? Which seems a dumb question. Let me put it this way: What reaction was there to Browder's arrest?

I've gotten some of the news about things from Virginia Johnson up to a while ago, but at present am befogged and ignorant awaiting the next materializing mail.

I'm sending along copies of some poems for your expert eye. What do you think? And please let me see some of yours. And I might add please don't wait quite as long to answer as it has taken me to get this letter off.

John

TO JOHN MALCOLM BRINNIN

Medford

December 26, 1939

[UD]

Dear John,

For such another Christmas card I should be thoroughly content to wait as long again for a reply, though, be it understood, I do not urge it.

I'm glad you like the book. I'm really almost visibly thrilled with the job Holt's has done on it. I did puzzle a bit myself anent Sara Henderson Hay, but beyond the fact that she is also Mrs. Holden as you undoubtedly know I can't see any reason for choosing her. Even then I don't see any reason for it. My choice would be to have her endorse Princess Pat cosmetics rather than poetry. She has the face for the one and very little for the other so far as I can see.

I'm happy too to know you approve of the exclusions, at least at first glance. There was a lot of bad stuff in the Hopwood ms. that I hope I've eliminated entirely from the book.

And how is Roethke? I've kept up a very widely spaced (six months to a year in between) correspondence with him, but haven't seen him for better than two years. But I don't imagine he's changed. It will be the death of a happy landmark if he has.

And to business: I'm afraid I haven't any picture of myself larger than a snapshot (excluding one in a Lord Fauntleroy suit age 5, and one at the time I graduated from high school—both censored). Nor I'm afraid much of any manuscript. I might be able to dig some up—I'll have to sort out a batch of papers at the bottom of my trunk—but mostly I make a practice of throwing out early drafts as soon as a later one is produced. I think I can scare up some scratchings however. I'll bring them out when I come.

Which brings me to that: I plan to arrive in Ann Arbor shortly after New Year's—sometime the first week in January certainly. And to be around for a couple of weeks at least. It will be good to get back, and your plans for display and reading make it sound downright impressive.* I shall of course be delighted—what else does a poet live for but to inflict his stuff on others?

But I generalize and that approaches dangerously close to philosophy. Let's have none of that. I'm glad you liked the poem in *Poetry* and that Dillon liked it. I've already had a batch of stuff out to them for five or six weeks now.

My congratulations on winning an award from *Poetry* and for smearing the field in the approaching Hopwoods. I have a note from Cowden saying that the competition in poetry should be keen this year, but I still predict an unquestionable walk away for you. Ginny Johnson sent me some copies of the *Perspectives,* which ran last year's poems. Your "Visiting Card for Emily" left me sort of mildly furious that you and not I had written it. Which is one way of spelling admiration. It's a swell poem. I enjoyed the others very much, but that one really took me—a beautiful touch all the way through.

Any guesses as to where this letter is heading? I write all my letters intuitively and stream of consciously so please don't be harassed if my continuity isn't always obvious.

Let me round it off and drop it into the mail. I've just time to catch the last collection I think. Thanks again for your card-letter. Will see you soon in Ann Arbor.

Until then,
John

*Brinnin operated a bookstore near campus called The Book Room, which specialized in avant-garde literature and occasional poetry readings.

TO JOHN MALCOLM BRINNIN

Kansas City
February 23, 1940
[UD]

Dear John,

I've had an envelope with your address written onto it and a stamp affixed staring me in the face for almost two weeks, but the general crush of things—classes, papers to correct, routine—all seemed to get in the way. Anyhow I have meant to write and I am writing, so forgive the fact that I've been too lazy or too tight to go out and buy letter paper when all I've had to do is use the University's—and here we go.

Jo Davis sent me a copy of the *Daily* containing the review which is quite a spread. What does Burrows mean by "working toward definition"? I'm not objecting—I simply want to know. If there's the germ of a concrete criticism there I'm anxious to know more about it. What definition? What I mean is—does it really mean anything more than critical jargon? And what does "identity with the world" mean? My impression was that the review lost itself in such phrases, but that perhaps he might have sensed a real weakness in the book. If he can spot it more definitely and say it more specifically I shall be eternally indebted to him. And in case anything in this might seem to hide a vein of sarcasm, I've been misread. Anyhow remember me to him (Burrows) and tell him I should be very happy to hear more.

Incidentally I just got a letter from *The Yale Review* saying they're using my poem in the next issue. Also that Untermeyer is reviewing the book in the same issue.

Also a letter from Ted Morrison offering a fellowship to the Writers' Conference. Bread Loaf, August 14–28. Of course I said yes. Also a rejection from *Poetry* after four months of hesitation. Must try again.

I haven't said anything about having landed a job here since I assume you've heard. Swell place. My only problem now is one of finding the time to get any writing done.

And also—not a problem but something you might be interested in—*The University Review* (somewhat like the *Yale Review* in intent, but so far not very well established) is published here at K.C.U. and I've been pressed to scare up material. I can't even urge it upon you since there's no pay. The magazine does have a decent format, a good editorial staff, and a circulation of about 5000-7000, many of whom could not, probably, be reached by more regular channels. Anything you can scare up—your own or any one else's around Ann Arbor—poems, stories, essays—would be more than welcome. . . . God, you should see the stuff that comes in. But of course you know having served an editorship. Well.

What goes on in Ann Arbor? Kansas City surprisingly enough is a real metropolis with people and skyscrapers. The skyscrapers are nice, but what people. With the exception of the faculty and a few people I've uncovered everyone seems to gush about *art,* and no one seems to know anything about it. I got my picture into the papers when I first got here and so far have received a letter soliciting poems from the S.P. Cruelty to Animals, an invitation to spend the summer on a Kansas estate, forty invitations to dinner—a few with overtones, and a bevy of phone calls. "Art" & "poet" are the magic words. Anyhow I've found a few interesting people and I've managed to shake off the rest.

I've exchanged a couple of very brief notes with Kimon. Also some postcards with Tom Boggs (do you know him?) who wants some poems from the book for an anthology he's editing, to be called *Lyric Moderns.* A hell of a name, but I told him to contact Holt's, and if he's willing to pay he can call the damn collection *Licorice Maudlins* for all of me.

I have a feeling that I'm fumbling toward a close, page three is the limit of imposition. But let me have a note when you can spare time.

John

TO ELLA (CIARDI) RUBERO

Kansas City
July 29, 1940
[ER]

Darling,

You're right about the heat—110, 105, 100, 110 etc. etc. etc. If it ever gets down below 100 I think I'll freeze to death.

And chiggers! Do you know what chiggers are? They're little red spiders, almost microscopic in size that live in the grass, and when somebody walks in the grass they climb up his leg and bore under the skin and live there raising a welt—sometimes a huge one. Some people have them as large as nickels. Luckily I don't appeal to them as much as some of our more toothsome citizens do, and when they do bite me it comes to not much more than a mosquito bite, but Jesus I did get covered with them for a while.

Well, it will be over soon: I'll be through here the end of this week and plan to leave the first of next week and by the time I get back the chiggers will be about gone—until next summer. Did you misread Ginny's [Virginia Johnson's] letter? She's coming down to pick me up and we're going to stop over at her mother's but she'll come along to Boston soon thereafter, if all goes by schedule.

I'm afraid though there won't be much time at home on the way in. I won't get there much before the 9th or 10th and I've got to be in Vermont the 14th. Anyhow it'll keep the family from getting sick of me.

Glad you closed up the shop—you need a rest. Anyhow behave yourself and love and love to the gang. Please tell Edith I'm not a skunk—I ordered her birthday present three weeks ago at the bookstore and the goddamn thing hasn't shown up yet—I'll probably have to bring it along with me—if it comes in time for that. Anyhow, love.

John

TO ELLA (CIARDI) RUBERO

Kansas City
December 4, 1940 [postmark]
[ER]

Darling,

There's not much news here. Things go on. I hope you'll finally get things straightened out between you and Joe. I have no advice left to offer that I haven't offered before and I'm too far away to know all of what goes on, which leaves it squarely up to you to act intelligently.

Your letter seems hurried and harassed. How is Cora's baby? I hope better, but let me know.

I wouldn't worry much about the vitamin tablets. One a day at $1.75 for 24 is only about 7½ cents. If you smoked you'd spend twice that and more for cigarettes. I don't know any way of getting them wholesale, but you should be able to discover someone connected with a drugstore that might give you a rake off. . . .

Just one thing. All things considered, it seems none of you can afford to do Xmas in any big way. Nor can I. Let's have it completely understood that we won't send any gifts. I want to send Mother a few dollars, but god knows it will be damn little I can squeeze out of the month when every meal sets me back 50¢ and every day piles up 25¢ or so for laundry etc. Anyhow at home I'll be able to contribute, when I get there, and that will help. So please—it's understood. Let's be intelligent about it. And please tell Mother not to make up any packages etc. We'll just forget it this year.

I'm rushed off my feet with a million things to do so I've got to run.

All my love and to Mom and the rest and see you all in February.

Love,
John

TO THEODORE ROETHKE

Kansas City
December 10, 1940
[UW]

Dear Roethke,

Nice to hear from you and glad to see the review (which I had not seen). Holts forwarded the letter to this heart of America (officially that as per Chamber of Commerce) where I've been doing freshman English and a few other courses, including a not very satisfying one in modern poetry, since last February.

John Holmes tells me Knopf has your book. Good stuff. I like very much the couple of things I've seen in the last six or eight months in *Poetry* as in one other—can't remember which. . . .

I'm leaving for Boston second semester. Want time to finish off some poems I've been accumulating in slap-dash. Are you going to Boston for MLA [Modern Language Association] this Xmas? I'm going, but not for MLA, but if you do go should like very much to see you again.

All best and thanks for the review. . . .

Cordially
John Ciardi

TO CLARENCE DECKER

Medford
March 4, 1941
[UMKC]

Dear Deck,

I hope this finds all things as you'd have them. Boston remains blustery and cold and waiting for spring. As do I, though I'm not blustering particularly these days.

I'm gathering in the final round of material I need for this Air Corps business and find myself at clause four in paragraph two: "this application shall be accompanied by three letters of recommendation." I hesitate to ask you for all of that, but would you be willing to stand as one of my recommenders to glory?

I'm off tomorrow, if all goes well, for two or three weeks in Michigan where I can pour over the finished manuscript of my would be new book of poems with Prof. Cowden. Then back here for the finishing touches on this Air Corps application and the physical. I don't know yet where I'll stay in Ann Arbor, but a letter here would be forwarded.

And so much for business. All best to (a) the Deckers, (b) the

University of Kansas City, (c) the various faculties, and (d) the student body.

Will you be East any time in April?

Faithfully,
Ciardi

Pres. Clarence R. Decker
The University of Kansas City
Kansas City, Missouri

TO JOHN MALCOLM BRINNIN

Medford
March 25, 1941
[UD]

Dear John,

Swell to hear from you again. And I'm glad of course you like the poem. And, also, thanks for writing of it.

I heard from Virginia Johnson that you had moved to New York. Laurel on all your ventures there. Your address sounds like the one Kimon had the last time I heard from him. Are you together? All best to him.

I've been thinking seriously of running down to NY some week-end in April. Which one I don't know but Tom Boggs (anthologist, poet, and wonderful company) and Rosemary (wife, stunner, and more wonderful company than Tom) have been asking me down and I've been hoping to do it in April. You may know Tom, or of him. If you haven't met him I think you'd enjoy doing so.

What have you been writing lately? I've declared myself a hermit, see none of the magazines unless I sell them a poem, and don't even read anymore. I've been working nights and every night at a ms. for a new book (*Elegy for the First America*), so far scheduled for publication next winter, but I want to get it into approximate form so that I can put it aside and try to work out a novel I have buzzing in my head.* My life would be perfect if I didn't resent the amount of typing that gets involved in it, but since I can't read my writing after three days, it just has to be on the typewriter.

Let me know where I can reach you when I do get to NY. It will be swell to see you again and I hope Kimon.

John

*Neither book was ever published.

TO JOHN MALCOLM BRINNIN

Kansas City
November 14, 1941
[UD]

Dear John—

So there you are. I had wanted several times to write you in New York, particularly since I was in and out of there several times last year, but I lost your address and wasn't able to sleuth you down. But tremendously glad to have it again, and to hear from you, and especially from Cambridge where I'll be able to see you, I hope, come February (I return home for the 2nd semester).

Thanks for liking the poem. It's one of the not enough poems that I can feel completely right about and sure of etc. One such a year and I'd be satisfied. Or maybe not. I don't know.

Good for Macmillan. It's a sound house and a good one to issue forth from. My sincerest congratulations. And on your general emergence come spring, what with Macmillan and New Directions. The coming out in spring of Osiris Brinnin.

And how goes Harvard? It's an odd place. One that seems to strike different people in different ways. I shall be interested in knowing how you take to it. I made some recordings for the poetry room at Widener last summer that you may like to hear. They're not very good recordings. I sound like a Mack truck grinding up hill in low gear. . . .

All best. I'll be looking for both new books in the newspapers, magazines and bookstores. Also for you in Cambridge sometime in February.

And write again.

Yours,
John

TO **ALAN SWALLOW**
Medford
June 4, 1942
[SU]

Dear Alan Swallow,

I'd like very much to have you see what I have for your article—and pleased that you'd want to. (Not false modesty—I'm simply happy to find someone who likes the poems.)

Do you want just published things? The point is that I no longer feel I want to be represented by the first book—it's horribly uneven and loose in all but a few poems I still like. I'm taking the liberty, therefore, of sending you the dummy manuscript of a book I recently finished, and that [Dwell, Sloan, and Pearce?] may do—if the war ever allows publishers to know what they want to do. About ½ the poems, as a matter of fact minus one of exactly half, have appeared in magazines.

My apologies for the state it's in. I used it as a dummy ms. and work book for several months. But I do think it will give you a better impression—for better or worse—of what I'm doing or trying to do, whereas the published book, I feel, is far behind in another time.

I will send both the book and the ms. by Express on Saturday—which will be my first chance to get to the Express office. I should like them back when you're through with them—I have only one other copy of the book—but there's no hurry whatsoever.

Isn't there an army training field near Albuquerque? I'm in the Air Corps Reserve waiting (for months yet I gather) to be called up for training. I'd like very much to look you up if I find myself in N. Mexico.

All best, and I'll be very happy to add anything you need to know for the article.

Cordially,
John Ciardi

TO JOHN MALCOLM BRINNIN

"darkest Louisiana"
January 31, 1943
[UD]

Dear John,

My furlough time was clipped by 20 days, so your letter reaches me in darkest Louisiana where I'm madly in process of becoming a navigator via the maddest curriculum ever known to man. Embellished with such niceties as wearing gas masks in meteorology classes etc. Anyhow your letter was all the more welcome for having arrived in mid-desert.

I'm sorry to hear you fell into a bout of down and under. And very sorry to have missed you. John Holmes wanted particularly to meet you, and it would have turned out to be a fine evening. But the next time.

Thanks for liking the *Y Review* poems. But I'm afraid, sadly, that they pre-date the life of action. Trying to write in the army has me badly baffled. I simply grow loud and profane. The job of maintaining poise and perspective at double time develops certain complications. I did manage one, I think, good prose piece, one fairish one, and one poem while home on furlough. And a number of sketchy things Virginia [Johnson] is typing out for me to overhaul.

Otherwise nothing. And no word re the book. I sent a batch of 30 poems to New Directions which (the poems) reappeared so hurriedly I didn't even bother to go down to the Railway Express to pick them up. . . .

All best,
John

TO PETER DE VRIES

Lowry Fd., Denver
November 19, 1943
[UC]

Dear Mr. De Vries,

Winning the Blumenthal Award is really very gratifying news. My sincerest and happiest thanks to you and to the editorial staff. And to *Poetry* magazine as an institution. It's really very exciting to be a small part. And twice so against a background of torn down machine guns and afternoon drill.

All best wishes for continued success.

Sincerely
(Pvt) John Ciardi

Mr. Peter De Vries
Poetry, A Magazine of Verse
232 East Erie St.
Chicago, Illinois

TO PETER DE VRIES

Walker Field, Victoria, Kansas
August 1, 1944
[UC]

Dear Mr. De Vries—

I don't think Marian Castleman's review of Thomas Hornsby Ferril's, *Trial by Time* should pass unchallenged. It's neither a fair summary nor a very critical one. Allowing—or trying to allow—all possible latitude for difference of opinion, I cannot agree that Ferril's is "supper music—limpid and melodic and as inconspicuous as it is possible for music to be."

I very often disagree with Ferril, too. But he's too good a poet to be brushed aside. He's pretty much a regionalist, and my view is that regionalism can too easily become a limitation. But not always. Colorado is his acre, but unlike Frost's New England there's neither a wall around it nor a No Trespassing sign. If he chooses to see the present as a link in a long chain that began when mountains began, that seems to me a reasonable attitude. I cannot find the complete abandonment of Now as Now that Miss Castleman stresses.

I like the way Ferril handles his local scene—the rush and spurt of it. The amazing fact that Denver was little more than pasture within his own lifetime. "Here in America nothing is long ago." It's a good poem and has at least one unforgettable line:

> The corn came so fast that Buffalo Bill lived to eat it
>   out of a can in a barber shop in Paris.

I feel it's a poor review. Not so much as a nod to the superb "Inner Song While Watching a Square Dance." Not a word to spare for "Harper's Ferry Floating Away"—in which, incidentally (and even while reserving some disagreements of my own) I find some very serious awarenesses.

And aside from regionalism, I wonder how many lyrics have appeared out of this war as moving and immediate as "No Mark?"....

Or am I wrong? I think it's a good book and I resent the review. (And very incidentally and privately I resent ending the review with a Milton sonnet. I don't really know why.)

Sincerely,
John Ciardi, 11069345
882nd Bomb Sq. . . .

P.S. I'll promise not to do this more than once in 28 years (my ratio to date) but I think the objection should be registered.

TO MARION STROBEL

Pacific Theater
November 25, 1944
[UC]

Poetry, A Magazine of Verse

Dear Miss Strobel—

As you will see from the address I have moved overseas. The uncertainties of overseas mail considered, I have worked out another arrangement that—provided it isn't too inconvenient for you—seems more practical to me. When the pieces you have of mine come up for publication will you send the author's copies and the check to:

Virginia H. Johnson
c/o Riggs Clinic
27 Fenn St.
Pittsfield, Massachusetts

Mrs. Johnson has a power of attorney from me and will be able to negotiate the check. . . .

Thank you. And all best wishes.

Sincerely,
John Ciardi

TO MARION STROBEL

Saipan
December 11, 1944
[UC]

Dear Miss Strobel,

Your letter of November 10 comes to hand a bit belatedly via several forwardings. You will understand my delay in acknowledging it.

My sincerest thanks to you and to the editorial staff. All the more thanks in that I value *Poetry's* judgment and recognition very highly.

And I especially like being the first to fall heir to the new Eunice Tietjens Award. May it prosper. And may *Poetry* magazine.

Very sincerely yours,
John Ciardi

Sgt. John Ciardi, 11069345
882nd Bomb Sq. . . .

TO CLARENCE DECKER

Medford
December 1, 1945
[UMKC]

Dear Deck,

I seem to have run through a lot of ponderous balancing and counterbalance. Let me ask you to forgive all this hesitation.

The longer I turn it over in my mind the more certain I become that I would like to get out to Kansas City for the semester. I have decided to take the Harvard offer in the fall, but if you can use me for the one semester I'd like very much to come.

I'm grateful to you for accepting my ponderings and indecisions so considerately. All best wishes, and may it work in with your plans for me to come out for the single semester.

Sincerely,
John

TO MARION STROBEL

Kansas City
July 9, 1946
[UC]

Dear Marion Strobel,

I'm sorry this reply to your June 20th letter has been delayed so long. I have been moving around the country and your letter came to me forwarded four times.

"Edged" seems right to me. I'm very ready to agree to it in place of "furred."

I shall be in Kansas City for the next three weeks at which time a personal apocalypse descends: I get married and leave immediately for the East. My address after the 25th will be

84 South Street
Medford 55, Massachusetts.

All best,
John Ciardi

TO CLARENCE DECKER

Medford
August 5, 1946
[UMKC]

Dear Deck,

Judith and I arrived yesterday after a gay and yet primarily sober week in Ann Arbor. Massachusetts is lushly green and not too hot, and we're bracing ourselves to start apartment hunting.

I found a letter on my desk from a Kate Beckett. She sent some poems to me in care of the *Review* sometime back and raises mild hell with me for not having answered. Especially since John Holmes took the trouble of recommending the *Review* to her, I'd like very much to see the things and write her an answer, whatever it is. Will you have them looked up and forwarded to me?

As a matter of fact, her letter brings home to me the fact that we'll have to have some sort of a system to avoid such confusions in the future. And the more I think of it, the more I feel we should get our routine stated and understood.

I know you'll see my point when I say that as long as I'm carried on the mast head as poetry editor, I have to insist on picking out what poetry we print. My name carried as poetry editor tells the reader that I selected the poetry. And I do have a reputation that stands for something; I want to keep that reputation meaning what I want it to mean.

Therefore I'd like to suggest this procedure:

1. All mss. specifically addressed to me instead of to the editors of the *Review* should be forwarded to me immediately.

2. The other editors shall be free to reject any poetry manuscript not specifically addressed to me, but no manuscript shall be accepted without my O.K. I think, too, I should insist on the right to accept a manuscript and to have my acceptance be final.

3. It might be wise to print my home address under my name on the mast head with a note that poetry mss. should be sent to me.

I don't insist on all this, but I don't see how my name can go on the magazine as poetry editor unless I have that much voice. If I'm poetry editor I have to select the poetry, and I have to be able to select it and accept it in Boston without cross country consultation. I'm sure you'll agree that that's reasonable, but if it strikes you as impractical or as cutting across your jurisdiction we can muddle through as is and you can carry my name as part of the editorial staff minus the "Poetry Editor."

That's a lot of business. Have done! How goes KCU? All best. And to Mary.

As always,
John

TO CLARENCE DECKER

Medford
August 13, 1946
[UMKC]

Dear Deck,

Good to get your letter. I really hadn't thought about the *Review* business as a matter of jurisdiction, but I can see your point about the difficulty of negotiating things by remote control. However, so long as I'm not carried on the masthead as poetry editor, the arrangement is certainly satisfactory.

It would help, however, in scouting up material from these parts if I could have your assurance that I'm free to accept things on the spot, and that what I accept will be published. I have twelve excellent poems of Cid Corman's for a section in the spring number with an introductory essay. Corman is on his way to the Michigan grad school and he's a cinch to knock off a good Hopwood check. I'll send the poems on in a few weeks with the introductory essay.

Can you send me proofs or copies of Win Scott's poems so I can get to work on the essay for his section?

Not much news from here. I enter the THIRD WEEK of marriage with amazing serenity; in fact I like it. Meanwhile we scout for apartments with no luck and gloat over my schedule: 9:00, 10:00, and 12:00 Monday and Wednesday. And that's all. If ever we get settled I look forward to getting large amounts of things written. . . .

Cordially,
John

TO CLARENCE DECKER

Medford
October 12, 1946
[FC]

Dear Deck,

As per my minor acidities of yesterday's note there come the questions of [Lindley Williams] Hubbell.* Who and what my colleagues are I leave Time to forget, but I can't escape the conviction that here (as in the case of the WT Scott poems—in re which my colleagues made the same sort of comments) the judgments are preconditioned by a kind of academic approach that I know quite thoroughly: know it because I can recognize it as a stage of my own development and further see it as a stage to be gotten through.

In the first place I can't see putting poetry to a vote. Case in point: the votes range all over the place on at least fifteen percent of the poems.

In the second place the approach is too casual between occasional harassments: a batch of poems appears in the mailbox, is dropped on a desk to be glanced at between the sessions of omnipotence that make the classroom gesture, and the judgments as likely as not depend on the lecture just delivered on Milton's prosody, or on the oration that just summed up and disposed of Crabbe, or just on what somebody had for breakfast that morning. It's too sterile.

And it tends to lean into that academic mind (as per paragraph one) that wants poems to reassert whatever classic proverbs of criticism one has collected from THE GREAT CRITICS.

I'm obviously being arrogant, but as a rhetorical gesture it will serve. Seriously, I must insist that a poem be judged on its own premises. And seriously, I must insist that it's enough for a poem to be interesting. I can't claim any greatness for this collection, but I most emphatically assert that they are interesting. I will even bow to convention and yield on "The Venus of Willendorf" if you think the phallic bent of the imagery is too strong for the *Review.* But I still want to do an introduction feature on this group. I'll wait, however, for your go ahead signal since there is a wide difference of opinion. Please let me know.

And while I'm being arrogant let me submit my last offer: a good poet is a better poetry editor than the standard college faculty. Let me run the *Review's* poetry at my own discretion and on my own authority for a year (meaning kill the backlog and let me start fresh) and see if you don't find visible results. My last arrogance is that you'll never find a better man for the job.

With all of which you're free to disagree, but I've been wanting to say it, and I'm glad, and what is life without differences of opinion?

Meanwhile, please let me know whether or not I may go ahead with writing Hubbell up. I'll have the Corman feature for you soon.

All best,
[John]

Pres. Clarence R. Decker
University of Kansas City
Kansas City, Mo.

*JC had met editorial objections to his inclusion of Hubbell's poems in the University of Kansas City *Review.*

TO CLARENCE DECKER

Medford
October 22, 1946
[FC]

Dear Deck,

Notes from the end of a limb.

Well, it was a good try. I grant, and you probably realize, that my little flare of invective was more a political chicanery than an effort at criticism. I obviously want to get my hands on the *Review,* and Hubbell seemed to provide an opening for plunging in with both feet (in my mouth).

I regret, from this end of the limb, any distaste my piece of bluster may have left in collective or individual mouths. Especially so since I respect, like, and admire at least certain facets of each of "my colleagues." That is seriously and literally so, and I should regret it if my over-the-beers invective appeared too solemn by book and bell in the black and white profundities of Remington #5.

As I was saying, it was a good try. Or at least a try. I do, very seriously, think something is dissipated in editing by ballot. I also think a "dictatorship" loses something. But I shall go right on plugging for the ballot as purely advisory and the final decision as one man's responsibility.

Which, as a matter of fact, is where I came in. I offer my colleagues my sincerest apologies and without reservation, but I would rather they understood the original intent in context, thereby making apology irrelevant.

All best,
[John]

TO EDWARD WEEKS
Medford
October 23, 1946
[FC]

Dear Edward Weeks,

I hope you'll forgive my mother-instinct about that manuscript, but I can't help feeling a bit unhappy about Time's winged chariots careening by me. It has been almost seven years since my first undernourished little volume and I'm impatient to get this one [*Other Skies*] into print.

My shrewdest guess is that you like the manuscript personally but can't get it approved by the Men at the Green Table. I hope I'm right about your liking it and I hope I'm wrong about the Guardians of the Cashbox. Certainly, having invested almost a year in your decision, I would hesitate to ask for the manuscript if you think there is any fair chance of its being published by Little Brown. By the same token I feel that for my own good I should ask for it back if your best estimate is unhopeful.

If you do return it, I'd be more than grateful for any leads you might give me in getting it placed. I'm frankly at loose ends if Little Brown won't do it, and any reasonably hopeful publishing prospect would be a point of departure.

It will hardly be necessary for me to say I shall be sorry if you decide to return the manuscript, but I'm sure you will have done all you could for it, and I shall remain grateful for your interest and counsel. . . .

I look forward to hearing from you and to seeing you somewhere about town.

Cordially,

Mr. Edward Weeks
The Atlantic Monthly
8 Arlington Street
Boston 16, Massachusetts

TO JOHN MALCOLM BRINNIN

Medford
October 31, 1946
[UD]

Dear John,

Let me say how much I liked your poems in the October *Poetry.* The language of "Fetes, Fates" is really something special, and "Around the Egg" builds itself around the refrain in a really memorable way. The two of them set a tremendous level from which "Angel Eye of Memory" declines not at all. Three really stunning poems: I hope you're finding many such.

I'm teaching English A at Harvard and resenting bitterly the way in which themes and conferences pile up on me stifling my time. I've written nothing worth saving since school started. But maybe I'll shake free soon.

All best wishes. And my sincerest admirations of some wonderfully moving poems.

John

TO MARION STROBEL

Medford

November 12, 1946

[UC]

Dear Miss Strobel,

I am gratefully indebted to you and to the editors of *Poetry*, and proud to add my name to the distinguished list of those who have received the Levinson Prize. I am glad, too, that the poem selected should be the 29th birthday poem, for which I have a very special feeling.

Will you convey my thanks and good wishes to the editorial staff?

Sincerely yours,
John Ciardi

TO CLARENCE DECKER

Medford

November 14, 1946

[FC]

Dear Deck,

I'll try to get the [Cid] Corman introduction finished and off to you this weekend. I have hit a fairly busy streak of things and have been badly rushed for time. I'm doing an essay for George Dillon for *Poetry* magazine and working up another series of things for French Radio diffusion. A busy time, but good. Many poems sold, and very gratifyingly, the Levinson Prize from *Poetry* magazine, my third and best from them. I enclose an essay that I think might well go in the *Review* as part of the project I have in mind to bring some specific notions of poetry to our readers.

And I must run. Frost is speaking in Cambridge this afternoon and I want to hear him.

All best, and please convey my fond regards to Mary.

Sincerely,
[John]

TO EDWARD WEEKS
Medford
November 26, 1946
[FC]

Dear Edward Weeks,

De profundis. Or notes from the rebirth (after long labor) of J. Ciardi, citizen-poet.

My room—and half the house—is littered with stray papers, cigarette butts, and somewhere my wife—but I think the new ms. makes sense. Constant intent reading brings me back very close to the poems and I have a very sure feeling about those that have survived deletion. I have read and pondered conscientiously Spencer's letter and comments. With a few emphatic exceptions I found I had deleted on my own many of the poems he suggested. His textual notes have left me unmoved, however, and I have felt no necessity to act upon them. We don't have the same notion of "professionalism," whereby I cannot let myself be bound by what seems to me essentially a private view of poetic technique. That is, aside from my own private view which I have stated in the introduction. I hope you will be able to approve it (the introduction) in its present form.

I have made the ms. as tight as possible. And even now I feel amputated. But I will go one step further and agree to delete any five poems you nominate. There are now 44 poems in the ms.

Let me ask you to read the book and apply one test—do the poems move you? If they do not, I want you to send them back—I mean that seriously—for if they fail as keen and sensitive a reader as you, they will fail other readers and fail me. . . .

All best wishes to you, and let me thank you again for your interest and cordiality.

Sincerely,
[John Ciardi]

TO JOHN MALCOLM BRINNIN

[Medford]
December 1, 1946
[UD]

Dear John,

My warmest thanks for kind words. Like you, I don't completely understand the basis on which *Poetry* makes its awards, and finally I'm reduced to a *de facto* declaration, knowing no way to quibble with a hale check well met.

Especially so since (I don't think I mentioned it before) I took unto myself a blonde and beautiful wife this summer. The title I am now competing for is America's Most Married Poet. It's probably a symptom of bourgeois decay, but I like it.

Unfortunately, we are near-orphans of the housing crisis, but if you get into Boston do let us know and I'll bet we can pull a pleasant visit out of somebody's hat.

All best,
John

TO JOHN FREDERICK NIMS

Medford
September 14, 1947
[IU]

Dear John:

I've been wonderfully moved to enthusiasm by "The Iron Pastoral." A truly impressive and enriching job of making language stand up and sparkle. I've had three readings of it over as many months and it just doesn't let down. A wonderful experience. I'm happy to report, too, that Bill Sloane and his wife (they were at Bread Loaf) share all my enthusiasms. May your publishers always be admirers—as they damn well should be.

Right now I'm thinking I very much want to do an article on you and the book. You may have known that I'm an editor of the Univ. of Kansas City *Review.* The *Review* is fairly new, but in my prejudiced eye a valuable little quarterly. It has run some good things and some good names.

Within the last year I have embarked on a series of so called introductions to contemporary poets. The function of the series is simple: to present valuable poets to our readers, and to preface the present action by some non-technical discussion that (we hope) will circulate some valid notions about modern poetry in general.

The form of the introductions, thus far, has been (a) a group of poems by the poet, (b) a brief *credo* by the poet setting forth his central objectives in a paragraph or two or three, and (c) an introductory essay by me.

The unhappy part of it all is that the *Review* does not pay and has a policy against reprinting. That leaves the undesirable crux of asking for unpublished poems free. I'm frankly apologetic for that and can seriously see every reason for refusing it. I think poets should be paid.

So far the only concession I've been able to force out of the magazine has been on agreement that the poet will receive twenty-five off-prints of the article and poems. I enclose one of W. T. Scott's introductions. God knows it's a poor introductory essay, in one way, yet I do believe it's fairly well-designed for our readers. I should want to do a considerably longer piece on you, if you think it worthwhile. There's a terrific chance to sell some real notions about diction in your poems.

Also on the credit side, I think it's seriously true that the *Review* reaches many people who have no other contacts with modern poetry. It's an audience of about 2500 people and I suspect most of them would not be reached in any other way.

If that sounds like anything you'd care to do, I can think of nothing I'd better like to tackle. If you do have anywhere from 3 to a dozen unpublished poems you can see your way to giving us free, I feel like a piker, but I would certainly grab them. Or even one or two. So far we've used fairly large batches of poems, but there's no real reason why we can't do with less.

I'd like, too, to have your permission to quote at least one or two whole poems from the book (in the text of the introduction) and quite a lot of excerpts to demonstrate the power of the diction primarily. The poetasters and poesyists need some electricity.

I know that's a lot to ask and there's nothing I could understand more readily than a refusal. My only justification for asking in the first place is that it provides me with a labor of love that I fondly believe can do good service for a better understanding of poetry, and that it provides you with a new audience.

In either case I remain an enthusiastic partisan. Here's hoping we get to split another beer before too long.

Cordially,
John Ciardi

TO MARION STROBEL

Medford
April 29, 1948
[UC]

Dear Marion:

. . . . Grinnell and the Writer's Conference turned out most pleasantly. Herman Sakinger whose good poems have appeared in *Poetry* was there—he teaches German at Grinnell. And E. L. Mayo came over from Des Moines (he's teaching at Drake). I got a night at Des Moines with Mayo and his pleasant wife and two daughters and small son. They're living at the Fort Des Moines housing project in what were once WAC barracks. We sat up till we were exhausted and talked about everything and nothing.

One of the things I remembered—though God knows how it came up—was the question "To whom do you write your poems? What do you visualize as an audience?" I've had my focus pretty clearly in mind for a long time now. I write to my much admired friend Virginia Johnson, as well stocked, sensitive, and interested a mind as I know, but not a literary specialist. She is an expert psychiatric social worker with a wide awareness of the world and of the arts. I don't think our times are likely to do better, and I like to think that using her as a touchstone I can get a reaction to a poem from a kind of ideal of the non-literary specialist mind.

Mayo's answer interested me. He carries a very definite memory of himself when he was very young—I think he said eight or ten—lying in bed looking at his walls and ceiling and thinking of the world and the future and deciding that he would report back to himself in that room stretched on that bed, as the rest of his life came at him. He thinks of his poems as those reports back to himself: this is what happened, this is what came out of the world. It seems a particularly rich illusion. . . .

I wonder what some other illusions are. I'd be curious to know what private addresses people carry in their minds for their poems. We battered that about for a while and talking about illusions generally I recall falling asleep in the easy chair about in the middle of saying something to the effect that the real illusion that informs poetry is that at the moment of the writing the poet convinces himself that the universe is seriously attending what he has to say and is really concerned with the verdict he will render it. I can't think of a better place to fall asleep, but even waking the next morning I found the feeling in my mind that it really was close to the matter.

Back at Harvard I found Robert Lowell scheduled to give a reading on the Morris Gray Fund lecture series here, which he did. The acoustics were not too good in the great vault of Emerson D, and Lowell's voice doesn't carry too well. From where I was sitting I got mixed impressions. I think I've heard poems read better and worse. I was especially struck by a trick Lowell has of throwing away the last line of a poem and shying away from it as if making good an escape. But whether or not a man puts forth a good platform performance is fairly irrelevant. The poems are what count. I sat with Theodore Morrison who had heard Lowell last summer at the Bread Loaf English School and he reports that Lowell's reading had improved a great pace since the summer. What was unmistakable through it all is that Lowell does put the heroic line through paces it hasn't performed for a long time. And that he probably gets more sea into his poems than any other poet I know. Hart Crane tried it, but most of the trouble with Hart Crane's sea is that Crane had never really gone to it and onto it. Lowell has, and his trick for capturing it is remarkable. . . .

Ever,
John

TO MARION STROBEL

Medford
June 2, 1948
[UC]

Dear Marion:

Foiled again, cuss it! Nobody will let me be malicious. And I have such lovely malices to sell.

Well.

I enclose the birthday poem, but I hope you take the "Guide [to Poetry"]—somebody has to get that feud started. I have very very strongly the feeling that if esoteric cultism gets much more encouragement, poetry is going to become about as robust as lesbianism. And about as valuable.*

Which will do for my daily exordium. I wish I were rich and twelve feet tall and were throwing a party in Chicago and everybody was happy-drunk and you were there.

John

*"A Guide to Poetry," with all its "lovely malices" intact, was first published in *Poetry* and later included in Ciardi's third book of poems, *Live Another Day* (1949).

TO MARION STROBEL

Medford
June 16, 1948
[UC]

Dear Marion:

I'm glad. And I'll provide any note you like. As, viz:

The malice in this piece ["A Guide to Poetry"] is mine, and I cherish it. The editors of *Poetry* thought at first they saw a kind of criticism in it but were honestly reluctant to publish it because of the way it put its big feet down. Whereupon I had to get righteous and scream that *Poetry* is a representative magazine, and that god knows there's enough malice in the current coteries so that a little more now and then needs some sort of representation. They finally had to take it under threat of a whispering campaign that Marion Strobel chews betel and that George Dillon was observed tipping his hat to an unidentified person reported by another unidentified person as being an unidentified Trotsky-ite. It's probably part of their revenge to print it in the prose section.

P.S. John Berryman needs testosterone.

Seriously, I'm awfully glad you're going to use it, and I will seriously sign any warrant of liability you choose, this one above or any other.

Love,
John

TO RICHARD WILBUR

Medford
December 5, 1948
[RW]

Dear Wilbur:

I tried to get a word with you at Dick Ellman's but couldn't penetrate to the corner you were in, and we had to leave early. I felt like such an ass after Matthiessen's when Judith identified you for me in the car going home. I had seen you about before that, but I hadn't attached your name to you.

I want to ask whether you would be interested in a Bread Loaf Fellowship. I don't have one to give, but I can make recommendations.

As you may know, the fellowship involves nothing in either money or duties. It's a pleasant two weeks' vacation in Vermont with good talk, probably too many martinis, and some rewarding people. Unhappily there is no conference provision for wives. The conference runs from the middle of August to the beginning of September.

I'd like to recommend you and Peter Viereck. Will you let me know if it sounds like anything you'd care to do?

All best,
John Ciardi

TO PETER VIERECK

Medford
December 15, 1948
[FC]

Dear Peter:

For heaven's sake! I hadn't realized you fired ray blasts into the fourth dimension too. Is this a passing shot or the visible part of a private iceberg? Fletcher Pratt and a gent named L. Sprague deKamp put forth a hell of a case annually for science-fiction (at Bread Loaf). Their case is mostly that they can make a comfortable living at it, but Fletcher also argues it as a literary form: a way of isolating an emotion so that it can be treated more analytically. He made me read a half dozen pieces of the stuff, and I had to confess I could feel the stirrings of something in it. Whereby I now read *Modern Science Fiction* instead of *Time* when I get on a train. That's as far as I've gone, but I discover the science-fiction brotherhood is not a reading public, but a fraternal order, and a secret one. All this is because I find myself wondering if you are one of the mystic brotherhood. Well. . . .

I'm delighted that you liked the off-print. I am in suspended process of doing a series of articles for the University of Kansas City *Review.* The article on style was a bit off the beaten track. Mostly the articles have been introductions-to-poets-you-should-know. I did four or five in the last couple of years, and then other things intervened and I've let it slide. I enclose one on E. L. Mayo and one on John Frederick Nims. And naturally the thought is in my mind now—How about Peter Viereck? . . . .

If . . . the notion and the handling of it make sense to you, I'd jump at the chance to write it up. I would need a few unpublished poems—as few or as many as you see fit—a brief credo (Nims wormed out of his, but I think it's a good feature), and permission to quote from *Terror and Decorum.*

Let me add . . . that there is every good reason for not letting yourself be plundered out of poems without payment. I can't urge any man to it. Whereby I'm with you come yes, come no. . . .

All best,
Sincerely,
[John]

TO JOHN HOLMES

Medford
January 15, 1949
[FC]

Dear John:

. . . I like the notion of an Eliot evening. As a matter of fact I'm scheduled to talk on T. S. Eliot at the Community Church on Jan. 27 on what they call a Great Books Series. And the more I think about it, the less I can find to say to the kind of audience I expect to be there. Let's by all means have the Eliot evening before Jan. 27. Maybe the talk will help get me oriented to the lecture. We're dated on the 16th and free otherwise. . . .

The *Kenyon Review* doesn't much surprise me. I don't know who

Flint is, but I begin to suspect that anybody that publishes where I do fares badly in the literary mags. I'm slick because I publish in the *NY'r,* vaguely lavender because I publish in the *Atlantic,* and obviously anemic because I work out in the *Yale Review* once every two years. Actually it's a school: Jarrell, Berryman, and whoever Flint is, are the guys that have lambasted the book [*Other Skies,* 1947; *Live Another Day* was not published until later in 1949]. J and B certainly fit together. I don't know Flint. But it doesn't much matter. You and I are not only nest builders; we have a stubborn streak in common. I insist these boys are wrong, and I'm willing to wait to prove it. . . .

All best from our house to your house.

[John]

TO CLARENCE DECKER

Medford
March 20, 1949
[UMKC]

Dear Deck:

I'm going to try to race off the Viereck piece, but I have a number of conflicts including a week coming up in New York for a series of conferences with a new publishing house (Twayne) of which I am now poetry editor. Will you let me know the *last possible date* for the piece? . . . .

I am going to be in Mo. in June. I'm taking Judith out late in May and mean to hole up there for a while to work at a long project that has begun to absorb me: I'm translating the *Inferno.* It's fascinating if laborious work. I'd love to drive over to KC and lecture unto the conference at some exorbitant fee.

All our best, and do let me know the last date for the article. I can use every day you can give me on it.

As ever,
John

TO THEODORE ROETHKE

Medford
April 20, 1949
[UW]

Dear Ted,

It has been a long time, and now it's business as well as pleasure, or rather business that is a pleasure. I'm at work on an anthology [*Mid-Century American Poets*] and I'm looking forward to some good Roethkeiana. The book will appear in late fall or early winter under the Twayne imprint (see enclosed brochure of our first book contest). Twayne is a brand new house with an active interest in poetry and I have high hopes of building up a list of really good poets in the years to come. I'd be damned grateful for any worthy ms. you can steer this way, yours or others'.

Oh, yes—payment: will be by proportional royalties on a page basis.

I am asking each poet to select ten of his own poems (or roughly 240 lines, whichever comes first) according to his own preferences, AND to prepare a statement of his own working principles. I hope the attached sheet will clarify both counts. My only suggestion is that the statement be on *your* working principles and not a general essay on the nature of poetry. And that the statement be as free as possible from the jargon of literary criticism. In any case the enclosure is not a binding form, but simply a list of suggestions.

If, however, you draw back from the labor of knocking your ideas into final form (I hope none of the poets will) will you treat the enclosure as a questionnaire, answering each question in whatever detail seems pertinent and allow me to lick it into shape? To discourage which, and because I am a pig, I will usurp half the royalties on those pages if you do it that way.

Seriously, the anthology is a highly selective one designed to represent the best poems of the better poets whose major work falls in the forties, and to present, insofar as possible, the working principles of versification that hold sway, if sway is what they hold. The poet's own statement would be the most valuable way of saying that, of course.

All best to you in Washington, and if the tall trees are shading any good poets, please ship some this way.

As ever,
John

TO MURIEL RUKEYSER
Medford
April 26, 1949
[LC]

Dear Muriel Rukeyser:

Swell! Haven't had time yet to assemble all the poems as a group but very much taken by "Night Feeding." I know it will be a strong group, however, from those whose titles I recognize.

I'm looking forward to your *How I Write* or rather *The Way I Work*—which is a good title. I'm especially eager to assemble these prose statements to see what they all add up to in terms of stating the practical prosody of today. I'm looking forward to a summarizing essay on that and it should amount to an important statement about what poetry is doing in the critics' and hell's despite. . . .

Sincerely,
[John Ciardi]

TO KARL SHAPIRO
Medford
April 29, 1949
[LC]

Dear Karl:

. . . . See if I can make myself clear re anthol: it began with a double notion:

1. To round up a good self-selection of the poets of the forties

whose poetry I admire. (Concession: one or two included because they have been recognized widely as poets of forties. I put them in to be representative even though I personally can't find their work moving.)

2. To round up with the poems statements of the practical working principles of each person. My idea was that a careful summary (the introduction to the whole book) of these working principles would in fact be a statement of THE practical prosody of the forties, and that that would be a very valuable document. My special concern is for the reader of poetry: I cannot escape a feeling that the poets must face the responsibility of providing themselves with a wider audience. That does not mean an all inclusive audience. I mean that with a little less spitting in the reader's eye, and with a little more frank statement of premises, dilemmas, theories, and hopes, a considerable and valuable number of readers could come much closer to understanding and participating in good poetry. (Maybe a wild hope, but I mean to explore it for what it's worth and with every possible device. Example: those UKC articles. Potentially horrible example: the preface to my forthcoming book [*Live Another Day*] in which my neck is more or less all the way out for what I attempt to define as the "reader of (some) general culture.")

In sum then, my idea was this: that if such a reader could be enlightened on what the poets are trying to do, he might come a lot closer to understanding it when he sees it done. . . . .

All best,
[John]

TO THEODORE ROETHKE

Medford
May 9, 1949
[UW]

Dear Ted:

Swell. I like the poems you've picked and I like the idea of the letter. No trouble at all about the length. Some questions have been raised on that by a couple of people who have longish things, and I've decided to raise the top length to convenience anyone who would feel cramped, making it read as high as 500 lines as imperative but suggesting 350 as a working maximum and 250–300 as a norm. What I'd like is to achieve a unit that permits maximum freedom to each contributor and still achieves the sense of equal representation.

The thing goes swimmingly, may I add: Wilbur, Viereck, Shapiro, Scott, Rukeyser, you, Nims, Mayo, Holmes, Jarrell, Eberhart, me are all checked in and some material on hand already. My major problems are now Lowell who is suffering a breakdown, and Elizabeth Bishop from whom I can't seem to raise a response. I suspect, however, that we'll be able to make it by early winter at the latest. . . .

All best,
John

TO JOHN HOLMES

Medford
January 15, 1949
[FC]

On April 26, 1949, Frank B. Ober, a Baltimore attorney, wrote a three-page letter to Harvard President James B. Conant complaining of two professors who were "giving aid and comfort to Communism." The professors were John Ciardi, who had spoken against an anti-subversive bill at a Progressive party meeting in Maryland, and Harlow Shapley, director of the Harvard College Observatory, who had appeared at the Cultural and Scientific Conference for World Peace in New York.

Ober confessed that he did not know what John Ciardi had said, nor whether he was a Communist, but he objected nonetheless on the grounds that any such meeting would gain "respectability" just by having a Harvard professor speak. Furthermore, he claimed Communism was no longer a "political movement" but had become a "criminal conspiracy," and therefore: "the test of a professor's actions ought not to be whether he can actually be proved guilty of a crime.

Reasonable grounds to doubt his loyalty to our government should disqualify him for the position. . . ."

The story was picked up by the United Press news service and widely distributed. *The Christian Science Monitor* ran a full page on the story in its issue of June 20, and the *New Republic* carried Harold L. Ickes' postmortem, "Hats Off to Harvard!" on July 11. All the New York papers covered the story in detail; it made the front page of the *New York Herald Tribune* on June 20, 1949.

President Conant acted quickly and decisively in support of his professors as well as the university. In a letter of May 11, he announced his position to Mr. Ober and added that he would have Mr. Grenville Clark, "a senior member of the Corporation and a leader in your profession," write a formal response, which followed on May 27—in eleven single-spaced pages of tightly reasoned defense.

TO GRENVILLE CLARK

Medford
May 31, 1949
[FC]

Mr. Grenville Clark
Dubling, New Hampshire

Dear Mr. Clark:

Herewith a copy of the letter I mentioned over the phone. [See next letter.] It and the other correspondence have been left with Mr. Bailey.

I am especially grateful that Harvard has not required a defense from me, but if it is at all possible to do so I should like my friends in the Harvard community to know unmistakably that however much my fringes may be painted pink I have too much respect for the free mind to submit it to the rigorous stupidities of anyone's party line whether it be Stalin's, *The Daily Worker*'s, or Ober's.

The converse of that needs also to be stated: that I find your reply a moving statement of the things the world would do well to cherish.

It is a valuable document at a time that needs exactly that sort of affirmation. My sincerest respects to you for having said so well what needed so badly to be said.

Sincerely,
[John Ciardi]

TO FRANK B. OBER

Medford
June 1, 1949
[FC]

[Letter printed in the Harvard *Alumni Bulletin*, June 1949.]

Mr. Frank B. Ober
640 Baltimore Trust Building
Baltimore 2, Maryland

Dear Mr. Ober:

Mr. Grenville Clark has been kind enough to show me copies of the correspondence that began when you wrote President Conant urging my dismissal from the Harvard faculty. My gratitude to Harvard for rejecting your proposal in the strongest terms is all the greater in that I was at no time required to defend myself against your charges. In the normal course of things, in fact, I should simply have ignored them.

With Mr. Conant's decision to publish this correspondence, however, the issue is made public, and I am accordingly moved to speak some word of my own to the students and to the general community of Harvard whose friendship I trust and value. Mr. Clark has written you a detailed and moving affirmation of the dignity and necessity of academic freedom in a democratic society. I cannot resist the urgency of the occasion to write you this open letter on my own account, addressing myself not to the necessity for academic freedom, but to some statement of the ideals that compel me, as one citizen (among many I hope), to oppose the principles you have elected to represent. I am all the more willing to do so since I can fairly conclude from your letter that these principles are not entirely known to you; and I may perhaps be especially justified in taking such a statement upon myself inasmuch as I am one of the two professors who would have been expelled with prejudice had Harvard accepted your point of view. There is a third and most urgent reason for such a statement: this correspondence makes public one more instance of a difference of opinion so important to the future of the free mind in America that no effort at clarification can conscientiously be shirked.

My personal gratitude to Harvard, however, does not in any way lend this letter official import. I write as one citizen to another in the fundamental hope that however much we may disagree on specific policy, we do in fact desire for others the same freedom and security that we covet for ourselves. I am forced to classify this as a hope rather than as a certainty in that your request for my dismissal was overtly an attempt to destroy both my freedom and my economic security. You do, nevertheless, "concede the right of self-appointed 'liberals' to fight particular laws against Communism, as there can be honest debate as to the method of handling the question." I do not understand why liberals must enter your mind surrounded by quotation marks, nor why they must be thought of as self-appointed, but since few if any of them ever win elections, self-appointment may be the only method of recruiting them to serve the public good. In any case such a concession as you make to the rights of others, if persistently adhered to, would certainly require extreme caution in limiting that right.

I should like to ask whether or not you have conscientiously exercised such caution in seeking my dismissal.

As I study your letter, I see that your request is based on one charge: that I appeared at a Progressive party meeting in Baltimore and spoke there against the enactment of a measure commonly known as the Ober Bill, of which you are the principal sponsor. You confess to lacking specific knowledge of what I said there, though the meeting was open to the public and the press, but you identify the meeting with communism, vilification, and distortion. If I read your letter rightly I gather a further implication that my opposition was all the more serious in that the General Assembly of Maryland had endorsed the measure with "but one dissenting vote."

I am forced to reply, to this last implication, that had the General Assembly endorsed the measure unanimously, I would still believe the legislation you have sponsored to be reckless and oppressive. Maryland can make it legal but it cannot make it wise. Nor can any overwhelming majority stifle the right of minority opposition under the democratic process.

Speaking specifically of the Ober Bill, I grant you that could some all wise and impartial judge supervise its application as law, it could (under these ideal conditions only) achieve the doubtful good of being harmless to the democratic process. The persons in whom an idea is born, however, can seldom be separated in practice from the consequences of that idea. You, as the principal sponsor of the bill and as a man prominent in Maryland affairs, are certain to be consulted in the administration of the measure of the law. Your personal attitudes toward these vital questions of freedom of thought and of the inviolability of impartial judicial process are therefore relevant. It is for this reason that I am alarmed, though not surprised, to find your attitudes so far from impartial that you are immediately willing to submit democratic process to the doctrine of "guilt by association," to charge your opponents with unspecified vilification, to resort to vilification of your own, and to demand economic sanctions against fellow Americans guilty only of what you interpret as "reasonable grounds" to believe them disloyal.

You, I submit, have done all these things in your letter. You have argued the known fact of the existence of Communists within the Progressive party as evidence that I must be—if not "legally" at least "reasonably"—a Communist. You have dismissed the Progressive party's publicly presented opposition as a campaign of vilification but have submitted no specific evidence of such vilification. You have yourself vilified when in referring to the meeting you wrote:

> the so-called "Progressive" (the quotation marks are again yours) campaign against the laws enacted in Maryland was not a debate, but vilification and falsehood

when you must have known (or have been recklessly ill-informed considering the charges you bring) that the meeting was officially called by the established Progressive party of Maryland and was publicly announced as a "rally" with no pretense at formal "debate." And without knowing any more about me than the simple fact that I appeared at that meeting and spoke against your bill you have taken it upon yourself to urge my dismissal from Harvard under circumstances that would almost certainly have destroyed my academic career had Harvard acceded to your request.

No legislation may be said to be perfect. In all of it there exists an element of discretionary power visited in those who must carry it out as law. Is not that discretionary power dangerously foregone when the principal sponsor of a bill, and one whose position in public life is practically certain to influence its administration as law, stands on such principles as these?

And is it possible that in declaring his loathing for these principles, any man disqualifies himself from the ideal of loyalty to the United States and from fitness to teach in a democratic society?

I am opposed to the Ober Bill not because it is against communism but because it is against my belief in democracy, a belief fundamental to the healthy atmosphere of the classroom and to the dignity of the human mind, for whenever any person takes upon himself the power to decide on so-called "reasonable" grounds that one set of ideas shall be desirable and that another shall be exterminated, the free exchange of the democratic classroom and forum are in serious danger. Who shall be made the judge of what is "reasonable"? And has it not been historically true that those who have been most willing to set themselves up as arbiters, have been the least willing to tolerate the slow process of democratic safeguards? One thinks of the commissar and of the bund-leader; never of, let us say, Jefferson or Chief Justice Hughes. I am opposed to the Ober Bill for these reasons, and I bring to my opposition the same loathing for "thought control" that motivates my unshakeable opposition to communism, to fascism, and to all repressive measures sought by distrustful Americans who have not yet learned that the real defense against totalitarianism abroad is not totalitarian measures at home but a vigorous and alert democracy; not suppression of unpopular opinion but freedom of utterance; not thought control but thought expansion.

It is true that I cannot exactly define myself politically except as a member of what I have come to refer to as the "middle muddle." Until recently I was a pessimistic member of the Progressive party. At present I am a liberal who finds himself unable to endorse any party conscientiously. I add this not as a defense, since I conceive no defense to be necessary, but rather to underscore the point that far from being, as you imply, a member of the Communist party or a sympathizer with the mindless rigidity of the Communist party line, I actually have no exact notion of what I am politically, except that I should like to think of myself as an undaunted liberal unsurrounded by quotation marks. I most certainly do know that I am opposed to the many items of legislation currently before many of our state assemblies in the hope of restricting freedom of belief and of utterance, and that I am most willing to state my opposition from the platform of any organization in which I can find—if I may paraphrase—reasonable grounds to suspect good faith.

Sincerely yours,
John Ciardi
Briggs-Copeland Assistant
Professor of Composition
Harvard College

TO **PETER VIERECK**

Medford

July 14, 1949

[LC]

Dear Peter:

Long overdue and my apologies. . . .

I have made all the changes you have written in the piece about poetry. With my wife in Missouri I can't get typing done, and I just can't give a whole day to banging away at this engine. I assure you, however, that as soon as my clerk comes home I shall put her on the typewriter. (Well, *soon after* she gets home.) In any case you will see a complete typescript of your part of the anthology. I shall probably have to forward it to your wife and have her forward it to you, but you shall have it.

I have read the *Soviet Reichswehr Alliance* with more than interest. This is brand-new to me. I needed no convincing that the Soviets were stupid and inhumanly rigid (same thing) but I really did believe that they were racial equalicists (Is there such a word?). With your permission I'd like to take these proofs to a friend of mine who will find them as interesting as I have found them. Another member of the middle muddle.

And thanks a million, Peter, for being willing to write on the Guggenheim business. I have the application blanks here and have to get to work on them. I'm tackling a translation of the *Inferno:* why I shall never know, but I'm almost through Canto VIII in first draft and as soon as I can get those banged up into a typescript with a statement of the principles of the translation which will be my project sheet, I'll complete the forms and shoot them in. No hurry on this. Applications don't close until October and you probably won't hear anything from them until after that.

Have a marvelous time in Europe. I'll look forward to hearing from you.

Best,
[John]

TO KARL SHAPIRO

Medford
August 2, 1949
[LC]

Dear Karl:

. . . . Actually I agree and disagree with your ideas. If by criticism is meant the spiritual, or psychological, or what have you—identification of the poet with the poem, the soul turmoil, I agree. But what

I am interested in here is not souls but *craft.* A flexible notion certainly, yet Da Vinci's notebooks for instance, and even the processes of Cellini (whom I refuse to despise) seem to me devotions and respectable devotions. It takes both love and mathematics. Of the love I think only the poem can speak, but I see no reason within myself why the mathematics shouldn't be open to discussion. What's that fine line of Marshall Schacht's?—"Love without arithmetic will fail." Well, there are all sorts of things that can be that symbolic "love," and there are all kinds of mathematics. But I have never felt I lost anything in trying to provide an admittedly faltering answer when someone asks "How did you mean the rhyme to function in this poem?" Or "Why in the hell did you use the word whatever-it-is in this way?" I write to be understood (as I'm certain you do) and if I can help anyone understand what I've written, I'm pleased.

Not, of course, that the poem comes out of the craft. All I can really talk about is notions out of past practice. How the hell do I know what I'm going to write next? And how the hell do I know what I'm writing now before I've finished it? Maybe I won't more than half-know then. There can be a block god knows: I'm at work translating the *Inferno* (as Viereck would say "for the hell of it." Really for the love of it). It's really quite an experience. Back to that symbolic "love"—the love is out of the writing. Dante had that as he wrote the poem. All I can give it as translator is the craft, whatever craft I can. And yet every now and then it catches fire and lights. And I find that happening in my own poems, and it's not a despicable way of writing.

What I'm getting at really is the question of entrails. It's not entrails I'm after at all, but a way of saying, a way of making clear.

And so to Emerson: "It's the not-me in my friend that delights me." . . . .

All best . . .
[John]

TO **THEODORE ROETHKE**

Medford

September 19, 1949

[UW]

Dear Ted:

Many thanks for the poems. I would like to include "Vernal Sentiment," "Child on Top a Greenhouse," "Academic," "The Heron," "My Papa's Waltz," "Interlude." Would like also to include "Elegy for Jane," but—as per Kenyon's decision will bow to the drift of things and yield with a grace to reason. A fine poem and I regret being done out of it by John Crowe Ransom who is at best a fine poet and at worst an academic son-of-a-bitch.

The anthology rounds into fine shape and advance copies should certainly be ready by December. The *Atlantic* will do part of my general preface, the *SRL* has already run a version of Viereck's somewhat questionable piece, and Shapiro (I saw him last week and he spoke very well of your poems) is withdrawing his somewhat sketchy first preface and is working away at a new lone piece in which he recants the position of "Essay on Rime." Those are simply selling points, of course. They are all to the good, but more important, the people that really matter have come through with some damned vital stuff for this collection and I do anticipate a reasonable profit for the contributors as well as the advantage of being perhaps better understood in future.

All of which is disorganized euphoria really. What matters is that the book is a good one as it shapes up.

Have I told you about the Twayne Library of Modern Poetry? I dreamed up the name myself and the project. I'm trying my damnedest to get good poetry together and to try promoting it on a subscription basis. So far we have six titles for this year's subscription: Holmes (a reprint of *Address to the Living*), my new book, *Clinical Sonnets* by Merrill Moore, *Walk through Two Landscapes* by Dilys Bennet Laing, *Horn in the Dust* by Selwyn Schwartz, and *Fingerboard* by Marshall Schacht (winner of our first book contest with a preface by F. O. Matthiessen). *Mid-Century American Poets* is being offered as a bonus book to anyone who subscribes to four or more titles.

So far our promotion is planned for mailing lists only but as we develop some sales we mean to advertise as widely as possible. Most important, we want to keep titles in print and to use each new list to promote all the books we have done: a kind of Modern Library in miniature.

At the moment I'm scraping for next year's list and foresee a book by E. L. Mayo, Holmes' new book, probably a book of my own, quite likely a selected Eberhart, maybe a selected light verse of David McCord, and if at all possible a book by Wilbur though he may be contractually tied up. My question as per my last letter: do you have any plans for the long poems you mentioned? Nine of them with a lead article by Kenneth Burke would make a hell of a good book. Please let me know if you have any plans for the book and if this one sounds at all attractive to you. I'd dearly love to wangle Roethke for our list, and though it is still new and relatively unknown, it is not going to be that long.

All best to you and thanks for the poems. Look forward to hearing from you.

Best,
John

TO THOMAS HART BENTON

[Medford]
May 18, 1950
[FC]

Dear Tom Benton:

The moral is: never let a good man rest.

I've just returned from NY where I broached a topic dear to my heart to the front office and they like it and are willing to spend money on it and I hope you will:

How about an outsize book reproducing all of your lithos, preferably with some comment by you about each one? I can guarantee you a real production on this. If it seems advisable to you, we'll have the plates made in KC where you can supervise them to be sure they are right. If possible, we can arrange to have them printed there, shipped here for binding.

At my last count you had 52 lithos, probably more in the last year. Decker tells me you don't have copies of all of them yourself. I know he has 36 of them. Certainly if you like this notion, as I hope you will, we can find the rest of them. Frankly as one of the admirers of the guts and people and mind you can put into a picture, I'm excited about this idea. To you it may seem less exciting. But I must ask.

What I especially would like to see is (a) a real good job of reproduction—that's expensive but worth it (b) your commentary on each picture.

I suppose I'm especially hepped on the latter point. I've just finished an anthology in which I got fifteen of the leading poets of my generation to pick out a group of their own poems and do a commentary of their own by way of preface. I'm now working on doing the same thing for the British poets. Partly, I guess, I'm soured at criticism by critics. My hope for Twayne is that it can do good work for the better understanding of what's alive in our art forms. My conviction is that the artists can do that job better than any critic. I'd certainly covet the chance to have a finger in producing this really monumental Thomas Hart Benton—all the lithos with the artist's commentary. It could be as rich a way as there is of teaching an audience to see with the right eyes.

As for the production: I have the NY office's promise to make it as good as your own specifications. I hope it's a thing you'll want to do.

All best,
John Ciardi

TO ROY W. COWDEN

Medford
August 2, 1950
[MHC]

Dear Prof. Cowden:

It suddenly dawns on me, alas, too late I'm afraid, that one of my students who has just graduated from Harvard would be exactly the kind of Hopwood material I suspect you would most like. I am bringing him to your attention late only because I had been led to believe earlier in the year that he had other plans. Only today I discover that he is just wandering and that he would welcome the idea of graduate school at Michigan and the Hopwood competition.

Is it too late to recommend him for admission to the graduate school? I know his grades at Harvard will qualify him satisfactorily. I can certainly speak enthusiastically for his talent. He has taken courses from me for three years and I've had the pleasure of watching him develop in a really remarkable way as a poet. I think too he is just trembling on the edge of real accomplishment: that he has just begun the business of really finding himself and should shoot wonderfully in the next year or two.

Unhappily, considering this late date, I think he will need some assistance. I should normally hesitate to bring this up at all at this point in the year were I not certain that you will share my enthusiasm for his ability. Unless I'm wrong he's exactly the sort of person you want for the Hopwoods. Name: Frank O'Hara, address: 72 Myrtle Street, Boston.

I'm sorry we got away from Ann Arbor without a chance to say goodbye. It was a hurly burly, but a wonderful time. How your farm does shine! And your face when you look at it. The army used to have a saying that "you can get the boy off the farm, but you can't get the farm out of the boy." Now I've seen it in action. Except that this boy couldn't be kept off the farm. Joy on it and in all you do, and my apologies if this letter is simply a late nuisance. I do think you'll find O'Hara's presence in the Hopwoods a considerable reward for any special exertions that may be required to get him there, a thing you know I would not say lightly.

Our warmest to Mrs. Cowden.

As ever,
John

TO **PETER VIERECK**
Medford
September 2, 1950
[LC]

Dear Peter:

Thanks for the look at your scrap book: I return herewith. I agree especially with your article about Russia: the U.S. is certainly committed to stopping Russian expansion, and painful and bloody as that must be, I think finally we must take on the job. My best hope is that absolute mop up in Korea coupled with just such a pronouncement as you suggest (that further aggression will be countered in exactly the same way) is our best last hope for a chance at peace. If we draw a line and say, "It's war the minute you step over it," the step may not be taken. . . .

I wish I were as sure I could agree with your literary wars. With the premises, yes. But damn it, Peter, I wish you'd stop journalizing. I don't trust your journalism: I suspect the better part of it is self-advertising. Anyhow, I've thought a number of times of writing something in support of your position, but I've finally decided I'm not going to do it. One, because I've lost my taste for literary wars. Two, because even Longinus couldn't be sublime in the newspapers and in the *SRL*. Three, because you can't write to a program anyway; all you can do is write what you find it possible to write. Four, because I like it better in my own garden.

I've decided therefore to ignore crusader Viereck, or journalist Viereck, in order that I may honor poet Viereck when he's at his best. All we can be is ourselves. Whereby my blessing on what you are, but if you let these journalistic crusades louse up any part of the gift that makes your best poems sing I shall curse you by bell, book, and candle unto seven generations.

This is my defensive line against Viereck, an inch over it and there we stop. God bless you, poet Viereck, and to hell with the journalist in you.

All of this in a purely Pickwickian sense and with all personal best from our house to your house.

[John]

TO MERRILL MOORE

Rome

May 21, 1951

[LC]

Dear Merrill,

Wonderful to hear from you. This is practically our last gasp in Rome: we'll be leaving in a few days for a gradual trip back to England via Florence, Cannes, and Paris, and the Queen Elizabeth on June 30.

I'm delighted that all goes so well, and your newses are certainly all good. I'm especially delighted that [illustrator, Ted] Gorey is getting this chance to launch himself: I have great faith in the final success of his little men. I think they will have to create and educate an audience for themselves, but I see no reason why they shouldn't. . . .

I hadn't known that Lowell's new book was out. I look forward to it most happily. There were the seeds of a potentially rich development from violence to calm in his last collection of poems. I shall look forward to seeing how the development has developed. My only reservation about the earlier poems was that the violence was always the same violence and that it was always there before the poem, so that one could with perfect ease yank one line out of each of twenty poems and have a twenty-first poem almost identical to the others. But what a damned good violence it is!

My own new opus, *From Time to Time,* will be out in June, according to Steinberg. My change is that I'm getting more difficult to understand: I find that I'm beginning to make friends with my own madness. Is that a serious symptom?*. . . .

Best ever,
John

*Dr. Moore was a practicing psychiatrist as well as a poet.

TO THEODORE ROETHKE

Medford
September 18, 1951
[UW]

Dear Ted:

Many thanks for keeping "The Lamb" in your head. That's good lodging for it.

As for Who's Who I'm very ready to put it in writing. viz. Roethke has 50 rhythms for every one Lowell manages. That's not crap: I believe it. Yours is the dance. And there's always K. Burke's agreement. That's certainly two extremes of taste represented. May you never get off the center.

Both our bests,
John

TO MERRILL MOORE

Medford
October 7, 1951
[LC]

Dear Merrill:

I've spent the week going over this last batch of sonnets. I am returning herewith those sonnets that I think should not be published. That leaves me about a dozen, none of which I would mark higher than B at the moment. I want to keep them and study them more carefully and again. . . .

That isn't many out of so many, but it's probably about your ratio. One of these days I'm going to buy you a six foot high wastebasket and send it to you as lesson one in English MM: Versification. The wastebasket is a necessary part of your method of writing: an improvisation can hit only now and then. I can't help feeling however that you would hit much more often if

a. You'd acquire a set of warning signals to light up when you have committed a cliché.

b. You stopped *lunging* from rhyme to rhyme in the course of racing through the poem. Many a good idea that could have become an interesting poem seems to me to die of one of those two faults or of both. Rhyme is an addition to the poem: it is not to be conceived of as a ring through the bull's nose.

There's another question in my mind. You want these for *More C[linical] S[onnets].* Question: what is a Clinical Sonnet? If you use a title I think it should be meaningful. As nearly as I can see there's damned little that's *clinical* about these. They are not *More Clinical Sonnets.* They're *More Moore.*

Let me say at once that this assumes some interest on your part in turning out a book of poems whose aim is some sort of aesthetic accomplishment. Every idea that goes through your mind and emerges in approximately 14 lines is not an aesthetic accomplishment. One in fifty or a hundred might be a sound ratio as measured by a strict eye. One in twenty-five by an indulgent one. On the other hand, if all you want is to turn out books, I can't argue. I'm in the publishing business. MM sells, and we will continue to publish MM as a good investment.

But only one of your egos wants that. There's another one, or a part of the same one, maybe its obverse, that fundamentally means to score the aesthetic accomplishment, as above.

I'm assuming that counts most with you. Therefore I'm being tough about it. I doubt that there are more than six out of this total batch that I would publish on that basis.

Should you want it loosened up, that's OK with me, but when it's loosened up my interest can no longer be aesthetic.

On the strict scale I would estimate that it will take 400 to 500 more sonnets . . . to mine a book of about 50. That as a minimum. It would be a better book were it selected from one to two thousand.

But the main point I want to make is that I'd like the *Clinical Sonnets* to be *Clinical,* psychiatrically clinical. After all, there *is* nobody else that has the fund of technical information to do that kind of sonnet. I think it's your strongest vein, and I want to urge you to mine it. . . .

How about coming over for an evening for a Moore-Ciardi clan meeting? We'll find a can of beans somewhere and a bottle of something and then we can hole up in the study and talk. We'd love to have Mrs. Moore if she can make it. I'll wait to hear from you.

Best,
John

TO MERRILL MOORE

Medford
October 16, 1951
[LC]

Dear Merrill:

Good to have yours of 15th & 16th. I agree with you about Gorey. Jack [Steinberg] and I are currently hot on the notion of an illustrated spoof book called *Gobbledygook: A Lexicon for Upper Echelon Gov't Workers.* 64 samples of Federal prose, 64 definitions, and 64 illustrations. Jack suggested Gorey, but I don't think he's orderly enough to depend on.

I'll hope to see him, however. He's a pleasant joker.

All best to you.

John

P.S. Top secret: We're going to have a baby! Judith doesn't want it known, but MD's can be told I should think. Is there any inside dope prospective parents should have? She's going to a Dr. Heels in

Cambridge and is reserved in at the Mt. Auburn Hospital for late March.

TO WALLY BROWN

[Twayne, NYC]
February 1, 1952
[FC]

Dear Wally:

Nice to hear and to know all goes well and that the long labor [a biography of eighteenth-century author Charles Churchill] comes to an end. I certainly have no doubt that it's a good book—you've certainly put enough work into it—the problem is to sell it, which in the case of literary titles is a tough one. Booksellers generally prefer rat poison to literary scholarship, unless it happens to be some age-encompassing basic book.

Which is to say I don't see how it could possibly work out on the general trade list. But I would be delighted to see it for the UKC imprint on some sort of, alas, subsidy basis. If that strikes you as possible, let me know how many copies you think should be printed, and I can give you the details. I wish that weren't the only way of handling scholarly books, but this side of the millennium I'm afraid it is. We can certainly assure you better distribution than you are likely to find through any other university press.

These have been tremendous days for us. Italy was tremendous and we got in a high month in Austria where I lectured at the Salzburg Seminar in American Studies. And between trains and drinks I finished off a first draft of a translation of the *Inferno* and wrote some poems. And, it seems, conceived a child: Judith is booked into the hospital for April 1, which retrospectively makes the child either French or English. All we know for sure is that it wasn't started on the Channel.

How goes with you? I'll look forward to hearing.

Much best,
John

TO FLETCHER PRATT

[Medford]

March 24, 1952

[FC]

Dear Fletcher:

. . . . Judith is a smiling vision on her bed of maternity (from which she is beginning to rise). Young Myra Judith began as an interesting microbe, but became beautiful yesterday. We have finally decided she has joined the human race, and rather lavishly. There is no fonder joy.

Much best,
[John]

TO M. G. "BUD" ORENSTEIN

Medford

May 12, 1952

[Peggy (Orenstein) Young]

Dear belosted:

I had all but abandoned you to the abysses of time and space. Not so much as a memory abided. But still a wan ghost of a memory, a shadow in the cellerage crying, "Remember me."

But there you are old mole and joyously received.

Ergo in primus: Wife Judith delivered unto us a child of rejoicings. Myra Judith Ciardi arrived March 19 in the seven pound class and made it immediately manifest that she was more beautiful than you could well believe from the telling, so I won't tell it. Next the Ford Foundation's Fund for the Advancement of Education decided it was willing to support us next year without my doing any work and I accepted pleasantly with a sense that I had already done my duty in populating the world anyhow and was entitled to subsidy. And as you can see [from the Twayne letterhead] I've drifted into the publishing business. (I enclose a list of our first list for your amusement, bemusement, enthusement, refusement—whatever it provides.) So far the business is much promise and no cash, but given time enough I'll manage to trade in my New Departure Coaster for an upholstered pogo-stick. And that's about the news except that I'm about to take off on a wide summer tour of the writers' conferences, but damn it not to Calif. I will get to Salt Lake in June, but that's a bit short of the mark, alas, and the schedule is too damned tight to play with. I'm scheduled to do a duty in Cambridge on the 16th, I will then fly into Salt Lake arriving in the wee hours of the 17th, remain till the 29th, go to Laramie for a one night stand on the 30th and to Boulder for another one night stand on the 1st of July and then to Florida before cutting up to Indiana on my way to Vermont. Why the hell don't you run up and insure Salt Lake City in the middle of June?

And while you're at it insure me. Also Twayne. You ask who distributes and the answer is the angels. We don't have a really hep West Coast outlet. Do you know any sharp rocks that want to take it on? We've got some pretty good titles forthcoming including two books by B. de Voto, an autobiography of Sidney Bechet that I picked up in Paris, and a thing called *The Great American Parade* by Henri-J. Duteil (a Frenchman looks at America with mingled feelings but a really sharp eye).

And that's enough Ciardi. What's by Orenstein? Why don't you get me a really fancy job lending *ton* to the picture business. Tell them I'm a non-participating technical consultant in unified field theory semantics and one of the few living survivors of post-prandial cybernetics. I am also sometimes known as Velakosky and occasionally as L. Ron Hubbard. Moreover I am the only tri-dimensional entity in this continuum who has manifestly experienced prenatal memories as far back as two weeks before the conception of my great grandmother Lulu on the Admiral Dewey side of my wife's family.

[John]

TO MAX GOLDBERG

[Twayne, NYC]
June 5, 1952
[UMA]

Dear Max:

. . . . For the next several months I'm a dead duck. Prentice-Hall sent back enthusiastic reports on the *Inferno* and want to use my version for their forthcoming World Lit Anthol but that means I have to do 11 cantos from the *Purgatorio* and the *Paradiso* by October 1 and meanwhile I've got a summer full of writers' conferences. I don't think I can deliver in time but I'm hoping I can make it close enough to being on time so that they have to play along with me. Anyhow it's a break and a good one. They are also pondering a deluxe trade edition and also lining up a pocket book edition. If all this goes through the world's a marzipan.

Incidentally do me a political favor will you? A whisper under the hat, so to speak. I note John Bruchard will be on your list of speakers. I'm angling for a job at MIT as the perfect solution of my problems. He seemed enthusiastic when I saw him several months ago but I've heard nothing from him since. Any discreet plug you can slip in will be repaid you with ichor in heaven and with alcohol when next we meet.

My love to Shirley and to all them there girls. Someday I want you to see the 11 pounds of girl we've achieved. An obviously amateur event in the eyes of you professionals but it looms large on our small scale. . . .

Best,
John

TO JACK STEINBERG

[Medford]

September 10, 1952

[FC]

Dear Jack:

Thanks for a fine letter. As you know, I have never felt any sense of division or of far reaching disagreement on any of the matters we have been airing. I think it is well to air them and to compare minds, and I'm grateful to you for patience, understanding, and concern.

As you know, I'm sure, I want more than anything else to be able to devote full time to Twayne, or at least to reduce my teaching to a nominal connection and to make Twayne the main issue. For I believe we have a good formula. The pocket books are going to do some far-reaching things to big publishing and the best-seller chase. I think if we stay alert to that we can profit from the situation, taking advantage of the fact that we are building a solid list of nonfiction which may never become spectacular but will tend to stay solid. . . . .

Much best to you and many thanks and we must certainly get together in December. Item: If you don't mind sleeping on a studio couch please stay with us. (Unless it seems urgent to be at the hotel with the convention.) In any case, you're most welcome and we'll look forward.

Best,
[John]

TO MERRILL MOORE

New York

September 25, 1952

[LC]

Dear Merrill:

. . . . . IF I ever finish the gd Dante, and IF I am still alive at the end of this hassle, I give you my solemn word that never by word, thought, or deed shall I incline, bend, stoop, approach, consider, involve, revolve, tort, retort and/or contort, nor encourage any other to do likewise in the matter of any translation of anything anywhere at anytime, so help me Guod Ruhtracam and the other backward demons.

As ever,
John

TO MERRILL MOORE

Medford
November 3, 1952
[LC]

Dear Merrill:

. . . . . At the moment I'm half-sad and half-mad. I've just finished telling Prentice-Hall to go to hell at the end of a long negotiation anent fees for including my *Inferno* in their *World Masterpieces* anthology. That may have been a bad guess, but promotion or no promotion, I want $20 per canto and the best the bastards would offer was $4. So fuck 'em.

That's spleen stored over from the letter I just finished and good to get out of my system. I know you won't mind.

Best,
John

TO MERRILL MOORE

Medford
November 6, 1952
[LC]

Dear Merrill:

. . . . . And oh brother! This is *top secret,* please. Judith doesn't want it known, although she won't be able to keep it secret for very long, but we slipped up somewhere and we're due for child #2 in May.

Personally, I like the idea, but it is a bit rough on her to have two so close together. Thank god she's a healthy beast. But oh the clamps that begin to close on the future. Ah well. (Let me repeat though: please keep that under your hat for a couple or three months. After that it will be very much out in the open I fear.)

Best,
John

TO J. FRANCIS MCCOMAS

[Medford]
December 8, 1952
[FC]

[Mr. J. Francis McComas and Mr. Anthony Boucher, editors of *Fantasy and Science Fiction,* accepted a story of Ciardi's called "The Hypnoglyph" published under the pseudonym John Anthony.]

Dear Mr. McComas:

My girl Friday has left for greener pastures, and I'm temporarily my own typist, which accounts for (a) the delay, and (b) the ragged—though I hope legible—typing on the enclosed.

I'm delighted of course that you like it, or at least come close to liking it, and I hope the changes I have made will seem the right ones.

The pseudonym is for hard cause. When my last book of poems came out, some of the reviewers had me down as a Philistine for having published in the *New Yorker.* I can imagine what they'd do if they found out I was taking a stab at stf [science fiction]. In absolutes, that's certainly an irrelevance, but this side of glory it makes reasonable sense.

I'll look forward to hearing from [you].

Cordially,
John Ciardi

TO ANTHONY BOUCHER

[Medford]
January 8, 1953
[FC]

Mr. Anthony Boucher
Fantasy and Science Fiction
2643 Dana Street
Berkeley 4, California

Dear Mr. Boucher:

I'm delighted, of course. All the more so since the story is my first stab at stf. For the moment I'm on a strait-jacket schedule of translating the *Inferno*—actually I'm on the *Purgatorio* now—and I foresee that I shall be dangling between heaven and hell for some time to come, but I certainly mean to take another whack at stf or fantasy once I've made it to heaven.

Your suggestion for a change from hypno-feely to hypnoglyph is a beauty. By all means. Will you catch the places in the text where it says hypno-feely? . . . .

Best wishes and my delights.

Sincerely,
John Ciardi

P.S. No, I have never used the John Anthony pseudonym before. Nor am I especially concerned with hiding out from myself. If you want to tell the reader that John Anthony is John Ciardi that's all right with me; I just want the different signature on it to indicate a different category as James Branch Cabell once changed to Branch Cabell to separate one set of books from another.

TO WILLIAM SLOANE

[Medford]
January 8, 1953
[FC]

Dear Bill:

. . . . Did you know that I am now officially an stf writer? Just for the hell of it I ripped off a story called the "Hypnoglyph," and when I sent it to *F and SF* they bought it. I don't mean to make a practice of it, whether I could or not, but I feel as if I had won a bet. I have, if only with myself. . . . .

Much best for the New Year and on, and to Julie. I'll hope to see you soon. . . .

As ever,
John Ciardi

TO CLARENCE DECKER

Medford
January 8, 1953
[FC]

Dear Deck:

Good to hear from you and a happy New Year. I have received two copies of the *Review* with the Dante translations and am delighted by its appearance. And delighted, of course, that Tom and Rita [Benton] and others are pleased by it. I may honestly say that I have really labored at it, and I think I may claim it's the first translation into idiomatic English. Well. I await anxiously those hundred off-prints so that I can scatter them about to get comments on them. . . . .

Joys,
John Ciardi

TO THEODORE ROETHKE

Medford

January 22, 1953

[UW]

Dear Ted:

I had hoped to see you last week. Flew into NY on my way to deep New Jersey, but as it turned out I only had three hours in town and was logged up in a big operation with printers and designers and then had to run like hell to get across the river and on south. . . .

Mid-Century Poets has more or less petered-out and I don't know what the exact figures are, but they're not nearly what I had hoped for. The salesman got enthusiastic about arguing bookstores into advance sale and it looked as if we were really hot until the returns began to come in. By returns I mean returned copies rather than election results. Or maybe I mean the same thing.

Anyhow shoot me a letter and I'll shoot it on to NY saying for Christ sake let's settle this one. Publishing is the goddamnedest juggle off the boards. If we paid all our bills we wouldn't have any money left to operate with. . . . .

I'm afraid I'm homebound for the next few months. Judith is mothering again in May and necessity and the psyche both speak for my roostering around the barnyard to protect the nest. Fathering is good stuff.

Do you know any really good poets under 30? MacLeish, Wilbur, and I are trustees under Amy Lowell's will to give away $2000 a year to young, able poets. With a big hitch: they have to take the $2000 and go to Europe for the year. So we've got to find young, able poets with some additional income. What the hell. Let me know how your act goes. . . . And happy benedictions.

John

TO RICHARD WILBUR

Medford
January 23, 1953
[RW]

Dear Multiple Wilburs:

I certainly see no profit in advertisements to Charlee [Richard Wilbur's wife] which are answered by Dick, but chin up, shoulders back, and bloody damned head unbowed. At this point it's good to hear even from Dick.

Glad to know you're in on the Amy Lowell thing. I have transmitted your acceptance to Harvey H. Budy of Choate, Hall & Stewart and you should receive a tinplated certificate of something or other in due course. . . . .

I goddamn know what you mean about drama. Haven't the slightest notion, after many attempts, how to start one. Guess I'll stick to the Dante which has made substantially no progress since. I've been at other things. Busy absorbing murdering things. One burst of writing a while back. After that just business. Well.

When do you get back? I just got some reprints of my first five Dante cantos which appeared in UKC *Review.* With many typos included, herewith. As set up for book it will have intro to each canto and notes to same. This is just the text. If you spot anything that outrages you, please sound off. One thing I'm not sure of: I've worked many lines so that they won't come out metrically unless they're read with meaningful emphasis. Sort of a steal from Frost (theory rather than practice).

It may stumble some readers. One commentator said I couldn't scan. Fuck him.

Myra is beautiful. Judith is ample. I am wondering if the roof will leak next year.

We anyhow have one meal taken care of: we accept the Wilbur's invitation to a really hot meal. You can't make it too hot for Judith. You can for me. Myra expresses no opinion and couldn't even have read more than half your letter before she threw it out of the high chair. A critic.

I love only Charlee and I conceive her husband (name's Dick isn't it?) and my wife (name of Judith) to be in a foul-spirited conspiracy aimed only at keeping us apart.

Love and X
John

TO JOHN HOLMES

[Medford]
January 30, 1953
[FC]

Dear John:

. . . . . I am quicksanded in the goddamn paper swamps.

Lectured at Andover last night.

Have a job offer from Rutgers. May go there. But details pend.

Myra is beautiful and has picked up a word: "Datin" pron. to rhyme with "Latin" but very trochaic and frequently repeated.

Judith has gone to her bulge doctor.

I am tired of science fiction and wish to find a really good title for the Twayne list.

Best,
[John]

TO RICHARD WILBUR

Medford
February 5, 1953
[RW]

Dear Dick:

. . . . . You'd make me very happy if you'd look at the enclosed poems (a section titled *Poems from Italy*) and give me some reaction to them. Scrawl on the sheets if you like. I miss those damn poets' meetings; worse, I doubt that we'll be around Boston next year. Ah, well.

This is really no job to knock yourself out on, but Jesus I'd like to get an outside eye on them. And fuck you if you try to be polite: go ahead and slash if you like. Why don't you send me some of yours so I can explain in detail what a shitty poet you are? You'd really be a frightful slob if it weren't for your wife, you know.

John

TO KARL SHAPIRO

Medford

February 6, 1953

[UC]

Dear Karl:

How goes it with you? Are you still commuting to Iowa? I'm loafing on a Ford grant this year, i.e., working like hell on the *Commedia,* but I stay home so the family has me down as loafing. Anyhow child #2 is underway (that's what I get for staying home too much).

Best to you and E.

John

TO FLETCHER PRATT

[Medford]

February 6, 1953

[FC]

Dear Fletcher:

. . . . . MIT has definitely fallen through. New considerations introduced into the negotiations make me unwilling to consider the job. So it looks like Rutgers if that comes through. In many ways I'll be happy to leave Boston, in some ways sad. In all ways I'll be happy to be near NY. And if Rutgers seems wholly untenable I guess we gamble on ravens, lectures, best-sellers, and odd-jobs. What is beginning to sour me on the academic picture is that some of my difficulty lies in being too good. You'll know what I mean. Old 2nd Lts. don't want any Captains appointed from outside. . . . .

Best
[John]

TO KARL SHAPIRO

Medford
February 19, 1953
[UC]

Dear Karl:

Very likely you're right about that last batch: I never know what I've written till I've had it around for longer than I've had those. How about this batch? Wilbur saw some of them and is announcing to all that I'm headed back to the church. I told him I was heading back to the *Golden Bough.* Anyhow herewith. In case you've any doubt of the references in "Sunday Morning," everyone is meticulously accurate—the poem was a sort of rummage over a week's reading.

All best and to E. Will you be in Chi this summer? I'm heading for Superior in mid-June.

Best
John

TO RICHARD WILBUR

[Medford]
March 4, 1953
[RW]

Dear Dick:

Yrs mit poems and comments arrived this morning and I'm tremendously grateful for your comments which I want to weigh into the soul further . . . but which make sound sense at first, second, and third sight, both giving and taking. Let's do more of this; it's damn near impossible to get a decent eye on things and I find it tremendously valuable. I won't send any more poems until you send some, but send some.

I like the bat-piece, especially the last stanza. One of your best touches, full of grace and poise and wit. And a terrific last line. The only two questions I am inclined to raise (and the first of them without much emphasis) touch stanza one. "Some bat"—would "a bat" be any more direct? Just the question for its own sake almost: either will work with me. I am less certain, however, of "*senseless* wit." The second meaning of "senseless" doesn't work for me. (Assuming, in this case, that "not involving the senses" is the second meaning, and that the primary here is "silly.") I guess it becomes a question of how literal a poem must be to fact: the fact is that the bat is using its senses to beat all hell. Would "witless wit" be too manufactured and Viereckiast? "Twittering wit?" I'm curious, too, to know your score on the bat-wit rhyme when all else rhymes so roundly. I have no objection whatever; just interested in your statement of policy. (See *Mid-Century American Poets.*)

I've been working like hell and scribbling bits of poems here and there but I haven't looked at them often enough to know what the hell they are. Have been working on getting the Dante ms. in final shape, and am delighted to report that New American Library (Mentor-Signet) has just taken it on for early '54 publication. It ain't exactly vast wealth since it will be a small edition as paper-bounds go (75,000 copies!!—and that's small they tell me) but much pleased withal, especially since that leaves me with the reprint rights undivided in my pocket.

Sadly, I must repeat that the chances of our being around these parts next year are very poor. It will be a while yet before Twayne can really support us and meanwhile we gotta eat. But maybe Charlee can come visit (somebody has to baby-sit after all). In the line of which we are anticipating May first with anticipatory anticipations. I want another girl and to hell with dynasty. Daughters are obviously a choicer sex. . . .

Anyhow thanks again that the eye is sharp and the finger true. I really feel enormously helped toward these Italian pieces. I doubt that it's a mood of poem I'm likely to be back in, but there is a certain feeling about the batch that I want to bring through.

Most best and leave us hear. As for example: poems, when do you get back? how goes?

And pray to be so kind monsieur as to direct to your wife the attestations of my passion the most distinct.

John

TO RICHARD WILBUR

Medford
March 29, 1953
[RW]

Dear Richard Wilbur:

I am a reader of your poems in the *NY'r,* and I must say I am surprised to enjoy them very much, especially after what my father keeps saying about you. Does your wife write them for you? My father says the only really creative thing in the Wilbur family is Charlee, which is your wife, and so I thought maybe she did, but you've probably gone to Washington—or is it Oregon?—to the Eberharts so I guess it doesn't matter since you may not receive this.

My father says he agrees with you about the poets for the Amy Lowell poetry but he can't raise an answer from Archie [MacLeish] nohow and to hell with it; it's supposed to be his baby too and if he ain't worried, why ever at all?

When are you going to send my father some of your wife's poems? He likes to read poems. He has been writing poems too. Only a few, but all of them immortal I think. I think my father is the immortalest damn man! Right now he's practically insufferable to live with on account of having sold his *Inferno* translation to Mentor Pocket Books. They keep telling him it won't be published till next year, but he keeps dragging me into drugstores and making me drink malteds while he sneaks a look at the magazine rack to see if they've got it yet. I don't like drinking 17 malteds every time we go for a walk!

When are you going to be coming back from Sandoval? My father is going out on a lecture tour starting the middle of June, and then it looks like as if he has to go to New Jersey to buy us a house because it looks like Rutgers for us. My father is plenty mad too. "Just when we had the Wilburs worked for a meal, we have to move!" he says. "I don't care if it is a good job," he says. "It's just a damn shame to let them off the hook!"

And when I look at that picture of my mother sitting on your lap, I'm sad too. I would like very much to sit on your lap. And here just as it looks as if my lap will come through, we have to go move to New Jersey. I think it must be fate, so please write a poem about me instead and I will understand what you mean between the lines the way my father understands Charlee. My father teaches me very much useful knowledge in this way.

Yours for a hell of a learning process,
Myra

TO RICHARD WILBUR

[Medford]
April 8, 1953
[RW]

Dear Dick:

Are you back from the far ouest? Wish we could have hitch-hiked it with you. The current *Poetry* is in with the review of [your] *Ceremony* which is largely full of shit; all these juiceless and joyless sons of bitches kneeling before poetry and praying for significance, God, and renunciation instead of enjoying it. I get more furious at that particular tone than at any other. Fuck the significance, friend; let's dance. This to say against the thin shadow of Thomas Cole that I like your dancing and that it's a damn sight more filling than Cole's aesthetic-religio crapicus. . . .

By the way, it's damned interesting to me to note how the little review reviewers love to pick out poems from the *NY'r.* Anybody that takes down one of them thar checks has sold out his significance for dirty dough. Reminds me of a roundup Delmore Schwartz once did for *Partisan:* the gist of it was that unless there's something wrong with you there's something wrong with you.

The only thing I regret about these angers and oppositions is that Peter Viereck would agree with them. Ergo there must be something wrong with them. Distrust everything. And beyond this disregard.

And send me some poems so I can decently send you some poems. Liked the last two in the *NY'r* very much. When do you get back? When does Charlee get back? Please answer the second question first.

Judith, for reasons obscure to me, sends love to you and Charlee. With a sense of much greater clarification, I send love to Charlee.

John

TO E. L. MAYO

(see letter of April 29, 1948)

[Medford]

April 9, 1953

[FC]

Dear Ed:

. . . . . I'm delighted you like "Flowering Quince." I think it succeeds and I think your point about the poem becoming a thing in itself is excellently taken. The *Writer* article is certainly no definitive piece. Actually it was a favor to the editor and was strictly a once-through-the-typewriter job. At $10 per article I couldn't afford to sweat at it.

As for the neutrality of nature, however, I must insist that right or wrong I believe in it. I guess fundamentally you're a religious man and I'm not. At least not in terms of God. In the illusion of writing I sometimes feel the great taskmaster's eye but for me it is a tenet of my own belief in the continuity of a tradition in whose presence I feel richer than I do in its absence.

I know what the religious argument could answer to that but it doesn't concern me. "Isn't that the same as a religious belief?" I'll say, OK if you want it that way, but I still stand by my belief in the neutral mindlessness of the universe and what I had in mind was not religious but a sense of wishing to identify with the long human tradition of art because I think it is the richest thing I can observe in the universe.

So round and round the metaphysical bush. But let all illusion be cherished if it bears fruit. . . . .

Yours,
[John]

TO VERNON SHEA

[Medford]
April 22, 1953
[FC]

Dear Vernon:

Good to hear. Actually I'm not sure whether congrats or condolences are in order anent my teaching shift. For the last seven years I've certainly had a beautiful academic graft at Harvard. Of the last five, in fact, I've been on paid leave for two years and only worked 3 afternoons a week when I did work. I'm probably hopelessly spoiled for honest toil. At Rutgers, alas, I shall have to work; but to balance the ledger, there are very good possibilities there. Worth a gamble anyhow. As a, by now, regularly installed collegiate tramp, I can always manage to fall out of the publishing business into somebody's faculty.

As for my fiction "career" *ça n'existe pas.* I had one short story, the first I wrote since undergrad days, in the KC *Review* about two years ago and was quite puffed up to have it honorably mentioned in

Martha Foley. Then, last year, I wrote a piece of sci-fic on a bet and sold it to *F and SF* (it will appear in the issue reaching the stands in June, pseudonymed John Anthony, titled "The Hypnoglyph." And that, sir, is my career in fiction in toto. . . . .

Yrs,
[John]

TO VERNON SHEA

Medford
May 19, 1953
[FC]

Dear Vernon:

As usual of late all is a mad rush and all is delayed. Did I tell you we've had a son? John Lyle Pritchett Ciardi, all of which arrived May 2 and is doing well and loudly. Wife Judith is flourishing. For some girls maternity is a beauty treatment, and, blessedly, she is some girl. . . . .

John

TO THEODORE ROETHKE

Medford
May 20, 1953
[UW]

Dear Ted:

Glad to hear of the new book. Looking forward to it. How do you like Naples, you lucky bastard? That's my home town.

Dept. of joyous news: unto us a son is born. John Lyle (for grandpa) Pritchett (for grandma). May 2. Judith flourishing. She does this sort of thing with high skill and ease.

Dept. of good news: my *Inferno* translation will be out as a Mentor pocketbook late this year or early next year.

Dept. of regrets: I'm afraid it's too late for [David] Wagoner this year, but am filing for next.

When do you get back? But why? I think you should stay in Naples and start a mob and fix me up a deal to run guns to you, or whatever gets the Ciardi family back between Sorrento and Pompeii.

Auguri,

John

And you may address me as sir, hereafter, by Jesus. You are now corresponding with a Fellow of the American Academy of Arts and Sciences, no less. I got elected on a little thing I did on Isotopic Analysis of the Morphology of Endocrinal Tissue of Bufo Vulgaris.— That and my good looks. Incidental intelligence: I'm going to Rutgers next year to organize a creative (it says) writing program.

TO KARL SHAPIRO

Medford

September 5, 1953

[UC]

Dear Karl:

All goes well, I hope. Ciardi's blossoming and Judith did me a son to go with her previous very superior job of daughtering. Hope you are the same.

This in transit. Will you pass it to the subscription dept. [of *Prairie Schooner*] and ask them to change mailing address for me to:

243 Frank Street
Bound Brook, NJ

I'm shifting to Rutgers to have a shot at organizing a creative writing program. Should you know of any geniuses who will write great literature which I can then pretend I taught them how, by all means throw them in this direction.

Best to you and Evelyn.

John

TO **ROY COWDEN**

Medford

December 23, 1953

[MHC]

Dear Professor Cowden:

It's good to have your card and it prompts me to make a fuller report than I got onto ours. I don't really remember where the report was when last entered, so I'll run through briefly.

13½ mos after Myra there arrived John Lyle Pritchett Ciardi, May 2, 1953. This summer I toured out to Superior, Wisconsin, to lecture at Teachers College there for a week, thence to Minneapolis to speak to the American Association of University Women, thence to Western Kentucky State College, thence to George Peabody College for Teachers in Nashville, thence to NJ to buy a house, thence to Medford to pack and prepare, thence to Bread Loaf, thence to Medford to attend to moving, thence back to NJ. (Judith and the children sat it out in Missouri.) The house is one of these new split-level boxes that look like television sets and are designed for people who think like television sets but without the view screen. Pleasant but a bit too pat.

That settled, school started, Judith returned and there set in a certain amount of dying for dear old Rutgers. It goes well and things are now in hand, but it's a dull school and I could do with souls to talk to. Except that I don't have time to talk to them anyhow.

Rutgers Press is going to do a hardcover edition of the Dante (*Inferno*) in May, Mentor is doing the paper-bound in June. As an act of folly I have committed myself to doing an introduction to poetry for Houghton Mifflin. Interesting to do, but ulcer-breeding with the number of other things that pile up.

Poems keep arriving but I keep suspecting them. It takes more time, and time is what I lack. Have just sold a couple to *Poetry*, three to the *Yale Review*, and given three to a new quarterly called the *Volusia Review* (Florida). I am also doing the poetry reviews for the *Nation*. And I have just returned from being PBK [Phi Beta Kappa] poet at Wm and Mary. Also I have just been elected a fellow of the Amer. Academy of Arts and Sciences.

You may enjoy the story of my happiest success of the year. In Feb. I argued with some science-fiction writers that any literate person could turn out the stuff and ended up with a $25 bet that I could whack out a story and sell it to one of the three top magazines in the field. That afternoon I wrote the story and sent it to *Fantasy and Science Fiction* (*The Magazine of*). They bought it, featured it in the July issue, paid me $100, added another $35 for foreign rights, and I am awaiting another check for $25, anthology fees for permission to reprint it in August Derleth's *Best Science Fiction of 1953.* The title: "The Hypnoglyph." The pseudonym: John Anthony. I rather relish all this.

Joys to you and to Mrs. Cowden on the farm.

Yours, as ever,
John

PART TWO

Eye of the Storm

January 14, 1954, to August 2, 1972

"If I am allowed to do my work, I can not only make SR *a real center of poetic discussion, but I can raise the whole level of poetry discussion in the U.S. I certainly cannot do so if the editor himself walks in spouting such random and irresponsible assertions."*

To Norman Cousins, February 16, 1957

"Now I learn—and from a news release—that Sandy [Martin] has been reappointed to the [Bread Loaf] conference as administrative director. I am left with a sense of having played a stupidly amateur role among professional politicians."

To President James Armstrong, Middlebury College, August 2, 1972

1954. *The Inferno,* translation of Dante.

Son Benn Anthony born, December 25.

1955. Harriet Monroe Memorial Prize, *Poetry.*

As If: Poems New and Selected.

Succeeded Ted Morrison as director of the Bread Loaf Writers Conference.

1956. Named poetry editor of *Saturday Review.*

Received *Prix de Rome* of American Academy of Arts and Letters in Rome to continue translating Dante.

1957. Elected Fellow, National Institute of Arts and Letters.

Published controversial review of Anne Morrow Lindbergh's *The Unicorn and Other Poems,* January 12.

1958. *I Marry You, A Sheaf of Love Poems.*

1959. *39 Poems.*

1960. *How Does a Poem Mean?,* textbook.

1961. *The Purgatorio,* translation of Dante.

In the Stoneworks, poems.

Resigned professorship at Rutgers.

1961–62. Hosted "Accent," CBS-TV.

1962. *In Fact,* poems.

1963. Awarded Honorary Doctorate, Wayne State University.

1964. Awarded Honorary Doctorate of Laws, Ursinus College.

Awarded Honorary Doctorate of Humane Letters, Kalamazoo College.

Person to Person, poems.

1966. *This Strangest Everything,* poems.

1967.	*An Alphabestiary: Twenty-Six Poems.*
	A Genesis: 15 Poems.
1970.	*The Paradiso,* translation of Dante.
	Awarded Honorary Doctorate of Humane Letters, Bates College.
1971.	*Lives of X,* an autobiographical poem.
	Awarded Honorary Doctorate of Humane Letters, Washington University.
	Awarded Honorary Doctorate of Humane Letters, Ohio Wesleyan University.
	Awarded Honorary Doctorate of Letters, University of Delaware.
1972.	Left Bread Loaf under pressure from Middlebury College administrators.

TO RICHARD WILBUR

Bound Brook

January 14, 1954

[RW]

Dear Dick:

What could I wish for more? I really didn't have Dante in mind in the *Review* poem, but I have been forming a notion, very largely stemming from close work on Dante, of a kind of poem in which the poetry is in the fidelity to the literal accuracy of the thing, in the precision of the saying. That sometimes clogs up the rhythm alas. And so grows the wastebasket. But I think the "3 Views" and the "Old Woman on a Doorstep," and some of those poems from Italy, manage to begin to manage it. A hope anyhow. In the nourishment of which I can't tell you how pleased I am to have you think exactly what you thought. I bow. . . . .

Judith joins in sending best love from here to there and from all to all, and strictly on my own, there be ardors to Charlee.

John

TO CLARENCE DECKER

[Bound Brook]

April 2, 1954

[FC]

Dear Deck:

I'm just back from a four day lecture-jog in Florida and delighted to find your letter.

I agree. The article [in the *Nation*] had to be written fast, and a great many second thoughts have come to me. I still defend the idea that if Americans can learn to say Go to Hell with the proper accent and emphasis, a great deal will have been accomplished. But the more I think of it, the more it seems to me that the most fruitful line is to argue over and over again and on every opportunity that one is opposed to McCarthy for the very reasons one is opposed to communism: because both are enemies of the free mind. Drew Pearson has provided further valuable ammo in his recent column to the effect that much of McCarthy's anti-army material not only followed the line of the new East German Nazi-Red pact, but was actually prepared at their smear hdqs. and mailed to him from Germany.

I think if I were called before the McC committee, and if I could keep my courage firm to my wish, I'd refuse to testify on the straightforward basis that I believe McC to be a traitor and that I believe it to be my duty as a citizen to be in contempt of any Congress that allows him to be included in its number. That means jail, of course, but I'm not sure but what I'd rather be in jail defending that principle than free without principles. Except that I'm not sure, either, that I'd have the courage. As Yvor Winters once wrote:

By a moment's calm beguiled,
I have got a wife and child.

Well. . . . .

As ever,
[John]

TO **ROY COWDEN**
Bound Brook
May 15, 1954
[MHC]

Dear Professor Cowden:

. . . . . All goes well, though a shade too rapidly. Twayne, reviews for the *Nation,* schoolwork, family, trying to get a book read, working on the Dante galleys, and trying to sneak in a poem now and then—all of which happens between flying lecture jaunts—has left me in too much of a whirl. I'm going to have to cut down on something. It's fine really to have a lot to do, but it should be better unified and more reflective than a lot of it is. The most price I pay is that there comes so little time in which to read with real care.

Besides which, we have a half-acre of bull-dozed New Jersey from which I am trying to coax a lawn. That, may I say, is no hobby, but a vocation.

Rutgers, I am delighted to report, goes very well. I am on as top associate with a full professorship around the bend and with pretty much a free hand. I find it all very pleasant and even fruitful, and the boys have turned out some really good stuff this last year. I look forward to sending some of them out to Michigan to bang away at the Hopwoods in another year or so.

Judith puts in her time being a very full-time mother these days, Myra in picking up vocabulary, and Jonnel in getting up onto his feet to pull things over. Hectic but good.

Our warmest to Mrs. Cowden and to you, and may all your acres bloom.

Cordially,
John Ciardi

TO DUDLEY FITTS

Bound Brook
July 7, 1954
[FC]

Dear Immaculate Conception:

Our lttrs. once more cross-coited in the male's, bursting the honey-gland for luxury that (as rcvd) my 39th Birthday Pome on my 38th Birthday reads to you somewhere between here and eternity. You're right about its being minestrone. I am defined, sir: a minestrone resisting bouillabaisse.

And still you are right. It isn't a final poem. It feels right, but right to the track rather than to the arrival. Somewhere in this simmering broth and the bubbles, it pops to sound I, as Jesus wept, am. . . .

Or am I talking through my second thoughts? For here we are, egad (and I demand your soul's vow to silence till at least September); [we] have done it again. On or about December 25 as the star returns, we are scheduled to go into terza rima. Judith has taken off for Missouri to visit the farm before the melon hangs clearly on the vine, and I sit here like a goddamn fool laboring mightily to avoid working at an intro to pottery text I have undertaken for the HMiff little crafts for little crafties series.

And by God, I rise panting at the thought of yr. dedicating the *Frogs* to *i Ciardi*. The only book I ever had dedicated to me (believe it or not) was a lousy ms. I labored to edit and which appeared last Jan under title—get this—*The American Sexual Tragedy*. . . .

In sooth soothly,
J. C.
INRI

TO JOHN HOLMES

Bound Brook
September 21, 1954
[FC]

Dear John:

Those were really my sentiments, or at least what I have seven times felt and seven times doubted about that piece. I know there is good stuff in it, but I do think it is no for an intro. Someday I would like to write the kind of intro you mention, but that will have to be a long way off, I'm afraid. As I'd like to do that autobiography, but also find it a long way off. I wish now I hadn't let Henry Thomas talk me into that *Intro to Poetry*, but I've got it about half done now, and hope to be able to deliver next Sept. Once that's out of the way and as soon as I can tap some foundation for a free year, I'm going to tackle the *Purgatorio*. Meanwhile, if things go on at the present rate, I shall have 13 children by the time I make the *Paradiso*. Things, let me hasten to add, have no notion of being continued at the present rate. Restaurant's closing. Hurry up, please. It's time. . . .

School here has already started. Opening day was last Thursday in fact. I have no Thursday classes and celebrated Friday by cutting my first classes to go to Columbia to read a paper "On Translation" for the English Institute. Quite a high powered outfit, with large numbers of stoop-shouldered Harvards and Yales: Levin, René Welleck, Wimsatt, Cleanth Brooks, etc. etc. Went pretty well and I managed to insert a fairly prominent ad announcing that I was indeed in the market for a grant.

I suspect the reason I'm so lousy a letter writer is that all my necessities drive me to answer 15 letters a day in ten words or less. Otherwise days could get lost just answering mail. . . .

Had a good letter from Archie [MacLeish], and my God his new book is a good one! Have forty books piled up to read. Have my English Institute talk to make up for publication. Today I gave the address at first Convocation, talking from notes, and now the Pres (Lewis Jones) wants me to get it written down (and up). And 87 attendant items. I'm becoming the divided man. . . .

I saw Frost at BL [Bread Loaf] on his return from Brazil. He's full of sad tales about Faulkner as a disgrace to the colors.

John, why don't we trade some poems and comments back and forth? I enclose a start. Thanks for comments on the intro, which are obviously right. Love . . . and general joys from our generalized generations.

[John]

TO READ BAIN

Bound Brook
December 29, 1954
[MHC]

Dear Mr. Bain:

Sorry for scrawl. Typewriter clacks and family is asleep. Your letter was forwarded from Harvard. (I've shifted to Rutgers while I ruin myself in the publishing business.)

Who can find heart to disagree with a man who lives his poems? But I must. I grant no tremendous enthusiasm for Jarrell (though his

"Death of the Ball Turret Gunner" stays strong for me) but I did not pick the entries, rather had them nominated as "representative." Otherwise I find pleasure in whole or in part in all the others (maybe least in Schwartz). Wilbur manages a tremendous manner to my reading. Viereck is a crazy bastard, an oaf, and a braggart sure—his conscious mind is less than a nickel's worth to my reading, but somewhere in the mess there is a bird that sings. After all nobody is good all the time. Much the same disagreements anent the others. I'll hold out strong, for example, for Eliz. Bishop. Roethke's a queer one, but take his poems for what they are—a man dancing his way out of madness (a recurring necessity for R, literarily compounded of the Elizabethan Rant, Smart's madsongs, Blake's prophetic stuff, etc.). Sure it's crazy, but it's human crazy. At least my human crazinesss recognizes it and seems ready to answer.

But then the thought occurs that you must be sane. Always that terrible doubt. Then I re-read your letter and am re-assured. (This is kidding. No pin-pricks in such as I often find in letters from literary pin-pricks.)

Hope someday we can have that drink. Couple of years back I had a short talk with one of your gents about coming to Miami for a short spell in the summer, but nothing came of it. Enclosure is to prove I'm virile, vigorous, vibrant—it says so in print.

Best to you, and thanks again
John Ciardi

TO DUDLEY FITTS

Bound Brook
January 5, 1955
[FC]

Dear Flaherty:

I was passing the time of day with Father Ignatius when that screaming broke out from the crypt, and damn me for a black hearted robe, if it didn't turn out the curate had piles after all, and, as you might say, behind all. So it was that the Christening was delayed, as you might well imagine. And the sad and sorry part of the whole thing, being the fee paid in advance, and now the curate balking. But, ill winds turning, I'll not regret a shilling or two ill spent, if it leaves time yet for you to pipe a lay, or phone her number down, or whatever at all.

Ye *Nation* allowed me but too few words. Given more time and space I'd have liked to develop the point at which I ended, viz., that what the poet says makes no anyhow so long as he digs the dog under the skin. Trouble with a great deal of crit. (modern and otherwise) is ye too-often assumption that a poem can be had at rationally. I'll claim no holy claims against incidental rationality, but beyond that the poem has to drop pebbles straight down the well and raise ripples out of sight, else no poem. Cummings makes the right ripples, and be damned to the rational. . . .

I will believe in the speaking and the summoning of the gland, in the suckling and the thumb of the need, and ever and on in the warm self of the masturbating egg. Why else is the man born bent?

Or digging ye academ. groove, I much believe aesthetically in something like the idea of a Jungian Uncon. through which the poem must echo. Cummings is for real in that he manages to sound into it. I think something like *pause and interval* is the most neglected key to it; pace, the rate at which the writing comes at you, or better: the rate at which the writing gets into you. The flip beneath the word. Or as A MacLeish onced it: If it's not a rhythm it's not a poem.

Wld like none better, heart's faith, than to have yr eye on the new ms, and mean absolutely what I say abt inviting yr most acerbities. Archie helped me form my mind on a number of poems I had half wanted to cut. Wld be ever gratefully thine for any disasters you can spot. 'Tis hard to be critical of one's own stuff. Sometimes I am too much so, sometimes not enough. . . .

Delighted to hear of *Three Theban Tales.* Paperbacks are no way, be assured, to great wealth. NAL pays me likewise 2¢ a copy on ye fifty cent edition (was originally 1.7¢ for a 35¢ book but price was upped). Anyhow 4% is ye rate on first (hold hats please) 140,000. Thereafter goes to 3¢ per copy or 6%. Having rcvd $1000 advance some two years ago, NAL is ahead of me till copy 50,001. On the other hand these things seem to sell at a great rate. With luck, I shld be able to count on $1000 or $1500 a year from text book sale for some years. Surprisingly too, ye newsstand sale seems to have been amazemently good, last being rumor only since I have no figures from NAL.

The enclosure is a piece I did many years agone and had forgotten. Found it in *Poetry* for Feb '48 and fell to revising it. Having reworked it once, my notion now is to cut it back to stanza five and try to close it out in one stanza from there, being six in all. What think you? Am I being stirred by the memory of that first fine feckless rupture, or is there a poem buried here?

Ye ms. (I have changed title to *A Specimen Ego*) is now at ye typists. Will get copy to you on arrival, and bate my breath. Jes. Mary and Jos. a rede ye.

Fr. Clancy, ofm

TO READ BAIN

Bound Brook
January 6, 1955
[MHC]

Dear Bain:

. . . . . Thanks for kind words, but if the light dims it won't be for avidity. We've acquired ourselves 3 kids in 3 years (a fast game of Vatican roulette), the last on Christmas, and Papa has to scrounge. But I don't hold with the lily-white gape. Energy is to spend, and life's as good as any to spend it in. If I go dry of the cradle rocking, it will have been a pretty poor water table to begin with.

Joys and thanks,
John Ciardi

TO JOHN HOLMES

Bound Brook
January 17, 1955
[FC]

Dear John:

The virtues that have come upon me leave even me astounded. To begin with, my goddamn hernia'd diaphragm began to kick up some considerable, whereupon ye MD oraculated that all that was truly needful was to take off a gross number of pounds, shrinking ye stomach back into place. Smilingly, thereupon he put me on a 1000 calorie diet. And in some sort of excess of passion I have been faithful unto the jot, book-keeping every goddamn last crunch of celery. Astonishingly, [with] accompaniment of hunger-killing pills, it is not unendurable. But in the course of the last week, said poundage having started perceptibly downward, I seem of all things to have become a man of disciplines.

So I have ministered unto my students, given finals, gone well into grading, finished many, many hours of editing a painful but very exciting ms. on Vikings in America, fed and burped the baby, walked the night, and here I am even answering your lttr the same week. Tis well: this NY'rs resolution I mean to keep. More of John Holmes.

As maybe a reward of virtue, I finally turned up the Shore poem and find myself very happy that I did. It was filed under "Mortgage Payments" having been paper-clip caught to the balance sheet, whence it fluttered gently when I drew out the folder to start jotting income taxables. Another reward for trying to be early. Oh, I tell you I have grown virtuous to the point of nausea! Anyhow, I like the poem and have decided to slip it into the new book.

Anent which, I see your point about the title [*A Specimen Ego*]. I haven't, alas, eliminated possible ambiguities. I feel very strongly, or, rather, not strongly but just natively, that if a writer gets deep enough into himself he reaches everyone. Somewhere at some point, maybe at what Jung thought of as the Unconscious, everybody has been with everybody else. With the baby's need of sucking, with Myra's . . . need to curl back babywise, with the need to love and be loved, and with the crazy wonderful lost-and-found sense of being amazingly oneself. Every ego, truly found, is, therefore, a specimen ego. I'd like to find enough of who I am to make the scratching really a specimen. So the title. . . . Nevertheless, you are right on your reaction to the sound of it, and I'll have to think again. I had had it as "The Statistician's Eye" and changed it. But I know what you mean about reviewers, though fuck 'em all. Did you see Kenner's review of the *Inf.* in last *Poetry*? His reasoning on "a hundred thousand/perils" and the attached footnote strikes me as a prodigy of something. On my own poems, I can shrug *de gustibus* when a reviewer no like. But having spent enough time on Dante to know more about the *Inf.* than Kenner will ever accumulate a bibliog. for, I'm ready to sound off sour on the subject of reviewers who automatically know all there is to know about a subject just by picking up the book. Growl, growl.

Delighted that you will read the ms. of the new book. It isn't finished yet (the new typescript) but I expect it soon.

Heavens, the U of Wyo. is getting loaded these days! The last fee they were offering, or at least what I got five years back, was $750. And I have just told Brewster Ghiselin I'd got to Utah, June 20–July 1 for $500. Normally, I would not have gone there for that, but there is a good chance we can unload the kids on Cora, Ella, Edith, whereupon Utah can be converted into a paid vacation for Judith, and that I am much for. . . .

The reward of all this virtue is that I haven't written a line in weeks. Moral: don't be virtuous if you mean to be a poet. I enclose a tear sheet sent to me by *Patterns,* which strikes me as one of the very good new mags.

Leave us hear,
[John]

TO GEORGE ABBE

Bound Brook
January 22, 1955
[FC]

[George Abbe founded a poetry book club and published a book by Frances Frost that Ciardi panned in *The Nation.* Abbe wrote and complained that the review had been "rather sweepingly harsh." Herewith Ciardi's reply.]

Dear George:

. . . . I thought of you as I did the [Frances] Frost review and I thought that something is wrong about the assumption attending any review. Take these two props. in reverse order:

You publish a book, a reviewer or poet [writes] the review, you are more or less either a bastard or a good guy not on your reasoning but on whether you were "cooperative" or not, or "favorable" or not. I began a May Sarton review with "I must file a dissenting report on May Sarton's new poems." The rest of the review was reasons and analyses as specific as I could make them of my reasons for the dissent. I know damn well that this was received not as a process of poetic discussion but as a stab in the back. That's wrong. I think *This Rowdy Heart,* as stated, is a bad book. I think the reasons for and sources of that badness may be reasonably demonstrated. And, as stated, I may be wrong. But any disagreement with my reasoning or analysis must be in terms of the specific evidence presented, or directed toward showing that I left out pertinent evidence. That is, before I can consider the disagreement to bear critical rather than personal weight.

But I do recognize the personal and it was much in my mind. I am hired, and infrequently paid, by *The Nation* to give my honest estimate of books I read. I take that to be an obligation. I assume no omniscience nor inviolable rightness in offering my opinions. They are merely offered. Anyone is free to disagree, and I know very well that the reviewer himself is subject to second-thought revision.

But look. I undertook a poetry list very much on your premises. We got all sorts of reviews which in retrospect I can only consider to have been unjustifiably good by way of encouragement. On that encouragement we went ahead to drop thousands and thousands of dollars.

Let's face it: it is a naive assumption that reviews sell books. Perhaps a *massive* accumulation of unusual reviews (good or bad) plus expensive promotion *may* sell a book, but I've been in this business long enough to know that a review in a limited circulation magazine has no bearing on anything but the author's, and maybe publisher's, sense of well being. As a matter of fact, no one living knows what does sell a book short of tailoring it to book club and best seller promotion, such tailoring having nothing to do with merit, and nothing whatever [with] the sale of poetry.

Let me tell you some of the things I think are wrong with your Book Club Plan, in which I hope to hell you have no money invested.

1. You are committed to finding mss. at regular intervals. This is the mistake I made and I regret it in detail. No one on earth can find a good book of poems, or even a fair one, available for publication every month, or every X months. As I was, you are forced into going for second and third bests. Not good, just the best available. And whatever your personal good will and enthusiasm, nobody but the poet's friends [will] shell out for second and third bests. *Ça n'existe pas.*

2. I don't know what your production costs are, but unless somebody is donating labor for love alone, that binding (beautiful) is an extravagance. Doubly extravagant when you hide it under so ordinary a dust jacket.

3. Your plan envisions building up a core of subscribers (so did ours), and you are trying mailings and so forth, are you not? If I may just read the crystal ball: you have sent out some mailings and the response has been disappointing but you are still hopeful. If only you could get X more subscribers . . . My advice is to face the fact that you won't get the subscribers you have set your heart on, and if you have as high as 1% returns on your mailings, that's as high as you're going to get.

I am discouraging, or arguing discouragement, but I am not reluctant to, because I have a handsome $16,000 Twayne deficit to inform me that you probably have a sure loser. Much as I like you, I suspect you're probably a damn lousy judge of poetry anyhow, being much too kind, and much too much a man of honorable conviction and commitment to an intellectual ideal. More poems, I shall insist, die of decency than of any other single aesthetic disease. I honor your decency, George; I cannot count it as a reliable aesthetic criterion. (And don't give me that chestnut about the danger of getting too academic about poetry. All analysis of reason has to take its point from some kind of measurement and we may as well call those measurements criteria. By now criteria has become an academic word, and academic has become an invidious label. What remains in or out of the academies is that incompetence always comes to the poem in a rush of feeling tending at once to give a sloppy performance, and that anyone who presumes to suggest that a good artist would have handled that emotional point further upstage or lower downstage is being damned academic about FEELING. No go. I'm all for love. But Marshall Schacht was right when he said, "Love without arithmetic will fail.")

By God am I declaring! Pardon.

I'd love to see you and would certainly like to get up to New Haven but I frankly doubt it. I don't even get into NY these days. Remember we have a babe in arms and two others at 20 mos. and 2½ years. Lots of life noises on these roosts, and a constant demand. As a matter of the acceptance of human limits and the impossibility of getting house-help in the 20th century I have to get home to take some load off Judith's shoulders.

Let me try, George. I may *have* to take a run to Boston. It may turn out I'll have to fly up and back in a matter of hours, but if I can manage time to drive it, we can maybe get an hour or two somewhere along the route. Would like to.

Best,
[John]

TO JOHN HOLMES

Bound Brook

January 22, 1955

[FC]

Dear John:

Ills flesh is heir to. No serious problem. I've been on this no-intake diet for a week now and dropped 5 lbs. If I can stick it out a week longer, I'll be some sort of sylph, no doubt.

All I need now is to have a Dr come in and tell me that I smoke too much and drink too much coffee, which I do. Insomnia, happily, I ain't got.

I suppose it may be a mistake to do book reviews. Somebody is always objecting to something. Alternatively, one may do it a la Wm. Rose Benet and like everything. The hell with. I call them as I see them and try to give reasons that strike me as sound, admitting that I may be wrong.

And you're right about the title. I have finally turned back to one I've had in mind for some time and which is very much in my mind as a poetic key-idea, and a life-idea: *As If.* All poetry is AS IF, and the sum of all AS IF's is IS (or maybe). Anyhow, that's the one I'm sticking to and damn all.

Benn Anthony eats sleeps cries eats sleeps, all in a constant tense of eliminate-at-will. Judith weathering through. My mother arrives tonight, which will be much considerable help.

Dick Wilbur, I hear through Choate, Hall, & Stewart will be homing this summer. All goes well? I may be coming to Boston soonish for a go-round conference on the Amy Lowell thing. Prize, prize, who gets the prize? Will hope so and hope to see you.

Much best,

[John]

TO JOHN HOLMES

Bound Brook
January 27, 1955
[FC]

Dear John:

The Amy Lowell thing would be yours so fast your back files of the *Atlantic* would start spinning, if there were any remote possibility of your being able to accept it.

Amy made the will out in the '20s and provided a generous chunk of cash to be paid to a poet of "promise or good standing" who would in return for quarterly payments of $500 leave "the continent of North America," payments to stop if recipient returns without good reason. Judges to decide good reason.

All very generous when writ, but damned tight today. We can (gladly) offer you $2000 if you would be good enough to get yourself and family the hell out of North America (getting crowded here) and stay out for the year. Taken? Archie and Dick Wilbur would certainly concur.

Why the hell don't you get Tufts to give you a handsome and handsomely deserved sabbatical?

I am very pleased that *As If* strikes you as right. I've even thought of doing a piece on AS IF as the true poetic mood. Prose is IS. Poetry is AS IF into which the poet when his powers are really functioning is able to inject, and thereby to enrich, some IS (i.e. statement). Came on it when I found myself doing a note on literal accuracy and the poetic AS IF in Dante. Suddenly came to it, that *as if* runs over and over through my poems, and through almost everyone else's.

I'm blessed if I know what to do about the publication of poetry these days. Jack S[teinberg] would have to settle whatever happens about the books still in print, but I will certainly do all I can to clear that track. Have you tried U of Indiana Poetry Series under Sam Yellen?

Yellen has knocked off some pretty damn loose and lousy titles to my reading—Yellen, Babcock, Padraic Colum, Charles G. (I am

America from a plane window) Bell. Also some good ones—Wagoner's *Dry Sun, Dry Wind* and your boy Humphries' *Gypsy Ballads of Garcia Lorca.* Ball-less Baldy, incidentally, seems to be in pretty solidly there. U of Ind. Press is doing his trans. of *The Metamorphoses.* They sent me some typescript excerpts for a blurb. I found them damn good and said so. Humph gets all sorts of good marks from me as a trans., but I am still damned if I can find anything I like in Collected Tinkles.

George Abbe is also promoting a Poetry Book of the Month Club which started off with a louzoola by Frances Frost. Strictly from rotten. The board may not have sense enough to know a good ms when they see it (and a selected may be too fat for their plans, but they do offer a yearly bonus book referred to in the brochure as an "anthology" but why not an anthology of Holmes?), but they are certainly in need of good mss. Why don't you get in touch with Abbe anyhow, and with Yellen at Ind. (either with or without a feeler in advance to Horace's ghost)?

When wld you wish to leave fr. Europe?

Yr friendly travel agent,
[John]

Notes from revolting developments: A note from one Alfonso Ciardi who runs a jewelry store in Dover NJ enclosing *a partial list* of 27 Ciardis living in and near Dover (including two Johns) and would I go tell the Lions Club about Dante Feb 22? Imagine discovering 27 plus Ciardis in one town in NJ. This I have to see. (Have checked with Mother, and they are all, it would seem, sprung from my father's cousin who came over at the same time Father did. What relation are 2nd generation descendants of one's father's first cousin?)

TO DAN JAFFE

Bound Brook
March 20, 1955
[DJ]

Dear Dan:

If Washington leaves you with the sense that Rutgers was a center of intellectual stimulation, then I can only conclude that you're not in the Air Force at all, but that you have died and gone to hell without noticing it. This is sad news to break to a man, but I tell myself you have to find it out sooner or later, and you might as well have it broken gently by a sympathetic soul. Alternatively, you may have to put up with the shock of reading it in the headlines, or getting it from the Arthur Godfrey show. . . .

When you have succeeded in filling that space-warp-transmitter-briefcase with Top Secret documents just turn the dial to *Kremlin* and start on another collection. The built in transmitter will deliver them automatically, and as soon thereafter as I get clearance from the you-know-what, I can release a ton or two of Moscow gold for the time being, pending final payment. Suggest you use this expense money trying to loosen up some of the govt. girls. Even if you don't get any secret documents from them, it will turn out to be invaluable experience for your Secret Agent file. Am temporarily out of boxtops or would have sent your badge by now.

Darkly
John

TO DUDLEY FITTS

Bound Brook
March 24, 1955
[FC]

Dear Father Birdsong:

For such turds as these are souls piddled. I told Miss ——— of ye Rutgers Press (a) to fuck herself (b) to take your letters and make her own goddamn blurb. She has underlined and copied the following wishes to work same into blurbania with some such surrend fodder as is italicked:

The qualities Dudley Fitts had in mind when he spoke of "the delight I find in Ciardi's acid human earthy stance, the good control of the melos, the apparatus of poetry which I take for granted," *and whose center he finds in* "a sense of the world both earthstruck and timestruck, a thing of great violence and of great control."

Had you written, "When piddle passes for high art Ciardi will surpiss all his generation" that would emerge just as you can foresee that it will. As in the piece that surpisseth superstanding as personified in ye poem of ye same name by R. Browning, sometime referred to as Papa Pisses, subtitle Misses frum the Old Manse.

Anyhow if nothing in paragraph 2 violences you I'll flag her that, and if you want to utter a final fuxis upon it all, soit, et mal y pense. I promise no more on this subject and ye have but to let this letter die unanswered to erase its passing from world and time.

Notes from the world's illusion: I let a goodish neighbor gent talk me into speaking to a local Kulturbund anent pometry t'other night: all very pleasantly and even alcoholic, and uv coarse slew the ladies to wit, wittily. Whereupon quod goodish neighbor gent: Jesus, do you always kill them this way? If I traveled around like you do, and if I killed them that way, and if I (quote) was (unquote) a (quote) cheating husband (quote) wouldn't I (quote) fuck up a furrow (end quote). I pass you the phrase "fuck up a furrow" (by analogy to "blow up a storm" I wiz) as a gem of purest ray, and the illusion wherefrom it were auspiced as ye final wasted fragrance.

Ah wot m' prostrate of m'will
Ye bonny braes were quaking still
An' ev'ry crag frum here to Ande
Wud roar wi' stours o' houghmagandie.

Or as Cecil wrote to Pomeroy after hiding all night b'neath his sister's bridal bed wi' note-pad in hand: "And would you believe, Pomeroy, this is the very woman who only yesterday reprimanded me for picking my nose."

Have been reading the *Selected Jarrell* with much admiration and much appallment at the bursting of his sentimentals. Times I bow and times again I burst. Is it the age of tears again, father?

Ah sooner lay me in ye sod
Wi' one crinked hair from me old bawd
    Ta tie about me nappie
Than here where stony angels weep
Lookin' far a the worrld like sheep
    Or Adelaide (Mac) Crap(s)ey.

Of the *Frogs* what word? To Cornelia high words and sweetly dutiful. I do commend me to m'lord.

Prince Michael Romanoff

TO DUDLEY FITTS
Bound Brook
August 3, 1955
[FC]

Dear Father Clanahan:

. . . . . Wilt be in Andover all summer, Father? Approxing Aug 14 we are due to migrate Bread Loafwise via Boston. I have hoped to find thy image before me, and to this end shall I direct my prayers.

I am pleased to announce, sir, that Jeffrey of Harding is in this month's *Ladies' Home Journal.* Rejoice in the lamb!

And from our far-flungs, further attested by AP and UP comes word, viz:

> Karachi, Pakistan: Police Commissioner A.T.Naqvi of Karachi has ordered forfeiture of all copies of Dante's *Inferno* a work by John Ciardi published by the New American Library. The work contains matter to outrage the religious feeling of Pakistan's Moslems. AAP.

See Canto XXVIII (Mahomet) for details. But think of it: Banned in Karachi! How many people do you know, even on your wife's side, who may reasonably pretend that they have been banned in Karachi? . . . .

Achitophel Cucakarachi

TO JOHN FREDERICK NIMS

Bound Brook

August 13, 1955

[IU]

Dear John:

. . . . Thanks for your happy words about the Dante. Starting it was an act of sheer brass, but staying with it was one of the richest things that has happened to me. I'm scratching like mad for a year off in which to dare the better waters, but so far no luck. Did I tell you we've acquired three kids since last I saw or wrote to you? Myra in '52, Jonnel (John Lyle Pritchett, etc.) in '53, Benn Anthony last Christmas Day. They'll do for problems. I seem to find lots of Bachelor deals for a year off, but none that budgets enough milk.

I (more often) and we (now and then) have been heading west from time to time but it seems to work out that during school year trips I have to fly to grab the check and get back for classes, and during summer jaunts I have to drive like hell to get the family settled down in Missouri before I take off. It's not hard to long for those first easy, revisable days. Luckily, it's not hard either to find the substitute blessings.

We certainly envy the hell out of your two years in Italy. Once Benn is walking and getting house-broken, I'll have to work some sort of revolution and get us over there.

No super urgent rush on the poems. I am leaving tomorrow for Bread Loaf, returning Sept 2. Then starts a hassle of legalities. And then on Sept 12 we move to our new (new to us) house. We're going from an antiseptic bulldozer split-level to a 60 year old plantation-style ramble with much more room and infinite (5½) baths. Address: 31 Graham Avenue, Metuchen, NJ. Any time after Sept 12. . . .

Bless,
John

TO DUDLEY FITTS
Bound Brook
September 2, 1955
[FC]

Dear Fodder:

It was when the hinges of hell came loose. For six weeks I had been saying no, I can't, lack time, can't afford it. Then after three days of long soul-talks I seen my duty and couldna shirk it, so am now officialwise director of the Bread Loaf Writers Conf. A loveslabor mostly. . . . .

Marster, it delights me to report that *As If* seems to exist though Bill Sloane snatched from me all copies but one at Bread Loaf on account of customers were paying cash at the bookstore for same. Likewise I am more than a bit uncertain anent a blurb thereon signed by one D. Fitts. I gave Page Spencer your two letters in comment on and she compiled a momentous puff from them which same strikes me as gilding the words in your mouth some. I pray ye will not be embarrassed by. . . .

My back aches from banging this damn dactylograph. Have slaved all day. I founder in virtue. Save me, Father. Write me some vice. But exclude fucking: will not admit it to any category but Aspiration these days.

As of Sept 12, the Ciardi's enmansion themselves in new address:

31 Graham Avenue
Metuchen, NJ.

Plethoras
Rasmus Donny Gual

TO LOUIS SIMPSON

Metuchen

September 9, 1955

[LC]

Dear Louis Simpson:

Please forgive a scrawl. We are moving Monday and the house is upside down. . . .

I am sorry to say I don't answer to this one.* You didn't ask for my two cents worth and I may be out of order in offering it, but if I may say so as an admirer of your work, I think this one is a mistake. You have a narrative poem, but without a real assault on the fictional obligation to tell a story interestingly, and the blank verse line which, to my reading, seems choppy, seems to rush you over the details of your perception. I must report, regretfully, that I don't find a place in the telling where the description, drama, or penetration really exceeds the expectation.

Well, you didn't, as noted, ask my opinion and I must apologize for thrusting it on you. I do hope very much you will let me see some shorter pieces where the form, rhyme, or whatever has compelled your attention more searchingly to each detail of the writing.

Apologies, regrets, admirations

John Ciardi

*Ciardi was at this time poetry editor of the annual *New World Writing* (#9).

TO KENNETH REXROTH

New York

October 14, 1955

[FC]

Dear Rexroth,

Thanks for the data on Mei Yao Chen. It is a rare thing to pick up a translation and to be given a real home experience across the years, miles, cultures. I certainly look forward to seeing more of him when your trans. come out.

New Directions has been doing impressively good jobs of translation. I like especially their most recent complete Baudelaire and Selected Lorca with the poems translated by various hands.

"Journey to Love" arrived for Review last week and I have it and the new Eliz Bishop in happy anticipation ahead but have had to stick close to Emily Dickinson for a deadline I just met—and a tight squeeze—yesterday. Harvard Press has just done Thomas H. Johnson's *Emily D, An Interpretive Biog.* and simultaneously a 3 vol. Variorum of the Poems by Johnson. Magnificent stuff. But with only two weeks in which to review it becomes murder. And still magnificent. Nobody will ever again have to meddle with the text, and I doubt that any one will ever again have to misread the Life except willfully.

Roger Shugg, the last Director of the [Rutgers] Press, left last April and went to Univ. of Chicago. The new Director is William Sloane whose William Sloane Associates was semi-pirated away from him by a fast shuffle of his creditors. I think he's a hell of a gent and publisher.

Meanwhile, nose to the mortgage wheel but good for these next twenty years, I am one-footedly in the publishing business, though I am fighting like hell to keep it down to one day in NY per week, and the idea of a book on the basic documents of American History strikes me as very interesting. Can you give me a brief of method and contents? If Rutgers Press has any first look rights on it, I shall respect those, as I think I must. But if they are not moving, I'd like a chance to see what Twayne can do with it. . . .

I heard about Weldon Kees. Unhappy. Poor Patchen certainly has had it on all counts. It's amazing that he somehow keeps going. I am looking forward to tomorrow night when Francis Fergusson throws a party for Kenneth Burke. The Eberharts are going to be there and I haven't seen them for several years.

I'd love to get out to the Coast. Haven't been in Calif. since I got discharged at Mather Field in '45. I've made it as far West as Salt Lake a couple of times, and there is an indefinite prospect of going to Montana sometime this year. If that comes through, I think I'll tap for a few weeks off and see if I can't bum my way West and South check-chasing the college route.

Yes, I know of Louis Ginsberg: he keeps popping up in the mail with rather sad stuff in the Poetry Society manner. I'm glad Allen is in revolt: he has a good cause to revolt from. I'll just bet he hates bluebirds: he'd have to: his father keeps cages full of them in his head. No progress this year on *Purgatorio* but I am scheming to get next year off and sail in.

Best.

Cordially,
John Ciardi

TO DUDLEY FITTS

Metuchen
October 18, 1955
[FC]

Wholely Fodder:

Aren't you overlooking the fact that despite various apocrypha to the contrary Christ not only stopped at Eboli but was actually born there? In heaven, it is writ, only dago sts. have full citizenship. Accept none other as the true the triple the immaculate McCoy.

Speaking of translation, sir (heavenly, that is), are you giving any serious thought to the call to Princeton. I saw R.P. Blackmur Sat night at a general gala sponsored by Francis Fergusson for K. Burke and others, and R.P. was concerned, . . . and were you well? Are you well? R.P.'s assumption seemed to be that you must be ill since you were not coming to Princeton, since obviously. He spoke as how it was a permanence did you so wish it. I speak of same since I obviously wish it, Andover [Mass.] being there, as distinct from P. which is practically here.

And speaking also of trans (heavenly) have just been chortled by an invite to fly to L.A. in Dec to be the main goose at the Integration Day festivities of Immaculate Heart College. "Lady Sister," I was tempted to pen, "when I get through Integrating this here now college you will have thought twice of this here now invite." I did in fact pen same in otherwises.

You may be sure, domino, that reading that jacket was, as we used to heiss it in Old Wien, traumatic. Learn, then, as writ Confucius, that many a light word falls from the mouth with force to break the foot wha spake it.

I am, yr relevance,
ever obdtly, affly, sincly, yrs
Mesmero Augenblick

Am on Shelley Mem Awd jury
for '56. Who gits it?
Patchen? His need be great,
his poems less so. Awd is for
"genius and need." Please remit
list of needy geniuses.

TO JOHN HOLMES

Metuchen
October 26, 1955
[FC]

Dear John:

All good and joys to hear. Delighted that things go well there. Here, we manage to stay frantic. Having taken on this big expensive house with a thumping mortgage note due every month I've had to scrub that much harder at check-bearing nonsenses at the same time that I find myself with a five-year fix-the-house program on my hands. In consequence, and also because I seem to have hit a dry spell, no writing seems to come. But so it goes. Something will light the lamp again. Meanwhile I rather like puttering away at ripping the windows apart to fix sash cords, get storm windows ready, touching up paint, etc. Trouble is, it's too absorbing. I have to set myself just so much time for it, else I'd end up doing nothing else. But really the right kind of house for us—big and easy to be in and right for the kids and with cubbyholes enough to escape into.

I saw Dick and Betty [Eberhart] recently at a party Francis Fergusson gave for Kenneth Burke. Quite a round up: Blackmur, R. W. B. Lewis, Daniel Aaron, and divers other items too numerous to mention. Dick is looking fine. We're hoping to get the Eberharts and the Lewises out here some weekend soon.

I'm especially glad to know you'll be heading down this way. Do you know when? Rutgers is in a damned bad way generally for general funds, but I will certainly do my best to see what can be latched onto. Certainly some fund should be shakeable for something. As soon as you have a date in mind let me know, and do plan to stay with us. Lots of room here.

Don Hall is doing well these days, as I am happy to note from time to time. I think the one thing I really miss in this shift to NJ is those poetry meetings.* Maybe I can yet manage to sit in on one of the current sessions.

Did I tell you that I edited the poetry selection for *NWW* #9? I really came on some tremendous stuff for it. So much so that I had to beg for half again as much room as I had been given. A really exciting bunch of poems I think, mostly by relatively unknown poets. I went through an enormous batch (batches) of mss. to get to them, but found myself really astonished and delighted by what came out of it.

No word from *As If* except from Kenneth Rexroth who got it for review and has been writing glowing letters about it. I'm thinking of him as a soul's bonanza. . . .

What else: Poem in November *LHJ* [*Ladies' Home Journal*]. This piece is a kid's poem. They have one other kid's poem yet to publish. And another which is not a kid's poem. If I sell them any more poems I'm going to get some small diamonds set in my front teeth—spiritually. In terms of cold fact, the proceeds turn into aluminum windows, paint, hardwood, and eventually (as in a dream gloriously) a power saw. I've hankered for one for years during which they have become more and more expensive alas! . . . . .

Yes, I think the pruning was right for *As If.* Too many of the poems in other books have been a kind of fooling around I enjoy, but they tend to obscure the poems that scratch real itches. I tried to isolate those as nearly as I could. There is also the fact that I have tried on a lot of different bathing suits in my various plunges. I think these go in bare ass, and better that way. I mean to become a crotchety old bastard whose function it is to tell Mrs. Featherhump that God wants me to ignore her and go to bed with her daughter. No, not that. That was a while back. What I really want is to know what I'm dying of. That's crotchety, but it's a praise too, and it begins with refusal, which is the rock on which acceptance has to stand. Bill Williams, bless his dying bones, really talks to me, though I think the bones might hit harder if they came shorter. But god those last two books! "The Artist" in *Desert Music* and "Of Asphodel That Greeny Flower" in the new book are magnificences. "The Artist" does it in containment, "Asphodel" does it asprawl, but Jesus the man knows how to die burning! . . . . .

[John]

*Ciardi, Holmes, Richard Wilbur, May Sarton, and sometimes others met at one another's home on an irregular but steady basis during their overlapping Cambridge and Medford years to discuss poems they were currently working on.

TO HENRY RAGO

Metuchen

October 30, 1955

[UC]

Dear Henry:

Thanks for joyous news. What could I be but delighted on all counts?—that the prize is in the name of Harriet Monroe, that it was these three poems (I think my best to date) that were cited, that it's from *Poetry,* that it's from your editorship. Thanks in all. . . .

Warmly, as ever
John

TO NORMAN COUSINS

Metuchen
December 29, 1955
[NC]

Mr. Norman Cousins
The Saturday Review
25 W 45th St
NYC

Dear Norman:

I hate long letters, too, and will attempt to curt-ify, but [it] seems well-advised to establish starting points clearly. Wld consider yr item-by-item reactions essential to clear understanding and right start. Items:

1. *Poetry now in file as accepted:*
   a. I have gone through the file and I see nothing to do but bounce it all back. Enclosure 1 is a form letter I have prepared for mimeo to accompany such returns.
   b. I understand there are some poems in the file you feel you *must* publish. I understand that *you* will select these and that they will *all* be published before I am announced as poetry editor, announcement to be delayed until those poems are out of the way. This point is very important to me.
   c. Properly pushed, I hope all such poems can be cleared in six or eight weeks which will allow me time to contact poets, spread the word, and have selections ready for whatever issue in which I take over as po ed.
2. *Discretion of poetry editor.*
   I take a personal pride in the fact that I stand for something, and I cannot permit that reputation to be blurred. Once announced as po ed, therefore, I must insist that I be consulted on all matters relevant to poetry. All in good faith, all in good reason, but if I am mastheaded as poetry editor it must follow that anything to do with poetry will be my doing. I must therefore be responsible for what I am answerable to.

3. *Poetry policy of* SR.

In recent years, poetry in the *SR* has served simply as filler. Is this a fixed policy or a happenstance? My faith is that poetry today is alive and vigorous in a remarkable way. With no thought of leaning toward the fancy lit quarterlies I want to see the *SR* reflecting that life and vigor, presenting good poetry and releasing ideas about it. You set the limits and I'll do the best I can within them, but I'd like to know what the limits are. Once I know those limits I can draw up ways of working my ideas within the scale and present them to you for hash-over.

4. *Poetry book reviews.*

Haven't yet had time to check the backlog. Will have to memo that later. I assume that X lead articles a year will be based on poetry, that to be determined by the nature of what gets published. If Thomas H. Johnson's tremendous 3 vol Emily Dickinson plus his more than tremendous biog are not too far gone, Emily could certainly make such a lead article. If they are too far gone the publication . . . of Jay Leider's *Emily Dickinson Log* will make a point for a real ED summing-up.*

5. *The dirty word—money.*

I have a high respect for the Great Themes. What we first discussed was a matter of a couple of evenings a month of running through submissions, Part A of the job, and $100 a month seemed fair for that. Part B of the same seems to me inseparable and is also very considerably more demanding. I think we need a discussion on that.

Hope few such letters at such length.

Yours,
John

*Jay Leyda's *The Years and Hours of Emily Dickinson* was not published until 1960.

TO JOHN HOLMES

Metuchen

December 29, 1955

[FC]

Dear John:

This in haste, but I want you to know what is not yet formally announced but what I would very much like to be spread about quietly among good people, that I have signed on as po ed of the *Sat Review.* I have insisted that the announcement be delayed until Amy Loveman's backlog is cleared, since I refuse to answer for her taste on anybody's masthead.

This in strictest confidence: I have insisted that all her acceptances (for more than a year ahead) be returned. Norman Cousins holds out for a certain number of sacred cows and the deal is that he may pick out his sacred cows, publish them promptly, and let me send back the rest. My name is not to go on the masthead until the last of the cows is through the fence. I foresee some yowling on that point, but let it lift. I have prepared a form letter accepting full responsibility for that decision and returning all accepted mss. unread by the simple process of having a sec. fold in the form letter and mail the poems back. Don't leak this, please.

By all means, however, go ahead and leak the fact that *SR* po policy is changed as of now including:

1. Poems alive are better than poems dead.
    sub 1: adjectives don't take the place of things.
2. Damn well more ventursomeness applicable. I'll be bucking some pretty fat attitudes and can't full throttle at once, but any similarity between future *SR* poetry and RPT Coffin will be just as dead as each other.
3. Prompt bounce if bounced and acceptance as prompt as can be (once I have waded through AL's piled-up boxes of unanswered stuff).

This in detail because, as you must know, I'd certainly value all suggestions you can make, good poets you can steer, ideas that may come to you. The mag has been poetically dead and I'd like to liven it up as best I can.

Have not yet had time to check the book review situation, but hope I may count on you, once I'm over the back-log bump. Wld welcome suggestions anent who might review what.

And naturally I want some poems from you once over the backlog. Haste, haste, haste, but want to get this to you. Best in all, to all, for all, and many NY's to come.

John

TO HENRY RAGO

Metuchen

January 1, 1956

[UC]

Dear Henry:

This isn't for announcement yet, but I'd like you to know I have just signed on as poetry editor of the *Sat Rev.* I hope you will understand that the *SR*'s poetry policy is changed as of now. . . . I certainly have no notion of trying to make the *SR* avant garde, but certainly hope to make its poetry appear more vigorous and responsive to the best of what is going. Should anyone come in on you when you're badly overstocked or with more good stuff than you can handle, I'd be most grateful for a referral (as they say in soc work). Will be delighted to recip. In time you will receive a formal notice of all this: meanwhile wld welcome its being leaked around unofficially. As best I am able, hope to make this some good to good poets today.

Best in all for NY & beyond

John

TO **PAUL CUBETA**

Metuchen

April 8, 1956

[MC]

[As Ciardi's assistant director at Bread Loaf, Paul Cubeta managed an endless stream of conference-related details.]

Dear Paul:

Two items and a news. Item 1. Funk and Wagnalls is adding a fellowship. Details later.

Item 2. Checking my own good impression against Bill Sloane's, I want to record a fellowship choice:

Paxton Davis
Washington & Lee University
Lexington, Virginia

He is the author of *Two Soldiers,* soon to be published by Simon & Shuster. Please send him a catalogue. How many fellowships will we have available?

News. The American Academy of Arts & Letters has offered me a fellowship to the American Academy in Rome from Sept. to Sept. of next year and I shall leave with the family soon after BL returning in time for BL '57. The year in Europe will compound some problems, but I am sure they will remain manageable. Still there will be much to discuss in advance.

Please make no public announcement until after May 23. The citation will be read at the Academy's May 23 meeting and they have asked that no prior announcements reach print.

Best,
John

TO DUDLEY FITTS

Metuchen
April 11, 1956
[FC]

Dear Father Divine:

I was thinking about you among my daisies. A glory sated hummingbird, fat from lilies, gave one a prod just now, and then streaked for comfortable heaven.

I made a moral of him. But I recited it to Sophinisba, as I call her, and now I have forgotten. Is immortality such a forgetting? Something I should be doing at night keeps pecking at my mind, but though I [lie] forever in the still, it will not come. Send me a glory, father; and only I fall, unloaded, by the wayside, too gross with hunger to rise again from my fat fall.

Thus communing, as I am pleased to tell you, a cowslip rang my number and from it a voice spoke saying child, would you like to cross the water? In the city of the Seven Hills, in a white academy intended for the sun but now overshadowed by a department store, there is a goodly fellowship and you may be one. Do thou but accept. And I: Voice that speaks to me, I do accept. And there my dream ended, and there arrived a confirming letter signed American Academy of Arts and Letters. So come September or a travel booking we pack the kids and dress the trunks and go again a-Romie-ing for the Purgatorial Hills. These be intelligences father. In thy name I praise them. We will be gone for about a year. Also I detect the fine hand of A. MacLeish in this.

Father, I would be thy child. Do thou tell me from the truth of thy mind a fact I must ponder. Have just read a review by R Jarrell of *As If*, and it seems I do nothing but steal my poems from Shapiro and Wallace Stevens, saith RJ. Now I fully realize a touch of personal animus 'twixt us, but allowing for how I don't like the man, I have perceived him at times to be perceptive and at other times not. I seek no brawl, but only the gift the giftie might and seldom give us. Assuming he over-charges me. I know full well I owe much to Wallace Stevens and am happy to acknowledge same. But I can't see that I steal from Shapiro. Do I in your reading? Even remotely? I'll fuck and be damned on many a score, but sincerely, even God save the mark, humbly, I want more than all else to be aware of what the hell I am trying to do in a poem, and full well I know myself capable of blindness. Call it a strange request and it is. But assuming me to be your worst enemy—who else would write you such letters—can you see grounds, however slight, to charge me with Shapiroing? Believe me, you need not apologize if your impression finds me guilty. But I would meditate it in the cell of myself and pray to learn from the stones. . . . .

Ever thy faithful Rosebud,
Clavia Clavicle

TO PAUL CUBETA

[Metuchen]
July 20, 1956
[MC]

Dear Paul:

1. Map and poop sheet. Well done. Yr prompt action in the face of enemy fire is in the best tradition of, and reflects great credit upon, you and the Service. Good bless you, son.

2. Temporary title for Bill Sloane: I shall always be happy to talk over anything with Steve Freeman.* I don't at the moment understand "hydra-headed conference," but I am sure Steve has something in mind that will be worth listening to. For whatever clarification it may provide in advance of our discussion, the following points seem meaningful in my mind.

a. That I shall be away and that Bill Sloane, out of devotion to the conference, has volunteered without stipend to undertake the necessary personal contacts and to do a great deal of letter writing—more even than the very considerable amount he has already turned out. Some sort of title such as associate director would immediately clarify the status of any letters he writes and save a paragraph of explanation in each one. It seems an efficient device.

b. I shall still be very much in touch with you, Steve, and Bill, via airmail, and the policy of the conference will be worked out exactly as it has been this year—by such consultation.

c. Bill's title as associate director would be for this coming year only and will add no cubit to his stature but will, rather, be a service to Bread Loaf.

3. Alan Collins is president of the Curtis Brown Agency, probably if not certainly the leading literary agency there is. He is an old friend of BL and has been present at many sessions. My understanding is that the fellowships Alan provides should be matched by outside funds, but I will ask for a clarification. I am sending your letter and a carbon of this one to Bill Sloane with a request for same.

John

*Freeman was the Middlebury College executive in charge of summer programs at Bread Loaf.

TO M. L. ROSENTHAL

Metuchen
August 8, 1956
[MLR]

Dear Mr. Rosenthal:

Bless you. It takes an outside eye. I saw your point instantly and I hope the condensations as enclosed will work for you. It always takes live surgery. Cut! Cut! Cut! I've said it a million times. Yet everyone falls guilty of clearing his throat for the first X lines of some-poem.

I am rushing these back out of some sort of sense that for these poems *The Nation* is the right place and also because I have so little time before B.L. and then my sailing. I must either do it this one free day or lose months in getting to it. I'd love to get these two nailed down before I go and I think I have pared them now, but for heaven's sake don't draw back from bouncing them if they don't work for you. As your opposite number at *SR*, I think I share enough of your griefs to make the common editor's shuffle-dodge superfluous.

I'd like to write a law forbidding editors to say any more than yes or no. But only for public defense. That law would have robbed me of good counsel for which I'm truly grateful to you.

But really don't hesitate. If they don't now *feel* right to you, knock them back.

Best wishes, gratefully
John Ciardi

TO PAUL CUBETA

Metuchen
August 31, 1956
[MC]

Dear Paul:

Hope that bug has unbugged itself. You've really had it, alas! All your work, and then to miss out on the most of the reward. Philosophy, son, philosophy. Seriously, though, it was a grand conference and I am really sorry you had to miss out on it.

Many things in mind and damn little time for it. One of my concerns, as you might guess, and as Bill Sloane and I discussed at much length, is that goddamn it Middlebury can't be paying you enough and that you'll be slipping off to greener pastures. We don't want to lose you, kid, and therefore I'm going to ask a favor: before you snap up any other offer that floats around will you give me a chance to kick (a) Middlebury's ass, and (b) that producing no result, Rutgers'? That ain't no snatch: I couldn't in conscience bid you away from Middlebury, but I don't want you to get snatched before the built-in snatch machinery gets a chance. Hein?

Do me a favor, will you? Please buzz the biz orifice and ask them to send my monthly check to me at the American Academy address on the Conf. address list through the June check, but not including the next July check, which same should be sent to me here in Metuch. Yes? Many thanks.

This is in haste with the world breathing down my neck. Expect no more till from Rome. But this for joys, toward hope and pleasure, and with a real honest to God thanks for everything you've done to make the conference the really tremendous success it was. Power to you, joy to you, and you'll be happy to know that Steve has all-but agreed to go to $750 for you. Steve's "all-but" is margin enough, god knows, but you have my promise that I'll push him.

Best, and thanks again, and love to Beth and boy-o's.

John

TO WILLIAM SLOANE AND PAUL CUBETA

Rome
November 3, 1956
[MC]

Dear Father William (Sloane) and Son Paul (Cubeta):
Letter follows:

Just back from Pompeii where I found occasion to think frequently of both of you, and where I also found among the graffiti of the lesser Lupanarium, scratched there in what was obviously an uncertain hand, a notice that seemed to refer either to a new method of dealing with sexual impotence or to a forthcoming Pompeii Writers' Conference. Both the choice of the language and the condition of the inscription left either rendering possible. I am even told that it is possible for both meanings to have been intended.

Naturally, therefore, I found myself somewhere, probably in the caboose, of what may be taken as a train of thought, in which, as in a dream darkly, I seemed to find myself in the company of one or both of you. At this point the guide seemed to require fifty lira and the train was concurrently derailed.

Among the wreckage these memos pried from the rigidly mortised hand of the engineer (or coal passer):

1. Do these bones live? Does Paul Cubeta gaze yet on the light? Why, among other memorabilia of history, have I received neither word nor check from BL? What exactly is the budget and when exactly must conclusions be concluded?

2. Father of man what dost thou? Has there been any word from Eudora Welty? The line up, committed or half committed at the end of BL '56, reads from past to future: Sloane, Raney, Lancaster, Walker, Miller, Guthrie, Adams, Frost.

Is Carl Carmer clinched? I'm inclined to do without Lincoln Barnett this session (your votes?). In a burst of euphoria I asked Van Atta back, but I hope Father thee can either avert or make it a one-night lecture. Bud Guthrie has just sold his new book to Hollywood for too much money and if he finds himself unable to come, I must say it might be well.

Bud writes in high recommend of one Robt O. Bowen, Montanan, Knopfite, author of *The Weight of the Cross* and *Bamboo.* Rec for a "sort of staff job." I have been learning (slowly) to adminstrate and replied with much cordial non-commitment that nothing but a fellowship available in the novel.

Our soft underbelly is the short-story and I much welcome all recommends anent. Also damned if I know what to do for another poet (for poetry).

These words the dying man let fall and shuddered and fell still.

Thine conclusively,
John

To Norman Cousins

Rome

November 21, 1956

[NC]

Dear Norman:

I note in the list Edith Kiernan just sent me of poems in the accepted file those seven clerihews by Fadiman.

My understanding was clear on these: they were to be used as captions for cartoons and were not to be run as poetry, which they are not, nor as light verse, which they are not good enough as, nor even as clerihews, which I can improvise better than instantly on two martinis. I had them taken out of the poems accepted file once on this understanding. I am asking Edith Kiernan to take them out again.

I call all this to your attention since it may easily have slipped your mind. Can you see to it that they are, as we agreed, used as cartoon captions? That would involve the (possible) nuisance of getting someone to draw the cartoons (Edward St. John Gorey who does book covers for Doubleday and who has done a couple of cartoon books could turn them out without much trouble), or maybe you could fob them off on Bennet Cerf (than whom even these would be an improvement), or you could maybe call Murder Inc. and have Fadiman quietly eliminated, but let me humbly pray and stubbornly insist that these botches must not run as straight *SR* poetry. In Shakespeare's name.

We're freezing to death in our marble tomb. Rome has winters like those of most of the rest of the hemisphere, but it seems to have a stubborn thing against admitting their existence.

Best
John

TO JUDSON JEROME

Rome
January 6, 1957
[BU]

Dear Judson Jerome:

I agree with all your premises and side-thoughts on the way, but I can't really agree with your conclusion because there are some more premises I want to weigh in before the conclusion.

I've never tried to defend poetry to the age. What good is it to defend? I'm ready to settle for it as a kind of addiction. If one is a drinking man, he needs no defense of bourbon: he's going to go on drinking it if it kills him. There's also the situation in which a bourbon-man gets invited to a party where nothing but sloe gin and pink-ladies are served (which is very much what happens with a lot of books—both now and in the past).

That's half-kidding but also half-serious. Lift the bourbon up a whole lot of symbolic notches and it becomes something from the human spirit—whatever that is—of which the poet is a part and which goes back a long way. Something that started before anybody knew it but something that was certainly alive and going by the time the Bible got written (alive and going in the West, that is). Something about a man trying to figure out what he's about not only in decrees but in a way of saying it that makes a shape.

About that Stevens poem—I certainly have no sense of whining about the age. I am telling it some part of what's wrong with it and also how it could get better, if it would bother to. I'm not even troubled by the fact that the age won't pay any attention. I'm talking to the people who can be talked to. In a way the poem says what I said once in a review: there's a line by Wallace Stevens that runs (about) "What has there been to love that I have not loved?" I suggest that all the E Pluribus Unum signs, all the Pentagon mottoes, all the big ringing slogan noises be taken down, and that that line be put on coinage, cornice, and letterhead. The suggestion damns the age for a failure but it offers an advice from love. Sure the age is bad and sure every age has been bad, but somebody has to keep saying why and what. And somebody will anyhow. And that's a good and saving act. We can't see our own poetry yet: the Elizabethans didn't even know they had a Shakespeare—they thought they had a sort of Rogers and Hammerstein—but you try to imagine the history of man's mind without what poetry has done to it, and you come up with a weird sort of thing.

And back to bourbon—it's just a good thing in itself.

I'm sorry about my editorial squeezes. Take a look at how little poetry *SR* publishes and try to imagine how much is submitted, and you can't miss the fact that I have to return a lot of good stuff. I like this poem, but at the moment I can't accept *anything* because of overstock. Let me hold it for a while. I'm trying to wangle a little more space, and if it comes through, I'll be freer.

Best,
John Ciardi

TO DONALD HALL

Rome
January 17, 1957
[UNH]

[Poet Donald Hall, perhaps Ciardi's finest writing student at Harvard in the late forties, had asked for help locating a teaching position.]

Dear Don:

Many thinks for "Now Side by Side" and "I Chop Down Trees" which I am snatching happily for *SR* and with many thanks. Two beauties.

Mason Gross, provost of Rutgers, writes me that Rudolf Kirk, acting head of English, is instructed to look you up at MLA or thereafter. Have you seen him? I very much hope, selfishly, that you can be wheedled to Rutgers. It would be fun to have you around and I think you'll find the proximity to NY a generally happy thing.

Clarence Decker, vice-pres of Fairleigh Dickinson writes that he's all set to latch on if I will write and assure him that you are a good teacher. I wrote him that I have had no opportunity to observe you as a teacher, but that I would certainly guess you to make a better one than he had ever managed to be. Well, not exactly that, but approximately that sense. The trouble with FD is that it is very small and very poor. If they come crashing through, you might do well to stall them a bit, keeping their offer in reserve, but I doubt that their salary scale will be especially tempting. Just guessing. Brooklyn's salaries are extraordinary, but the rate of advancement is correspondingly slow.

I'm sorry to say I have practically no control over the actual appearance of poems. Accepted poems are set and proofs are filed while the metal is held in Phila. Then layout patches the issue together and when a hole shows up they pick out a poem that fits into that hole. The dirty word, I'm afraid is "filler."

A couple of letters from Bob Pack. We're hoping to see them in Florence if I can ever fight clear of this time-flail I'm under.

Best,
John

TO DONALD HALL

Rome
January 19, 1957
[UNH]

Dear Don:

Yrs to hand and joys indeed. I'm delighted that it all has gone so well so quickly and I very much hope selfishly for my sake and unselfishly for your own that you take it. Rutgers does in fact have a great deal of room at the top and as fast as I can buy cyanide it's going to have more. Seriously, quite a number of gents in the Full Bracket are up for retirement within the next five or six years. Happily, we'll lose a couple of duds that way. Sadly, one major dud will survive and will be in line for head. (I promise you he won't get it alive.) But that's only to say that the dept divides into Young Turks and Old Guard, and the Old Guard is due to muster out soon.

All of which is really irrelevant. Five or six years from now, enrollments will be so swollen they'll be kidnapping street car conductors to teach electronics and Jehovah's Witnesses to teach comparative philosophy. I'll bet my shirt that nobody today can even approximately guess how unpredictably wide open it's all going to be then. It is certainly not a point that need occupy you.

All right, then, what's a fair statement of things?

First that Rutgers men are not Harvard men. There are no snobs, there are plenty of slobs. Rutgers is wakening from a long hibernation (some of which still has tenure); it has ended a long, slow process of change by becoming the state university of NJ, and it is therefore suffering from the NJ High School system more than would a non state-U. You won't find any brittle-brilliant lads around. You will find, however, under the confused manners, social uncertainties, and confused unsophistication of our boys that the good ones are surprisingly good. I think they have been improving slowly, by and large, but come the anticipated flood and that trend may very well reverse.

Second, the Young Turks. It's a good department that way. Some good, sharp, younger gents. We're even on the way to being pretty hot.

Third, being a state university, Rutgers offers some advantages. Public Employees Retirement plan is a dandy. Also there hasn't been a year since the flood that didn't produce some sort of increment. At the same time, Rutgers preserves a long tradition as a private college, and largely in consequence of that, we have what I think is a damn good administration. Lewis Webster Jones is president, Mason Gross is provost, and I'm all for both of them. Their ideas, attitudes, ambitions, plans—all strike me as just damn good and right. They also serve good liquor.

To my way of seeing it, accessibility to NY is a damned big thing. Many gents commute to Rutgers from NY. Anyhow it can be made in about 30–35 minutes on the through trains, 45–65 if you mess up the time table and find yourself on an all-stops local. Distance 30 miles. And don't let anybody kid you—the streets of NY are, I find, honest and truly lined with gold. You'll make contacts, man—as the song says.

Also, Rutgers is a place that's waking up. Has awakened, in fact, has a good sense of what's ahead of it this day, and is out to get it down. I think it's a real opportunity for you, but that is finally an outside guess, and that sort of thing has to be decided inside oneself. Speaking for myself, I have turned down a lot more money offered by various schools, and have recently turned down what amounts to a sub-dept chair in creative writing at Brown. There are a lot of jobs floating around, but I'm going to stay put.

Well. Let me know how your talk with Kirk comes out. I hope you'll say yes. I'm pretty well convinced you won't regret it.

Joys,
John

TO NORMAN COUSINS

Rome
February 7, 1957
[NC]

Dear Norman:

There have been some misunderstandings of letters but no real disagreements. Peter [Ritner, *SR*'s feature editor] sent me galleys of the "Letter to an Avalanche" piece two days ago, and I returned them immediately with full approval of his cuts.* He was dead right in them—as I saw the instant he pointed.

I confess that I personally hatched this controversy with Ray Walters, but certainly with no sense of making *SR* my personal squawk-box. My notion was that such a controversy was necessary for clearing some of the national air and [was] thereby potentially valuable both to *SR* and to the general—and far reaching—shadow of ideas it casts.

It is possible, I know, that in seeking to stir up the controversy, I might have borne down too heavily and gone thereby that shade beyond reason. I can only reply that I really sweated over that Lindbergh review, in my effort to keep the disagreement impersonal. There is one other chapter I want to add to this record, and that will be a piece for the May poetry issue: "The Morality of Poetry"—the positive statement of what has been opened here negatively.**

Believe me, I did not join up with *SR* and accept its money with any idea of working *against* it. I *have* joined and I have endorsed and cashed the checks, and that as I see it has to be understood as a pledge, else I'm a swindler. Blast away at anything you disagree with, substance or emphasis. I am hard to offend in a discussion of principles. If I think necessary I'll blast back. But all in good will, I assure you.

From which, best
John

*Ciardi's critical review of Anne Morrow Lindbergh's *The Unicorn and Other Poems* had appeared in *SR* on January 12. It provoked hundreds of mostly angry letters to the editor and was followed by Ciardi's self-defense, "The Reviewer's Duty to Damn: Letter to an Avalanche" (February 16).

**"The Morality of Poetry: Epilogue to an Avalanche" appeared in the March 30 issue.

TO NORMAN COUSINS

Rome

February 13, 1957

[NC]

Dear Norman:

I have received and read with care the February 16 issue and I am sorry not only to report the strongest possible disagreement with your article but that it raises a serious question as to my ability to continue as poetry editor of *SR.**

I shall not here analyze the reasons for my disagreement but I shall be happy to do so in detail if you wish.

Meanwhile you have identified the fact [that] I will not willingly endure an ambiguous position, and I am grateful to you for that insight and for stating it well. The fact is, as I see it, that you have put me in a decidedly ambiguous position and in a way that touches directly upon my discretion and ability as a literary critic. I do not feel that I can endure this position. To make matters worse, it seems to me that your article now makes it more or less embarrassing to both of us for me to resign now.

Let me add that I do not really want to resign, but that I must certainly do so unless we can work out a clear and firm understanding. If I am to continue I shall require some public statement of this understanding, much as I dislike the idea of protracting this Lindbergh business any further through the turn you have given it. I am willing to work out a mutually satisfactory wording, but let me point out that time presses. I enclose a draft of a statement that covers my side of the case in what I hope is a neutral way. Please assume that this statement is part of the present letter and that it is signed herewith.

Since time is short and since the distance is long, may I ask that you reply to what I have said rather than in some other set of terms? There is always a temptation to reply to such a letter as this beginning: "Hell, let's be reasonable about this, you're a good fellow." I'm not really a good fellow; in my own way, I am trying to be a measuring and disciplined sort of fellow. I ask you to believe that I am seriously disturbed by your concept of measurement.

Sincerely,
John Ciardi

Enc. Draft of statement

*The "article" was actually an editorial by Cousins ("John Ciardi and the Readers") in which he found it expedient to publicly question Ciardi's "basis" for criticizing Mrs. Lindbergh's *Unicorn.*

Statement of Understanding Between John Ciardi and Norman Cousins. To Be Published When Agreed Upon. To Be Agreed Upon Reasonably Soon.

In *SR* for February 16, 1957, Norman Cousins published an article entitled "John Ciardi and the Readers." I find it necessary to reject this article and to disassociate myself from its principles, assumptions, and conclusions. I offer as a working substitute the following formula: Norman Cousins is not responsible for what I think and I am not responsible for what Norman Cousins thinks.

I can continue as poetry editor of *SR* only on the understanding of autonomy on all matters pertaining to poetry, subject only to space limitations. In accepting this agreement, Mr. Cousins affirms his belief that I am capable of exercising such autonomy in a principled and responsible way for the good of *SR.* He also understands that the principles I have thus far established in this magazine are the principles upon which I shall continue to base its poetry policy. When he feels that he can no longer so affirm, it is clearly his duty to accept the resignation I offer him herewith.

I affirm his central responsibility as the coordinator of this magazine. I cannot accept him, despite his many other accomplishments, as properly qualified to correct me on matters of literary criticism. When the discussion is based on stated principles, developed by analysis, and supported by evidence, any man may enter it and be held to be competent according to the competence of the principles, analyses, and evidence he offers. I do not, in my turn, mean to chastise Mr. Cousins. His many accomplishments will speak his praise in better terms than I can summon. I must, however, reject his right to offer unsupported assertions, even in the name of general good-will, in reply to a discussion that has been opened on firm and documented critical grounds.

John Ciardi

TO NORMAN COUSINS

Rome

February 16, 1957

[NC]

Dear Norman:

I think—my wife having persuaded me—that I should offer you a detailed statement of why I am so powerfully distressed by your piece about me.

You have a perfect right to kill any article that you think will damage *SR* or to call me in and ask why I did a certain piece in a certain way and raise objections for discussion. In such cases I may agree or disagree, but I should always leave the final arbitration of total policy to you. It is remotely possible that under such handling our differences might be such as to become unbridgeable, but such a case would only suggest the necessity for an amicable parting of the ways. It would not question your essential right to edit the magazine.

In this case, however, your objection has been both *a posteriori* and public. Had you called me in or phoned before the fact, I should have registered the most powerful objection but I should have been satisfied to have left it in private. You have now made the thing public in a way that is powerfully offensive to me, and I therefore demand some public acknowledgement of the fact that I reject your views. For the following reasons:

1. I resent your charge that I have violated good manners. I took pains to detach Mrs. Lindbergh from the discussion and to point out that the issue was serious (a) in that this book would certainly win a considerable following, and (b) that it would certainly receive mildly approving notice in the press, thereby winning approval of what I insist is a most pernicious view of poetry. Having apologized to Mrs. Lindbergh as a person, I see no need to apologize to Mrs. L as a writer who has offered shoddy goods for sale. I find your charge both serious and unwarranted and even libelous.

2. You charge me with the implication of having scoffed off all my critics as not knowing anything about poetry. I point out to you that my second piece was addressed specifically to a large volume of letters, none of which, as far as I could see, had anything to say about poetry. The letters I saw were addressed to the fact that I was a low character and Mrs. Lindbergh was a sacred symbol. When the discussion is of poetry I grant anyone his right to enter it according to the merit of his principles and methods of discussion, analysis, and documentation. May I point out to you that I do not spend most of my life teaching the young the fundamentals of disciplined intellectual discussion in order to abandon those fundamentals for journalistic purposes.

3. You proceed next to tell me in public and with the peculiar authority of your editorship's last word that I am unqualified as a literary critic by a kind of literalism that makes me blind to the total significance of the poem. I am, I take it, an X-rayer of the literal without breadth enough or depth enough of understanding to respond to that larger spectrum of meaning which is, of course, instantly clear to your more acute critical intelligence. I could address this point in a much stronger way were I to let myself go, but let me suggest only that it may be a mistake for an editor to set himself up as an expert in everything, adding that if you really believed me to be possessed of such limitations you would obviously be out of order in retaining as your poetry editor a man so poorly qualified for his duties. I utterly reject both your qualification and your moral right to make such a statement.

Let me suggest, for example, the sort of terms in which you reasonably might have disagreed, *viz.*:

> It is no part of an editor's duty to be omniscient. We hired Mr. Ciardi as our poetry editor because his accomplishments clearly make him an authoritative voice. We know his disagreement was seriously taken and seriously addressed in open honesty. Our personal feeling may at times incline us to disagree with his opinions, [but] never to doubt his sincerity nor the integrity of his method of discussion. In this case we are reluctant to endorse all of his view, but we can neither repudiate it nor his right to advance it honestly. The function of a magazine of ideas in a democracy is to preserve an open market of ideas in which any man of integrity and qualification may advance his views on stated principles and supported by evidence that must speak for itself. We regret the distress his view has caused our readers, but we are sure they will endorse the reasons that lead us to support his right to his views.

I merely suggest a tone in this. The necessary assumptions of such a tone would be (a) that I am in all likelihood more competent than you in this particular discussion, (b) that I have made my points sincerely and for reasons that must speak for themselves, and (c) that the *SR* stands for something more than the omnipotence of its subscription list.

May I suggest, Norman, that it is unwise to want everyone to love you. I doubt that the readers will love you for such bones as you have thrown me. And I certainly find it very difficult to love you for them.

4. You assert that "few living authors . . . are using the English language more sensitively than" Mrs. L. "or with more genuine appeal." As a literalist with a small X-ray eye, may I suggest that you check this mis-use of "appeal" in Fowler and/or Webster. As a moralist I am utterly shocked by this statement. Have you even *read* my review? I point out to you that had I said no word of my own in it but only used the quotations I inserted—the quotations and nothing more—that this assertion placed alongside those undiscussed quotations would be as absurd as a giraffe in a Volkswagon?

Even assuming that I had sinned in my review in the way the letters charge me with sin, is it so impossible to see that my intention in total policy is to provide *SR* readers and even the nation's book reviewers with critical principles that can serve viably to measure poetic performance? *SR* has a terrific educational possibility and responsibility. If I am allowed to do my work, I can not only make *SR* a real center of poetic discussion, but I can raise the whole level of poetry discussion in the U.S. I certainly cannot do so if the editor himself walks in spouting such random and irresponsible assertions.

These are my basic objections. *Time* magazine and several newspapers have been after me on all this business and I have firmly refused to let them in on these reactions. I feel all the more entitled, therefore, to state them to you in strong terms, secure in their privacy. I can only conclude that your piece was written in haste, without taking the time to analyze the total context, and without enough thought of me. In whatever way it was written, it has been made public in a way that I can only find offensive and even libelous to my professional qualification.

Believe me, I have no wish to embarrass you, but I, too, have a career, and I point out to you that my name and reputation have every bit as much meaning as yours, and considerably more in matters of poetry. I certainly did not sign on at *SR* to fight with you. But I certainly did not sign on either with any sense of being subject to your public criticism or in any way junior to you. I must, therefore, insist on my utter disagreement with you, upon my rejection of your views, and on my insistence that if I continue at *SR* I do so—as already stated—autonomously though always willing to discuss any *a priori* criticism you wish to make and subject always to your final right to kill any piece that does not fit into your plans for the good of *SR*. I must insist on that statement, and I must insist that it be made publicly.

I hope this statement can be made in mutually acceptable terms. I confess to you that I do not want to quit. But these objections are matters of strongest principle with me and I mean, without qualification, to put them first.

Sincerely
John

TO M. L. ROSENTHAL

Rome
February 17, 1957
[MLR]

Dear Mr. Rosenthal:

You're down in my book as some sort of a miracle. You have never made a comment on any poem of mine that hasn't immediately helped me to see what it was immediately obvious I should have seen. I am returning a much revised copy of the "After an Evening with an Italian Novelist" piece. God knows you are not responsible for the changes I have made, but I do feel it shapes better now, and my thanks to you.

I can't tell you how impressed I am by the rightness of your insights. I wish I could find a pretext for sending everything I write to *The Nation* in the hope of getting more of your reactions.

What I am thinking instead is this: I am in process of preparing a new collection of poems [*I Marry You*] for Rutgers University Press. I can think of nothing I would rather have than your eye upon them. Would you be willing for some necessarily inadequate fee to read a manuscript copy and to pencil your reactions on the pages with no thought of diplomacy? (The best criticisms I've ever had were by Dudley Fitts and consisted largely of marginal comments such as "Oh, for Chrissake, John!" or just "Stupid bastard!")

It will be at least two months before I could have a ms. in sufficient shape to send, and God knows I cannot pay you what your comments would be worth to me, but I could promise to find $100 for that, and if we have any bank balance left at that point I should want to make it more.

I hope you don't mind my asking this. I hope very much in fact that you will say Yes. If it is not a good idea, as it strikes you, please accept it at least as an admiration.

Cordially,
John Ciardi

TO JUDSON JEROME

Rome

February 21, 1957

[BU]

Dear Jud:

I'm delighted to hear that your reviews are going to rip, and pleased as punch to think I might have sparked it. I personally have some real admiration for some—not by any means all—of Rexroth's stuff, but he can take it. I'm sorry John Hall Wheelock has to take a pasting, though you are right beyond question. His poetry is damned thin stuff, but I hope you will mention that he has served a real idea of poetry in his editing and encouragement of young talents. He has not done that flawlessly, but he has done it warmly, generously, and toward a total good, as I sense it. His *Poets of Today* series is a good thing, I think.

If I may reiterate my personal feeling on the necessity of stinging reviews, I think they should ask first if there is any possibility that the stuff reviewed is likely to be taken seriously. . . . .

Best,
John

PS Couldn't agree more about the fact that a poem has to *move.* I don't care what rhythm, but a rhythm. MacLeish said it well once: "If it ain't a rhythm, it ain't a poem."

TO NORMAN COUSINS

Rome

February 25, 1957

[NC]

Dear Norman:

I am glad to have your letter. As you may well imagine, I have thought carefully about this whole thing, as it is obvious you have. World as it is, everyman's native gesture is to see his own right. We have a disagreement, and I am sure we also have basic goodwill between us under that disagreement, and obviously, too, there is right on both sides. As you say, moreover, the whole discussion is complicated by the fact that we are oceans apart physically, and hence what could be easily settled over a drink and a talk takes a kind of awkward carefulness.

Let me say I am grateful for the care you have taken in this. And let me also say at once that I withdraw my demand for a public statement. I realize, of course, that my first draft is impossible. What I have since had to conclude is that no draft is possible: I have worked at many and all of them sound like a fight, no matter how carefully one draws up the words.

I don't really want a fight with you. I did not sign up to fight. I joined your staff and I have accepted your money, and I understand both actions to be a moral guarantee that I am bound to serve the best interests of *SR*.

I cannot escape the feeling, however, that if you truly and finally view poetry—and the arts in general—in the terms and on the principles clearly implicit in your editorial, then we cannot hope for any meeting of minds on literary criticism. I take the essence of your position to be (a) that a poem is independent of its parts, and (b) that the statement of "significant human insights" is enough for a poem, whether or not the poet has paid whole attention to his formal aesthetic responsibilities. I have to hold this to be not only an impoverishing view, but a doubly dangerous one in that it can be made to seem so plausible. It would seem to follow, then, that if I pursue my course to the extent that we profess clearly conflicting doctrines, our views are bound to conflict.

I am especially glad that your letter offers me a way in which I can continue with you and with *SR*. I want to and you know that I want to, and I shall certainly labor to do my best. I believe *SR* is ideally situated to take on a really vital job of education as far as poetic and general aesthetic attitudes are concerned.

Back to the paragraph before the last then: if I pursue what I believe to be essential, one central part of my work must be to preach against those very attitudes I take to be central to your view. Forgetting the general percussiveness of this isolated AML [Anne Morrow Lindbergh] incident, let's pretend that the following propositions are raised as questions in the purest Platonic tone: (1) Are you willing to have me preach against what I take to be your doctrine? and (2) What happens when we disagree again?

Anent question 2, let me make it clear that I have no notion of being the world's hatchet man. I do intend, as the occasion makes necessary from time to time, to speak out strongly. I think *SR* has a major responsibility to speak out on the current state of reviewing and to do so at times with names and the accumulated record. If it becomes known, for instance, that *SR* is watch-dogging both the insolence of publishers' blurbs and the inadequacy of general reviewing, I believe that the resulting effect is bound to be good for the national level of reviewing, that the publishers themselves will more than welcome a call to abandon their crazy purple prose, and that *SR* is bound to grow in stature as it serves the cause of good intellectual order. Thus, I have no least intention to be a murderer, but I certainly mean to slug the offensive in poetry. I read my primer at Benny Blessed DeVoto's knee: "Make sure of your grounds: then say it straight." I mean that for both gentleness and toughness, and I certainly mean to be gentle whenever gentleness can serve good intellectual order.

I cannot, however, accept a situation in which you are free to walk in with the weight and authority of your editorship and disagree in the terms of, say, the editorial on this AML business. You can slug the hell out of me so long as this discussion is on stated principle and entered on evidence. I cannot accept simple assertions of this order. That, in fact, is the whole gist of it. I should have swallowed it all if you hadn't offered AML as a master (mistress?) of the English language.

Well, peace. Let X be a symbol for shaking hands in open good fellowship, and let me write—herewith—XX. Then let me speak to just one more point:

You refer to the fact that Ray and I—it was really my doing, Ray let himself be persuaded—cooked up the idea of a clobbering review and then lay in wait. That is one way of putting it, but not really a true description. In my overall concern for what I certainly believe to be the bad state of reviewing in the larger media, I pointed out to Ray that one hardly ever sees an unfavorable review, and I said that *SR* had a moral responsibility to face this issue, and that I was going to say by chapter and text exactly what I thought was wrong with the next really bad book that came along by a known-name author.

The review was long (1) because a bad review has to be detailed: when you call names you have to prove they fit, (2) because the book was certainly due for prominence—when a publisher runs off 50,000 copies of a book of poems, that's an event, and (3) because AML's is exactly the kind of badness that perverts most because it seems so surface-attractive—or in terms of my piece on the Morality of Poetry, because it is so right to the World's Six of the 7 Deadly Sins and so damned wrong to the Poem's doom by Acedia.

I think any one of those three reasons would have justified the emphasis, but there is one other. I feel very strongly that available review space is whacked up among too many books. One reason reviewing is so bad is that the reviewer hardly ever has enough space to stay with it. As an article of policy (not yet discussed with Ray and with you, but one I mean to discuss and to push for), I feel strongly that we should stop parceling out our review space for poetry a few hundred words to a book and concentrate it more on significant books, cutting the incidental reviews to perhaps a quarterly round up with one to three sentences per book. That is a tricky thing to handle, I know, but it can be handled. Because it is tricky, I am not trying to do anything about it from this distance. I shall pursue it when I get back, however. Meanwhile, I am more and more inclined experimentally to try to get central books centrally reviewed, good or bad. I think of the *Unicorn* as central to a kind of badness, but central. Hence, subject to a central review.

Well, peace. I promise you in open faith to do the best I can for both *SR* and for what I believe to be a living view of poetry. Sometime next September—or if there is time between our landing on August 1 and Bread Loaf on August 14—I promise to let you buy me a hamburger if you will promise to let me spout for about ¾ of an hour after it has been chewed.

All best.

And still yours,
John Ciardi

TO HORACE GREGORY

Rome
April 8, 1957
[SU]

Dear Horace Gregory:

I don't recall what MBT [?] said nor what I said to her. I think what I said was that I had received a more or less cantankerous letter from you saying that I was insulting you by asking you to write reviews for *SR*. I think I recall her saying she had a letter from you or from Mrs. Gregory saying that my reply was also more or less cantankerous.

I certainly hope I haven't slandered anyone in this. I have a good shot of cantankerousness myself. I think I may openly say we both qualify on that score. I am just lousy at being abject and I happily respect your own lack of merit badges thataway.

Yes, I can agree that you are one of the few critics with real authority. I have a very real admiration for a large part of what you do. I have to confess my admiration stops short of veneration, and I am not sure I can fall in love with every kitten in the litter. In honest frankness, I have to confess that that Humphries review in the *Times* seemed to me a job of clubbing rather than of criticism. And I have to confess that there seemed to me to be a bit of random flailing in the Graves article.

Honest, I am not trying to get your dander up. On other tacks I'm practically ready to confess that you're next door to omniscient. I find myself thinking that like everyone else practically, you write some considered pieces and some hasty ones. Also I confess I don't like being growled at—and I think you will confess there was a growl in your note to me. Maybe we're partly dogs of a feather. If you will tell me that your Auden piece and your Crane piece are considered pieces rather than Donnybrook Fairs (Is it Donniebrook?—no English dictionary here), I happily accept them herewith, and sight unseen, and delighted to have them.

I have tried to be as open as I can be. I think you can see this as neither an apology nor an attempt to start a fight. I think it is obvious that a great deal of respect goes with [it]. I owe thanks, too, to Mrs. Gregory. I hope she will find that this letter answers hers as well. Let me add my good wishes.

Sincerely.
John Ciardi

TO JOHN FREDERICK NIMS

Rome
April 16, 1957
[IU]

Dear John:

Thanks for the carbon of your review of Fitts' poems from the Greek anthology.

I think it's a helluva fine, perceptive, balanced, and informed review. I must confess, however, that I am frankly afraid of either the Greek quotations or the same transliterated for *SR.* I have already had so many angry letters accusing me of trying to be a goddamn highbrow, etc. etc. that I'm frankly being cowardly before the foreseeable blast, rather than following my personal inclination and admiration.

Would it be possible to make the same points by comparing the Fitts translation not to the Greek but to the other translators? Would it be possible at least where the Greek text (transliterated) is especially pertinent to add in parentheses a literal English rendering? . . . . .

This is obviously a semi-quizzle, but I do hope you will see the point. Not I but the wind (from the readers) alas.

All best to you. I shall hope
for forgiveness in advance.
John

TO JOHN FREDERICK NIMS

Rome

April 26, 1957

[IU]

Dear John:

Many thanks for your forbearance. I have marked-in the changes you approved and forwarded my copy of the review to NY. I hope the wheels will grind it through without annoying delay and I have marked it for soonest insertion, though all such markings tend to be hopes rather than bank balances.

I really feel a number of things, including a little shame, at having had to ask you for these changes, but there is the nature of the beast to consider, I am persuaded—or at least have decided to function *as if* persuaded—that there is hope of training the beast that reads *SR* into some semblance of a human response, and my feeling is not to insult the beast unless necessary. Why the beast should feel itself insulted at the sight of Greek, I don't know, but I cannot blink the conclusion that it would. Hence a *little* Greek is fodder for its better wonderment. Meanwhile good solid points made about the nature of poetic performance—that's what reviews badly need. An appraisal seriously made on specific evidence so treated that data of perception may begin to accumulate in the beast's head. Thanks.

Some time ago, partly in defense, and partly for self-evident reasons, I made a firm rule against publishing translated poetry. We have so little room, I argued, we need to save it for our own poets. But what good is a rule one can't violate for better reason? I have held "Sonnet Right Off the Bat" under cover of the defensive rule, but clearly it argues better than the rule, and I want it. I am forwarding it to NY as accepted. Sometime within the next 87 months you will receive an inadequate check for its delayed publication. But what a lovely piece!

As always we have damn little room for poetry, and not enough really good poems for it. By now I think I have learned not to be indulgent or hopeful. With the backlog still pressing for publication, that learning process will not be evident for a long while yet, but I am resolved to get tough as hell about what little poetry we can accept. I'd like a rejection slip that reads "Go do your hoping somewhere else: I find it possible to live without this poem and therefore the hell with it. If you or your friends have any poems I cannot live without please submit those instead of these." What a lovely dream!

Seriously, there is always a shortage of good poems. I hope in time to wheedle slightly better space rates (ours stink). Meanwhile I just hope to wheedle. Please send anything immortal you have on hand. I'd be grateful for any immortalities by others you can steer this way.

And thanks again—on many counts.

John

TO ZUBEL AND IRMA KACHADOORIAN

Metuchen

November 10, 1957

[Irma Cavat]

[At the American Academy in Rome, the Ciardis had struck up a warm friendship with artists Zubel and Irma Kachadoorian.]

Dear Zubel and Irma:

. . . . Judith . . . has her kitchen arriving into a little dream world of its own. But oh the rate of arrival and oh my broken back! We're pushing the figure I had had in mind for the total cost and so far practically nothing has happened except preparations for getting started (wall knocked out, new windows in, floor leveled, walls squared). Soon now we may hope to see these here now carpenters begin on the cabinet. Incubi, by god. $60 a day incubi.

To rescue something like balance from the world of imbalances I have been racing around like a real whirler. Classes on Monday, airport right after class, lecture on Tuesday somewhere between Maine and Texas, back by sleeper or night plane to NJ for Wednesday classes, back to the airport Wednesday night and return for Friday maybe stopping off in NY to fill up my briefcase at *SR* in case I might have nothing else to do on Sunday, and so it goes. Once in a week or two a Tuesday or a Thursday shows up uncommitted, so I go into NY for *SR* and there's that. If there be blessings in all this, number one is that these carpenters haven't bankrupted us. I can even stay ahead of the bastards in a sprint, but if this becomes a marathon I'm going to cross the finish line daid. . . . .

Did I tell you about our time with NY customs? Doc Klompus had gotten someone to write a letter for us. We landed with our mound of stuff and found a customs man paging us. The head of NY customs had written a letter asking that we be extended every courtesy, and man were the courtesies extended. We were out of there in no time. Then the next day the Doc called and said, "If you were thinking of writing Mr. Walsh (or whateverthehell his name was) a thank you letter, don't: he doesn't know that he wrote that letter for you." Bless the Doc. Let us know when you land and we'll see about cooking up another letter. . . .

Well. Basta, chiarissimi, carassimi ed illustrissimi.

Yourn affly
John

TO JOHN HOLMES

Metuchen
February 15, 1958
[FC?]

Dear John:

I'd like nothing whatever better than to do one of the Steinman Lectures at Tufts. Even without all that lovely money. And double with it. And for many long reasons. And all good and all deep. Yes. With most pleasure. . . .

It's great that you're leading off with Archie. I am just reviewing his *J.B.*, and this certainly is the year of his most greatness. What a play! What a poem! This is The Great American Poetic Drama and it's the future of American Poetic Drama. Magnificent. . . .

Joys
John

TO THEODORE ROETHKE

Metuchen
April 19, 1958
[UW]

Dear Ted:

Eliz Kray probably over-billed me out of her own sweetness. She called and asked me to fill-in for you, and it seemed a shame to let the occasion go by without a nod to the gent whose candle I was carrying. I read a few of the early short pieces from *Open House* as an anchor point. Then I read one or two of the later lyrics, especially "My Papa's Waltz" by way of demonstrating what a tremendous increase in charge you had learned to put into the tight lyric. And then I read "The Lost Son" as an example of what I have to call your dance-poem or many-rhythmed poem or suite-poem or whatever you want it called. It wasn't hard to make them stick: they carry their own charge and I kept my own comments to a minimum. The poems really scored. I enjoyed hearing them on the air myself, though I'd much rather hear you read them. I tend to hold back when I read and your poems need that "more" that you give them.

How is it going? And when do you get East? My busted sacro-iliac, my hernia of the diaphragm, and my general debilitude all bowed when you called me a rugged bastard, but I cherish the illusion.

News that your *Collected* will be out in the fall is good news. I'll be watching for it and waiting to give it a signal in *SR*. How about some poems for this miserable-pay sheet? I have a hell of a time working in anything but short poems, but if you have a homeless long-one I'll break down a door and get it in somehow. I'll hope.

All best to you,
John

TO ARNO BADER

Metuchen
April 19, 1958
[UML]

Dear Mr. Bader:

I have indeed been gathering thoughts for the Hopwood talk and I think I should like to title it The Silences of the Poem. Some few days back I wrote Mr. Rice of a problem that had come up in my mind. The paper I find myself working out seems rather too technical for best effect from a platform. Would there be any objection to my leaving the paper technical for purposes of publication but of *talking* it in a less technical way from the platform? In my status as an old spielman, I hate to bore an audience unnecessarily and I recoil from the thought of "reading" a paper. My thought is that I should prefer to communicate with the audience in audience-terms and with the reader in reader-terms, but I shall be happy to be guided by you in this.

It gives me very great pleasure to hear you speak so highly of Daniel Jaffe. I shall look forward to seeing him in May, and all the more happily should he indeed turn up in the winner's circle.

Yours faithfully,
John Ciardi

TO ZUBEL AND IRMA KACHADOORIAN

Metuchen
June 4, 1958
[Irma Cavat]

Dear Irma, and Karin, and—what is your husband's name, darling?—
(I do recall him as a very pleasant type in an indistinct sort of way—)

Well, as the feller said when his landlady slipped into bed with him, things seem to be happening. If you people keep hanging your canvases all over them Roman galleries you're going to end up as Exhibitionists. . . .

And what's this about broke chillun? Old Daddy Warbucks Ciardi has been printing the stuff almost as fast as his carpenters, his wife, and his peculiar views of life have been erasing it. Do you need any and how much? Seriously, I'm loaded. I've been hitting the lecture circuit from here to there like a schizophrenic centipede and making them pay till anybody but me would be ashamed. What's a feller to do, fellers? I keep raising my rates and they keep saying yes. My only regret is that I seem to have reached the summit: at this point the next step up is sky. If it weren't for Judith I'd have resigned from Rutgers this past year. Why teach school when two lectures come to over a month's pay. I'll just give six lectures and sit back and eat pork chops the rest of the time while Daisy Mae is out splitting the cord wood.

Anyhow lemme know if you need any and check will be en route. . . . .

I have a wife. She appends.

I conclude,
mit aff.
John

TO GLORIA ODEN

Metuchen
September 6, 1958
[GO]

[Gloria Oden, poet and professor, met John Ciardi after one of his poetry readings in New York City. Among other things, they discussed the problems of black writers.]

Dear Miss Oden:

I'm sorry I was bugged out. Still am, alas, but starting back to the world step by step.

Let me hope for a chance to phone you next week, but please don't make me the villain of the piece if it doesn't work out till the week after. I teach at Rutgers, school is starting up next week, and I simply cannot plan my time in the scramble of registration and odd chores that always attend school-opening. I must get into NY soon for I am mountainous piles of stuff behind. And I have to be a lousy letter writer, else do nothing but write letters. Believe me that's not a brush-off but a matter of survival.

Yes, I'm not wholly ignorant of your problem. In my own terms I've been there myself; i.e., so dedicated to a conviction that what I wrote turned out to be rhetoric and argumentation rather than poetry. From where we all sit it is the problem that has always beset the Negro poet in the US. I went to school at Bates with Owen Dodson. He never found a whole answer to it. I think maybe Langston Hughes at his best has come closest to solving it. And M. B. Tolson to some extent. The specimen case, I think, is Countee Cullen: He got himself caught in the dilemma of not knowing whether to write white or black and made the mistake of thinking he could answer himself by being more Keats than Keats.

The last thing on earth I could pretend is that I know how to make the answer work, but I think the answer itself is obvious. There can be no Negro poetry, nor white poetry, nor any but human poetry. A poem has to speak into the silences of every mortal being, into those silences deeper than skin. Write on the skin and you can always pick up a big, fast encouragement. I think the critics are all deeply persuaded that there is a great body of poetic song locked up in the American Negro, and all of them are ready to pop up and yell hurrah at any shadow of a hope that here comes the poet who will unlock it. I think that big, ready built-in hurrah has done a lot of damage.

Well, you can see this rambles. Is there any point, however badly put, in what I'm laboring to say? I think you have to make the poem good enough to drop into my coffin when there's nothing left there but bones and no way of knowing what skin wrapped them. We've all got bones. Maybe the only final communication is bone to bone. How you take someone who has had psychic tomatoes thrown at him all his life and ask him to ignore the tomatoes and just sniff the breeze is what I don't know. That calls for a size I don't come in. But I think maybe one can find the size he had to be if he really has to be it and wants to be it.

Oh, hell, I sound like somebody else pontificating to three other people. Forgive the tone, the wrongness of the way it gets said, and try to find the grain of truth or half-truth in it. Don't write propaganda. Sure, those kids in Little Rock are brave, and bravery is a good enough subject for anybody's poem, but remember one thing about it: bravery is the commonest commodity. Or at least it's among the commonest. I put in my time as a gunner on a B-29 during the late-great [war] and never quite recovered from my amazement at seeing what an 18-year-old kid will pitch into, smiling. There was a wisp of a kid fresh out of high school who worked the guns across the ship from me. There he was in his first job, a sgt. in the Air Corps on a B-29 and he had a couple of medals and boy would the girls turn around when he got back home, and for no more than that sense of importance he happily volunteered himself for everything in sight until he volunteered himself to death.

I'm not remotely tempted to minimize what it takes for one of those kids to walk to school. All I'm saying is that whatever they do is *human,* not white or black, and that human beings as I have observed them work on motivations that have never been treated with justice on any billboard.

Well. . . . I'll hope I can make it into NY next week. Probably on Thurs. if at all.

Best,
John Ciardi

TO DAN JAFFE

Metuchen
October 5, 1958
[DJ]

Dear Dan:

Are you absolutely sure it isn't Omaha after all? No matter: everyone starts teaching in the wrong city. I knew you're somewhere out there because Karl Shapiro has sent me a couple of notes (he took some poems for *P[rairie] Schooner*) and mentioned you and liking a poem you had shown him.

Well, how is teaching? Are you loaded down? In my youth and

vigor I started my first semester (U of Kansas City) with 150 freshmen—five sections. I hope they've treated you more gently. Well, you can always binge your mind clean by reading Yeats as if you were going on a drunk. And dig them metrics. Never mind being a poet: just learn metrics. Write anything you damn please, but learn metrics. Ignore metrics when you're writing—if you must—but learn what you're ignoring. End of 30¢ sermon.

I've been having a binge of selling poems—*Nation, Atlantic, LH Journal, Harper's,* maybe one to *New Yorker* if I can work out a compromise with them. I even sold two to *SR* and that editor is a bastard. And wildest of all, Eunice Blake bought my book of children's verse for Lippincott. I'm practically a rich poet.

Write and let me know how it's coming when you find time. I'm lost to all system, but sooner or later I'll manage to answer.

Judith sends best. We've had to hide the Erector Set because Benn decided the pieces were ammunition. Learn to shun children. Those one cannot avoid should be kept in respectful terror.

Best
John

TO LOVELL THOMPSON

Metuchen
November 10, 1958
[FC]

Mr. Lovell Thompson
Houghton Mifflin Co.
2 Park Street
Boston 7, Massachusetts

Dear Lovell:

May I borrow your ear in the hope I may pick your brains with it?

This directorial business leads on to problems, and not knowing what to do with them, I am transmitting them to various friends of

Bread Loaf and hoping. Our current problem—and it seems ready to stay current for a few years—is the age level of the BL customer. The only answer I see is a fund for making scholarships available to the promising young who need help. We are getting too many well-spread ladies whose husbands are doing well and who have more spending money and leisure than fiery promise.

But there is obviously no point in racing around hat in hand every year, and the only answer I see to that is a scholarship endowment fund. We are getting ready to launch a loud cry to all surviving Bread Loafians. We then hope.

Question 1: May I use your name as a luminous and honorable on the mailing piece? Sponsor, Association of Bread Loaf—whatever it gets called? This is not a pitch for cash. I am asking if you will lend yourself for window dressing.

Question 2: Can you think of anything useful to tell me in my ignorance as I (tremblingly) launch this thing?

Aside from the scholarship thing, there is the question of fellowships. Marsden Perry has given strong indications that he will endow the Fletcher Pratt Fellowship for $5,000, which will 4% at $200 a year. I am not within a dream of imagining that Houghton Mifflin can justify itself in shelling out on that scale for the De Voto Fellowship, but will it consider carrying it for another year or two, or—better—would it consider endowing some part of it if I manage between now and then to raise the rest for it?

One further question I shall be asking all the world: do you know any well-disposed person in the right tax brackets who would like a very handsome bronze plaque on the BL premises to announce to all time that he had endowed the XYZ Fellowship or Scholarship? If he has a spare statue of himself we'll put that prominently anywhere.

All best to Kay. Don't let this be a chore, but I should much welcome your thoughts.

Best,
John Ciardi

TO JUDSON JEROME

[Metuchen]
December 2, 1958
[BU]

Dear Jud:

I have mentioned NCW [?] to Rutgers Press, and I don't know whether or not anything can be hoped for there, but it might be possible. If I get any more definite indication of interest from them, I will certainly let you know.

That was quite a poetic bang-up at Baltimore. I could never have imagined that Marianne Moore would have let my review of her *Fables [The Fables of La Fontaine]* rankle for so many years. Very soon after the book was published she turned to me on the platform at Mount Holyoke and belabored me with a reading of that review, most of which, god knows, was favorable. A queer world.

I agree about Cummings' *95 Poems.* It is mostly warmed-over hash. It will almost certainly win the National Book Award. And that, alas, is a confusion. For his career, yes; for this book, no. Well, mistake or not, it will be a good mistake, I guess.

I can't tell you how pleased I am that you like the *Atlantic* poem. I didn't really expect Weeks to take it and was especially delighted when he did.

Was Ransom doddering into senility when he read? I heard him in New York, and he sounded as if he had been dead for three months.

May I say that it is the greatest pleasure *not* to be your president? The last thing on earth I want is college administration. It is all I can take to work some sort of part-time for the Ivy halls. Why don't you take the job and become a shaper of the future and a name to be carved on stone?

Any poems?

All best,
John

TO ZUBEL AND IRMA KACHADOORIAN

Metuchen
February 6, 1959
[Irma Cavat]

Dear K's:

You children obviously need a chaperone. Here we leave two of you and all at once there's four of you coming around the corner! So who's complaining. If you're not, we're singing joys with you and running valentines up the flagpoles. Will you get it born in Italia and import it? Or will you smuggle it back in the original container? (Assuming Zubel still has the original container.)

More important, how are you weathering the years? All this family stuff and cratage and haulage can get expensive. Well, you're probably selling canvases like mad and living it up like rich Americani. Nevertheless if you need the lend of a loan say the word and I'll speak to my rich wife. (Seriously, for a' that.). . . .

It's all mad enough here. I've taken the semester off and violated all my religious scruples by taking it without pay. Oh well, hit the lecture platform and let it roll. Meanwhile, the prayer is to finish *Purgatory*. That would be a lot easier to do if I could just get started (the last ¼ of it remains to do), but day by day goes by and other things keep coming up. Well, sooner or later.

Do you ever see Luciana (our once upon a maid) or her brother? Give her our love if you cross. We should send her some sort of wedding present, but I've lost her address. Do you know it?

And tell us more. When do you get back? How? Where do you go? Can we pick you up and get you off the pier?

Have fun.

Love
John

TO RICHARD WILBUR

Metuchen
February 14, 1959
[RW]

Dear Dick:

First things first, will Charlee be my Valentine? And will you not stand in the way, like a good fellow?

More elegiacally, yes, I'm not exactly delighted by those half-ass rhymes in the Dante. I am managing to use fewer of them, but some are inescapable. They are not a choice; they are a price that has to be paid every now and then for an indispensable word. Or so it has seemed to work out. Needless to say, I couldn't be more pleased that the Venture Canto seems good to you. Bless.

And delighted again to have BL reconfirmed. You are assured hereby that no mss. were contemplated. Come on up, join the party, give us an evening talk, (and I hope one during the day) and let a glass be poured. We're great in poetry this year. Frost, Nims, Roethke, and I will be yr team-mates. I wish we were as well heeled in all departments. Aside from utility-men Sloane and Raney, we've got Nancy Hale and Ralph Ellison for fiction, Walter Teller and Richard Gehman (of *Cosmopolitan*) for non-f. and Eunice Blake for juv's. I am casting for one more real shiner in fiction and could use one in non-f.

I hope the *Candide* lyrics come, and I hope to hell you aren't fractioning yrslf as I have been doing this last year. I've taken the semester off from Rutgers in the hope of finishing *Purgatory*, but I'm doing so damn much lecturing (I'm on unpd leave) that it works out to very nearly the same thing as teaching, though rather more profitable.

Joys to you all.

John

TO **M. L. ROSENTHAL**

Metuchen

March 14, 1959

[MLR]

Dear Mack:

After much delay I enclose the ms. of *In the Year of the Longest Cadillac* on which I am very eager to have your detailed comments. Please feel no hesitation necessary. Pull no punches. Write right on the page in whatever detail you like. I think you know how I feel about it. First, I respect your opinions. Second, I want to keep this sort of thing on a strictly professional basis. I'd like to think I am retaining you (assuming you are still willing) as one might retain a lawyer. One doesn't pay a lawyer to toss him bouquets. I truly want to know what you think, in whatever detail you are able to manage, but if you can't detail your reasons, write STINKS in the margin and I'll buy that.

About the retainer. I wrote you from Italy that I could scare up $100 for sure and probably $150 for the whole ms. *I Marry You* was originally part of that ms. and I sent you $50 for your welcome comments on that. Will it be satisfactory if I enclose $50 now and send you $50 later for your trouble with this ms.? It's no way of getting rich, God knows, but I hope you'll be willing to take it on at that fee. Considering what poetry is likely to earn, I can't go any higher, though I well know there just is no way to put a value on the kind of help you have been able to give me. Add sincere gratitude, for that truly goes with [it].

And really—kick me if I need it. The whole point of the fee, in one very real sense, is to put you in the position of feeling immoral if you try to fob off friendly compliments.

I'm feeling brisk today. Houghton Mifflin just sent me copies of my newest book, *How Does a Poem Mean?* They are putting it out as a $2.00 paperback separately, and as ¼ of a general intro to lit in hardcovers. The HM salesman will no doubt be around to see you, but if they don't send you a copy, please let me know, and I'll see that you get one. I'd love to know what you think of it.

Joys, thanks. And needless to say, I shall be looking forward to hearing from you. Rutgers Press is planning the book for the fall.

Friendliest and best
John

May I send you 10–20 poems later for your thought as to whether or not they should be added?

TO MARK MUSA

Metuchen
May 5, 1959
[FC]

Mr. Mark Musa
Graduate School
Johns Hopkins
Baltimore Maryland

Dear Mark:

I think you did a good job on that Pirandello review [in *SR*]. Some of the people around thought it was a little "academic heavy" and others thought it had "real substance." If you mean to seek the real balance between those two (and I do think both comments had point), that search is not something you will be done with in ten years, or twenty. For myself, I was all with it. Sure, we're a popular medium, but it was more than good to see a piece that was really loaded with right information. More power to you.

I am sorry that my views may have brought you into conflict with [Charles] Singleton's. I know him only very slightly, and he me ditto. When I showed him some first Cantos of the *Inferno* he replied to the effect that having spent many years trying to teach students exactly what was in Dante he felt he should disqualify himself from an opinion on what I was doing.

I think I can locate the crux there. Or, better, in Dudley Fitts' distinction between "strictness" and "faithfulness" in translation. Singleton's a scholar. All I've ever tried to be, and without scholarly preparation, is a translator of the *Divine Comedy.* I think three kinds of translation are possible:

1. A prose literal intended to serve as a trot to the original.

2. A poetic translation that will respect the poetic possibilities of both languages and thereby be committed to the constant balancing of the strict and the faithful. In any case the assumption of this sort of translation is that the reader cannot read the original but is entitled to a poetic experience approximating the original at whatever cost of distortion.

3. The fish-out-of-water poetic translation. This is the sort of thing scholars go for when a text book salesman nudges them. They pretend they are translating for someone who cannot read the original, but they are constantly covering themselves against the possibility of attack by fellow-scholars who can read the original. The result is always purée of balls.

With Singleton, you have no real business (I am only guessing here) thinking of any but prose-literal rendering. I may be doing him an injustice, and if so I apologize sincerely, but I sense that what he wants is scholarly exactness. Why shouldn't he: that's his profession, he is good at it, and the profession is honorable.

I am thinking rather of you and of the fact that you can do yourself no good with Singleton trying to hold out for my notion of what's poetic. Singleton is your master now and you've got to throw me away. Maybe when you've gone Singleton's road long enough to come to your own, you'll want some of the shrubbery that grows along other roads. But that's not the point now. You've chosen to walk a certain way with S and it is now your job to walk it. You have my full permission and blessing to renounce me and denounce me. After all, you've undertaken an academic marriage. Forsaking all others, etc. Exactness, man, exactness. . . .

As ever,
John Ciardi

TO ZUBEL AND IRMA KACHADOORIAN

Metuchen
May 8, 1959
[Irma Cavat]

Dear K's: (Kaach, Kavat, and Karin)

. . . . . And ain't the world been just the busiest? The whole damn gang is popping every which way. I got 3 fucking books coming out this year (one already out—*How Does a Poem Mean?*—of which you were sent a copy—leave me know if it made it) and two coming in the fall (a book of poems called *In the Year of the Longest Cadillac* and a book of children's poems called *The Reason for the Pelican*). *Purgatory* is due in 1960 and I have also finished, sold, and signed another (very thin) children's book to be pub'd in 1960.

Just back from three days in Detroit—ah, that lovely overflowing check-bearing lecture circuit. I'm gonna be a rich poet if I don't shut up! (And catch me shutting up!)—and great larks. I talked to the Friends of the Library and took in a terrific sculpture show at the Art Institute. It was the Hirshhorn collection: room after room full of Epstein, Lipchitz, Giacometti, Arp, Henry Moore, Rodin—you name it he got it. And ain't it wonderful what 130 million bucks will do for a man? Though he's modest about it. ("My name is Joe.") I had lunch with him at Charles Feinberg's and I swear no more than 101 of his 130 million were really noticeable. ("I bought 14 Henry Moores last week, 8 Lipchitz, and 19 Giacomettis but I didn't have much time.") Actually, he is an impressive gent. A rough diamond but he actually *knows* what he buys.

Also met Ab Lerner, which same spoke of you. Lerner is curator of the Hirshhorn collection. Man, has he got stuff to play with!

Avidly, you may be sure, I look fwd to the most beautiful cart part of all time.* Nobody ever knew me when I wasn't greedy. And about cart-parts, I'm gone. They dig me the most. The only thing I'm avider than is anent my title as billiard champ of the universal world and where the HELL do you get off signing love from the billiard champ and his daughter when all you can reasonably lay claim to is a spavincued stumble bum, which, though he manages to paint real good, shouldn't be let into a pool room without taking off his shoes to keep from profaning the temple, already. BILLIARD CHAMP? My grandmother already—and she's 33 years dead—could beat him with a bent knitting needle for a cue. TAKE IT BACK! TAKE IT BACK, I SAID!

Oh, well, the poor bastard probably needs a morale booster. Leave him dream.

Speaking of dreams, are you art-for-art's-sake types solvent? Remember you got an emergency fund here you can tap whenever. (Just submit a statement signed by any 11 doctors that you haven't eaten for 18 days and that certified medical tests prove it.)

Seriously, if you find yourselves getting low, make known. This side of unforeseeable disaster, we can always bail you out. (Ah, those lovely lecture checks: I can't make no $$ selling poems but I can sure make them pay through the nose to hear me explain what they won't buy.) Just tell me you've sold me a picture and let me know how much I owe you.

And keep the flag flying high. Ever yrs.

John

Wayne State University Press has just published (already!) *John Ciardi: A Bibliography.* (Wanna touch me?)

*Ciardi made a casual hobby of collecting fragments of ornate Italian horse carts and setting them about his home.

TO M. L. ROSENTHAL

Metuchen

June 22, 1959

[MLR]

Dear Mack:

Thanks for forbearance. My record keeping wins no prizes, and I wasn't sure whether I had sent you $50 or $100 with the ms. Herewith the other $50 with pleasure. Never was money better spent. It's a joy to cheat you, sir.

I have had to hold out for my own eccentricities in a number of places, and the result may disappoint you in some instances, but I hope you will forgive me that pigheadedness that strives to be a faith, however mangled. Your comments have led to a number of precious cuts and revisions. At least the cuts are precious. Of the revisions, God knows. But I did weed out a couple of "meats" [and] cut the Wallace Stevens poem as you suggested (a special thanks for that) and several others.

I think the points at which I balked most were the points at which you seemed to be hearing echoes I could not hear in my own ear. I could only guess I hadn't made my own movement clear and made some punctuation changes in several instances. I hope the changes will emphasize my intended reading.

The ms. was mailed to the designer today still titled *39 Poems*. I am not wholly delighted by that title, but I have always wanted to do a book called *Poems*, and why not now? Certainly there could be no more honest title.

I've had to race things & by the time galleys appear I may have pondered myself to your view on some of the points I've had to resist. But even when I had to resist, your points always struck me as perceptive and fruitful. A sincere thanks for all.

Best to you
John

TO ZUBEL AND IRMA KACHADOORIAN

Metuchen
July 30, 1959
[Irma Cavat]

Dear Zubelonians:

In the name of the mercy of Allah and toward the piece that surpasseth understanding—Shantih. . . . .

Chillun, we has mounted that there Canto IX in the dead center of the living room, and daddy's been saying his prayers there. Damn if we ain't turning into a happy moozeum. The Hebalds got here with all the loot of the ages and we are hopelessly in debt to them for the next forty years for the load of stuff we bought from them. Lovely stuff. But you know me and my greedy ways. We got angels, now, but we ain't never going to have enough angels and if you-all latch on to any excess angels, we-uns is just the chillun to buy them off'n you. We may even have some money in a couple of months, once I get back on the lecture circuit. Right now I done flattened us cold by up an buying a Cadillac. And thereby hangs a tale.

Hold your hats: it ain't new. I was out looking for a cheap station wagon, but the best I could do on a new Chevy was two-thirds of a gold-mine. When suddenly a friend of mine that's a lawyer showed up with an estate he was settling, and within five minutes I'd bought a '56 Cadillac from him for less than half what the Chevy would have cost. So now we're rich, if only in the economy size package. Come on over for a ride. We even got push-button windows. And self-dispensing prophylactics in the back seat . . .

Send news. We love you, but we ain't sane nor civilized and you gotta forgive us all strange lapses, on account of it's that world.

(Judith has gone to Boston with the kids. When she gets back we all go to Bread Loaf for two weeks, then I dump them off here and head for South Bend briefly, then home again, with ten whole days before I start getting crazy again.)

Love,
John

TO READ BAIN

Metuchen
August 7, 1959
[MHC]

HEADQUARTERS
CIS ALPINE STRATEGIC WOLF PACK
31 Graham Avenue
Metuchen
N.J.

Tactical Ideological Team
7 August 1959

Reply to
attn. of: TIT

Subject: TAT
To: 2 Lt. Read Bain
Miami University Fld. HQ.
Oxford, Ohio.

1. 2 Lt. Read Bain (ex) will stand for commendation on preparation of recent morning report.

CITATION: For extraordinary achievement in both perception and the taming of the adjective, and for assured rhythmic consequences, despite a certain fulsomeness for which this HQ is nonetheless grateful, 2 Lt. Read Bain (ex) is hereby granted a three-day pass, without *per diem.*

2. In reply to questions addressed from TAT to TIT:

(a) Ref: Mother:

2 Lt. R. Bain is directed to re-read "Three Views of a Mother." Not exactly a fixation there, it is confessed, but for reasons apparent . . . she stopped being my mother and became my child so long ago that there remains nothing but mercies between us.

3. (b) Ref: Father:

The 2 Lt. has something there, but with missing pieces. My

father was killed in an auto wreck when I was not yet three. I hardly knew him, but as the only son, I was immediately elected to take his place in the family and entirely encouraged in all my first fantasies and confusion to be my father. No hate whatever, there. Rather, identity. I spent most of my childhood and good parts of my adolescence attaching myself to any large male that would allow me to hero-worship. I still find myself talking to my father sometimes when I'm really talking to myself.

(c) Ref: Sandburg, Frost.

2 Lt. Read Bain is directed to read "Mowing" by Robert Frost and to underline "Anything more than the truth would have seemed too weak." He is then directed to read as much Sandburg as an honest man can consort with, measuring the writing against that one line by Frost. This stolid-hard-bitten Italian thinks that florid over-operatic Swede has portions of moldy cheese in his pre-frontal lobe.

(d) Ref: Lowell, Roethke.

In my book they go for real.

(e) Ref: R. P. Lister, McGinley, Ogden Nash.

Ditto, but it matters much less.

(f) Ref: Bread Loaf

$1000 a year to direct a headache is not an inducement. The 2. Lt. may think of it as love: B.L. is the best goddamn two-week house-party in the western hemisphere. If I had the money, I'd underwrite it myself.

(g) Ref: Teaching.

Have just finished a semester on unpaid leave and am starting a year of the same to be followed almost certainly by another. Reasons: first: that students are beginning to bore the hell out of me; second: that colleagues are beginning to be more boring than the students; third: avarice, in that I can get most or all of a month's pay for a single free-lance lecture; fourth: for the fun of it, in that I like tooting around the country on airplanes; fifth: avarice again—how many rich poets do you know? Having just completed a quick survey, I discover that E. Guest, A. MacLeish, and I are the only poets in America who drive Cadillacs.

Per CO, TIT, CASWOP
John Ciardi

TO JOHN HOLMES
Metuchen
September 23, 1959
[TU]

Dear John:

Delighted to hear that all goes well. I'm having a racing good time of things. So much so that I'm reluctant to think of going back to teaching again. I shall—for many reasons—but only on a very special, very limited part-time, one-seminar-a-week basis.

Slowly, I am picking away at the ms. of the *Purgatorio,* and with luck and only a few busted arteries, I shld have it ready for publication next year. In the meanwhiles of interstices, I've been working away at children's poems and having a ball, as they say. Lippincott just sent me the contract for a little thing called *Scrappy* (he's a pup)—a 900 wd. book. In fact there are more words in the contract than there are in the book—about 7 times more.

Also I have a growing folder of children's poems for the next Lippincott book (1961) and I really am happily excited about them. I have enough for a book now, but I want to wait and do more and pick out the ones with a slightly grim touch. No "grim" isn't the word for it. But I think I have found a tone I want and value for itself, and I want them to be on that tone.

Also I have put together for Houghton Mifflin a book of children's poems on a basic word list. A really fun thing to do: to start with the words on the I and II lists for first-graders and to build the poems on those, using rhyme, context, trick devices, and special illustrations to work in new poems. I've got more than enough poems for that one, but they haven't been selected and put into final order yet.

And Rutgers is doing a new book of poems titled simply *39 Poems* for November release. Galley and page proofs are checked and the book is in production. I am reasonably pleased with this collection. Who can get pleased? But there are some poems I feel very right about in the total. And they are MY poems. No fooling about that. My poems in my own way. . . . .

Joys in all
John

TO MASON GROSS

Metuchen
November 4, 1959
[FC]

Dear Mason:

Let me try to make this as brief as possible as a memo of what I think we talked about at lunch (pleasantly, may I say) today:

First my feeling is that I neither want to cheat Rutgers nor to give the impression that I am cheating. My situation is that my moonlighting has become so much more lucrative than teaching that I cannot conscientiously take on a full-schedule nor the responsibilities that seem to be implied in being a professor. At the same time there are some things I can do easily that can turn out for the good of the university, and perhaps they are even things that no one else could do quite as simply.

I suggest therefore that we consider the possibility of changing my title to something like Poet in Residence (or should I say Poet in Transit?).

I do want to do some teaching, but I don't see how I can manage more than one day a week firmly scheduled, with some roving time on other days for conferences.

I must report my disappointment in the number and the quality of writing students of late. I do not think I justify either my salary or the expenditure of my own time with such classes as I have had in the last two years. Increasingly, too, I have become absorbed in the problem of teaching teachers to teach poetry.

I should like to try next year to put in a seminar for teachers on the teaching of poetry, to meet on the graduate level. I don't know whether that should go as school of education or English department.

Perhaps we could work out a satisfactory temporary arrangement by alternating that seminar for teachers and a seminar in writing, alternate annually that is. I think I could perform a good service additionally by giving a number of talks on poetry to various groups through the year—but please understand I suggest this without insistence. I am afraid I am something of a roving delegate by nature: should my way of doing things create any friction I want all parties concerned to know that I should much prefer to step out sooner than damage the cause.

I am saying that I want to do what is possible because I seriously value the work there is to do at Rutgers, but that I am forced to leave myself reasonably free to take advantage of the loot available on the lecture platform.

Best to you,
John Ciardi

TO M. G. ("BUD") AND FLORENCE ORENSTEIN

Metuchen

December 10, 1959

[Peggy (Orenstein) Young]

Dear Bud & Florence:

. . . . The world goes slowly but it goes. I'm going to make it out to Calif. yet, but damn it those West Coast colleges just ain't used to shelling out and I like to be expensive. It's a hobby of mine. I had one chance to go to SF for a week in June but was already committed for that week. Maybe another time.

All else ages on schedule. I age a bit faster. Myra is in 2nd grade, Jonnel in 1st, Benn in kindergarten. I am seriously thinking of leaving teaching. Judith wants to go to Europe. Nixon wants to go to the White House. Khrushchev wants to go to the moon. Me, I want to stay home and pour bourbon for Bud & Florence when they come to NY.

Merry X
John

TO DAN JAFFE

Metuchen
December 12, 1959
[DJ]

Dear Dan:

Congratulations on the sale to *LHJ* [*Ladies' Home Journal*]. By happy coincidence I had just made a sale there myself: they bought a couple of my children's poems.

Consider, too, that you have walked in easy. They began by paying me $7.00 a line and only worked me up to $10 slowly. May it always be so.

And then there are always the beasts of chagrin. A while back when I had collected a fat $10-a-line check from *LHJ* I ran into Phyllis McGinley who was aglow with *LHJ* gelt and was saying "What lovely rates!" Whereupon I was chortling back right with her, in such wise as, e.g.: "Boy, kiddo, you said a mouthful!" or words similar. Whereupon in the happy bubbling of both our percolators I heard her say in the same tone: "Imagine, $750 for two sonnets!"

Christ what bitter coffee. But learn ye, in this, my son, that many are soiled, but somebody's always filthier than you are.

No, I won't throw you out of house & garden and home beautiful. Don't you know I'm a rich poet? As an aging and intemperate heap, moreover, I have learned to insist on comfort on the road, and believe me, $6.00 is pre-war rates for any sort of decent hotel room these days. We can fix the exact dates and how many of them later, but get me the best they have and whatever they charge won't be too much. Besides, it's deductible.

I am not sure yet, but I may be driving. I shall be on a two-months tour that starts mid-Feb. Judith and I drive to Florida where I lecture for two weeks while we cadge a vacation. We then drive to Virginia for two days. She flies home. I drive to Memphis. Lv car. Take plane to SW Texas for four days/fly back to Memphis/drive to St. Louis for a lecture, then to Chicago for two weeks at Roosevelt University/then to several scattered lectures en route to Nebraska, then to Colo for Air Force Acad, U of Denver, and U of Colo at Fort Collins, and then home by way of three lectures en route. The whole thing is so spaced out that a car seems the right weapon for it, though I may decide to do it by plane and pullman in the hope of getting some reading [done].

Let me know your plans about jobs etc. Are you definitely not going to PHudnick [to pursue a Ph.D.]? What courses have you been teaching? Send me a bibliog, too. I mean keep me armed in case there is a job I might be able to shoot down for you. . . .

Love to Yvonne.
John

TO CONCETTA CIARDI

Metuchen

January 9, 1960

[Ella (Ciardi) Rubero]

Dear Ma:

I hope this finds you feeling better, and also that it finds you settled back in your own room, as Cora mentioned in her letter. I know you don't mind, but anyone is bound to feel more comfortable in his own nest.

I seem to be forever late in writing to you, and here I am late again. Please forgive that. You know it's not because I don't care. I'm just never caught up. I just got back from Pittsburgh. And I'm going to be making at least one trip every week until the middle of

February. Then Judith and I go to Florida for two weeks. She comes back early in March, but I won't get home till the middle of April.

Over the holidays I worked like a fool at an article for the *Saturday Evening Post* and just got the handsomest check for it—$2500. And just in time to endorse it over to Uncle Sam for income tax! Anyhow it gets me off the hook, so for heaven sake if you need any money, say so. Is there any treatment that leaves you feeling better?* Please ask the doctor if there is anything. Would a sun-lamp help? I'd love to get you one. Or he may think special hot baths or massage. I'm just guessing. But please, ask him if there is *anything* at all that you might *try.* Even if it doesn't work. Then let me know. Or ask him to write to me. Please do me this favor. It would be such a pleasure to be able to do a little something to help you feel better. Nothing is guaranteed, to be sure. But if the doctor thinks there is anything worth trying, let's do it.

Well, I've got to get to work. And there's company coming tonight. Lots of love to all of you.

John

*Mrs. Ciardi was suffering from arthritis.

TO WILLIAM SLOANE AND PAUL CUBETA

Metuchen

January 26, 1960

[MC]

Dear Father:

Our mutual acquaintance, a Mr. P. Cubeta writes: "Will you see Sloane about asking Funk and Wagnalls about renewing their fellowship, or do you want me to ask him?" A very curious question.

Affectionately,
J. Ciardi, Son.

Dear Son:

If this letter goes astray, I guess you'll have to see him about it after all.

Affectionately,
J. Ciardi, Father.

TO CONCETTA CIARDI

Chicago
March 17, 1960
[Ella (Ciardi) Rubero]

Dear Ma:

I assume Judith has written you what news there is. I am in Chicago for 2 weeks after which I head out to Colorado and then home. The trip has been fun but tiring and the weather has been bad all the way. It will be April 12 or 13 before I get home again. Let me hope there will be a little springtime by then.

In case you haven't seen it get a copy of the *Saturday Evening Post* for March 19. I have an article in it and they have run a full page photo with the article.

I shall be running up to Boston May 17 to talk at M.I.T. and again about June 10 or 11 to attend the Tufts commencement on the 12th. So I'll get a chance to see you before terribly long.

I gave Ella some money for you when she came down, but I've been so crazy I can't remember now whether she came in January or February. If it was in February I gave her some money for March but I can't be sure. Here's $20 anyhow and if I gave Ella your money for March call this for April. Or just call it extra. Please don't hesitate to let me know if you need any money for anything. God knows the way I keep racing around there is very little I can do for you except to send you a little money. Please let me know if you need any, or if there is anything you'd like to have.

And how about flying down to St. Petersburg to visit Pat and Jo? I know you wouldn't like to go alone, but why can't Cora fly down with you? It would do you both good. And if you go down together you could do it for 1½ fares on family plan. I'd love to pay for the tickets. Please think about it. But do it fast if you want to do it. Pretty soon it will be getting too hot in Florida. I'll be here until March 25. Please let me know by then. After that I'll be traveling to Colorado with a lot of one-day stops along the way and I'll be hard to reach.

Lots of love to all of you, and a double kiss for you.

John

TO PAUL CUBETA

New York

c. August 25, 1960

[MC]

Dear Paul:

Look! Look!
See the asst. director!
What fun he is having!
He gets to write so many nice letters!
He meets such nice people!
He gets so much sympathy from the director!

What are you going to be when you grow up?
I am going to be a cow-inseminator!
I am going to be an assistant pickle-taster for Heinz!
I am going to be a child vivisectionist!

Yes, those are all nice things to be, but
I am going to be an assistant director.
Then I shall get to write letters.
And I shall meet nice people.
And I shall get sympathy from the director.
What fun that will be!

Yrs. between disaster and mourning
John

TO DAN JAFFE

Metuchen

October 22, 1960

[DJ]

Dear Dan:

You tell me that girl is helium. That much I could see at a glance. If this poem is representative, she's also something else. I guess it takes the girls to bring out the man in a boy—though let me bless, too, those that bring out the boy in a man.

Anyhow with this poem you get your commission and your poetic razor. You may now don the cloak & begin to shave. You don't have to be in an all-fired hurry to grow a beard, but today you are a man. It's a good poem. No frivols about it—a good poem. Keep at it. We're proud of you Herr Doktor Colleague. Your membership in Parnassus Local 1 is hereby confirmed. *Ad* aspirin *per aspera.* Your dues are to be paid to Yvonne.

I don't know whether or not I can make it to Salem in Jan. Rather doubt. But in any case not to talk. In my decline and avarice I just won't talk for less than my $500 + expenses & Salem, Oregon, if it is any part of the West Coast, won't ante. If I decide to go on to SF, I'll certainly make it via Salem, but for that promised steak.

Well 4:10 A.M. and a class tomorrow (Sat) at 11:00. No matter. One need not be awake to teach school-teachers. I've been doing revisions on *Purgatorio.* The damned thing will definitely be off my hands by Jan 1 or sooner.

Am also shuffling poems toward a new book to be titled *In the Stoneworks.* The poems are written, but no final order yet. I've been sending them out & sold gobs of them. A long one due in Nov. *Atlantic.* One in *Harper's.* Two in *SR* (I have a pull). One in *N Yorker.* Several in *Ladies' Home Journal.* A group in *Poetry.* And ten or so in various little mags.

I still seem to have a fair batch unpubl'd but the markets seem to have dried up. Where do I go from here except to more give-aways? Ah, well.

Children's poems are still fun. *I Met a Man* (Houghton Miff) is delivered & will be out in Spring. Robt Osborne is illustrating. And Lippincott will do *The Man Who Sang the Sillies* in the fall. . . .

Stay well, stay busy, stay not too busy. Love to Yvonne.

John

TO MILLER WILLIAMS

New York

May 18, 1961

[MW]

Dear Miller:

The Bread Loaf Writers Conference runs from August 16 to August 30 this year, and if you can get away for two weeks in Vermont I want very much to urge you to accept a fellowship. The fellowship covers all conference expenses, but you will have to take care of your own transportation. If you are interested in drinking, you would also be expected to kick in to the communal martini fund in some reasonable proportion to the intake, and it might be reasonable to budget five or ten dollars for tips, but that would be about the total cost.

That aside, I think it would be a powerful thing for you as a person and a damned useful thing to you professionally, to have the experience of the conference under your belt. There will be all sorts of editors and publishers around, as well as a tremendous list of good American writers to bang heads with. This year's poets, for example, are Dudley Fitts, Howard Nemerov, and John Frederick Nims, with a couple of appearances by Frost and a couple by me when I can stop counting directorial paper clips long enough.

I hope you will give it some serious thought. I am urging it as something that could possibly be very valuable to you for a long time to come. I am sorry to say that fellowship accommodations do not include wives, though I should do my best to find out what the wife-charge would be if you wanted to add that grace to the occasion. Do let me know your thoughts.

All best to you,
John

TO JOHN HOLMES

Metuchen
July 18, 1961
[FC]

Dear John:

I hope my little *SR* piece of thanks to you and Cowden reached you and that you will accept it as honestly meant if too-long delayed.

Today I rcvd one beautiful pre-flight test-pilot's copy of *The Man Who Sang the Sillies* which contains the poem to Margaret Nash and the one to Evan Kirk. You may be sure you are on the list to get one as soon as Lippincott gets busy about sending out things. They haven't sent me my copies yet.

And soon now I am expecting the Rutgers Press books of *In the Stoneworks*. . . .

I've been so scattered I don't know when I've written you what. Did I tell you that I had resigned from Rutgers and that I was a prof. no more? They want to keep me on the list and are working out an annual one week visit as visiting poet, but otherwise I'm now—at least—a freelance. Anybody you want to have lanced?

All goes very well, I'm happy to say. Austin Olney wrote me from Houghton Mifflin that *I Met a Man* has done over 7,000 copies in less than 3 months and seems to be picking up rather than slowing down. And *How Does a Poem Mean?* has been going better than well. I finally got the final revised ultimate never-again ms. of *Purgatorio* to Mentor, mailing it from Missouri on my way to the West Coast about 10 days ago and that is due sometime late this year. Christ, that makes four books in 1961 and time for a vacation.

We are all planning on going to Italy (we hope, doubt, but still hope) at the end of 1962 for (probably, if we go at all) two years! That's (it says) in order to get through *Paradiso* and finish the *Comedy.* If. But how we'd love to. Trouble is I've got to live on airplanes between now and then, looting the lecture trail so I can pour large checks at Our Uncle and try to hold out enough to float us to and in Rome and back. Jesus, we could just about live there on what I'm paying Uncle! Well, let Uncle but be right, and I'll begrudge him no penny of it. Mentor has in any case agreed to advance me $6000 a year if we go for the two years. That won't, I know too well, do it for 5 people and school problems, but it gets the luxuries taken care of if I can manage to loot the necessities from the lecture-trail.

The trouble is I'm becoming a damned illiterate these days. Running so hard I can't find time to sit and hold a book. The fact and the thought of it both hurt. I swear to reform.

Well, it's 1:15 and I've been going for 13 hours with practically no let up and I'm tired and this rambles, but let love ramble with it from our house to yours,

and joys,
John

TO MILLER WILLIAMS

Metuchen
December 12, 1961
[MW]

Dear Miller:

Damn! How poorly heaven does! Poor Lucy. Please give her my love and tell her to get well soon. A hospital room is a thin Christmas.

What's all this about insulation? I thought you were going to be with a newspaper. At that there is certainly more cash future in selling [insulation] than on a paper. Sell a lot of it & keep the weather outside—where it belongs.

Don't rush Rago. I do want to do that page of poems but it can't be made to happen fast. It will take time to fight out the space.

I can't say you miss much in missing "Accent." It's a good show, but TV is a thin medium at best. My best hope for it personally is that one insane year of it may provide us with enough money for two [years]—or most of two—in Italy in which to get the *Paradiso* done. If all goes well I should be leaving by the end of '62. If you're in NY by then we can talk seriously about your doing the first reading, though that, at best, is a very part-time thing & *SR* won't go more than $100 a month for it. It wouldn't in fact involve more than three or four afternoons a month. Most of the poems can be chucked out at a glance and you could avoid getting sucked into any large scale letter writing. My secretary would handle that. In any case it's a possible crumb.

You've had a year of it, haven't you? Have you stayed in touch with Eunice Blake? Them Lippincott mills grind slowly, but they might grind. May '62 be writ large. Nemerov's intro & a book publication are a fine banner to see flying ahead.

Please give my love to Lucy. And all best to all of you.

John

TO DON V. R. DRENNER

Metuchen
March 11, 1962
[KSU]

[Don V. R. Drenner met John Ciardi at the University of Kansas City before the war. Over the years, Drenner maintained a high-quality printing operation called The Zauberberg Press: Coffeyville, and wanted to publish a limited edition book of Ciardi poetry. Though they were both willing, they found it impossible to settle on titles because so many poems were tied up at Rutgers University Press. However, Ciardi did offer a short verse drama, "Mother and Father: An Interlude," which Drenner decided against.]

Dear Drenner:

I returned home last night to find your letter waiting. I certainly do like the *Graphics of Love*. A beautiful book. It's lovely paper. And the Bulmer works beautifully with that much space around it. I am happily a partisan of a plainly stated page that pleases by grace and by the proportion of type to space rather than by scrollery and curlycue. I speak as mildly as the amateur must, but I speak in pleasure.

It's harder to speak meaningfully about the poetry. The eye can be pleased or rebuffed almost at a glance. A poem takes living into. Every man, moreover, has his own predilection. I try to avoid literary reference and to achieve the voice of the most readily spoken language. You like references and rhetorical flourishes in alternation with a heightened more literary way of speaking. So we have a difference of premises in common. I cannot, certainly, say that my premises are better: only that they are mine and that my predilection rides with them. Let me have more time with them.

No, there is no need to send a review copy to *SR.* If I can work in a piece for my column, I shall do so gladly. I can't promise it. But I want to try to work it in. It could take me a long time to find the right way of getting it said. But I'll find it.

No need to return the ms. of the "Interlude." If you think it will make a book by itself—fine. That would please me much. It would also get me off a hook. I am due to enter six months of insane activity. According to present plans I am due to leave for Europe about May 1 for some frantic work taping TV shows for CBS. I'm not sure I can manage a sane thought in those six months, and I have exactly 17 days at home before I leave, with 17 million details to tend to. If the play makes sense to you as a book, that would spare me a series of decisions about mss. that I simply haven't time to make competently. . . .

All best to you,
John

TO MILLER WILLIAMS

New York
April 5, 1962
[MW]

Dear Miller:

I am delighted to write to Dr. Kirby and will do so at once. While I'm at it, let me include a letter from a former student of yours: a real, certified fan letter, begod. I also have a very strange letter from the Deep South Writers' Conference, Inc., wanting me to certify you as a fit and proper person to speak to them. The fact that the bastards are paying nothing seems only to heighten their exclusiveness. I shall write them that you are a Communist and a homosexual as well as a heroin addict, but that I forgive these faults in you because you are such a fine specimen of the militant Afro-American.

Well, all right—I'll send them the kind of pablum they are able to gum, since they obviously lack spiritual teeth.

Please kiss Lucy for me. It's grand to hear that she has recovered and is back pounding the keyboard. All best, and thanks too for the photo of Karen, Cindy, and Myra. How about some more poems?

Joys,
[John]

TO LUCY WILLIAMS

Metuchen
May 2, 1962
[MW]

Dear Lucy:

Yes, Bill Sloane just told me. But you mustn't be despondent. Sloane didn't turn the book down on merit. Every publication has to be approved by the Press Council of the Univ. & the Council just didn't see why the press should lose money on a non-Rutgers connection.

It's a mistake to pin so much hope on publishing a book of poems. I fluked into my first publication in 1940 by winning a prize & then it took me 7 years and literally over 100 mag publications—way over—before I could talk another publisher into losing his money on me. —That's what a publisher has to agree to do. He has to say, "all right let's lose $2000 worth of the firm's money publishing Miller Williams because we like him $2000 worth."

The points I'm trying to make are:

1. Even with as good a man as Nemerov willing to do a preface it may take a long time to connect. All you can do is keep bucking. But

if every rejection is a cause for grief, there's too much emotion riding on it & too many causes for grief ahead.

2. If you take it that hard, eventual publication will itself be a cause for grief because you will probably expect much too much from it. What *do* you think happens when you publish a first book? The answer is mostly—*nothing*. Nothing at all. Next to nothing. Maybe a big puff in the local paper—probably not. A few scattered reviews. About 400 copies sold—that's about 1 to every ½ million people in the U.S. A few letters from friends.

And that's all.

The phone doesn't jump with job offers. The publishers will not pant for a second volume. The Nobel Prize Committee does not convene on it. Your pay doesn't go up. You begin to think publication is one of the best kept secrets in the country. Later you discover it is.

That's all. Ironic maybe. Maybe a poet chooses an ironic life. Certainly a poet's wife does. But you find enough that's worth it. Love & grace and knowing what you do is human, good, and a damned sight better than banking. —There's that to think of. Think it gladly.

And bless.

Love
John

TO PAUL CUBETA

[Metuchen]
c. May 12, 1962
[MC]

Dear Paul:

I haven't had any luck running down a fictionizer but I'll keep trying. Have you borne in mind that Walter Ross is primarily a fiction man? He can take some of the mss. He, Raney, and Sloane will all carry some of the fictive spasms.

Let me know how the mss. run and if we absolutely must have another man, for I confess the fishing has been awful goddamn lousy.

If the impossible must be swung somehow, let it swing. But let me know.

More grief. CBS, after killing "Accent," has brought it back to life and is moving it to a coveted slot, 7:30 P.M. Thurs. for the summer (June 7–Sept 13). I am plugging hard for a program on BL and begin to think it can be managed, especially if I can persuade RF [Robert Frost] to sit for a half-hour tape to be shot on the same trip. But to get our programs, the unit has to go crazy and all over the country from now until then. I haven't the slightest notion what our sched will be except that it will be far gone, long gone, and crazy as usual. I'm wondering where the hell I'll be and if I'll be when the fellowship/scholarship mss. hit in. How much preliminary screening do you normally do? If I am absolutely dead lost with CBS in Las Vegas, L.A., Sea Island, Ga., or Hannibal, Mo.—to mention a few of the spots on the shooting schedule, is there any chance that you could do the picking if I promise to endorse your decisions without question and with whole approval and even to claim that they were mine if you want?

What I'm asking is would that be a hell of a lot more work than you do already in screening? I'll be here next week, but my damn trouble is that after May 20 I don't know where the hell I'll be nor for how long. That leaves me in the damned box of knowing it has to be done and in some homage to time without knowing whether or not I'll be in any position to do it.

Please tell me what would be involved in your doing it if you had to and suggest any arrangement you can see as possible. I hate to put you in this spot & I will most urgently hope I can do it myself as usual, but in case I'm left on the desperate end of the impossible rope, please let me know your thoughts in whatever detail.

Item: Please send a fellowship blank to Byron Vazakas, Suite 30, 1699 Cambridge St., Cambridge 38, Mass. with a note saying I am eager to nominate him for a fellowship and will he please fill out? Add there is no need to send books or mss. I want to bring him up to Bread Loaf. He's really a bit far along having been publishing a long time. But I like the twisted bastard; he writes a good poem, and if you will permit me a directorial fiat I want to put him down as a Fellow in Poetry as of now.

(Not the Frost Fellowship, however. I doubt he and RF would hit it off.) He will make a queer one around the edges of the mt. (he takes long walks) but I think he can both give to and take from Bread Loaf, and besides Judith thinks he's cute in a sort of girlish Savonarola way, if you can visualize a decayed tonsure on a corrupted Jesuit.

Best in alas always too much goddamn it haste, but best withal,

John

TO CORLISS LAMONT

Metuchen

September 22, 1962

[FC]

[Corliss Lamont had written to invite Ciardi to speak at a meeting of the Emergency Civil Liberties Committee.]

Dear Corliss:

Frankly, I was dodging more than just a date. Some time ago, after a number of years of chasing around after good causes, I came to a decision in which I have by now grown confirmed: I am a writer, my work is what I do, and once I have survived the distractions of making a living, my writing gets my energy. My sympathies are with you, but to put it bluntly, they are even more with my workbook. If I can capture a thing there as it should be captured, it will stay captured and said, and that capture and saying, I must insist, is also a public cause. With you, I could recite long arguments on both sides, but that's where I mean to live and in the long run I'll somehow manage to dodge every change of address because I have to.

I don't know how you will feel about my saying this, but I hope you will at least believe I say it seriously, with all good will, but firm in the belief that my cause, whatever it is, is here.

Cordially,

John Ciardi

TO WILLIAM RANEY

Metuchen
September 19, 1963
[FC]

Mr. William Raney
Editor-in-Chief
Bobbs Merrill Co.
3 W. 57th Street
NYC 19

Dear Bill:

I need hardly tell you that Bread Loaf is running into problems. I feel, and I am sure you will agree, that the content of the conference gets better year by year, while enrollment falls off. This year we were knocked over by 54 last minute cancellations.

At the same time a number of the publishers and magazines and friends who have been supporting our Fellowship and Special Programs on a year to year basis for a limited number of years have reached their limit.

The hell of it is that I could fill the mountain by destroying the program. If I went for a fusty staff of old plug horses who are by now extinct in terms of where American writing is going but who are yet enshrined in the hearts of the old blue hairs, we could load the mountain.

Bread Loaf, as I know you will agree, is too important for that. I must therefore cry for help. One of our jobs is to discover talent and to get it in touch with publishers, editors, and agents who need talent. That is not our whole job, to be sure, nor even our first job, but it is an important one, and to do it we must be able to dig among more promising ores than the white-heads test out to.

I enclose a memo on some of our most urgent needs. Could Bobbs Merrill see its way to helping Bread Loaf, I think there is sound reason to believe that the investment will be returned with interest over the years, for there will certainly be many good writers arriving at the conference from year to year, and some of them will certainly turn out to be valuable literary properties.

At the same time let me urge again the possibility of arranging for a junior editor or for some young writer the firm hopes to develop. . . .

Let me add one item: To any publisher who will endow a fellowship or scholarship . . . I can offer this arrangement. If the firm will pledge $1000 a year for four years, I can manage to pay for the year-to-year cost by one form of beggary or another, and thereby permit the firm to appoint an editor or author beginning in 1964. That is, the endowment will be treated as if it were paid up from the time it is pledged. At the end of four years it would be fully paid up and thereby able to function forever—this side, that is, of any dangerous inflation.

All best to you.

Cordially,
John Ciardi

TO BEATRICE ROETHKE

Metuchen
September 28, 1963
[UW]

Dear Beatrice:

I am home for only a few hours between two legs of a lecture tour that will keep me lost to the world until late November. Meanwhile, my marvelous secretary had forwarded photo copies of your letter and the poems.

I am terribly sorry to have missed you in NY. I got in from Cleveland this afternoon and leave for Boston tomorrow, alas.

Bless you for liking my piece on Ted. No one page could do him near-justice, but it was meant in love and admiration.

And thanks, too, for the poems. I think "Saginaw" is pure Ted and a true song, but I'm boxed in by house rules whereby I'm just not allowed, even in love, a poem that pees and farts, damn it.

I am in no box, however, about "The Pike" and the "The Chums" and I grab them in avid pleasure for *SR.* Our rates of pay are, alas, lousy, but I'll buck for as much of a bonus as I can get. They more than deserve it.

Forgive me for slapdashing out what I wish I might write at the pace of a proper pleasure. This tour doesn't head toward Seattle, but I'll hope the next one may and that I may see you there.

Let me wish you joy in a sweet memory.

Yours,
John

TO MILLER WILLIAMS

Metuchen
December 2, 1963
[MW]

Dear Miller:

Please don't count the days from letter to reply! I shan't even try to explain what you wouldn't believe anyhow. But let it begin with 8 weeks on the lecture circuit, a week at Tufts, and a mosquito swarm of chores to be done.

By way of refusing the world I have flatly decided I work for 4 hours every day before looking at the mail. The legacy of that decision is now two large cartons of varied mail. But I *am* making some progress toward a book of poems—though none yet toward a title unless I decide to call it "Person to Person."

Your time sounds as marvelous as mine sounds impoverished. Learn not to get busy. And don't for Christ Sake slide into being a Figure without first building a wall around it. There must be something better for suburban wives to do than to send me their diaries for a comment. At that the only comment would be No Thanks.

So far not a damned inch toward the *Paradiso.* God how far I am behind hope's schedule. . . . .

I'm dreaming I shall finally fight clear of the mosquitoes by Christmas and give myself 8 whole weeks in which to do nothing, nothing, nothing except what matters. *Orare!* . . . .

Love to Lucy. I ain't got no serenities of my own to send from this madhouse but let me wish you all you can come by yourself.

Fondly
John

TO MILLER WILLIAMS

Metuchen
January 25, 1964
[MW]

Dear Miller:

. . . . Have you ever quit smoking? I'm on my second day into the jitters and just broke down and fished the old butts out of the ash tray. Even they tasted like the wind of heaven's asphodel, goddamn it. No man does well to saddle himself with character. But this time I am turning stubborn. I'm going to make it stick.

Yrs for character aspiration devotion sincerity L&M's sobriety virginity tarrytons prudence wisdom fortitude oldgoldspinfilters charity reverence cleanliness godliness winstons and plain crap.

Seriously, I'm delighted to hear about the LSU proposal. I think a U Press can sell as many copies of a book of poems as any big press and I have even turned down two big houses that seemed willing to do my poems in order to stay with Rutgers. I just sent Rutgers the ms. of my new book, *Person to Person,* and sent a carbon to Dudley Fitts for his eagle-eye. He generally raised hell with it and ended up giving me something like C–/D– on it, with which grade I walked the floor for two days, reading and re-reading, and finally decided it was no go and that I would let it stand exactly as submitted to Rutgers. It takes some sort of madman to veto D Fitts on every point, but it was either that or try to turn into someone else and by now it's too late for me to try.

Love to Lucy. I am delighted to note how good a year this is turning out to be for the Williamses. May there be an endless row of such lined up bumper to bumper.

Joys
John

TO **WILLIAM SLOANE**

Metuchen

September 14, 1964

[FC]

Dear Bill:

Your letter long to hand and long in thought while this top spun on.

I am against radio and TV writing at Bread Loaf. I'm willing to be persuaded on evidence, but what evidence? One of the first things I said as dir. was that there would be no TV and no radio writing workshops because Bread Loaf was concerned with putting mind on paper. I can't see either of these as writing occupations. It *is* possible, of course, to write humanely about human beings for radio and TV, but what the medium is out for is simply something to fill out the advertising. God knows there is nothing so special to meeting the technical requirements of radio and TV and if a man can write he can write for the media, but where does such mechanical scissoring fit into Bread Loaf? As above, I'll listen. But not to the fact that people think they want such courses. I have to be persuaded first that [it] *is* writing, and off hand I don't believe it.

As for theater, I have long resisted because of the nature of the beast. Get half a dozen would-be playwrights on hand and there will inevitably be a skit with people being dragooned into taking part, and I don't see how two weeks offers enough time for that. Remember when we had skits? Gaaaawwwd! I think forty-seven or forty-eight was the last of them and I certainly haven't missed them. . . . .

And, yes, we have to do something about getting the fellows back to us. We have, frankly, been experimenting, and this year's experiment worked beautifully for the fellows but badly for us. I am tempted to let the whole pack jam back into Treman and let it ride. With half a break as far as the weather is concerned it could work. Loud, maybe, but the right loud. I've missed those sessions, too.

Kitty Bowen is a fine thought and a long one with me, too, but if the best she can do is a weekend—as it turned out her last two years with us—it isn't enough. I'd love to get her back on the staff, but a visit solves nothing really. I'll write her, of course, and if all we can get is a visit, so be it, but what we need is Kitty for the full session.

Which is to say thanks for some thoughts that counted. I haven't spoken to all your points. Some go on file for next year (anent late comers to lectures, for instance). But all noted. And it takes exactly this crossing of impressions before we can see what's shaping.

Am I flat wrong about radio and TV? If you think I need persuading, persuade me. And aside from what I said above, where do we fit the lectures and workshops into the schedule?

Best to you and Julie and Julie Ann, Anne, or Julianne (or how does she spell it?).

And thanks, Dad.

Yours ever,
John

TO CATHERINE DRINKER BOWEN

Metuchen
September 14, 1964
[MC]

Dear Kitty:

Another Bread Loaf put by and no Kitty though Bill Sloane and I mentioned you often as the world changed out from under us. We both left the mountain with a weary sense that it was changing out of its own memory. Bill goes back to the late thirties and I go back to a fellowship in 1940 and there simply is no one else left to remember how it used to be. Not on the staff. Avis De Voto is with us and she does. And so does Mary Moore Molony. And Inga Pratt comes up for a day or two.

But nothing remains a greater need upon us, as I feel it, than those who remember how it used to be and can carry that memory [into the present]—which is good, even perhaps better than it has been, but still lacking something you could help us give it. I just hate to see the past of the place change even into a better present without leaving more mark on that present.

That's one reason for my special hope that we might be able to lure you back in 1965. Bill Sloane tells me you have some hope of being through with your new book by conference time. If you are, I can think of nothing that would do more for us than to have you back on the staff to the greater glory of everything. Will you bear it in mind and let us hope?

May the book go well. And may hope flourish.

Toward hope,
John

to Edward "Sandy" Martin

Metuchen
September 21, 1964
[FC]

Dear Sandy:

[President James] Armstrong just phoned me to say you had accepted the Bread Loaf job [assistant director of the conference]. I guess you might have guessed that we wanted you for it, and we did, and very much, but having is a better thing than hoping, and all of us have a feeling of coming home winners. Welcome, sir.

Paul [Cubeta, former assistant director] knows infinitely more than I about the details of it and I don't have to tell you that anything he tells you about it is 200 proof, but it is your show, as I know Armstrong has made clear, and Paul will be in on it for this year only and as an advisor.

I certainly don't need to tell you how much we hate the thought of losing Paul. I have the comfort of having known for a long time that there was no way of keeping him forever. And there is a long friendship and long affection. But never doubt that it is your show. Nor that you are the gent we wanted and the one we'll all be there to welcome come the next mountain-madness.

Welcome again, and let me hope it may be for as long as I know it will be happy.

With rejoicements,
yours,
John

TO PAUL CUBETA
[Metuchen]
September 21, 1964
[FC]

Dear Paul:

Jim Armstrong just called to tell me that Sandy is in and that you will stay on for this year as his advisor, and so fade out.

I don't see how we could have done better than we did in getting Sandy, and obviously I mustn't drown his welcome in tears for you. They would, at that, be selfish tears. I've known for a long time—for longer, I think, than you may have known it—that you were too much bigger than the job to be holdable to it forever. And in some sense that softens the blow. You will be having a show of your own—as you should. And certainly Armstrong has made it clear that you are a big man on his campus. That's all good, and all right, and any tears have to be followed by cheers for the good you are going to.

So let me just say thanks. It's a long thanks, as you know, and it involves respect and long friendship and all the ways in which the Ciardis love the Cubetas. And if you must fade out to the academic set, that's certainly no reason for not zooming back in, and long, and often, once *the people* take over the mountain.

Love from all of us to all of you. I certainly have no way of forgetting that it was your management of the conference that made the attendance zoom the first year you took over. Don't be modest about that; I know it is so. I may have picked up a customer here and there on my lecture tours. But the bulk of that jump was the direct result of the fact that every letter addressed to the conference got an immediate and well-considered answer.

We'll always owe you that, and if we have to owe it to you among many other things, that's because you're an easy man to owe a lot to. We do, and thanks for all.

And joys to come and as they come.

Ever, and as ever,
John

TO RICHARD EBERHART

[Metuchen]
May 28, 1965
[DC]

Dear Dick:

The "Vastness & Indifference" is a true thing & of course I want it for *SR.* Many thanks, as ever.

It was great seeing you at Lewis Mumford's Anschluss, but a little sad because we don't see you enough and I could get nostalgic for Cambridge in whatever golden age it was when we were all around the corner from one another with something like a real garden for our imaginary toads to hop in.

Love to all of you from all of us.

John

TO MILTON HEBALD

Metuchen
April 11, 1966
[MH]

Dear Milton:

Don't ask me how it got to be April 11. Don't, in fact, ask me what world this is. It spins too fast for me. Ten seconds ago as the psyche ticks we were looking forward to seeing you. And 8 secs. ago as the same clock goes you were heading back for Italy and we had hardly had a glimpse of you. And here it is months later and I still haven't come to rest from one spinning tour after another. Where in hell do these worlds spin to?

Anyhow you were hardly gone when my agent started to take over and I have hardly surfaced since. Nor can I expect to until well into May. Blessedly, May, June, and July are a free gift of time—well, the last half of May. I shall be tied to my desk doing Dante once I get off the loot circuit. And then in July we head for a whole month on Nantucket. Golf and a swim in the morning, Dante in the afternoon, and so to bed. It seems a beautiful dream.

I got home from a month long tour of one-night stands just long enough to be checked over by our friend Doc Klompus and, by God, I pass as healthy. Judith dunt git to spend my life insurance yet. Old sweetie-pie says she dunt wanna spend my life insurance. She says she wants to enjoy me. That's where I caught up with her. Given a choice between me and my money what sane woman would take me? Ergo: she is either insane or a liar. Right? So I do believe her. Right? So she's crazy. Right? And now you know why I love her and hope you are the same. . . . .

How are things going with your studio on the lake and with the house? Judith and I have a bug in the ear about getting to Italy next year. I have been made an honorary citizen of Manocalzati in Avellino, I will have you know, and we'd just like to get over and have a look at the home town. But there are so damned many imponderables. We'll have to wait and see.

Give our love to Cele (and keep as much for yourself) and come back soon and stay longer. What with your crazy schedule and my crazy schedule we hardly got a glimpse of you. We have been making vague gestures toward buying a great big old house with 6½ acres of land not too far from here—a vest-pocket estate, b'gad, with scads of guest rooms. If we buy it, we'd love to install you for a leisure spell. . . .

Deh, ciao, carissimi. Stay well, be happy, work joyously, e mangiati bene.

[John]

TO MILTON HEBALD

Metuchen

May 23, 1966

[MH]

Eregio:

Congratulations on the construction of your new *potere.* It looks great and I hope you will find endless blessed hours in it. I have been racing around the country again and too much, but you understand I do it only for the purest of motives—greed.

Then having got rich I blew myself to a new Caddy. Man, it's pure exhibitionism! And with more gadgets than Rube Goldberg's imagination. It even has an automatic wife-coaxer that turns on at the end of a long drive, about five miles out from the motel. By the time you've checked in, she has been tickled pink and is ready to go. Marvels of science!

And yes, by God, we will make it to Europe and Bracciano, but first I must finish the Dante. Which means we probably can't do it until a year from now. Though, with luck, and if we can get the kids sat with, we might just be able to do it in Feb., though I doubt that. Anyhow, I am working hard at it and hope for good progress. (We are going to Nantucket for July and there is nothing there to distract me from a solid month of dig-dig-dig.). . . .

Love to both of you from both of us,
as ever,
John

TO WILLIAM DENEEN

Metuchen
June 19, 1966
[LC]

Mr. William Deneen
Encyc. Britt. Films.
425 No. Michigan Ave
Chicago, Ill. 60611

Dear Mr. Deneen:

Yours is a letter for a man to sit long to, and a hard one to reply to, though certainly the beginning is thanks.

Certainly, I did not mean to haggle. My principle is simple. I work at my writing with no regard to what I get paid for it: it is simply what I do. To support it, I take on the lecture trail, grabbing large wads of cash fast in order to be able to stop racing around and get back to my desk. It's a selfish principle but a sound one: anything that takes me away from the central purpose of writing has to pay off in a large way because that is the fastest way back to the writing. I am, of course, spoiled by the lecture platform, and I love it. My agent stands ready to leave me with $3500 to $4500 after all expenses and commissions for almost any week I will give him. That makes a hard market.

Certainly, too, it would be fun to do this pair of films. But suppose you burst the ultimate gusset in swelling the budget and that I committed myself to it, and then it did not work out? —I am, after all, not experienced enough to guarantee results. On all counts, I'd hate to get us bound to an awkward commitment.

I am, moreover, nailed down for the summer. I shall be on Nantucket all of July, leaving June 27 for Wauwinet, and I shall be in New Hampshire and Vermont all of August. I have set myself a daily schedule of work on my translation of the *Paradiso* and I have no choice but to honor that long-standing commitment first. But suppose I take the thought of these two films along as something to turn to for variation's sake. Then let me see what I come back with.

I only have about 32,000 things to do in September, so that month is relatively free. If I have the right makings of two scripts by then in whatever rough-out form, perhaps I can get together with John Barnes and whatever resident-suggestors are at hand, and we can perhaps play it from there.

The thing might just pick out a groove and follow it home. I'll promise to do what I can to scratch a groove for it.

May I ask you to buzz me early in September?

Hopefully,
John Ciardi

TO DORIS HOLMES

Metuchen
October 7, 1966
[Doris (Holmes) Eyges]

Dear Doris:

In a word, we are NUTS. I'm leaving Monday for a month on the lecher circus, pecking worriedly at Dante before popping off, got myself slathered into agreeing to do two films for Ency. Britt. Educ. Films Inc., and wish I could get out of it, and have bought another house cross town. Haven't sold this damned ark, don't know what the hell we're doing really, but we seem to be due to move plus or minus Thanksgiving, and I think I'll simplify matters by just plain blowing my damn brains out, as if I had any to get myself involved in another house moving. Ah well, t'aint nawthin a million bucks wouldn't make easy. . . .

Books are off to Don Brodine. I'm off to who knows what. If this letter sounds scattered, there's cause. I'm due to talk at BU OCT 27, Hayden Hall, 8:00 P.M. Buy you a drink?

Love,
John

TO RICHARD EBERHART

Metuchen
January 17, 1967
[DC]

Dear Dick:

I hope the new address will explain why we have been unheard from when the Christmas cards were flying: we moved on Dec 19 and chaos has been general, but now settling into a nice house—big and rambly.

Rutgers Press has just put out my new book (Dec 5) *This Strangest Everything*—which is as close as I have come yet to describing the world. I'm asking them to send you a copy and hope you will find it worth your eyes, though no need to acknowledge: the world will yet die of letter writing. (I wish we could find a bottle to sit over and gab toward civilization.)

Love to all of you from all of us.

John

TO DAN JAFFE

Metuchen
January 23, 1967
[DJ]

Dear Dan:

It was great to get a look at you those 97 years ago last Christmas, and I owe you an apology for being blank when you spoke of *Aloud to Alma Mater.**

As I have just discovered today, the book had been sent, arriving while I was away. I found it today in Jonnel's room. He had assumed I had read it, had taken it off to read for himself, and had stuck it into his bookcase. Family life.

It's odd to read oneself through other eyes and generous ones. Did I really walk down the street with my briefcase on my head? Item: it was John Holmes, not MacLeish, who wrote "Haunts you, Hell: make it haunt me." And surely, I couldn't have had your raunchy crew as cowed as all that? Or could I have had? Man, what a sense of power, if only in retrospect.

But dust motes aside, I am touched, sir, and grateful to you. If you give me more than I deserve, that is only more cause for gratitude: far be it from me to demand justice when mercy is available. Nostalgically, too, the piece takes me back to other days and makes me remember they were good ones. Dammit, had Rutgers been able to produce another crop or two of students half as good as that first harvest, I might have stayed in academe. There was a rather fair second blooming a few years after you left, but then never again.

That much, however, is just the nostalgia musing on by free association. What I want to say is simply that I am moved by the piece, grateful to you for it, and glad I have it. It is also—at least as far as I am able to detach myself from it, which is never easy—a damned good piece of writing. Shall I take that as evidence that you were well taught? Let's say instead you were the hoped-for learner. And bless you for having stayed so.

Joys to you in all and to Yvonne and the flowering sprouts.

And thanks, Dan.

Yours,
John

*Jaffe had written a piece on Ciardi in this anthology celebrating Rutgers.

TO NORMAN COUSINS

Metuchen
January 26, 1967
[NC]

Dear Norman:

I haven't been able to coincide with you to talk things over so let me try another of my dreary letters. When we last talked you suggested that I say what I think I should have from *SR* and that you would consider possibilities. I'll try.

The basic question in my mind follows a basic condition I am glad to find myself in. I like it at *SR:* I like the people, I like the freedom to chase my own tail, I like writing the column, even allowing myself at times to think I will eventually manage to do something worth doing with what is left of the familiar essay, and I like the responsiveness of *SR* readers, with whom I seem to have a natural entente. All of which adds up to the fact that I want very much to make a career at *SR,* to keep it rewarding to my own sense of writing, and to make it useful to the quality and growth of the magazine. These are good conditions. The question that follows from them is simply: "What does a career at *SR* come to?" I have been here 12 years now and I have accrued nothing beyond the next piece of copy I turn in. If I stay another 12 or another 24, will I come to the same audit? If so, I submit I shall not have had a career but only rental mileage.

You tell me that I do have certain benefits accrued. Well, yes, I am sure *SR* would carry me for a few months were I to fall ill with the expectation of coming back to work. Certainly, however, I have no expectation that *SR* could or would carry me were I to be permanently disabled, or that my family would receive any death benefits, or that I could expect retirement benefits for bribing nymphs in my lecherous (well, hopefully) old age.

I think it would be not particularly enlightened but only standard twentieth-century employment practice for a great corporation to ask itself the questions I am asking. I am assuming, perhaps arrogantly, that I am worth something to *SR* and thereby to *McCall's.* And I am asking what *McCall's* is worth to me in terms of how my life is to be lived. Every great corporation I know anything about provides retirement benefits, annuities, stock options, and other fringe benefits in some mix. I have been harping on this point for years now, and nothing happens. I remain an independent contractor and, with the possible exception of being carried for a few months in case of a passing illness, I have accrued nothing that is worth a dime ten minutes after I fail to pass in my copy. Call that repetition for emphasis. I do submit it is a factual answer to your demurrer.

It is as an independent contractor, therefore, that I switch back to paragraph one and say what I think I should have. I will contract to deliver to you 26 columns a year at $1000 apiece, all columns in addition to 26 to be paid for at $500 apiece. I do not propose to limit myself to 26 columns but to think of the column as a weekly assignment. Until I finish my work on Dante, however, I may not be able to go over the annual 26. It is also possible that I may become absorbed in another book manuscript and have to limit myself to 26.

While you are getting your eyebrows down from the top of your head again, let me say that nothing less will make any real difference to me. I guess I can simmer along at *SR* for a while longer while I make my living on the lecture platform. Eventually, however, it has to come to a choice of energies. My hoped for choice would be to work at *SR* and at my own desk here, at my own writing, with only incidental lecturing. Alternatively, I can hit the lecture trail hard—my take in 1967, for example, after agent's commissions and expenses, is going to be almost $60,000. But that is three solid exhausting months of one-night stands plus another month of visiting professorships, etc.

With royalties and miscellaneous that means something like $100,000 this year, which is obviously insane as a way of life, but without *SR* to think about, it would leave me almost eight months of the year free at my own desk and still allow me to accumulate capital for the Ciardi Memorial Old Age and Widows and Orphans Benevolent Association, and there is nothing insane in that thought: give me five years of that and with any sort of hopeful market I should have most of a million and be free to sneer at money.

But it *is* insane to try to carry *SR,* my own desk, *and* a full lecture schedule. Something has to give. On the terms I suggest (I hope your eyebrows are back by now) I can keep the lecturing incidental. On anything less it is *SR* that has to become incidental and more and more so to a foreseeable vanishing point.

One last point: committed as I am to this year's lecture schedule I could not undertake even the contract I have suggested until the end of the year. Meanwhile, of course, [agent] Harry Walker will be lining things up for 1968 unless I put the brakes on him. So there is time and there isn't. I'd like to cut down on the lecturing. If you can see your way to what I suggest, I can cut down. Otherwise, it simply has to be *SR* I cut down on: there just is no way of hacking it three ways, I will not give up time for my own writing, and I will not forego the comfort of family security and the problems of a substantial estate—or not willingly.*

But willingly yours,
John

*Cousins replied on February 7 with a counter-offer. He suggested $1,000 each for four lead articles per year plus an increase to $500 per month for being poetry editor. He also recommended to the board that Ciardi be given stock options and be included in the retirement program, neither of which ever developed.

TO EDITH (CIARDI) ROSI

Metuchen
July 15, 1967
[Ella (Ciardi) Rubero]

Dear Mrs. Rosi,

. . . . How's you? In flight from the bill collectors, we're taking off for a week while I golf and [Judith] sits. Our carpenter stays on in residence. Infernal Revenue has given me permission to claim him as a dependent along with his wife, children, in-laws, grandparents, and 13 cousins. Last week the tree surgeons were in. That closes the cycle. After shelling out to the lumber yards, now I start paying for the trees. By me, they are for the birds. Trouble is that unless I get them tooken care of the birds won't be able to find them. I am also listing as a dependent one huge ancient American elm that ain't been blighted yet. I'm told that if I can keep it on twenty-four hour private nursing care it might live. Trouble is my pulse is getting lower than the tree's.

How's your old man? Still chasing chicks? Men—baah! Women—baah! Me—eh! Jonnel is on Nantucket as a month of July baby sitter. Not a bad way of unloading him, but I'm afraid he will be coming back. Myra is hard at the guitar and still working up her song list: my daughter the folk-singer. Benn still keeps coming by to tell me how good he is going to be and how hard he is going to work—that's in between raising hell and doing nothing.

Big doings. The mayor of Manocalzati, provincia d'Avellino came by yesterday with a traveling delegation and presented me with the fanciest scroll you ever saw declaring thereby that I am an Honorary Citizen of said Manocalzati in said Avellino. It was really very touching. You may refer to me hereafter as Signor Comapaesano Cittadino Onoraria. . . .

Hoppita days,
e auguri santi
John

TO DAN JAFFE
Metuchen
July 15, 1967
[DJ]

Dear Lad of the Golden West:

Dan Freeman came by cantankering in a rumpled suit, still claiming he was #1, but I keep thinking his author is. Why don't you file as the first man to mine real poetry out of Nebraska? Seems to me you've got a clean claim. I just wouldn't have believed a real thing could be made of such material, but you've done it b'God, and as far as I know you've invented a genre.

It's a compelling book, Dan. And not just in bringing a highly flavored old curmudgeon to life but—and marvelously—to poetry, grand poetry. I'm with you in this way of going. Lyric condensation of the soul's insides is powerfully possible stuff and the world has not run out of need and appetite for it, but what I think poetry needs at this turning is a way and a form of statement that will allow it to clutch facts to it, and their specification and detail, on the scale the novel is able to. Not in the way of the novel, but on the scale of it.

Tight lyric tends to rely on symbolisms already tightened for it. It has a hell of a time escaping what has been standardized for it. And it does make glorious escapes, capturing single moments of gorgeously cut detail. But it has few resources for dealing with the crazy-kook-wonderful strew of facts the world and experience spout. And poetry needs a way of gathering that strew to itself.

You've taken a fine, full strew of Dan Freeman and made order of it—it is poetry that adds to itself in the act of adding fact to itself. That's much to do and well done. Salve!

Yours
John

TO MILLER WILLIAMS

Metuchen
July 29, 1967
[MW]

Dear Miller:

I couldn't have foreseen how hard it would be to thank you for your introduction [the typescript introduction to Williams' *Achievement of John Ciardi*, published in 1969]. You've said some powerful fine things about me and if I say how right your portrait seems I'll seem to be saying all those kudos are simply appropriate, and over the corpses of several torn up letters, I don't mean that. For the praises, I don't know of any human possibility but to be grateful and I am.

But even more, I'm left to feel—hell, I *know*—you must have read me more carefully than any man living; and how does one address that mystical entity *The Most Careful Reader*? You loom upon me as a spirit and essence. . . .

What is there about being read that carefully that gets to a man? I am touched, and of course grateful, but more than that, somehow identified by you and to you. I won't make a Chinese debt of that—save my life and you become responsible for it, identify me and ditto—and yet that makes you terribly important to me. And for my part, of course, gladly in debt to, the great thing being always to choose most wisely those to whom you owe most & not to owe much to such as you would not be indebted to.

Oddly, since you say so much about identities, I've been partly delayed in answering you by a rare little ceremony in which the mayor of my mother's birthplace (Manocalzati, prov. of Avellino) came by and presented me with a fabulously illuminated parchment proclaiming me an honorary citizen. Somehow that parchment and your intro come together in my feelings. Pieces of some identity, whatever it is, but guessfully of the son of man.

You've said it for me, Miller, and damned well, and generously,, but in the psychic profile accurately and even in a way that helps bring it together for me. And how does one say thanks for that? Except that it goes gladly. . . .

I'll be looking forward to seeing you at Bread Loaf . . . and best, and bless gratefully.

As ever
John

TO MILLER WILLIAMS

Metuchen
October 28, 1967
[MW]

Dear Miller:

I'm glad it will be the *New Orleans Review.* A plain speaking, sensible name. How about *Lagniappe, the New Orleans Review.* "Lagniappe" is such a damned good NO word.

And now sadly. I really thought I was about to bust out of *SR* and was beginning to be happy about it, but after a long wrestle with Cousins I agreed to have a try at his suggestion of a column a month for *McCall's*—after all, $1500 for 1500 words a month ain't hay. I told him I couldn't get on schedule for a year or so until I caught up with my desk but that I would try it. Since that makes a column a month for *McC* and at least one a month for *SR*, I'm afraid I just won't be able to do one a quarter for *NOR*, not at least till I get my insanities organized, but let me hope I can dig up poems for you. One of those long ones would be more than a column. When will you be kicking off? I'd like to send you one to see what you think.

All joys
John

TO MILLER WILLIAMS
Metuchen
November 30, 1967
[MW]

Dear Miller:

For once I got a thing done before I was prodded. Your letter just in, and only yesterday I sent you the typescript of one of the long autobiog poems. You may not like it and certainly you don't have to. If I ever see it magazined, I may find I need to change it. But in any case I do have you in mind.

If you *do* like these poems, perhaps I can ride on *them* for a few issues until I see how it goes here in the effort to write for both *SR* & *McCall's*. I haven't made much of a start. I haven't even finished the fucking lecture circuit—one more week starting in 2 days.

Then nothing till I finish the *Paradiso*—not reason, not responsibility, not social commitment—nothing till I get the hell out of heaven. . . . .

Light, more light!

Shine thou
John

TO MILLER WILLIAMS

Metuchen
December 18, 1967
[MW]

Dear Miller:

. . . . What are you writing? *SR* aside, and if you're not swallowed into too much else, I'm thinking I'd like to try trading some letters with you about poems: you send me some of yours to pick and prod at and I'll send you some of mine. It isn't quite as good as hashing them out over a bottle, but it's something I'd value enormously if you've a mind to it and the time for it. Don't, of course, hesitate to say no if you can't but let me hope you can.

And either way—

best to you on the high road,
Yrs
John

TO MILLER WILLIAMS

Metuchen
January 18, 1968
[MW]

Dear Miller:

Bless you for your letter. I had just caught up with *Poetry* for December and was feeling rather dumped by William Meredith's review. The dog might at least have disliked the book (*Strangest Everything*). But to be dismissed as some sort of resident literary figure and incidentally, maybe, a poet, is grating. I don't know why I mind being inaned at, but I confess I do, though not for long: there's too much to do. At that, *Poetry* is the only literary magazine (aside from a notice in *SR*'s quarterly round-up) to review that damn book within 12 months of its publication.

Anyhow I am grateful for kind words and won't even insist on their being true, though I can say honestly that I'd sooner have your praise than any going.

I've been working on a longish thing called "Letter to an Indolent Norn" and I think I've worked myself to a blind stop on it. I can't see it any more and have to put it aside till I can get far enough out of it. If it's not good, it has to be very bad. And at this point I just can't tell. Only hope.

If you're in any mood to look at it, I'd love to know what you think. And send me something of yours. I'd love to trade poem talk with you. . . . .

Tell Cindy I'm glad she got back safe and sound.

And fond best from all of us to all of you,
John

TO MILLER WILLIAMS

Metuchen
February 19, 1968
[MW]

Dear Miller:

In a few hours I'm to take the shuttle to Washington for a talk at Ascension Academy in Alexandria (Are we being ecumenical or wooing the apostate?), but now I've been re-reading "Letter to an Indolent Norn" after a many-eth reworking and I'm beginning to dare to guess I think I've got it. Would you mind taking another look?

Am I being a nuisance? I don't think I can tell you what a gift you give me in letting me pick your mind this way. It has been ten years since there was anyone I could send a poem to and get back a reaction I could build to, and there never has been as good an eye as yours to me. I am endlessly greedy for this good from you. All I can hope is that you will let me try my less deft hand at your poems as they come. Both ways, this exchange will be a feast to a long hunger. . . . .

Shalom—
John

TO MILLER WILLIAMS

Metuchen
March 1, 1968
[MW]

Dear Miller:

I'm leaving for California for a few quickies and back Wednesday for a talk at a local community college on Thursday. I won't try to digest and act on your suggestions about the "Letter to an Indolent Norn" in what harried small time I have before I leave. You have a great touch on the tiller and I bless and thank you for it.

What I want to say is how deeply moved I am by what you wrote of Lucy and of Becky.* You already know you have the categorizing world to buck, but you also know that feeling won't go by categories. I don't see how you could have worked out a difficult relationship in a more compassionate way toward all needs. I honor you for it, Miller.

Will you allow me to go into a possible difficulty bearing from it? I have Bread Loaf in mind. I hope I'm not dead yet but the fact is I have entered the age at which people do drop dead. I mean to keep undropped for as long as I can, but it is the prudence of my duty to Bread Loaf to bear a succession in mind.

I have done as much in the past, trying always to keep in mind someone who could take over if I had to resign or did just drop dead. You can believe I have been ruthless about this in changing my mind for what I believed to be cause. In this connection I can consider only what would be good for Bread Loaf and no personal feeling could be allowed to intervene.

I am thinking now, and I absolutely will not promise not to change my mind, that you are the man. Bread Loaf has been an important place to you. I am sure you share my feeling for it, for both of us have found it a place from which we have drawn treasured friendships, as both of us have found it a place from which roads opened.

As I say I have had various people in mind in the past. But let me add you are the only one I have ever spoken to about it. When it comes time for me to turn in my uniform, I think you could make a great director.

In the practicalities of the goddamned world, however, Becky could be a problem in this. Not as a warm, fine, attractive human being, but within the goddamn artificial categories of the director's non-wife. The words, dammit, sound hideous at it: to describe the world is to damn it. I can just see the administration of Middlebury gulping.

Well, sir, I'm not dead yet; things have a way of working out, and for all I know you'll be too damned important for the job by the time I sign out, and who knows but what I may be playing the sad harmonica (metaphorical: I can't play the literal one) over your grave.

But grant me your faith that I have fumbled honestly toward this thought, which I must, of course, beg you to keep secret. And this summer at Bread Loaf let's sneak off and chew it a bit. I'd like to be able to leave on file with Prexy Jim Armstrong the thought that if Judith becomes a rich widow, he should have you in mind. I can, of course, only propose to his disposals, but I have a feeling all would be well enough in order if you were willing to come up alone for the two weeks.

Such, alas, is the category tax.

(Incidentally, I don't at all mean come up alone this summer—I mean in the event that. I also promise to struggle against the event, at least as a near thing.)

As a matter of fact, I'm tempted to rip this out of the typewriter and to start over. But, no, I won't. You are generous enough and kind enough and I will trust you for a high enough opinion of me to read it as intended. Without faith there can be no communication. . . .

And so to Calif.

But not before I say you're a good man, Miller. I'm richer for your friendship and I wish you all of this hard won happiness. Life's to live glad and a balanced man's compassion gives height and breadth to gladness. Give Becky our love.

As ever,
John

*Rebecca Jordan Hall, who became Williams's second wife.

TO MILLER WILLIAMS

Metuchen

c. October 1, 1968

[MW]

Dear Miller:

Your reaction to that dangling participle left me with a thought I think I want to build into a column:

> A man should never be ashamed of being human.
> Or perhaps he should always be. But it's no
> good to be off and on about [it]. Whatever he did
> wrong, it won't qualify for a patent.

Well, maybe it won't work out, but I smell something possible there. Fact is, I felt the same way about some of your points about the poems. It only takes the right light on it to make [it] visible. But Jesus how the whole universe can hide in a crack till that light comes.

There is, of course, another light in which I try the whole thing on your sensibility, and I shall never finish telling you what a blessing it is to me to have that light and to have it from *you*. How many men in one life time can a man love, and honor, and admire? For me John Holmes was one. Roy Cowden at Michigan was another. Fletcher Pratt was one. And in some crazy way Bill Sloane is. But I've never felt as close in mind and feeling to any of them as I do to you. And only John was a poet, and a good one. And even there you are a tougher (and therefore larger and more compassionate) talent.

And no, Miller, you mustn't do my biography. Not at least until there comes a time—should there come a time—when it would serve your academic purposes. Constance Le Brun once approached me about doing Rico Le Brun's biography and I told her that in selfishness I could not, that I loved the feel and the talent of Rico's work but that I had my own work to do. You have your own work to do and may you never come to so dry a season that clerking my biography seems more to you than the poems on your desk. There will be clerks to do it. You have you to do. —And you know I bless you for the thought. . . . .

With heart's thanks,
John

TO DAN JAFFE

Metuchen
October 26, 1968
[DJ]

Dear Dan:

It's hard to face up to a thing like that but love must intend realities, a man has to do what his manhood brings him to, and you're a man, a decent person, and with the gift and obligation of language in you. There's nothing to hate and only the faulting of love to grieve, not love itself. It's Yvonne who shrinks in this. Could she prevent her own shrinking? She could, of course, if she loved enough. But if she loved enough there would be no shrinkage.

Put it by, past both bitterness and nostalgia. It's done and with time yet—and to spare—for a better coming together. You'll choose better next time because there will be more of you to choose with. Pax.

I was in the hospital last week to have some tail bones whittled. I was suffering from pressure on a nerve, had gone lame, and the kids were threatening to shoot me for the estate. The operation was a breeze and I'm stretching the convalescence into a lazy lounge till year's end. I could be up and off sooner, but why? I love being totally free to woo my desk.

Come see us at Christmas & bring the kids, but don't get out of the car if the dog is running loose. He likes to eat people from automobiles but his warning is loud enough to summon me and he does obey me.

We'll be looking forward. You look forward, too—there's nothing to look back to now.

As ever,
John

TO MILLER WILLIAMS
Metuchen
November 15, 1968
[MW]

Dear Miller:

I should have written long since, but I binged off into a series of poems for the autobiography . . . 2 new ones about 10 typescript pages each, and some heavy revision on another. I need some time now to take stock and see where the book is and if these new ones are right, but I do feel the thing coming together with a good sense that it's right and even true enough to be all new: a way of reclaiming into poetry the kind of detail it could once manage but allowed fiction to usurp. I know I hit it in the one you published and in "The River," just published by *SR.* I'm waiting for others to come into focus. . . . .

I'll send you the new poems when/if I dare.

Fondly, as ever—
John

TO RICHARD EBERHART
Metuchen/New York
December 13, 1968
[DC]

Dear Dick:

Forgive indirection. My secretary comes out from New York, I dictate, she takes the stuff back to New York, types it and mails it out from there. . . .

Many thanks for the poems. Of them, I especially like "Will" and yet, if it isn't a stupid thing to say, and it probably is, I keep stumbling on the end. I think it does a magnificent job of gathering its forces. Then it tells me that no one can imagine big or wide or far or universal till he has gone sailing in Maine waters, and I just can't keep myself from being stopped by a still small voice that says, "Tell it to Emily Dickinson." Heaven knows I may be dead wrong in the voices I hear, but, alas, I am stuck with them.

Thanks and all best to all of you for the season and long beyond and for many more to come.

As ever,
John Ciardi

[signed by secretary]

TO NORMAN COUSINS

Metuchen
January 14, 1969
[NC]

Dear Norman:

. . . . . I note your thoughts on Mailer. I have twice written a column on him, then ripped up the copy. It's hard to get the true balance on him. Trouble is, he's not only the worst writer on the scene, he's also, damn him gratefully, the best, or something close thereto.

I'll hope to see you before forever.

Best
John

TO MILLER WILLIAMS

Metuchen
March 19, 1969
[MW]

Dear Miller:

The world is an odd confluence. I had been panting (Myra calls it an ego kick) to see the *Achiev.* [*The Achievement of John Ciardi*]. Then, in the same mail your inscribed copy arrived and with it, two copies from S-F [Scott, Foresman and Company].

I'm grateful to you on many counts. I had, of course, read your intro, but I like it again on re-reading. If I say it feels right to me and that I can't disagree at any point, that would seem a dull way to respond to high praises. What I mean is that you've identified a lot of intents and even made visible for me some intentions I knew by feel, wouldn't have put exactly as you did, yet end up accepting in your phrasing of them. It's an odd sensation to come on yourself so. I come back to thinking you know me better than does any man alive, and I love you for that. How could I dare not to? Yet seriously, and gladly, and with an honoring sense of the luck it is to have the friendship of a man who is to respect and admire as well as be fond of.

You have also refreshed a lot of poems for me. Poems I had more or less put by and no longer had a firm sense of. The fact that you chose them brings them back to me, and time and again as I read I'm grateful to you for your choosing.

Alas, then, I find myself feeling guilty that I have yet to write about your poems. I got so fouled up here at home that I took them to *SR* to scribble on there, and I've been so fouled up at *SR* that I must bring them back to scribble on here. I won't detail my schedule—even it wouldn't be excuse enough—but between lecture hops I am absorbed in getting that autobiographical book rounded out, and at the same time I have been sorting poems for a new children's book.

Please don't take my failures as intents. Even busyness can win through to purpose.

Myra is 17 today. Judith and I are taking her out to dinner with a bunch of her friends. Good cause—but there goes one more evening at no desk.

Bless & thanks and love to all of you.

John

TO MILLER WILLIAMS

Metuchen

April 3, 1969

[MW]

Dear Miller:

What could be sweeter news? May you and Becky share the good of a long life. Together, I know you will make it a happy one. I don't mean that signing some papers and arranging some certificates will make any soul's difference. You have already found a full and compassionate arrangement of your lives and of Lucy's. But this—now—is the way you have wanted it, and it is warming to know it has come to you. We drink to your happiness.

I wish I could be here for your reading but if you insist on being in provincial New York instead of in the four-square center of Mankato, Minnesota, there just isn't anything I can do about it. In fact there's not much I can do about anything much until I fall off the other end of this tour in mid-May.

Miller, do you know of a fictioneer-poet who might do an ambidextrous job at B.L. this summer? I'm waiting for Sandy's report on enrollment & chances are we'll need someone like Hollis Summers (not available) who can double well in both fiction & poetry.

I must apologize all over again for goofing on those poems. Please send me copies. I certainly want some of them for *SR*. Christ, I had put them aside to talk about during your Christmas visit. That's why I didn't get to them at once. At some point I must have filed them for safe keeping—always a disaster. You have a right to feel slighted but give me a chance to offer amends.

And live forever, forever singing, and sober only when it's your mood to be.

Love from all of us
John

P.S. To whom should I write to order some *Achievements*?

TO MILLER WILLIAMS

New York
April 11, 1969
[MW]

Dear Miller:

I returned from God knows where last night to find several letters from you waiting at home (I'll write you from there tomorrow). Here at *SR* I have just finished reading your quarterly review and I think it's a dandy. Many thanks. Just to maintain my reputation as an idiot, I seem to have goofed. In the same mail came a review of Wilbur by Louis Untermeyer. Your review, as you might reasonably have guessed, is a damn sight better than Louis's. I've just finished writing him more abjectly than is natural for me and I hope he won't stink up too much about it. Yours is certainly the one I want to use. The only hitch I can imagine is that Louis might get Norman Cousins steamed up over my booboo (I did tell Louis it would be all right to review Wilbur and then forgot it), but if it's absolutely necessary to offend the man, that is a bearable thought.

This here desk looks like the bottom of an avalanche. I'm taking this occasion to confess my sins. By tomorrow I shall have forgotten them and hope to write you in a more genial way.

Ever fondly,
John

TO MILLER WILLIAMS

[Metuchen]
June 8, 1969
[MW]

Dear Miller:

We're off to Europe on the 12th and I have chores by the scores but sit here working at a poem, if it is a poem. Is it? Is it anything?

It has been long since your last. We hope all flourishes. No hurry on this poem: we'll be gone till July 24, by which time I'll be ready for the poor house (in anticipation of which I have ordered a new Cadillac for our return. Always go to the poor house in style, pappy told me.).

It seems too long & too far to everything. I wish I were staying home to sweat at the *Paradiso* instead of traipsing Europe at $100 a minute on sore feet, but what's a man to do, having married an energy & begotten frenzies? Thinking of the *Paradiso* typescript, time suddenly seems too short. A man is a maunder. In any case it is getting on to mountain* time and that thought does shine. We'll have the martini bowl ready for you.

Love and joys from our house to yours.

John

*Bread Loaf

TO IRV KLOMPUS

Middlebury
August 18, 1969
[IK]

[Irv Klompus, M.D., was Ciardi's friend and Metuchen neighbor as well as staff physician at Bread Loaf where he and Ciardi regularly squared off at the cribbage board. After moving to San Francisco, Klompus was replaced at the conference by Dr. John Stone of Atlanta.]

Dear Doc:

We've been waiting ever since we got back to have your SF address—

trust you to end up in Leavenworth. But it isn't really justice we want for you. We'll even go beyond justice—all is forgiven; come on home.

A quiet conference this year. This Doc Stone—just to establish a new precedent—is a cultural type. Writes pomes. Miller Williams learned to play cribbage out of the Encyc. Brit. (the article didn't teach him anything about sneaky plays). He points out that it has taken 2 men to replace you—one to be doc, one to play cribbage. The hell of it is I can't allow Miller to bet—he doesn't know enough.

We could, if it comes right down to it, get along without you, but it's plain indecent of you to keep Ruth way out there. Give her our love. And hello to you.

How is this silly ass sabbatical going? Is it going to be a sabbatical or do you mean to stay stubborn in your indolence and crap it up in SF forever? Remember, all is forgiven. Come home. Bring Ruth. Bring money.

There are some people around here who seem to remember you but they are of no real consequence, as I suppose you know.

Fifteen two and a run of three
and last card for seventeen!
John

TO IRV KLOMPUS
Metuchen
September 4, 1969
[IK]

[The following letter was handwritten on graph paper.]

Karo Klomp:

I'd rather play Ruth or consequences—and she certainly does write a better letter than most medics with boils on their butts. I should even go upstairs and do Beauty some immortalities—I could even think of typing this. Trouble is, I can't seem to break the inertia of my

237 lbs of solid flab, so there being this paper and a pen to hand, I says to myself, says I, I says (quote) I will pen a correspondence-type epistle to that square Klompus on the most appropriate letter paper ever conceived by man (end quote). That is because of all the squares through which I am writing [I am writing] to the squarest. Which is a joke ha-ha.

Well Old Bess my fat wife with the disapproving look is back home at last and I with her—more or less like the tail trying to wag the dog—which is a bitch in this case—and she says to me (Quote) I swear you are fat as a spring sow and but for the mirror you will never see your toes again unless you put down that bottle and put yourself on a diet! (End quote). Well I was 235 lbs at the time and I could see the string was getting tighter so I did put down the bottle and I went on that diet 3 days ago and by golly I haven't gained but 2 pounds since—which is strictly in line with what I always did think of the value of being virtuous, but I have determined to fight it out on these lines till another corpse or two is brought in as proof that the good die young in size 52 Freeman-Hickeys or Hickey-Freemans, as the case may be.

We had a good conf. this year though marred at the end by an accident to one of the fellows who drove off the road into the ravine one whiskey morning at about 4:30. Those state troopers are sharp: spotted the tracks in the dark and had him in the Burlington Hospital by about 6:30, reported in with a broken leg, head lacerations, some exposure but entered in good condition, but he developed embolisms almost at once—marrows I guess—went into coma and was on the critical list. Three days later when we left he was still in coma. [Assistant director] Sandy [Martin] promised to let me know of any change, but so far no word. He's young (33ish) and in pretty good condition but at best it's going to be a near thing. . . .

No flips. We were on the verge of one with the least pleasant most mooching goddamn fellow in conf history, but Doc. John Stone, your Atlanta understudy, talked him into accepting some sedation, which soon settled him down to being just obnoxious without psychobatics. Psycobatics is a term we professionals use for acrobatics of the psyche.

I know how you feel about Junior Lafayette and that Banto Bob.

By patting their skulls gently with a two by four—to treat dandruff—I've kept ours down to a moderately grotesque wet mop effect but screw the younger generation says I. I've heard of the generation gap but this fucking abyss is ridiculous.

In good conscience I can report that I have done about .001 work (on a scale of 10,000) since we went Europating. Now back from B.L. I keep thinking "Today" but I'm damned if I can break the inertia. Please send some anti-inertia pills 'cause I got deadlines and time is running.

What about this sabbatical? Is it going to become the Golden Years out West or do you still think you might manage the courage to pack your cribbage board and come back East?

Please buy stocks heavily. The market needs you. Even we need you, though we'll settle for Ruth. Judith joins me in hoping it doesn't get you in the end.

Fatso to Fatso
John

TO MILLER WILLIAMS

Metuchen
October 23, 1969
[MW]

Dear Miller:

Back from the road awhile and beginning to sort back toward sanity, or so I hope. Some day I shall find the character to say no to easy money. But, then, how is a man to be a poet till he has been tempted, yielded, and come to comfortable repentance on the proceeds of his sin?

Flash: Robert Lowell woke this morning without feeling guilty. Was heard to whistle as he went down to breakfast. Suddenly caught himself in mid-stride in the act of not feeling guilt. Now he has that to feel guilty about and is back to being himself.

How goes the *NOR [New Orleans Review]*? Is it on or off? Are those jeebies beginning to learn mountain music. Zing that fiddle at 'em!

I haven't made nearly enough progress on the final revisions to *Paradiso.* Have been working at poems instead. It's a helluva Lowellian thing when I come close to feeling guilty for fiddling at poems when I should be doing me clerical duties. Screw! But what a sigh of joy it will be to mail the fucking thing off!

Normal sorts of things to report from here, meaning nothing much, except minor tremors when Myra, now a driver, takes off in $9000 worth of Fleetwood and Benn (he has a job now) banks money for a motorcycle he is going to buy as soon as he is seventeen. I'll probably have to bribe him away from a bike with a Maseratti. Be of good cheer, friend father. Send not to ask for whom the grimoire was written: it weaves for thee.

Daily mail; letter from Colo:

Mr. C—

Discovered "Song for an Allegorical Play." Lost it. Can't find it. Love it. Send it.

Cheryl Mares.

Dear Miss M—

Poem in *In the Stoneworks.* Rutgers. Bookstore. Find it. Buy it.

J. Ciardi

If you find time and inclination I enclose a revise of the crossing the desert poem and 3 new ones. Eager for your thoughts. Will you be coming this way for Xmas? 'Twould be great to do that houseparty again. We'll hope.

Love to all,
John

TO MILLER WILLIAMS

Metuchen
March 1, 1970
[MW]

Dear Miller:

Your letter came just as I fell ass-first into my second bad bout of the season with the viruses. It seems to take forever to fight off those new bugs. Which has something to do with the generation gap, I'm sure.

It's good to know you are finally settled in and with what should be a great rich time ahead of you. We certainly are counting on you for B.L. Shane Stevens will be aboard this year and was asking for you. Is there anyone anywhere like him? . . . .

I'm about ready to give Rutgers *The Lives of X* with some feelings of terror. Perhaps I've read myself out on it. I'm moved to fierce doubts about it and lean heavily on your assurances as my stay. What an insanity it is to be a writer.

I sold a poem to the *New Yorker*—"An Emeritus Addresses the School," which you have seen. Or I think I've sold it. Howard Moss suggested 5 changes and I couldn't go along on any of them so he may send it back.

Miller, we hope all of you make a great and flowering season of this time in Mexico. We certainly do want to fly down and visit. So far nothing works out, but something will have to. Even if I have to pay for the tickets myself—which is, of course, immoral.

Bless, flower, shine
as ever
John

TO MILLER WILLIAMS

Metuchen
April 7, 1970
[MW]

Dear Miller:

. . . . Yesterday I delivered *Lives of X* to Sloane. I had stewed at it a long time, think I have tightened it. And I cut the chapter called "Innocence, Experience, Innocence." After many fretful readings of the ms. I discovered that was the piece that was really fretting me. What a trail it is to the simplest discovery! I like the book much better with that fret out of it. With your permission I want to dedicate the book to you—for many reasons, all of them good enough to stand with or without your permission, but say yes to what love asks. . . .

Love to all your house from all of mine.

John

TO MILLER WILLIAMS

Metuchen
May 3, 1970
[MW]

Dear Miller:

Jonnel was 17 yesterday and I seem to be committed to buying him a car as soon as he gets his license. Myra has been accepted at Swarthmore—to us, a thrilling outcome of the college sweepstakes. The air has been let out of our (Judith and my) fantasy balloon. We had been making plans for Mexico City in great spate when my agent's office called about something else and added, "Oh, by the way, that May 20th date is for 1971."

I was almost ready to commit the unforgivable and to pay for transportation myself, but too much, alas, is piling on. I have promised Myra, I have promised Jonnel, I have promised the revenuers, Judith is buying furniture again, and aside from having the string pulled on my anus by the stock market, I have to estimate I'm taking in about $30,000 less than last year. It's not so bad that I've stopped drinking, nor so bad that I am driven to drink more. Call it crimped affluence: there comes a time to start counting the thousand-dollar bills, if not the pennies, and this seems to be the time.

Myra meanwhile is fevering for a trip to Mexico City to visit Cindy, has written her, and I write again herewith. We'd like it to be her graduation present and her reward for getting Swarthmore. Could you be descended upon by her and her guitar about June 20-something? I'm sure she and Cindy could have a ball. Please don't hesitate to say it won't work if it won't work. If it can work, it would overjoy her and please us much.

Thanks for word anent the dedication of *Lives of X.* I like the way you care, brother Miller, and don't need to pledge myself to care with you, though I will gladly. If for no other reason, and there are many, [than that] the book is your godson and should be named for you by all rights. I have leaned on you for encouragement when I needed it, and for the kind of criticism I have always needed and you have always supplied.

Yours gratefully. . . . .
John

TO GERTRUDE AND LEONARD KASLE

Metuchen
July ?, 1970
[GK]

Dear Gertrude & Leonard:

. . . . . Judith has been in Missouri visiting her parents—returning, probably about the time you get this. As a favor to two old friends, I am on standby to go to Chautauqua for the second week of August. Edw Weeks, formerly of the *Atlantic,* is due to speak there and family illness makes it uncertain he can go. For *auld lang syne* and as a favor to Curtis Haug director of Chautauqua, I said I'd stand by to fill in if Weeks can't come, provided I know yea or nay by Aug. 1. On Aug. 6, Jimmy Orenstein, young son of Bud Orenstein, copilot of my WWII crew, arrives to visit. We'll take him to Chautauqua if we go and then to Bread Loaf and then put him on a jet back to L.A. You can see it looks full.

And I'm glad of it in one way. I have fallen, as into an addiction, into playing golf (oh how badly!), gardening (so-so), and—of all things—gin rummy—the last being the silliest decay of time and mind since the invention of television. Let me think of it as a way to get a lot of mindlessness out of my system. But I do love gardening when it isn't too sticky-hot, and though I am furious at my inability to put together a decent round of golf, I do feel well for having taken all those turns around the course. So there are bonuses.

I haven't spent time enough at my desk these past weeks but I'm happy to say the galleys of *Paradiso* came and have been proofread. The galleys of the new Rutgers book of autobiographical poems (*Lives of X*) are here and have to be proofread. Loathesome work!

May your summer be as rewarding as it is far-flung. When will you get to NYC? I have had JoAnne White bring the work out here, hence haven't been into the city (thank God) for about five weeks. The last time was to have lunch with Norman Cousins and to say I had to have $500 a column, or else, and got it (which is a $200 raise)—and I figured I couldn't do much better than that for a while so why go through the misery of going to NYC—unless, of course, you are going to be in town. . . . .

Have a marvelous time in all them places and get back soon to where we can see you.

Much love
John

TO MILLER WILLIAMS

[Metuchen]
July 28, 1970
[MW]

Dear Miller:

Forgive me for too-long silence. The Imp of the Perverse has been sitting on my shoulder these two months. I've managed a lick and a promise at my desk, but by and large I have fallen into a stretch of busy indolence. Day by day I have come up from sleep with things I meant to do, slipped out to look at the flowers, started gardening, and come to four hours later thinking, "Hell, I may as well go to the golf course." There after 18 holes I've showered, started to gamble at gin rummy, decided to have dinner at the club, gone on gambling, and made it home at 3:00 A.M.

That's a routine, I submit, that describes its own insanity. I have, of course, been aware of. I've simply left it to run its course as some sort of mindless release I've sensed a need of without knowing why.

I am thinking of myself now as being back in the world. I mean to go on gardening some—I love it. And golfing some—if only I improved instead of just practicing all my bad habits into place! But I am justly bored with 10 hours at a stretch in the gin rummy casino. Call it a madness that had to be purged.

This catharsis has left me a million man hours behind my desk, alas. I still have bills unpaid and checks uncashed that go back two months. And some columns to get ridden. (An interesting typo that!)

Will you accept this little from a perverse compulsive to say we love you all—at least with the better part of what nature has been given—and that once I make it back to mind and more sensate identification, I want very much to write a civilized letter.

I have been reading galleys on *Lives of X* and I come back to hoping for it. Have also read page proofs of *Paradiso* for Nov. publication. I await daily copies of Lippincott's Kinderbuch—*Someone Could Win a Polar Bear* yclept.

As creatures stir to their natures I sniff the air and feel Bread Loaf coming. I'll be going to Chautauqua first (week of the 9th) then back here, then to Bread Loaf. It will be great to see you and Becky there.

Love
John

TO MILLER WILLIAMS

Metuchen
October 26, 1970
[MW]

Dear Miller:

. . . . . I doubt that international hot-lines have been flashing with the fact that the House Internal Security Committee has labeled me a "radical." Their given reason is that I once let the National Committee to Abolish the House Un-Am Comm. use my name. The idea of the release, I gather, is to keep radicals from getting dates on the college circuit. Irony: choice of speakers has definitely passed from faculty to students and I have practically no bookings because I'm neither an ecologist nor out on bail. . . .

Anyhow HISC has given me a chance to do an article on the subject for *SR*—Nov. 7 issue—and I think I have to value the occasion that led me to that place. It feels good to me.

All goes well. I had one of those in-office operations to remove a skin-growth, technically a cancer, but not one of the spreading kind. The same sort of thing Frost had several of. (You can see there would be a kinship.). . . .

Benn [had] to go to court. Jonnel has the male lead in the senior class play. Myra hit a funk at Swarthmore and has come home for a few days of rest and reassurance. The earth's orbit is irregularly around the sun which is approximately 93,000,000 miles away (average mean distance). *Cogelo soave, hermano, pero cogelo*

And shantih
John

TO DAN JAFFE

Metuchen
November 20, 1970
[DJ]

Dear Dan:

I heard from your father and wrote him my thanks. Probably because of his persuasion Rep. Patten writes me that he will take the floor of the House to say some kind words anent me. I don't know anything to say in favor of my character but I'm glad for all that reads FUCK HISC.

Delighted by your piece on the war poets—a good solid job of critical sympathy in the best sense.

I wish I could feel as sure of the love poem. I think you're too much in love. Admirable and beautiful and enviable and God bless, but bliss lowers the rejection threshold for clichés. Don't write another love poem till you hate someone. Blessed as you are, you should confine yourself to poetic invective (I'm available) since you must have enough esthetic detachment for that. (I'm more than half serious—re-read that poem as if Hitler had written it and see if you're entirely happy about all his phrasing.)

I do love you, but I was a bastard first, and old habit clings.

I'd love to join you for that kosher dinner if you promise me *no kasha.* Trouble is I'm not traveling as I used to. I'll have to find an excuse for making it to KC.

All joys
John

TO MILLER WILLIAMS

Metuchen
December 11, 1970
[MW]

Dear Miller:

. . . . Busy times here. Jonnel, after endless goofing, has settled down and *mirabile dictu.*: he's on the basketball team, has the lead in the sr. class play, is on the principal's sr. advisory council, & came home with 4 A's & 2 B's. He even got a haircut (in order to play basketball) and looks human! Ah the joys of patient fatherhood!

Myra is having a real grind at Swarthmore. A tough, tough school. (Her French assignment was: 1st week, read "La Condition Humaine;" 2nd week, read "L'Espoir." Four such courses, two chorale groups, and private voice lessons make a busy & too-busy girl. She's reeling but holding on.)

I've made history! My congressman delivered an official apology to me on the floor of the House & had it inserted in the *Congressional Record.* Then on Dec. 9 HISC dropped eight names, including mine, from its list of "radicals." I don't think the McCarthyites have ever been squeezed this hard before, damn their eyes. I did an article in reply in *SR* and have picked up some lovely $ from newspapers that have reprinted it. (Off print enclosed.). . . .

All the best
John

TO F. ANDRE PAQUETTE

Metuchen
January 7, 1971
[FC]

[Andre Paquette had recently begun a short term as director of the language schools at Middlebury College.]

Dear Andy:

I look forward to a chance to talk to you about the conference. I think that you will find our staff people are easy-going (I have weeded out as much temperament as possible), drunken (there wasn't much sobriety to weed out), loyal, unacademic, a touch iconoclastic, two touches ironic, and very much *inside*—a sort of club of spiny types who respect one another's spines and who come to Bread Loaf, basically, for a tone they exchange there with one another.

I do admire the briskness of your new broom, but I beg you not to be administratively brisk with the conference irregulars, which is to say the staff. Sandy [Martin] has forwarded me copies of your proposed forms and I'm obliged to say they just won't do for us.

We are not a school and the staff is not up for a faculty appointment.

I must veto anything that says "salary" followed by a blank. The implication there is that salaries can vary. It is fixed principle at the conference—to avoid possible jealousies—that all staff members receive exactly the same pay.

I don't want my people bugged to fill out forms that don't apply to them in the first place. As I say, we have an odd and spiny damn good crew and it just won't sit still for the kinds of forms and systems of brisk administration. It spoils an essential tone of things that I must labor to preserve. We're just not a saluting and form filling crew. I submit it's a good crew and worth keeping. If forms and systems turn out to be the essence, you're going to end up needing a new crew and a new captain.

It would be just as well, too, if you let me do the communicating with the staff, and would save me a certain amount of time. Sloane and Meredith sent me copies of your letters to them commending them for their "extra effort" and the gist of their letters to me was, "What the hell is this—a merit badge?" I'm trying to say that you will get the best results from us if you think of us as oddballs and leave us alone. A certain distrust of administrative procedures is built into all writers: the less administration they see, the better it will go.

Thanks for listening. It has to be said, and now is better than later.

All best.

Yours,

TO MILLER WILLIAMS

Metuchen
January 26, 1971
[MW]

Dear Miller:

A joy to have your first letter from home. It is Tuesday night. Tomorrow morning I leave for Detroit and then Chicago anent some promotion New Am Lib has worked up for *Paradiso*. Tonight I am trying to claw through a desk inches high with overdue mail, which mostly fuck, though I must scrawl something at it. If only good people would realize what hell they impose by writing their goddamn good-people letters and leave the mailbox for what counts and desk time for what counts! As if I need tell you.

I've been on a compulsive binge of children's poems. I get up, have coffee, start to scribble, and then it's two A.M. I must have a hundred on hand (started more than somewhat by your Arkansas bear) and if every fifth one is as good as I hope they all are, I have a book of rejoicements underway.

> There was a man who lived in Perth.
> He had about five dollars worth
> Of boys and girls at three for a dollar.
> The less they were worth the more they would holler.
> The more they would holler the less they were worth.
>
> For two cents cash I'd send you to Perth!

I'm foolishly happy about that one. And about one that begins:

> Your dog? What dog? You mean it? —That!
> I was about to leave a note
> Pinned to a fish to warn my cat
> To watch for a mouse in an overcoat!

Something about these things does me. Am I forsaking the world's doomsday, my heritage of sorrow, the rad-lib chorus of human dolefuls? Am I in retreat? I know I'm happily riding a mood, that I've done nothing else with this glad fit on me, and I find myself dreaming I'm going to leave something boys and girls will want to say because they are happy saying it. Well, ask me again at mood's end. I'm unreliable and behind in everything else, but this fit I must ride out.

As part of the fit, I haven't read *The Only World There Is* as it should be read. I've glanced and happied but need to wait. I haven't read anything at all, as a matter of fact. I don't want any rhythms in my head but the ones that seem to get started there by morning coffee. Forbear me this compulsion a while, frater. It obviously can't last, but I'm afraid to touch it while it's in process.

Serves you right for knowing crazy people.

I join you in not fathoming Sandy's letter. You probably know I've had problems with him. Half the time when I think I'm director it turns out that Peggy is and that Sandy is her assistant. I wish I could explain to them that staff, program, and policy are my responsibility and that bulletin, housing, budget tending, etc. are theirs. I don't see how I could have made the point more strongly to Sandy, but that's his deaf ear.

It does make me wary of sequences when it comes time to hand over the conference. Sandy is marvelously good at his thing, and marvelously too busy about what isn't really his thing, and could make local pressures for his view of things. That's something we would do well to drink a quiet drink on when next. Nonce-wise I will say only that his sentiments are strictly his own and that Vermont heads ain't easily entered. . . . .

Kiss Becky for me. Worthily, if you please.

Is the enclosure worth working on? Is it my voice? The fact itself got to me so that I may be mistaking the fact of the fact for the fact of the voice. But I worry about its being not entirely the right voice, or entirely mine, but if not mine, whose?

As ever,
John

TO MILLER WILLIAMS

Metuchen
March 12, 1971
[MW]

Dear Miller:

Too little but much good and now the goddamn world closing in. I've just completed the lovely business of a G-I series, complete with castor oil, endless enemas, barium, etc. And now I have to do it all over again. Science has found a shadow on the X-ray plates and doesn't know whether it's a polyp or a stray piece of shit. That, I submit, is the situation of science. I hope I won't have to cancel what few lectures I have lined up. I'm due to leave for Phoenix on Saturday, returning Tuesday, to go to the Virgin Islands on Thurs to get back on Monday to leave for Texas on Tuesday and thence to the Middle West and home about April 4. If, that is, a polyp can wait most of a month.

Meanwhile, goddamn it, I have to assemble tax lies for my man to work on. What a howling destruction of time and sequence the world is.

Tell Becky I love her. Her voice was the sweetest possible pause in the dark hours. Erratum: For "pause" read "brightening."

Please don't think less of me if I go into what may seem to be a stubborn and sullen silence these next few weeks. I'll either be riding the whirlwind as above, or will have canceled and gone polyp hunting. I'll know when the doc tells me. In any case nothing serious, though a nuisance.

Thanks for being generous about the dedication and note. (To *Lives of X*). More would have been to the point. Less would have been an affront to gratitude and love.

Which, take
John

The doc says the follow-up can wait till I get back in April.

TO MILLER WILLIAMS

Metuchen
April 23, 1971
[MW]

Dear Miller:

It has been much too long since I'm not at all sure what I've done with the last month or so. There was some traveling, quite a bit for a while, then a pause, then a bit more traveling, and here's the start of a cold May, or the cold start of a hot May, and I can't think of anything I did in April that was worth doing, except to note that I am running out of energy these days and so putter away more time than I use. My desk is covered with abandoned starts of all sorts but with nothing brought through to itself, and I am more and more often moved to leave the desk and just plain fart around. Well, a season for all things.

How goes it with you & Becky and the kids? Jonnel, I am delighted to say, has been accepted at Tufts. A happy solution. Now, if we can somehow manage to get Benn into a good school come next year, I will somehow feel we have made it into the golden years.

Any progress on the anthology? I had Jo Anne [Blair, his secretary] photocopy "Manner of Speaking"* and send you the columns. She brought me a set a few days ago, and I've been browsing and doubting. I just can't seem to see what sort of book, if any, a selection of them might make. A bedside browser? Seems dull. I think I'd rather get back to the children's poems (I've scarcely looked at them since you were here) and see what groupings they want to fall into. I will, of course, keep browsing the "M of S" columns and see if I re-see.

Send me a poem or two to pick at. It has been too long.

Love to all of you
John

*Ciardi's column in the *Saturday Review.*

TO MILLER WILLIAMS

Metuchen
May 1, 1971
[MW]

Dear Miller:

. . . . I'm going through a lousy time. Next week I have to get set for another G-I series. I suspect the polyp they think they discovered in the last series is a polyp in fact and not a shit-shadow. Everytime I sit at my desk for a stint of work I begin to feel blah and end up getting next to nothing done. I don't guess there's anything fatal in a gut polyp, but if that's what it is, it's time to get on the table and let the night of the long knives in.

I told Jo Anne to make those Xerox's of "M-of-S" long ago and she finally got to it. I've been frowning through them wondering if there is/isn't a book to be made of them and still have no formed opinion. If you're in any mood for a like-browse why don't you put a check mark on the ones you think might stand reprinting. Maybe 50 or 60 of them might stand. I can't make myself sure. Who uses bedside readers these days?

Lives of X has had good advance notices. Rutgers has certainly splurged the ads—a big one in yesterdays *NY Times* book section. And even the Book of the Month Club magazine reviewed it—a sort of pallid puff but likely to sell some copies. Bill tells me it has an advance sale of over 3000!

I have been shuffling the children's poems at odd moments and I think they fall into three piles, the working labels of the piles currently being *Sort of Sweet, Insults, & Hopefully Mysterious* (with dark edges). I will get to typing copies. I just don't feel up to facing this contraption for more than a bit at a time. Right now I'm hoping they'll get this gut thing identified next week and that they will then know what to do about it.

Joys to the world. Love to all.

Ever yours,
John

TO **MILLER WILLIAMS**

Frankford, Missouri

June 1, 1971

[MW]

Dear Miller:

Just flew in from L.A. & Denver to meet Judith & Myra on the farm. We go to St. Louis June 4th where I get an honorary from Washington U., then home (probably Sunday night). This is a field expedient scrawl (let anything say love). I wish there were time to loop south to Fayetteville but calendar says no. Blessing on your house and bright the day you bought it. I left the X-rays with my MD & left for California. Sufficient unto the polyp is the pruning thereof. Stanley Burnshaw wrote me a beautifully glowing letter about *Lives of X,* bless him.

And bless all of you.

John

Just left John Wms, Sy Epstein, & Zeke Mphalele—all well. It looks like a great Bread Loaf coming.

TO **STANLEY BURNSHAW**

Frankford, Missouri

June 1, 1971

[UT]

Dear Stanley:

I've been in L.A. & Denver briefly. Yesterday I flew in to St. Louis & met Judith & Myra who had driven in from N.J. On the 4th we go to St. Louis (we're now at my father-in-law's farm) and I get an honorary from Washington Univ & then we drive home.

This scrawl located, I hope I can tell you how much I value your letter (and the one Bill Sloane sent me a copy of). There have been a couple of laudatory (and generally vacuous) reviews. I suppose all praise is good to the ego—part of that total bodily reaction you web seamlessly but praise from *you* is for the soul. I'm not at all sure about being orphic or anti-Cartesian, but if I can be Burnshavian, then I'm on the human nervous system and that's the one thicket I want to be born & bred to.

I do feel strongly about this book. Counting some non-books, it's my 30th title. In some ways it's my first. I had to find a way of dealing with this material, and I feel that the material took me into ways recent poetry has turned from but that should be reopened. Subjectivity is a louse. In a real sense, I have been gambling that I wouldn't fall—as some have told me—into prosiness. Believe me, I have sweated over that risk. In the end I had to stake it on my own ear and feeling without ever being anything but desperately (which is to say not entirely) sure. Bless you for an assurance I have badly wanted: if it works for you then it works, and after having been told by Virginia Kirkus and a couple of local newspaper reviews that "this is really prose"—well, I could call them stupid bastards, but being the author and blind how could I help wondering if they were right? Now you tell me I was right, and despite the fact that I *want* to believe that, the point is that when you say it I *can* believe it.

That's much to thank you for and I thank you much. Cum blessings.

Will you be on the Vineyard all summer? We may go to Nantucket to visit the Fredlands (my old roommate) briefly, but that's in doubt.

Joys & thanks,
John

TO MILLER WILLIAMS

Metuchen
c. June 7, 1971
[MW]

Dear Miller:

Notes from an aimless estimation: I have been gardening fairly well, golfing badly, and spending fantastic and foolish amounts of time playing cards. My desk has been untouched for weeks, letters unanswered, bills not paid, checks not deposited—I haven't even invented my expense account for my various trips.

There is, I think I observe, a *force* of indolence. Some indolence can be static, I suppose. Mine is compulsive: I work harder at it than I do at work. Besides I have been dieting—very hard with small results though some—and aside from keeping myself astir in my bepiddlements I seem to enjoy them, until I'm done, and then I wonder why I bepiddled all that. No word from the lower colon. The M.D. got the X-rays. I told him to let me know if I needed doing to. He has let loose no word. The symptoms seem to have vanished. I'll let him worry about it.

It feels good to be sitting here at my desk again and two-fingering at you again. I think I may have come to the end of this cycle that has been compelling me nowhere. A fit of mindlessness can be purgative. I must get back to the *kinderdichter* still stacked on my desk untouched though separated into three manuscripts that I think may cohere. . . .

We are going to Nantucket over the July 4th weekend. July 28 is our 25th anniversary and I must start thinking about going somewhere that will please Judith, though it will probably bore the hell out of me. And then Bread Loaf. A light shining soon.

Miller, those poems are fine, pure baguettes, if that's the term, not central gems, but flawless small stones for setting the central gems. Nothing could improve them nor enlarge them. You must by all means keep them and use them, for themselves, for their purity, and to show any doubtful bastard you can be a lapidary as well as sculptor. . . . .

With love to all of you.

Till soon,
John

TO IRV KLOMPUS

Metuchen
August 1, 1971
[IK]

Dear Irv:

. . . . . I have fallen into a fantastic period of indolence. We took a week-long trip to Nantucket. And before that I had one sort of busy jaunt to L.A., Denver, and Missouri. But since I got back I have done nothing, period, nothing and not even visited my study. I have gardened some and we are now eating our own tomatoes and admiring our own flowers—glads, dahlias, lilies, and many more. But basically I have become a bum. I hit a hot streak at gin rummy (which I have been playing to the point of idiocy) and bought a color TV (which I have been dawdling in front of) and playing some golf (which I do with improving badness) and solving all the puzzles in all the magazines (at which I am maniacal) but bills are unpaid, checks undeposited, records unkept, manuscripts unlooked at, and the summer rainy.

I am, I see, an obsessive. In the spring I ran a 40-day streak in which I didn't even get out of pajamas because I was too busy writing. It might have lasted indefinitely but the trip to Calif-Denver-Mo broke the streak. Now I'm on another obsession and maybe writing this letter will break that streak. If not, maybe Bread Loaf will. Let 'er ride. Though we wish you two were riding with it. Can we lure you back next summer? Shucks, man, you can't hide out in them tuna boats forever. . . .

We love Ruth.

Joys,
John

TO IRV KLOMPUS

Metuchen
October 2, 1971
[IK]

Dear Irv:

. . . . The house sounds beautiful. Wear it in good health, landsman. And be happy you went up the mountain. We've had something like six hours of sun in seven weeks. All those girl-named storms seem to have bowled up this way just off the coast shaking their wet skirts out here. The interims have been filled with local showers. When we got back from Bread Loaf that grass was eight inches high and too wet to cut. In the steamy intervals it got up to fourteen inches while Sears Roebuck took a month to produce missing tractor parts for the power mower. I got most of it hacked by hand with the Lawn Boy, then mangled the rest with the tractor working into the night with my lights on and too exhausted to rake when I finished. So naturally it rained like hell last night and half of today, gluing the cuttings to the lawn. Is it worth it?

I just ain't no hombre no more. An hour or two of working up a sweat and I'm bushed. Know a good doctor? I'm too damned heavy, short of breath, the few teeth I have anchoring this goldplated engineering in my mouth are coming loose, and it turns out that I have a polyp on my lower colon. I jam the brakes as hard as I can but this thing keeps rolling down hill. Screw it. *Dum spiro spero* and with bourbon I can even dream. With luck I may yet find a nice Jewish boy to marry—the way they do it in San Francisco, though I'm not sure I can find nineteen more boys for bridesmaids.

Bread Loaf was bad this year. Not only the cold that knocked me out of half of it but Sandy's goddamn (strictly between us) maneuvering to make the conference over in his own undergraduate image. In a way a good thing, though, for it brought matters to a head. He has the word and can stay on with the clear understanding that he does not make policy but implements mine whether he likes it or not. Or he can resign with military honors as a case of conscience. Or he can get his ass fired off the mountain. I hope he chooses military honors, but I'll settle for his becoming ass-director with utterly no co-director nonsense about it. So screw that, too. . . . .

Benn is organizing a combo. He turns out to be pretty damn good (and too damn loud) on the electric guitar. Jonnel is at Tufts and overspending his budget (as I knew he would but let him suffer the consequences as part of the learning process). Myra had her tonsils out a month ago (at Lenox Hill), is beginning to get her voice back, and has the tearing miseries, having just had a break-up with her one-true-love-forever, a handsome, blond-bearded beast that once into every maiden heart must reign. Not that the foolish tears hurt any less than the ones that hurt more.

I'm off for a quickie to Sioux Falls, S.D. There's not much left of the lecture circuit and I see nothing in sight for SF but I keep hoping for a chance to get out there with Judith so we can eat lemons off your tree.

Are you still writing up your stuff anent the drug clinic? That material is too good to waste. Hurry up with it so I can offer you a fellowship at Bread Loaf: The Ruth Klompus Fellowship in Non-Fictitious Doctoring.

Tell the lady she is loved. Goddamn it, we miss you two expatriates. Whyncha go back where you came from?

Love,
John

TO MILLER WILLIAMS

Metuchen
October 13, 1971
[MW]

Dear Miller:

I have been absorbed in a number of things, including a painfully long series of letters anent Bread Loaf that have finally come to a head.* This must be in absolute soul confidence and Judith is the only other who knows. Please hug it to your bosom alone. After offering Sandy every opportunity to stay on with the condition that he leave conference policy to me, or to resign on his own initiative as a matter of conscience, and receiving from him only more flak, I have asked him to resign and so informed Armstrong and Paquette. I've had it.

What comes up next is a meticulous business of getting related to a new assistant director and of rebuilding Bread Loaf as the kind of learning excitement it can be. I plan a substantially new staff (half new and half rotated) and I am afraid I am going to be flooding the world with memos. I particularly want to have regular sessions with the staff to discuss how things are going. We can meet an hour early for cocktails, discuss the day's lecture, and try to re-establish a common vocabulary. Well, many more such things. There will be a lot to do.

That Hayden Carruth review is one of the things one has to live with. He has always enjoyed wielding his little hatchet. Bear in mind the psychiatrist who got into an elevator with a friend. Another gent in the elevator goosed the psychiatrist 3 times on the way down, a fact observed by the friend. "But why didn't you do something?" said the friend in the lobby. "Why should I?" said the psychiatrist. "—it's *his* problem."

Many, many thanks for the suggested outline of the *Manner of Speaking* book. I've talked about it with Sloane. I have been having a helluva time getting it into focus. Your suggested table of contents helps much. I am happy to say Bill wants to do the book and I am especially glad of that. With your suggestions and his and Helen Stewart's, I've got three damn good editors going for me. Thanks much too for notes on "A Prayer to the Mountain." They help. I suspect I can't really get it nailed down until I solve "watch through tears." Daedalus, spiraling down around the line of Icarus's crash, is not only crying for his son as he flies down as fast as he can while still staying in flight trim, but the wind of his flight would inevitably make his eyes water. Well, I'll have to sit up with it.

Joys to Becky birthday girl. May the two of you sing to many more.

It's 3:00 A.M. and I have a lecture to give tomorrow at Union College.

Love till cock crow and then all day.

John

*These letters have not surfaced.

TO WILLIAM MEREDITH

Metuchen

c. October 17, 1971

[WM]

Dear Bill:

I'm sorry about the Clarence Major books. I keep a messy study. Put any book down and it gets covered. I'll give them to my sec to mail back next time she comes out.

I'm sorry I can't find much to admire in the poems. Nor am I ready to accept a plan for "integrating" the conference. It is already open to any black writer who will come as an auditor and pay the fees. It is available to black fellows and scholars if their writing makes it in open competition. I have done my best to recruit black staff members whose work I thought worthy. And I have not been riled when a group of blacks formed in the corner and did nothing but glower at the dumb whiteys. That is as integrated as I mean to get. If you think skin color can be put ahead of writing ability we are at unconquerable odds.

Can we put one more difference between us and remain friends? If so, I'd like to return to your first decision not to return, and to accept it. I respect your conscience but I remain a bit reluctant to accept it as mine. I am determined to reorganize Bread Loaf and I can't believe you would approve of the overhaul. I suspect rather that our two views would conflict. I have had enough of trying to conduct the orchestra with another baton going at the same time. I've got to try my uncontested sense of it, and your conscience would necessarily contest what I think has to be done.

Let me seek comfort in the fact that it is a large universe and that it has room enough in it for more disagreements than there are between the two of us. Let disagreements be kept honor to honor and I don't think all will be lost.

There does remain the martini bowl and I hope you will come to sip often.

Joys,
John

TO STANLEY BURNSHAW

Metuchen
November 12, 1971
[UT]

Dear Stanley:

Your letter has sat lonely while I rode around the South and Southwest looting the lecher circus for never really enough money, but yet for fair to middling wolf-sops. God knows, I never meant to be rich and the accident of it keeps surprising me, though this market may yet bust me back to even.

Who doesn't know that echoing silence that follows a book of poems. *Lives of X* got a rare review by Edmund Fuller in (of all places) the *Wall Street Journal.* The BOM Bulletin gave it a puff and offered it as an alternate choice. *SR* ran a fulsome piece. And the *Boston Globe* gave it an uncertain dither. And that's all of it. I'll cry tomorrow: the book has sold over 5000 to date and I have your letter about it and one from MacLeish to warm my soul at. Besides which I won a bit over $700 playing gin rummy last night. What's to weep? . . . . .

God knows how any election comes out but you got my vote for the Nat Inst. I'll be hoping with you. Joys to you and to Leda, north and south. Judith and I will be looking fwd to seeing you in Florida. Bring Nixon along.

Best
John

P.S. Watch *SR*. The new management feels exciting!

TO IRV KLOMPUS

Metuchen
November 12, 1971
[IK]

Dear Irv:

Since much of this concerns the [children's] trust, I'll address it to you, but always with the thought of Ruth as the shining presence. I wish I could foresee a way to get us to San Fran and up the hill to your eagle's ledge. It sounds great and we'll make it yet, if I don't get too fat to get out the door. I've really become a terrible short winded, fat slob. Ah, well.

What can I possibly advise you to do in this crazy market? If a decision makes sense to you, it makes sense to me, and bless you for taking the thing on in the first place. I guess I just write to each publisher to say royalty payments, if any, revert to me. Should I see Norman about winding up the trust or will the accountant handle it and bill me for the service?

The checks came and many thanks. Jonnel is loving Tufts—a really happy lad. He has decided—if only *pro tem*—to major in philosophy. He may change, but Judith and I went up there three weeks ago and he showed me a helluva good paper he had written on Protagoras—so good in fact that it persuades me he means it. He is still thinking of law school & damned if I know why philosophy ain't a good pre-law.

Myra came home for the weekend hating Swarthmore, which means her love affair has gone sour, and how the hell long does the world have to be arranged and rearranged because she is in or out of love? She's a lovely child and bless her bubbles, but Shee-it, man!

Benn is still lost to all but his combo, which is getting to be fair. Me, I'll settle for an hour's silence. It's 1:00 A.M. as I write in the attic and the house is being rocked by amplification. Nobody ever told me a man could screw himself into this many problems. . . .

I have cut way down on the lecture circuit. Just got back from Texas, the two Carolinas & Penna. Pretty well worn out. Who needs it? Let me get the kids out of the nest and I might even follow you out to the Sun—though, who the hell could conceivably move the stuff out of this house? I went happily mad a while back, sold some stock and bought a $14,000 painting by Adolph Gottlieb. Judith doesn't like it. I tell her to bless anything we sold stock to buy.

You have your excuse for Bread Loaf '72 but not for '73. Make it soon. I've been talking with Middlebury about it being time to look for a new director. It has been 16 years now & time for a change.

Keep your lemons polished.

Love from all of us
John

I won $687 playing gin rummy last week! (Let's hope I don't lose it all back next week.)

TO MILLER WILLIAMS

New York
December 6, 1971
[MW]

Dear Miller:

The whole bloody family just made it disastrously back from Missouri. We had to fly Jonnel in from Boston and Myra in from Philadelphia, and Judith and Benn and Dippy and I drove out, somehow arriving at the St. Louis airport on a coordinated schedule, and so to Thanksgiving on the farm, which wasn't really the occasion but the coincidence—the real campaign being to attend Judith's parents' 50th anniversary party. Thank god we don't have to do that for another 50 years. It was a desolate trip, my mother-in-law being some flustery with excitement, but just naturally cantankerous. Nothing seems to suit her daydreams, even after everyone is knocked cold trying to please her. I got back home in total exhaustion, forgot to check my calendar, and simply ignored a lecture date in Baltimore. The fact is I had forgotten there was a calendar. I have written them to say I would give them a free program by way of apology, and I hope that will get me off the hook. It's the first time in 31 years of lecturing that I've pulled that boner, and I guess some penance is due.

I'm not sure what's happening at *SR.* We have been told that there will be a substantial editorial expansion but I guess it is to be evolved toward. I don't know what is holding up Jim's [James Whitehead's] quarterly review but it should be scheduled soon. Everything is sort of up in the air, waiting to see how the new editor works things. I am not particularly pessimistic about it and even think it could be a good thing on balance. If it should turn out to be messy, it will be simple enough to quit. For years Norman urged me to make my living elsewhere and to do *SR* on the side, and having taken his advice I am not now forced to critical choices. In general, I think Charney may be a bit hucksterish but that he is generally intelligent. I don't much care what he peddles in the magazine—if it remains a congenial place in which to write as I please, I'll be happy to settle for that.

Sandy has officially resigned as assistant director and the search is on for a replacement.

All best to all of you.

Yours,
John Ciardi

[Signed by secretary in Ciardi's absence.]

TO MILLER WILLIAMS

Metuchen
December 17, 1971
[MW]

Dear Miller,

Your heavy handed and god-bitten father must be an ambiguous figure to you, even now. All fathers, I suppose, are congenital ambiguities. Mine got simplified to death before I knew much of anything about these things and I don't know what I inherit. Through all the ambiguities you got yourself a helluva birthright from the preacher and you carry it, honcho. May it, goddamn it, not be too much to carry.

I know something about backs, dread what I know, and count myself among the luckiest for the success of my patch-job. Nevertheless, it's still there. I get up in the morning and have to creak myself erect. I get out of a chair and the message gets flashed. It's only a creak these days. But I remember when it was a hot poker. And even the creak is enough to carry the message.

Spare nothing to get it doctored. If there is a specialist you haven't seen yet, go see him. Fortitude is of the spirit, and bless it, but a man has to live in his body and that belongs to the medics. For chrissake use them.

I can't tell you what an impression Norman Cousins made on me in recovering from that infection he brought back from Russia. Even the best specialists in Sodom on the Hudson had given him up as a cripple. His joints were clogging, his muscular tissue deteriorating. They were fitting him for a wheel chair. He finally talked the doctor into massive—more than massive, unheard of—vitamin injections, and damned if he isn't some sort of athlete again. Sometimes there *is* something that can be done. And sometimes the bastards have to be pushed to try it.

I am beginning to have something like a real faith in vitamins. This year is the first time I have made it into December without a crippling flu. I thought in fact it had hit me last week. But I have been swallowing large doses of vitamin C and by God I made it through the incipient colly-wobbles. At least so far. May it hold.

I don't know (speaking of Cousins) what goes on at *SR*. Chaner and Veronis, the new owners, keep hiring new crews of people, most of the gents young, bell-bottomed, and bushy; most of the gals long-haired, veloured, or hot-pantsed; boys and girls much turned on and basically illiterate. It doesn't feel like an office anymore, but like a hotel in which four different conventions are meeting in the same hall.

Nor do I know what comes next. I have a feeling I'll know fairly soon whether I go or stay. Either could be all right. . . .

I have true warm feelings for Bill Meredith but essential disagreements re Bread Loaf. I welcome blacks to staff and membership but insist on choosing them as writers who happen to be black and as writers aside from blackness, whiteness, and pinkness. And I will not surrender the idea of writing disciplines (staff described but self-imposed) to the idea of "deep, solemn, human encounter." If you get a look at next week's issue of *SR* and a column entitled "Generation Gap" you will recognize sentiments, disguised occasions, and a bit of privacy in which I have stolen your own remarks. Stolen, I say: never borrow. What is borrowed still belongs to someone else. To steal is to make a thing one's own.

May you never run out of bourbon under the bed.

Do you recognize this as a Christmas Card? See: It says "Love to you and to Becky and to everyone in your house from everyone in our house, and a Joy-Ox Newel. Plus ho-ho-ho!"

Poem (and love) enclosed
John

TO MILLER WILLIAMS

Metuchen
May 16, 1972
[MW]

Dear Miller:

I have gone to bed four times tonight (last night) and nothing came of it. It's now 9:50 and I'm too groggy for anything but to regret insanity as a way of life. I think of you often and make gestures toward writing you, but every time I get to my desk it is buried in papers and before I clear a space for doing what matters I'm lost in something else.

I've left *SR*. This letterhead is old paper; NC has a new magazine called *World* and I'll be doing a bi-weekly column for it but no poetry. Maybe later if the thing gets off the ground I can persuade him to add poetry.

It's good to know Nemerov is warm toward BL. I spoke to him

last year and he was for it, but I couldn't work him in this year. Be sure I'll do my damnedest to get him back. Sloane phoned to say Rust Hills—if you recall him from last year—has a BL article in *Audience* and that Judith and I come out as nasties. I haven't seen it. . . .

It's pointless for me to say I mean to get squared away with the goddamned world. I keep saying it, but when do I get squared away? Yet someday. I have a dream, as the saying goes. Ah, for a tidy desk and my life in order. May both be yours.

Love
John

TO MILLER WILLIAMS

Metuchen
c. June 1, 1972
[MW]

Dear Miller:

. . . . Department of mixed feelings: I've been back and forth with Jim Armstrong at Middlebury, Pack has agreed to take over Bread Loaf after this conf., and here we go to swan song. Well so, I guess. I think the kids will miss it more than I will. It's all turning into ghosts anyhow. . . .

Pace in terram,
John

John the extinct

Who's Rust Hills?

TO JOHN STONE

Metuchen

June 9, 1972

[JS]

Dear John:

There is always a price to be paid. I don't see that a sclerosed, stenotic, deformed pump valve is too much for a firmly licentious, drunken, and deceitful life. As a matter of fact I do pretty well with the drinking and have no trouble being deceitful. It's that firmly licentious life I crave and can't seem to get to. It's what I do really want but I can't pass the physical. Please send the right pills.

I'm done with *SR* and have signed on at *World Magazine* with Norman Cousins.

I'm also bowing out of Bread Loaf. Pack has agreed to take on the job and I'm happy to pass the flab to new muscle. This conference will be my last. I'm especially glad, therefore, that you'll be on hand.

All joys
John

TO MILLER WILLIAMS

Metuchen

June 25, 1972

[MW]

Dear Miller:

As of yesterday I'm 56 yrs old—no wiser, though obviously sweeter. Thanks for going over "Magician" and spotting that redundant line, that obviously of course redundant line—once a good eye has focused on it. It is always fantastic how little we see of what is so obvious, once it is pointed out.

Just between us and for no other, as I will say it to no other, I'm a touch miffed about Bread Loaf. What it comes down to is that I finally got rid of Sandy, and he got rid of me. So goes the administrative mind. Since I had to get rid of my assistant, it's time to get rid of me. Well, in one sound sense, yes. I should have dumped him two years ago and was a bad administrator for not doing so. That aside, it's time, God knows, & I have to believe Middleburry is right in thinking Bob is a good man for the job. *C'est ça.* Tomorrow to burnt hills and pastures sere. . . .

Project. Would you have any interest in joining me on a re-do of *How Does a Poem Mean?* The book has had a good run—over 300,000 copies, but is becoming dated (so saith Houghton-Mifflin). They have sent various instructors here and there to report on their feelings about it. Some of the reports make sense. Some don't. I will not, for instance, include "poems" by Bob Dylan because some asshole instructor thinks that would grab the young.

And there are poems I know must be dropped. "The Congo" for one. What I realize is that I'm out of touch with these college generations. You, on the other hand, are with them. . . .

I'll be in Chicago June 27–28 and in Mississippi the week of July 12. Otherwise free and unemployed. We'll all be looking forward to seeing you at Bread Loaf.

Ever as ever
John

TO JAMES ARMSTRONG

Metuchen
August 2, 1972
[FC]

Pres. James I. Armstrong
Middlebury College
Middlebury, Vermont 05753

Dear Jim:

When Sandy resisted my plans and did his best to take the conference in directions I thought would defeat its purpose, I resisted him, explained the reasons for my resistance to you, and thought I had your understanding and approval.

Your answer was to pick up my open resignation despite the fact that I had asked for a year or two in which to reset the switches Sandy had thrown open, and to put the conference back on what I thought was the right track.

I made myself approve your decision, telling myself you had to keep in mind a college-wide range of problems invisible to me.

Now I learn—and from a news release—that Sandy has been reappointed to the conference as administrative director. I am left with a sense of having played a stupidly amateur role among professional politicians.

In any case, Sandy has his conference, undergraduate types will have their soul sessions and their chance to pound a podium half the night, and I have your pragmatic estimate of what my judgment is worth. You will forgive me if I say I cannot thank you for it. It is the conference and the idea of the conference I weep for. There was a time when a hopeful writer could come to Bread Loaf and find a kind of professional guidance available, as far as I know, no where else. Perhaps Bob Pack can keep that sort of guidance as the center of his conference, but he will certainly find that Sandy will push him in other directions. Forgive me if I am dismayed by the thought of a Bread Loaf that turns out to be a summer camp for souls.

Above all, I ask that there be no ceremonial gestures in honor of my services to Bread Loaf. Your more practical estimate has been rendered. I must accept it, and I would have to reject any other as window dressing.

Regretfully,
John Ciardi

cc William Sloane
Paul Cubeta
Because they have been
closest to me at Bread Loaf.

PART THREE

Felonious Footnotery

September 11, 1972, to March 28, 1986

"I become an increasingly private person and find myself wishing I had made it sooner to this bent hermitage. I never suspected I had such a taste for grubbing among dusty old footnotes, but I have; it is what I do with my days, and I am happy at [it]."

To Stanley Epstein, May 14, 1979

"My days are a madness. I have been typing, literally 10–12 hours a day, racing toward my deadline for Browser's II, *always in fear that I can't make it. I should never have undertaken a second volume in 2 years. In future I shall insist on at least a 4–5 year interval, thus permitting myself the obsession but not at the damned cost of everything else—including, to my great guilt, poetry."*

To Miller Williams, February 8, 1982

1972–73. Named contributing editor of *World Magazine.*

1974. *The Little That Is All,* poems.

1977. *The Divine Comedy,* complete translation in one volume.
Awarded Honorary Doctorate, Kean College of New Jersey.

1978. *Limericks: Too Gross,* with Isaac Asimov.

1979. *For Instance,* poems.

1980. *A Browser's Dictionary,* etymologies.

1981. *A Grossery of Limericks,* with Isaac Asimov.

1983. *A Second Browser's Dictionary,* etymologies.

1984. *Selected Poems.*

1985. *The Birds of Pompeii,* poems.
Ohio Valley Writers Conference, October 21–25.

1986. Died March 30.

Posthumous publications include:

1987. *Good Words to You,* etymologies.

1988. *Saipan: The War Diary of John Ciardi.*
Poems of Love and Marriage.

1989. *Echoes: Poems Left Behind.*
Ciardi Himself: Fifteen Essays in the Reading, Writing, and Teaching of Poetry.

1991. *The Selected Letters of John Ciardi.*

TO JOHN FREDERICK NIMS

Metuchen

September 11, 1972

Dear John:

Bless. Your letter is good for my soul and sadness. And how oddly the world works. On the night of the same day you and Sy [Epstein] met on the Ohio Tpke he wrote me a lovely and moving letter from his motel, and yours and his arrived on the same day.

I guess you know I left Bread Loaf with a certain weight of sadness and with less than happiest feelings for Middlebury & Jim Armstrong. Your letter, and Sy's, tell me it's all right where it counts. I'm happy in any case that Bob [Pack] has it. He is an hombre and will do well. I hope he will do well enough to ask you back often. I won't be there again but I cannot help but think often of the mountain and it will be good to know that many of the right people are there. Judith is absolutely disconsolate. I can see I'm going to have to take her to Europe next year to get her mind off Bread Loaf.

I'm off tomorrow for lectures in Michigan & then Kansas until about Sept. 21. I'll not make it to Chicago this time, but will hope for another.

How lovely your girls grow! Joy of them. And in all.

As ever
John

TO MILLER WILLIAMS

[Metuchen]
c. July 1, 1973
[MW]

Dear Miller:

I've heard you talk often of your father and I think I have some notion of what son you are of what man. And above all that you know it. Every father is an ambivalence to be buried. As he would agree, I'm sure, it is better that the son bury the father than that the father bury the son. It was a long life with a mind to it. It ended short of agony. May someone find it possible to say the same for me. . . . .

John

TO MILLER WILLIAMS

Metuchen
July 20, 1973
[MW]

Dear Miller:

. . . . . I'm pleased to hear that the Mexico Conf idea lives on but twitchily uneasy about any conference that offers academic credit. I may even be panicked by the thought. Academic credit *has* to mean school teachers; how can it be for credit unless they come as contributors? What sort of mss. could one expect? How could anyone flunk? How would it be possible to establish a useful conversation about writing in two weeks with a grade to be given? I will listen to all persuasion and hope I can see a way to change my mind, but my first reaction is that I wouldn't touch it if it is to be for college credit. If it ever gets to the planning board and if I am invited to discuss it, I want very much to speak against credit. As urgently, I want to urge that every effort be made to *isolate* the conference in order to keep the writers from wandering away from the discussion to other things and to keep other things from wandering into the discussion. Isolation is,

I believe, the real secret of Bread Loaf's success. No other conference is sufficiently isolated and no other conference has achieved the Bread Loaf effect. That's a pondered conclusion from thirty years of watching the strange miracle happen on the mountain and not happen anywhere else.

Item: I've begun to jot toward a new very personal book of words, phrases, their origins, and uses. This may turn out to be a ninety project, but it came to me at a most-miserable Chautauqua where I filled three large notebooks in two weeks of defensive withdrawal. One of those notes is about your father's expression, "I can borrow salt in any town in the county." Please write me a note on borrowing salt and about what you know of that usage, and its origins.

Do you know anything about a gent named Kelsey? I keep hearing "hotter than Kelsey's nuts . . . queer as Kelsey's rooster . . . bigger than Kelsey's cock." Who the hell is Kelsey? . . . .

Joys
John

TO EDWARD CIFELLI

Metuchen
December 14, 1973
[EC]

Dear Ed:

Your article about my poem was a wonderful surprise.* I am grateful to you for wanting to do it and grateful again that you should do it so well. Many thanks.

I have a form letter from Southern Mississippi saying that the interview is going to be published and they will send galleys.** I may be in Florida when they arrive and they may be delayed in forwarding. Certainly I will look forward to receiving them, but in case of delay, please accept my permission to make revisions, corrections, etc., as you see fit. I am going to the University of Florida as poet in residence. . . .

Is it possible to get another tearsheet or two of that article? I am quite set up by it and would love to send copies to a couple of people I care about. Once more, my happiest thanks.

All best for the season and long beyond.

Yours,
John

*"The Size of John Ciardi's Song." *CEA Critic,* 36 (November 1973), 21–27.

**"Ciardi on Frost: An Interview." In *Frost: Centennial Essays.* Jackson, Ms.: University Press of Mississippi, 1974, pp. 471–95.

TO NORMAN COUSINS

Metuchen
September 3, 1974
[NC]

Dear Norman:

I agree. Kill the Nixon piece. Someone, however, must insist (you?) with no appetite for blood that to let Nixon off the hook while Mitchell, Haldeman, Ehrlichman, Magruder, Dean *et al.,* stay in or go into the chum bucket is a mockery.

Those were great anniversary issues. You have every right to glow inside both for your triumphs and the manner of them.

I'm glowing a bit myself: I shed 35 lbs this summer. I'm still not exactly John of Gaunt, but I'll need a pillow to play Falstaff.

Joys
John

TO **JOHN WILLIAMS**

Metuchen

September 4, 1974

[JW]

Dear John:

. . . . . Thanks for saying yes to being an advisor to the Nat. Soc. of Arts and Letters. You won't find the duties onerous and I am sure you will find the cause good. I enclose a copy of my letter to Mrs. Erskine who will get you written to by the NSAL president and get you listed on the masthead or whatever you and I get listed on, in, with, for, and about. I spoke to the NSAL convention in Washington this year and can attest that the ladies are better than clubby, though there is always, to be sure, the little old one from Dubuque. The world's good is done by many hands and could use more.

Bill Sloane has been badly beset and several times operated upon for cancer. He is down to a shadow of Twiggy. The last operation had to go through some nerves that impair his never overly-clear articulation; he is having to learn to swallow with a different set of muscles. I am much afraid it is the brink. But if mind is the man, he's all there and insists on working away at mss. and on regular conferences with Helen Stewart who is running the press. No one at Middlebury saw it (I pleaded for years to get the college to give him an honorary degree and got the fish eye in return) but the man has dignity and purpose and I love him.

Have you got dignity and purpose? I'd be glad of any reason you can supply me for my feelings toward you—probably an instinctual malfunction.

Bless.

[John]

TO JOHN STONE

Metuchen
October 10, 1974
[JS]

Dear John:

. . . . Things go as things go. Norman Cousins just wrote to say the cost squeeze (price of paper is up 115% in 20 months) means a slimmer mag and all columns must be once a month only. I seem to be becoming unemployed faster than any man in town. Ah, well. My mind to me a (dwindling) kingdom is.

Joys
John

TO NORMAN COUSINS

Metuchen
October 10, 1974
[NC]

Dear Norman:

I know the bind. I'm in it myself. And may hope triumph.

I know how busy you have to be with all these problems, but may I beg favors? *viz.*

1. I've thought for some time of the possibility of syndicating a daily paragraph about words, the working title being "A Word to the Wise." You know everybody except God (and I suspect you've had lunch with his chief exec): is there anything you can tell me or anyone you can put me in touch with?

2. I've prowled endless bookstores looking for Matthews' *Dict of Am Eng on Hist Principles* and it just ain't to be had. On the assumption that you do not dip into it regularly will you lend me yours—the word is *lend*—until I can track one down (which I will)? I'm piled high with dictionaries and reference books but I keep needing that

one badly. I pledge myself not to rip you off and to return it to you as soon as my various booksellers come up with it.

Item: Rutgers has said it would send you a copy of my new book of poems (*The Little That Is All*), but Bill Sloane's death has upset things and they have been erratic. If it hasn't reached you, please let me know and I'll see that you get one suitable for framing.

To the lean years: may they fatten and not flab.

Best,
[John]

TO DONALD HALL

Metuchen
December 17, 1974
[UNH]

Dear Don:

I think the poems are powerful and right, both the prose-poem and the sweetly formal "Goldenhair," and I'd jump at the chance to publish them did *SR/W** publish poetry, and had it a poetry editor, and were I it, all of which it and I ain't, alas. I am something called a contributing editor, which is a no-voice-in-things with a reserved space for nothing-really-to-say once a month. Which I mail in from NJ, having become the hermit of my own attic (which I like) except for lecture trips (which I some like but mostly have two kids in college as a consequence of some fine first careless raptures). Apologies therefore for sending the poems back.

But I am glad by your letter and the sound of happiness in it. Like an old biddy I'm big on happy marriages. I've had one and somehow find the world confirmed in sensing that others are having one of their own. Are you out of teaching forever? Like you, I once *wanted* to be a teacher and worked at it but came in time to want my mind to myself and its work (or just its churnings). I like the thought of your getting the farm. I hope it includes that box full of string too short to be saved. I like my days in my attic study but New Jersey has no roots—not for me/I doubt for anyone—and you have the better of it in having a root place to go to. (Sometimes I think mine is on a mountain just behind Vesuvius, where I have sat drinking wine and talking with the old men in their execrable dialect, but after a while I come to realize I'm only a tourist shopping for nostalgia, and that I have no roots.) I'm trying to say I wish you all the good of your deep place. And of writing. That's a lot to be glad for. . . .

Joys. And as Dudley Fitts used to say

tutti bestorum
John

I'm working obsessively (have been for several years) on a sort of dictionary. I don't know yet what sort, but I see it will take the rest of my life—if I live that long.

*Norman Cousins merged two magazines and called the new one *Saturday Review/World.*

TO DONALD HALL

Metuchen
January 7, 1975
[UNH]

Dear Don:

The lecher circus certainly has fallen off. H. Walker [Ciardi's agent] got me one date for '75, but I had been picking my own and use him only when he ties in. The mail—bless it—keeps popping enough invitations to stock the bar, though with sub-vintages. And still your decision has the right ring to it. Happy welkins for it to ring in.

No, Boston has no real roots of mine left. In memory yes. But even-handed progress has blanked all facts. I'm not sure there is a place left to which I could go and say, "It was here, just as this place is now." —And do I want to? I guess I'd like to know there was such a place in case I should want to go to it—which is no great compulsion upon me. Why make up problems? I'm 58. 70 is a fair life expectancy. My one problem is what to do with + or - 12 years. Which gets it down from infinity to something small enough to taste. And the taste stays good.

I'm tentatively due to talk about something or other in Michigan next October. I was hoping I might see you then but you'll be in N.H. Which is good, and only my timing bad.

Cutting poetry was not my decision but one enforced by the economics of a new mag. Even if I worked for nothing, office space and a secretary would run to about $1500 a month which = 2 issues and give-or-take 2 poems per issue (+ 7¢ each to the poets). It's a miserable sort of addition.

Many additions—and all of them better—to you.

John

TO DONALD HALL

Metuchen

January 17, 1975

[UNH]

Dear Don:

Apologies. My letter said I was returning the poems but I find them still clipped to your letter. Let not your hand know what your mouth is saying.

I am feeling rejubilant. The Nat. Council Teachers of English just did an elaborate nationwide survey of poems liked by 4-5-6th grade children. They voted on their 25 most liked poems, and #1 in their hit parade turns out to be "Mommy Slept Late & Daddy Fixed Breakfast"—by me! I like the jury!

Joys to you
John

TO MILLER WILLIAMS

Metuchen

August ?, 1975

[MW]

Dear Miller:

You're right. And thanks for putting your finger on that wrong last line. How does the new ending strike you? Working on it, I spun off a new poem ("Universal T&T") and I think I like it at first blush, though first-blush makes poor lenses.

We have just returned from a week at a writers' conf. at Wm. Paterson College in NJ. Phil Cioffari (if, perhaps, you remember him from BL) started it but was rushed to the hospital (and is all right but a near thing) and had to be substituted for.

It went fairly well. Howard Nemerov was a pleasure (the next issue of *Poetry* is all-Nemerov and good). Among others, Stanley Elkin. And Diane Wakoski. . . .

The parties at the conf. were dull, so I sat in my room and poems came. First the revision. Then U. T. & T., then Guilt, Birthday, a Nap, and 7:00 A.M. I enclose the lot and welcome your pointer but don't feel you must scour every page. . . . .

John

TO DAN JAFFE

Metuchen

c. January 15, 1977

[DJ]

Dear Dan:

. . . . . We bought a shack in Key West and leave for it Jan 20 till April. None too soon. It has been a drab-drugged winter. I feel dull and heavy. Am just completing a tiresome round of dentistry down to full choppers and find the mouthful of hardware a painful nuisance. I'm ready to sit in Fla., take off my clothes, spit out these choppers, gum my mush, and just lie in the sun.

Watch your record shop for Myra Ciardi sings "Do You Ever Think of Me?" on the Polydor label, to be released as a single about Feb. 1. Our little girl is a recording artist! Pester your local D.J.s. Beat down their doors. Any immoderate enthusiasm will do as an adequate beginning.

When do you come East? It has been too long.

Love to all of you,
John

TO MILLER WILLIAMS

Metuchen
April 1, 1977
[MW]

Dear Miller:

Judith and I are just back from Fla. We're half unpacked and I'm in a psychic litter of accumulated mail. As chance would have it, your letter lay right next to one by Osvaldo Ramous from whom I hadn't heard in many years, and he included a pamphlet of poems in Italian with English translations that seem to me exactly designed to your cats' and dogs' specifications.* I take the poems fast to my feeling and think you will.

I hadn't thought of that deadness of Italian poetry as an operatic influence, ma con questi stupidi poeti tutto e possibile. I had thought of it as that inane "lingua scelta" the acadamicians have imposed on Italian literature (and French too), but the two are certainly related. Years ago Phillippe Jones of Belgium (*Journal des poetes*) made much of the fact that I said "monkey wrench" in a poem. In France, he insisted, such language would be dismissed as unworthy of poetry. (He was envying my freedom to say such things.) Anyhow I think you will find Osvaldo Ramous cat-and-doggy enough for your liking and I hope he will send you the pamphlet.

What happens to time? I meant to put together a children's book and a senile one** in Fla. (God knows I have poems enough to choose from.) Instead, I got hung up on two jobs I had to do: some radio programs for Nat Pub Radio, and an intro to *The Divine Comedy* (WW Norton is publishing a gift edition of the whole *Divine Comedy* for Christmas. It will probably be a $25.00 book. They think they can sell 15,000, which will come to about $45,000 in royalties—!!—and will at least [explain] why I put other things aside—and gladly to settle for half.)

I haven't put my hands on that particular issue of the *NY'r* but have often been out of touch with Howard Moss's taste. He hits some great ones now and then, but too often strikes me with blahs.

Myra's recording, a 45 rpm single, has been issued by Polydor, a big international ("Do You Ever Think of Me" by Richie Baron, and on the flip side her own song "It Happens"). She had top pick reviews in *Variety* and *Billboard* and has been on the road for weeks calling on disc jockeys in the hope of making the charts in about six months. If that happens—a mystical ritual—Polydor and Marx Music Pubs. will pay to put an instrumental group behind her and get her some bookings while she works up an album (where the money is/none in singles). It's a damned consuming ritual, an enormous disaster if she fails to "make the charts." But live and gamble.

There is much to be said for going to a U press that keeps books in print. Rutgers has done extremely well at distributing my books. I may, however, go to WW Norton. They will be doing the Dante. They want a word-book I am eager to get at. And they have said they'd like me on their poetry list. All's yet to decide.

I still want to do a book of limericks.

There once was a fast-talking Druid.
Whose manner of living was luid.
He'd engage Druid Lasses
In small talk—no passes,
But the first thing they knew they'd been scruid.

Or:

Said Sophocles putting his X
To the contract for Oedipus Rex,
    I predict this will run
    Until the Year One,
If the shooting script plays up the sex.

I have 144 and want to call it *A Gross of Limericks.* May your year continue to flower. Love to Jordan.

As ever
John

Judith and I will be proud to appear on your dedication page. She's a rather good wench, you know.

*Williams had written Ciardi that he wanted a poetry that dogs and cats could understand.

**"Senile" as opposed to "juvenile," Ciardi's standing joke to distinguish adult poetry from children's poetry.

TO ANDREI SERGEIEV

Metuchen
April 1, 1977
[FC]

My dear Andrei:

It is always a pleasure to hear from you. I envy you, of course, your command of both our languages. More than that, however, I sense a kinship. How marvelous it would be to see the ideological barriers removed between Americans and Russians. In my few days in Leningrad some years ago, I sensed that Americans and Russians have much in common. Both walk as if they owned the earth: so at least I felt when I went strolling. And at the Moscow airport I had a marvelous sympathetic conversation with an English-speaking young

Russian student. We traded lapel pins and I still have his—a vermillion glow on which are the profiles of Marx, Engels, and Lenin. The button I gave him read: Support Your Local Poet.

I am delighted by the choice of poems you have made, especially so to see "Requisitioning" included. I have long been bemused by the fact that American business jargon is full of terms from theology: good will, promised delivery, days of grace (in paying a bill), confirmation (of an order to buy), credit substantiation, conversion (of assets), redemption (of bonds), manifestation (the listing of items on an order)—and so on. I don't know what to make of this vocabulary but it did prompt the poem. (Perhaps to show that business is the religion of America; or perhaps that religion in America is a business—but, of course, I am being mildly cynical.)

You ask for suggestions, and I recommend to you as a poem I am pleased by, "Washing Your Feet." I think of it as my most successful effort at writing a minimal poem that manages to enlarge within its minimals. . . .

We have just returned from Florida, and there, last week, I met and later heard your magnificent Lasar Behrman—*horoshon* (is that the word?)—certainly one of the great giants of the piano.

I agree with what you have to say about fragmentation and disintegration. Our young poets are too often drawn to what I have to call "the trip culture." "Trip" is a term of the (now happily fading) drug generation. It means, at root, the hallucinatory experience (trip, voyage) brought on by drugs. It implies an eagerness for self-excitation (or drug excitation) of the mind. In poetry it seems to suggest (to the young) that all one needs to be a poet is the excitation of his own ignorance. Discipline and a true respect for the art, it follows, would stifle the overflow of one's excited feelings. The result is pap, but many young idiots, rejoicing in one another ("relating" to one another, as they call it) praise such clatter—because, as I suspect, they have never formed an attention capable of responding to the real thing. Whether it is the oratorical shouting of an Yevtushenko or the soul-spilling of a hallucinator, it is a self-exalting ignorance, and I can find in it nothing to hope for. I take my text from William Butler Yeats' poem, "Adam's Curse":

A line may take us hours maybe,
Yet if it does not seem a moment's thought,
Our stitching and unstitching has been naught.
Better get down upon your marrow bones
And scrub a kitchen pavement, or break stones
Like an old pauper in all sorts of weather,
For to articulate sweet sounds together
Is to work harder than all these, and yet
Be thought an idler by the noisy set
Of bankers, schoolmasters, and clergymen
The martyrs call the world.*

As I once said to a student: "I, too, want the impromptu, but I find that it's what begins to happen about the twentieth draft."

All good things to you.

Faithfully,
John Ciardi

*Ciardi always quoted from memory and was almost always letter perfect—or nearly so, as he is here.

TO STANLEY BURNSHAW

Metuchen
July 25, 1977
[UT]

Dear Stanley:

Bless you for forbearance. Please believe that I have been distraught but not surly. Even aside from family upheavals that have left me low in spirit and with the leaden conviction that I have turned out to be a lousy father (though, Lord, I have tried lovingly)—even aside from this depression of soul, this has been a blurred year.

Your book came, I read the first four poems, loved them—I mean with the real excitement—and then galleys began to arrive. WW

Norton is doing (this fall) the first hard cover edition of my version of *The Divine Comedy.* God, how I hate galleys—and they're such tough ones. Packages kept arriving every three days for over a month, and I was never through the last set before the next came along. Along with writing the column for *SR* and working up some (possible) National Public Radio programs on word and phrase origins, I lived in pajamas from late March (return from Fla.) to mid-June, with a few quick junkets here and there to snatch what little (and necessary) cash there is on the lecture circuit these days.

In mid-June Judith and I drove to U of Denver where I did a two-week seminar, then a week in Missouri to close out details of my father-in-law's meager estate, then a week in Chautauqua—a swelter all the way.

On August 20 we sail on the *Q.E.II* for England returning Sept 13. I didn't want to go. We went last year (our passage in return for two lectures at sea), and London was unbearable. This year Cunard's man phoned to repeat the offer, I was away, and Judith said yes for me. Meanwhile I am waiting for page proofs—and also for several crates of books I must read as one of the members of the Nat Institute's awards committee.

Do you know of some non-violent (and if possible lucrative) crime that would get me say three years in one of those minimum security federal prison camps where people get a small room to themselves? I feel Frost's line—

Back out of all this now too much for us—

That's not it exactly, I'm afraid, but close. . . .

Sweet breezes to your island.

Ever fondly
John

TO MILLER WILLIAMS

Metuchen
October 29, 1977
[MW]

Dear Miller:

Your letter made my day. I feel strongly right about "Minus One" and this is the first time anyone has had a word to say about it. It shouldn't matter, but it does. And thanks. . . .

I had a chat with Walker Percy last Monday—we're on a committee for the Nat. Inst.—and he spoke well of you. I told him you were my brother and after a reflexive moment in which he seemed to fear a Yankee invasion, I think he reclassified me as an honorary Southerner (Neapolitan style) and seemed to approve.

Almost as much love to you as to Jordan.

John

TO JOHN FREDERICK NIMS

Metuchen
November 18, 1977
[IU]

Dear John:

The (always) pleasure of hearing from you aside, there could hardly be happier news than this of yr. re-editorship of *Poetry.* I have never met Hine.* One of his first acts as editor was to send me a letter telling me not to submit any poems. It wasn't quite that blatant. The letter said *Poetry* wanted to stress younger poets, and would I therefore not seek to clutter up its pages. Nor in the more or less decade of Hine's editorship was I ever reviewed in *Poetry*—no, I'll take that back: my last book *The Little That Is All* was mentioned in a round-up.

All this has been a sadness to me. I shrugged as one must and told myself everyone has to take his losses, and that I had plenty else to think about. Now your letter changes everything, and I realize I really have felt more strongly than I had admitted about being shut out of *Poetry* and the long happy association I had had [with] it.

Let that explain what may seem my over-reaction in sending you so many poems. I have gone into a sort of hermitage about pushing publication, but I have mounds of poems on hand. Except that I hate typing and am poor at it, I might have sent you 100. As is, it took me most of yesterday to mistype these. Naturally, I hope you will find something here you will want to publish, for few things could please me more than to see some of my poems in *Poetry* again. Though the typing is crude, I believe you will find them legible.

I'd love to get to Chicago and a visit with you—and with Studs Terkel, of whom I have been enormously fond since the first time I laid eyes on him. I'll hope. I am flying to Milwaukee the A.M. of the 20th and, that night, to Chi. but only to make a connection for Minn'p'lis and thence to Spokane. A mad schedule, but after months on low loot on the lecher circus Nov. has turned lootfull and I chase apace, trying for winter fat to take me thru the time I will be sitting on my patio in Key West.

I am inclined to agree with you about UFla. It was beautiful before it suffered atmospheric pollution. Now. . . . ? As they say in Little Italy, "I ron' know." You know, of course, how south Italians favor a d-r shift between two vowels, as maronna for madonna, but I'd like you to meet Mrs. Petacci, who sometimes refers to her son as "the stupor iriot."

Great times to you, to the ed. of *Poetry*, and to our lovely friend Bonnie.

John

*Daryl Hine, editor of Poetry, 1969–1977.

TO MILLER WILLIAMS

Key West
March 7, 1978
[MW]

Dear Miller:

I left chilblains to return to more of the same—a raw, nasty week.

. . . John and Nancy Williams came a-guesting, and greatly welcome except that we have no guest room. We gave them ours. Judith slept on a make-do. I slept on the sofa. It was impossible to get anything done with four people in one closet. (This is the *tiniest* shack: every gut-rumble resounds through it.) But joy abounding: John and Nancy house-hunted and ended up buying a place about 4 blocks away. So add one more to the happy colony. When are we going to make beach combers of you and Jordan?

I am dizzied by the number of things that have piled up on me—including the annual torture of preparing fictions for IRS. I think I'd like a deal whereby my income gets paid to the US of A, and it sends me what's left over, if anything.

Those were lovely days with you and Jordan. Even enough to justify that hairy flight from Tulsa. Toward joys, I returned to find a letter from John Nims who has taken four poems for *Poetry:* "For Instance," "The Lungfish," "Machine," and "Censorship"—all in the ms. In re which, I enclose the missing carbon from "Being Called." Will I ever get it pruned down to a semi-coherent book? Don't know. And IRS insists on coming first.

We leave here c. Mar. 29., go to Hattiesburg for a talk, cut for home about April 8. Judith loved that shawl you and Jordan sent. She'll write, but let me say I like it too.

Joys to your house, sir, and madam. We are into some lovely days, sun-drenched breakfasts on the patio. Beautiful. If it holds for the rest of the month, we're blessed. Thanks for all.

With love, as ever,
John

TO ERIC SWENSON

Metuchen

March 20, 1978

[FC]

Mr. Eric Swenson
W.W. Norton
500 Fifth Avenue
NYC 10036

Dear Eric:

I'm delighted that the limerick book is in the works. The advance of $2500 does more than please me: it comes like a transfusion at the critical point of an IRSectomy scheduled for April 14. . . . .

How about *Too Gross* as a title? The first 144 can be labeled *Limericks, A Gross,* the second: *Limericks, Too Gross.* "Gross" is the indisputable collective noun for limericks. I look fwd to seeing you in April.

All best,
John

TO MILLER WILLIAMS

Metuchen

June 5, 1978

[MW]

Dear Miller:

Your beautiful letter of 4/29 about the long poems in the ms. and the small fine packet of your poems make me ashamed of these 5 last weeks. They have been smashed time. A trip to Boston, one to Illinois, another to Minn., some crap to shovel in NY, and I'm due to go back to Boston June 9 to receive a gold medal from the Dante Alighieri society. (I have a couple of "gold" medals stamped "bronze" on the rim, but this one, I am told, is actually gold-plated—and how can I turn that down?)

I have some radio chit chats to get ready for a taping session for Nat. Pub. Radio—a series (irregular) to be called "A Word in Your Ear." (See your local paper.)

W.W. Norton is doing *Too Gross* (288 limericks by Asimov & Ciardi) and wants a foreword and I'm breaking my head on it and it won't come right.

—All this by way of apology. Once back from Boston I shall have most of a clear month in the hope of becoming a born-again human being.

I wrote Gordon Ray who misunderstood my letter so I'll write him again—if that is, you are planning to apply again next year.* I can at least keep him needed. Let me know.

July 10 I start 2 weeks at Chautauqua, then one at Bemidji, Minn., then one at a NJ writers' conference (at Paterson College). Then the fall looks clear. No lecture checks in sight, but time to work—and more in Fla. It foresees well, and blessed by a fat nest egg for $5000 worth of bank stock I bought in '66, the bank being acquired by a larger bank that will pay $46,000 for my originals plus my dividend shares. So, even at these prices, we'll eat (after we put a new roof on the house etc.). —Have you ever sat and figured how much it costs you per day for basic breathing? I add my various taxes, house repairs & maintenance, food, utilities, clothing etc. and come up with just under $200. —It can't be: I don't make that much (or do I?)—and yet I can't find anything wrong with my figures. Even if I'm way off, the total is appalling. And fuck it.

I'll really write once back from Boston. Kiss Jordan—at least once for me.

Love
John

*For a Guggenheim fellowship.

TO GEORGE GARRETT

Metuchen

June 14, 1978

[GG]

Dear George:

You are a beautiful man. I will certainly send [George] Core some poems. At this point of my slovenly bookkeeping, I have about 20 out to various magazines and I'm not sure which are where. I don't dare risk the embarrassment of having a poem accepted and then having to say "Oops, sorry." I'll wait a bit till my chickens come home to roost and then do it—gladly, gratefully.

Thanks for telling me about Brendan Galvin. As I noted earlier, I haven't cause to complain, but I put a lot into *Lives of X* and can't help but feel much pleased when anyone approves it.

I'm not sure my life makes sense. I seem always to have one more commitment to fight free from—all of them half-nonsense. As life is, I suppose.

Joys to you. I'll not fail to send Core some poems as soon as I know what I have free.

Fondly
John

TO GEORGE GARRETT

Metuchen

June 18, 1978

[GG]

Dear George:

I want you to know I have just sent to George Core six poems of less than 30 lines each as he stipulated. I've never published in *Sewanee* and would be delighted to get an acceptance from him. I told him you were that rare man one could both love and respect & that much is not subject to rejection.

I am a cheapskate (which is to say cheap "shit" < Old Eng. *scittan* with the "c-kappa" by way of Scot. and dialect skite, skyte, skate. "He played me daughter Kate a de'lish skyte" for "He done her shitty.") and use old letter heads.* I am also—as you see—obsessive about these crazy-beautiful etymologies.

Bless,
John

*This letter is written on *SR* letterhead.

To George Garrett

Metuchen
June 24, 1978
[GG]

Dear George,

. . . . . I bombed with George Core from whom I received a brisk the-editor-is-final-judge-of-things letter. He tells me I write light verse and instructs me to sing. (A fine bit of advice to a Raven.) I thanked him, cited passionate preferences as honorable things, and reckoned we were divided by ours.

Will you be in Maine in October? Judith and I were thinking of an Autumn leaves tour into upper N.H.—and why not into Maine, if you're there?

Thanks, and all joys.
John

TO GEORGE GARRETT

Metuchen
July 1, 1978
[GG]

Dear George:

You have—I pledge you—absolutely nothing to apologize for anent George Core. May no man ever find need to apologize for having done me a kindness. Nor is it so grave with Core. Nothing is easier for an editorial poop than to assume that "this person, by submitting his work to my editorial consideration, appoints me as his intellectual and esthetic superior, and I shall pronounce." Core told me my poems are light verse—which they are, though with Robin Goodfellow jamming the ass's ears on my head with hat pins. I sent him a polite note. He wrote back to ask me to review *The Oxford Book of Light Verse* (the bastard) and asking to see some of the longer poems I had mentioned. I said no to the review but have sent him more poems. All very polite. Nor did I bother to tell him I think he's an ass. I deal willingly enough with asses. To quote from one of my old poems.

> Anyone can learn from a wiseman.
> But learn to learn from a fool and the whole world
> Is your faculty.

My only distress is that you have been so distressed and I beg you not to be at the same time that I honor your sentiments. It is one of the more congenial failures of the civilized. Confronted by a fool, the decent person tends to say, "Oh, Lord, what is my fault?" It is often as fair a response to think, "What's wrong with this goddamn lout?" And with no need to counter.

You and I have reached an age not exactly terminal, I will insist, but tending. I, for one, feel I have paid my dues and have a right to retire into myself, ideally into some enlarging self. But I have no overwhelming large problem. I feel rather securely [?] for ten more years and I might edge toward twenty, but I think anything more would be fantasizing. I set 10–15 as the gist of it and my total problem is simply what to do day by day for that much time. I also insist that "what to do" must include enough damn-foolery to keep my ego-ape from growing sullen.

My ape and I are both proud of our place in your personal anthology. I don't have to tell you you have a place in mine—a tone and a way of seeing and saying that rings movingly true. So much that I see seems forced. The art—and you have it—is to make real without stomping it. . . .

Have you sent some things to John Nims at *Poetry*? It feels so damn good to have him back in the chair after Daryl Hine. Nims is, I think, our true scholar-poet, with both the toughness and the dispassion of the man who has thought and read enough. —That will do for a tower in an age when the kids seem to think the single prerequisite is the excitation of one's own ignorance. Or of a "cause."

Shit—that sounds as if I were writing not to you but through you to some future editor. I apologize. Without realizing it, I fell into quoting myself again. It's that goddamned ape. (But I join him in being happy that Nims is back. I used to think of *Poetry* as the house I lived in once. Then *those others* moved in. And now John Nims, and I can visit again.)

Judith & I will be looking forward to October.

Fondly
John

P.S. Good lord, I haven't said anything about what you have done to line up people to write about my things. What *can* one say? I have long known that my reputation is partly that of a noisy fraud—"a cultural headwaiter" as one of the reference books put it. I know I am guilty of having published too much—a lot of which I wish unpublished. I've told myself I have no cause to complain, that I've been egregiously rewarded for doing my own thing. That should be enough for a man, but I confess my ape doesn't like it. Even *he* hasn't ever really meant to be a fraud—except when he was trying to maneuver girls into bed. And by now, having all but achieved the dignity of impotence, that is in the past. And yet we'd all like to be paid attention to. "And always the soft idiot softly 'me.'" That's Auden, but I may be mangling the quote. I'm grateful.

TO MILLER WILLIAMS

August 5, 1978

[MW]

Dear Miller:

The writers conf. at Wm. Paterson Collich was X'd for lack of enrollment, which pisses me off a bit on accounta (a) I turned down a $2500 week to honor my W.P. commitment, and (b) Am now out the $1300 I turned it down for, but at least I've had a whole extra week to get 11% caught up in, and I guess my life will not be significantly altered one way or the other. This seems, in fact, my season for refusing $$$. The Franklin Mint Library offered me $2500 for a book club use of the *Div. Com.* (they could have been worked up to $5000, the pikers) and I had to turn the offer over to W.W. Norton on the fair assumption that the book club use would compete with the Norton edition. Maybe they will decide it won't and I can reach for the goodies, but if they say it would be competition I'd have to say that I think so too and stand for honor before cash, a generally shitty choice.

I am going to do a long interview with MacLeish in Sept. for Nat. Pub. Radio and plan to spend this month re-reading him and working at the final-final draft of the new book of poems. Rutgers Press is phasing out poetry. I'll send it either to Harper's or to Norton. Norton has decided that the *Browser's Dictionary* is not in their line but Harper's has shown what is called "interest."

I returned to find your comments on the poems, and bless you for them. The one point I can't settle (I think) is the line:

were all of her—and, of course, Internal Revenue.

You read Revenue as /-/ and make it six feet: I read it as /—, a double feminine, and argue five feet. Well, I'll bounce it around in my head.

Well it's 5:26 and time I thought about getting drunk and going to bed. Goo night, Miller, Goo night, Jordan. Goo night, all.

EEEyawwwwwwwwn
John

TO JOHN FREDERICK NIMS

Metuchen
October 15, 1978
[IU]

Dear John:

I've been scrubbing about for something I might offer to the Poetry Day auction and I'm afraid I come up empty. I'll have to ask you to settle for the enclosed small check as my contribution. . . .

Nothing would please me more than to see an article in *Poetry*.* I think I may fairly say I was never once mentioned in Hine's time. One shrugs, but I'll confess it felt a bit like having strangers living in a house that held warm memories once.

I am frankly astonished that Diane Wakoski came up with the idea. I rather like her but we're such continents apart! But whyever not? I like it more the more I think of it. I'd be honored.

Yes, I have been at work. WW Norton recently brought out (about a year ago) a hard-cover edition of the whole *Div. Comedy* with a new intro. In Nov. Norton is releasing a non-book, a collaboration with Isaac Asimov. He did 1 gross of original limericks and I did another—which gives us the title: *Too Gross*. My new book of poems *For Instance*—you ran the title poem—is going to be published by Norton (just signed the pub. agreement). And I have a contract with Harper and Row to deliver a first volume of word origins (*A Browser's Dictionary, And Native's Guide to the Unknown American Language*) April 15, next. I got a fairly good advance for it but doubt it will entirely pay for the typing, alas. Worse yet, I'm going to have to do most of it myself, which is a recipe for disaster.

I won't be so stupid as to offer you any advice on *Poetry* off the top of my head. It feels warm again. I enjoy reading it as I never did under Hine. Poetry today is forever in danger of being locked up in the graduate schools, which to be sure, are not the worst of prisons, but neither are they the ideal environment. I have a happy sense that your mood, mind, and breadth have opened it to first airs again. I certainly will pass on to you, for what little they may be worth, any comments I come up with, I mean any comment more specific than my general approval, the sense of which is strong in me. . . .

Love from our house to your house,

John

*Nims had written Ciardi on October 7 to say Diane Wakoski "liked your work, thought you underrated" and that he had asked her to say as much in an article for *Poetry.*

TO VINCE CLEMENTE

Metuchen

November 10, 1978

[VC]

Dear Vince:

Thanks for much: for your kindness to me, and especially for *Songs from Puccini:* good poems, and Marino has given them fine voice in Italian, music for music and measure for measure.

I like the sense of the project you suggest.* I find myself, however, oddly blocked by "the Am-It esthetic." Can another word be found? I am not sure there is such a thing; and if there is I doubt I have it. It isn't that I am l'Italiano dirazzato, though I guess I am. Though I also know I am not. I have poured out endless poems about the Italian "roots." Yet Jefferson, Tom Paine, and even—God save the mark, Emerson—are as much at the roots of my mind and feeling as the It. of my Am.

I am saying that I have always relished the part of me I have held over from my parents, but that it is more nearly a memory of first things than a state of being. No—I've said that badly—but in any case I don't know of any way to think of it as an esthetic. The only time I have a sense of that Italian fraction is when I am at a specifically It-Am gathering, as I am once or twice a year, and which I always enjoy. Then, and whenever a poem summons up pieces of my childhood, pieces for which I am always grateful when I can make them work. A feeling of good belonging. And yet that feeling is just as strongly upon me when I drive across the Rockies again. A good feeling, rich and right, but nothing I can make myself feel as an esthetic.

I had a more specifically ethnic sense when I was the Wop kid in a primarily Irish suburb. That came to some years of trading black eyes and bloody noses, but that, too, faded as we began to play on the same teams and the town became full of Irish-Italian couples. When we have a family reunion, the Fennessey clan and the Elkins outnumber the Ciardis by many. My own kids are English, Scotch, Irish, Penna. Dutch, middle-border, southern pioneer stock on their mother's side. I took the whole crew to Italy some years back to give them that memory, but when my surviving cousins began to overflow upon us, they couldn't believe it. I confess that even I felt I had time-machined back to the egg and been born again in the Middle Ages. And add that, in part, I loved it. Yet it is no longer my way. I know how to let it echo in me like memory I am glad to have summoned. I don't know how to make of it anything that could be called an esthetic. Can you suggest some other term—one I might focus on without this sense of being blocked?

You mention the complexity of being an ethnic. I have acquaintances who tell me they have had problems in being categorized as Italian and suspect. Have I been so arrogantly introspective that I never noticed? I am an American man of letters. My most revered, dear friend is Archibald MacLeish. I kid him for wearing a Scotch cap and we laugh together. Perhaps I've been blinded by habituation. Now and then on a lecture in west Texas an old local will look at me as some sort of strange foreign intrusion, but to me he looks like a gopher peeping out of his dry hole. Perhaps it is an arrogant indifference: there are not many people whose opinions matter to me. . . .

You see, I am fumbling. Something about that one phrase makes me uncertain. Whatever I am feeling about my roots is not an esthetic: a nostalgia maybe, a rush of memories I am happy to summon, but always somehow a long-ago and not a present frame of mind, and not an esthetic.

I lectured at the Univ of the Philippines about 15 years back—no probably longer—and as I drove to Baguio and saw the native villages I wondered what it would be like to enter one of them as a native and sense and enter the life there. When I first entered my mother's home town (Manocalzati in Avellino), I remembered those Philippine villages with a sense of having entered Manocalzati and the Middle Ages as somehow a native son. I was delighted to the point of being almost reborn to find I could summon the dialect, or some of it anyhow, and recognize the emotional patterns, which weren't mine, and yet they were. It is a loveliest ghost and its loss would impoverish me. But can one make an esthetic of that?

I would, of course, love to join your project. God knows I have poured out enough poems on my Italian roots. I could write an intro piece that might answer, but only, I think, if you will let me get that word "esthetic" out of my head, and go for memory as it comes, as honestly as I can summon it. Does that seem reasonable?

I'll be here till a bit after Christmas, then in Key West till about April pecking away at a book manuscript I owe Harper and Row in April. I can't in any case do anything until I get this book off my hands.

Does any of this make sense to you? As Dudley Fitts used to sign himself,

ganz tutti bestorum,
John

Give my best to Lew Turco if you see him; a good man and a good poet.

*The project was to be a collection of poems and commentary by Italian-American poets who were to describe how their common background helped to form their poetic consciousness. It never developed into a book.

TO VINCE CLEMENTE

Metuchen
November 15, 1978
[VC]

Dear Vince:

This question about the project: who wants it? Who will read it? Poetry is for the few who read poetry, and who among them reads poetry for ethnic roots? The ethnic roots would reach for an Italo-Am. readership, and it is my conviction that there is no readership as such. I flirted with being a publisher once, and I think I learned that only books of Jewish subjects can expect a readership. (An ethnic one that is.) We are the children *del cafone*. We may have found a cultural continuity by ourselves, but it is not an ethnic tradition. When *I-Am** started up with expensive backing and high hopes, I pledged myself to do what I could, but warned that the magazine would never find enough subscribers. And it did fail—expensively and within two years.

I am not throwing wet blankets at random. I am assessing a literary publication and coming to the conclusion that it is foredoomed as a publishing venture. Someone is going to drop a bundle of money on it. If you feel it is worth pursuing for personal reasons despite the certain financial loss, so be it, but it has to lose.

The next question: is it worth doing for its literary value? I don't know. I don't know of anyone who thinks in terms of Italo-Am poets. I had a longish poem about Italy in the *Atlantic* some years back, and when Robert Lowell wrote to praise its Italo-Am voice, I took offense. Did the s.o.b. suppose I had used an Am. Eng. inferior to his, or that I had inherited and made mine less Am. Eng. than his? Well, even the good ones can be fools.

My book *Lives of X* was autobiographical and so went as deep as I could reach into roots. I gave it everything I had. I will even claim that I brought to XX [th century] Am poetry a kind of fictional technique that amounted to a notable technical expansion. No book of mine was more important to me and none was ever more thoroughly ignored.

I write this for you to ponder before you commit yourself to an impassioned failure. If you are sure you want to pursue it, I will do what I can. But these things I submit you must ponder soul-deep.

Thanks for your kindness. It would be fun to see Montauk Point again, but Long Island, alas, is a traffic jam I will not willingly face.

All best to you
John

*A magazine; short for Italian-American.

TO GEORGE GARRETT
Metuchen
November 29, 1978
[GG]

Dear George:

You have been feasting the printers! And they you. Good type is a pleasure. And becoming, alas, a rarity. Good poems well set. I am delighted by them. They stick: "Home is wherever/you are going." —Simple, right, and fine. And good barbed sardonics. I wish there were more satire in our times. Trouble is that satire requires a norm and who has one? But that's no reason to put away nice, nasty invective. Lay it on. As a gent told me once (about Robert Herrick) "If you're a midget/The world is full of crotches." —Too good a turn to forego: I have used it as the end of an invective poem.

I've been not quite under the weather these last days, physically stale and profitless. It will be good to get to Key West and get out of doors. I'm having a love-hate thing with my word book. I love sniffing out the roots but detest the typing. When I get back from Fla. I may take a fling and go for Xerox's $3000 typewriter: you type on an electronic screen, correct, edit, shift around by push button, then push DESTRUCT and the thing rattles off up to 120 flawless characters a second. If only they had one for sex. But enough nostalgia.

I hope the limericks got to you and are some fun. When do we two meet again? '79 must not pass withouten.

Joys,
John

I got a pretty fair poem today—I think (it will probably look horrible tomorrow).

TO **MILLER WILLIAMS**

Metuchen

December 13, 1978

[MW]

Dear Merry-Happies:

The clock is ticking and I begin to be restless about getting to Fla. Judith and the kids have a big thing about Xmas. I insist they could learn to adjust their nostalgias to a fat check sent from Key West, which, if they insisted (without being urged) they could use to fly down and carol under the palms. But I was born to lose this one. I wish we had gone down in Nov. As it is we'll leave prob. Jan 2 and arrive via many stops prob. Jan 8-9-10. If time seems anyway manageable, I'd love to get in a visit with the Stones but am reluctant simply to use them as a motel. We'll see.

I have fallen into a queer rut. I hardly get out of the house for ten days or more at a time. I keep falling into the word book and still falling behind schedule. I smoke too much, drink too much, and am getting to be plain obese.

And stale. Something about these felonious footnotes chokes Erato. But not always. I've got a batch of things I finally decided to type up and I'm not sure what to think of them. They still need work. I am in fact looking forward to Fla. and to working on them there. I would, however, love to have your reactions, suggestions, approvals, or howls of rage as the case may be.

All of these are slight, but I have no other subject. I sometimes think it would be just dandy to work up a big fat fervor. Then I read the fevers of the fervent and decide I'd rather be slight. If only the personages hadn't brow-beaten and chest-thumped poetry all those centuries, the tradition might have gone closer to the species. What we need is imaginary parties with some real farts in them.

The Nat Inst put me on a committee to make up the slate for the Gold Medal in Poetry. I discovered that MacLeish had never had it and take that to be conclusive, but the climate demanded that Tate, Penn Warren (!), Kunitz, and Eliz. Bishop be put on the ballot. Then damned if I didn't receive an out of the blue effusion from Muriel Rukeyser. "This is just to say . . ." Ah, well, everybody wants.

You and George Garrett and Stanley Burnshaw are on the ballot for membership but the vote is not in yet. You should be a member. If not this time, the next. I can't predict anything about this queer club, but a membership, I suggest, might reasonably be U of A [University of Arkansas] grounds for a raise. I'll settle for 5%. Hell, I'll settle for less.

Have happy everythings. I'll look forward to hearing from you.

John

TO MILLER WILLIAMS

Key West

January 15, 1979

[MW]

Dear Miller:

We have been here six days and I have not smoked for five of them so be careful how you talk to me because I'm cocked to take heads off at the first slant word. . . . .

The average length of the erect male penis is 6.27 inches. The average depth of the vagina is 6.531 inches. Problem: compute by states and counties and with allowances for celibacy due to all causes, the amount of unused vagina at any given point in time. . . . .

I want a cigarette.

Much to my surprise, I find it is quite possible to want one and to be indifferent to wanting. This may not work but it is instructive. My advice to young men is don't light up a cigarette: fuck. Now, if only I could practice what I preach. . . .

The weather is lovely here. Picked a marvelously ripe and quite special very large papaya off our tree. Also some avocados. My fig tree grows but will yet take years to bear gracefully. This year no bananas: we had a lovely bunch last year. Why don't you sell Ark. and buy Cuba?—it's only 90 mi. across to Havana. We could start a good neighbor policy.

The social season is slow: have seen the Wilburs and John Williams: otherwise I type dict. entries and think defilement. Minus the entries, hope you are the same.

Love
John

TO GEORGE GARRETT

Key West
February 2, 1979
[GG]

Dear George:

This is an invocation. Our letters must have crossed in the mail. I must tell you that nothing could have given me more pleasure than your letter about *Lives of X.* I invested much in that book—and had almost to invent the form for it—or at least to renew some lapsed inventions. Yet I've never published a book that was so systematically ignored. As I recall, it got one notice in a Boston paper—and that is all.

Had it been overpraised—as does sometimes happen—I could be remoter about my pleasure in your praise. As is, to have it so thoroughly ignored but then praised by one whose praise matters—well, it does matter. And thank you, sir.

Trust nothing I say. I have quit smoking. Not a weed in weeks. But I'm not yet entirely relaxed about it. In fact, I get jumpy now and then (but only passingly). It's a disappoint[ment] to find that virtue is not really as big a pain in the ass as I was sure it would be.

May you avoid all virtue—or at least not suffer by it.

Love
John

TO JOHN FREDERICK NIMS

Key West
February 9 (?), 1979
[IU]

Dear John:

Yrs. has wafted among the bougainvillea and palms & surceased under the papaya. We're here until April and I have but to damn myself for a fool for accepting a talk-date in Omaha Feb 19. It would serve me right to be frozen into a slow glacier in Nebraska or Kansas City. Hereafter, I get south of the frost line by at least Dec. 1 and stay there until at least April 1. U of Richmond wrote about a seminar in Feb 1980 and I said no on these here now same principles.

This blushing pink paper is from work in progress. I have a contract to deliver the first volume of my *Browser's Dictionary* to Harper and Row on April ?, and I am amusing myself by keeping the carbons on rainbow paper—pink, yellow, green, blue, etc. Toward a more colorful prose. Whereupon there came to me that John Nims, blanched and chilblained by Chi. could stand some colorful prose. Wherewith-which herewith.

Aside from some junk-in-passage to be quick-noted, I've had two reviews in *Chi. Trib*—and several articles on word origins (and one on the limerick). One review was the round-up [on] Shapiro and I did have something to say. The other was the River Poems of that guy whose name evades me as much as nuance evades him. The Shapiro was a natural. John Blades asked if I'd do Rukeyser, and I said no: I'd be forced to say things she would not like and there would follow tension. So with Red Warren. I like the guy, like some of his poems, very much dislike the rest, and I don't want to say so in public. . . . .

Norton, incidentally, will be doing the new book of poems. *For Instance* : it's in process. At least 7 of the poems in it have or will have appeared in *Poetry.* Born, one might say, under a mighty aegis. Dick Wilbur was saying the other night how much he feels *Poetry* has improved under yr. tillage—as indeed anything would have been an improvement, but yrs vastly.

It matters to me. Under Hine I felt I was shut out of an important house by usurpers. You bring it around to being home again. That's important. Hine forgot what Harriet Monroe started, and you won't forget. If I can help, I will and gladly.

The Key West garbage trucks carry signs that read: FREE SNOW REMOVAL. How little it costs to lend a helping shovel when all's clear. I vow never to go near Chi. between say Oct. 1 and April 1. My last wintering there was—can we ever forget?—with you, and I thought to die of it.

If Allen Sundry is still around, give him our love. We are a-building a new house on land I bought here. John Williams, Peter Taylor, Jim Merrill, and much else are here and hereabout.

Bea Goodcheer.
John

TO JOHN FREDERICK NIMS

Key West
February 26, 1979
[IU]

Dear John:

I honor your intention to memorialize Tate and I have passed on the project to Dick Wilbur, John Williams, and the Taylors without, alas, eliciting much response. I have myself thought about it and have had to conclude that I am not the right man for it. I have simply never responded to Tate, starting with an early sense that he was austerely constricted in ways that did nothing to my nerve ends—a sense I might have to revise on a careful re-reading, though probably not. That is to say, I might be doing him an injustice. (As I once thought I was doing an injustice to every girl I had not been in bed with, but so it is between Tate and my psyche—the invitation was never there and all doors bolted against it.)

This is the deadly season of compiling tax returns. Loathsome, maggoty, soul-retching. I propose to have all payments go to the government and to have it make me an allowance.

Have you come across *A Modern Dunciad* by Richard Nason? It drifted by and I found it as utterly stupid as any book of poems I have seen of late. What I found saddest in it is the fact that he engages his stupidities in categories that seem real to him but that I did not know existed. Is there really a movement that can be labeled California-is-the-future-and-the-effete-East-reviles-it-in-self-destroying-envy? Ah, well, none of us has finished inventing the ways in which we will be wrong.

I think *Poetry* needs an office in Key West. I have every faith in your discernment (Miller tells me you've taken 5 of his grand Belli translations—that's fair evidence), but even you would do better while perusing poems in a floating desk in the swimming pool from Xmas to April's Fool. I came on a poem by Diane Wakoski a few days back and was reminded of what you said about her wanting to do a piece about me. Is she serious? I'm fascinated by the thought, as if from a least likely source. Did Rutgers Prep send you any sort of check? I told them I'd give them a day if they would send *Poetry* a check. I don't suppose it will be for much—if they do send it. But I'm curious to see if they will pledge for me at least 40% of what I have to pay a plumber. . . .

Would you believe that *prehistoric* does not occur in English until 1850 and that its use then in a book on Scottish archeology moved many pulpits to thunder and damnation? You can see why, but what a least footnote to the fundamentalist society! . . . . .

Take seriously the thought of a Key West winter office/ we'll start a new Athens here on Gay Key. I saw Eberhart on the way through

Gainesville. He's a marvelous pixie but a disastrous teacher. What's there to say about an English department that let you go to keep Joy A., and let me go to keep Dick E.? The times are out of joint, but thank you quite that I was never born to set them right.

Joys in all, son of man.

As ever—which is with great affection,

John

TO MILLER WILLIAMS

Key West

February 27, 1979

[MW]

Dear Miller:

Omaha is easier to get to than to get out of, but I've been and gone, stalled there for an extra day by an ice storm. Call it a learning experience. What I learned is: once you get south of the frost line, stay there. . . .

Have you any strong feelings anent Allen Tate? John Nims is getting set to do an issue on Tate and says he is looking for essays, notes, poems, memoirs, etc. I'm not the gent for a chunk of it. But you might go for the thought.

The day I was delayed in Omaha and trying to walk on [glare?] ice while balancing a suitcase and then collapsing across airport vistas to sit and pant while my knees shook—that day, for the first time unblinkably, I knew I am an old man. Not just a fat slob, but an old fat slob.

The thought struck home—as we say—*impactfully.* But after I had had another drink I discovered it didn't really make much of a difference.

I have been digging away at the *Browser's Dictionary* and whatever book this first book is to be is just about done! I've got to stop to do my fucking income taxes but once that's over and done, I'll jot the last title and send the typescript off to Harper & Row.

I think U Ark should establish a southern campus for winter quarter translation in Key West. Love to Jordan.

Hold on!

John

TO LEWIS TURCO

Key West
February 28, 1979
[LT]

Dear Lew:

I am in the inner wrangle of pure hatred that always comes of trying to make out the annual fictions required by I.R.S. May ½ , ⅓, or 2/7 of their life expectancy, whichever is first, but not exceeding the total of lines 47A and 13C, be subtracted from their accruable pensions (p. 14, line 136B) unless they are fired beforehand as stipulated on p. 64, ¶s 13A-C-D, in which case goddamn 'em anyway.

I haven't heard from Clemente. I have had a couple of over-breezy notes from Brian Swann. I really don't know what to make of so much Italo-Am. I've never thought in terms of I-Am poetry. I don't know any I-Am poets, as such. Lew Turco is an Am. poet who happened to have It. parents. T. Roethke is a ditto with Ger. parents. If the human race could not somehow have managed to evade its parents we'd all be fed. bureaucrats. Well, I'll try.

Thanks for standing in awe. There's nothing I like better than to inspire terror. At my country club I hire guys to spread the word of how to-be-feared I am. That way, when I enter a room, people grovel as they say "Hey you old fart—where ya been?" (The answer my friend is blowing on the wind.)

I just got back from Alas-Omaha, and two days late returning after being iced in. It's good to hear the icicles are beginning to drop off your toes. In the old crockery of my 60s my joints have gone barometric and thermal and I mean, hereafter, to stay safely south of the frost line come winter. Go thou forth Lew Hardy to slay the Ice

King's dragons: I'm all for dozing among the pussy cats of the creamy islands.

Joys in all
John

TO LEWIS TURCO

Metuchen
April 16, 1979
[LT]

Dear Lew:

My sins upon me: *TV Guide* called and asked for X words as notes of a TV watcher. They offered $250 for writing the piece against $1000 if they accepted it. So I did some typing at about $500 an hour. I like that.

Nor am I bemoaning for myself. I have in fact been egregiously lucky. Having done everything in this world to guarantee monkish vows of poverty, I found people lining up to pay me for my dumb jokes. No, I have no personal lament, but a grief for lost causes—among them literacy. In one sense it can't make any difference to me—I expect to go to my grave without having skipped any meals (my wife and my waist line, in fact, say I should). It's some sort of grief of seeing much that I have valued most being discarded as irrelevant. Like walking around the back yard of the museum and watching good paintings dropped into the shredder. Well, someday I'll study metaphor and come up with the right one.

You're right about Rexroth. I have been fond of him for years and admired his brilliance in so many areas, but he really is a goddamn Californian; just the sort of guy who would run a writers' workshop as a group therapy encounter session: begin by taking off your shoes and touching one another's feet sole to sole: now add an adjective. I have never understood why he should be all NOW.

As a matter of fact I was watching color TV—a brand new one. I played cards my second night back and when Judith complained that our TV set was lousy, I flipped her $500 (I had won $600) and she and Benn drove off and came back with a new set. So next time I'll lose my $600 and Judith will say, "Well, you're even." What she does not understand is that no one is ever even but only a) not rich yet, and b) not broke yet. And among this world's jokes would you believe that the limerick book I did with Isaac Asimov, pub'd last Nov. sold 12,000 copies by mid-Feb.? Crazy—but I love it.

John

TO GEORGE GARRETT

Metuchen

April 17/18, 1979

[GG]

Dear George:

. . . . . I'm at some sort of loose ends. I seem to have enough work to last me the rest of my life—if I live that long—but is that what I want to do?—just day after day at this desk? I am thinking seriously of spending six months without writing a word.

I have finally quit smoking—for keeps, after many backslides—and I've paid for it by becoming grossly obese. I may just declare six months of nothing but golf & diet to get more or less back into shape. But what does one do with an obsession?

All joys
John

TO STANLEY EPSTEIN

Metuchen

May 14, 1979

[SE]

Dear Stan:

It's good of you to wish me a column but I am happily out of it. I become an increasingly private person and find myself wishing I had made it sooner to this bent hermitage. I never suspected I had such a taste for grubbing among dusty old footnotes, but I have; it is what I do with my days, and I am happy at [it]. Sam Johnson described himself once as "a harmless drudge"—and such have I become.

My one regret is in not having the column for sending out an S.O.S. when I get stuck. Several times in the past I have sent out a call for help and received every sort of ref. and photo-stat from readers. I still have my little weekly radio spot on National Public Radio and do send out distress calls through it, and have picked up some help. . . .

I don't think the word book will turn enough sales to buy a house in Key West—it's an expensive place—but I had a bit of luck with shares acquired by another company and with the stock I bought at 13 being taken over at 40(!). I can now manage to have a roof put on the house.

Meanwhile, the fun is where the words are. For example our word *liquid* is based on the 8000 yr. old Indo. European root *leikw-*, to leave. How's that for a mental connection?—a liquid is, at root, "that which leaves." (By flowing away? By evaporation? By being absorbed?) Language is the way an ethnic mind works. . . .

Hang in there. All best to you and to Honey.

John

TO LEWIS TURCO

Metuchen

May 16, 1979

[LT]

Dear Lew:

Book binding strikes me as a lovely hobby.* Most books today are either slighted or garish. The Franklin Mint Library did an edition of my trans. of the *Div. Com.* for $40 to subscribers only—felt leather, gold stamped, moiré end papers, page numbers in red, red ribbon place-marked: a really impressive bit of book making—but with the old stale Doré illustrations, and those from worn-out plates.

That's the world isn't it?—at least one serving of turd salad at every banquet? . . . .

Best, as always
John

*Turco's hobby.

TO GEORGE GARRETT
Metuchen
May 23, 1979
[GG]

Dear George:

By way of example I have just received a generous check from Brendan Galvin, and also in your name, for a poem called "By a Bush in Half Twilight." I find (1) That I have no least recollection of sending a poem. (2) That I don't remember and cannot find such a poem or one so titled.

What that is an example of, I'm not sure, but it begins to describe what may be a general loosening of my screws. A broker with whom I have had some confused conversations over the phone called to say he was closing out the short term trade we had been talking about and today sent me a statement showing I had netted a touch over $3000. —For what? I note that it seems to turn out well, but shouldn't I be present when I'm doing something?

At any rate, I would not have you think that I am purposefully delaying my reply to your letter and invitation: I keep finding myself out of touch with myself. Is that ominous?—or only the world recognized? I would love to make it to York Harbor and am afraid I can't until the fall. I'm snarled here for most of June. Then off to Birmingham, Alabama. Then to Chautauqua. Sometime in October I am to speak for the Boston Public Library. Then, if there is gasoline available in this world, would be a fine time. Or will you be off somewhere come Oct.? I much hope not.

I have about given up cigarettes. —Since about Feb. 20. But when does the ache stop? I have put on an enormous lot of weight by compensatory nibbling. And I still damn crave and feel lousy. Ah well.

I shall be looking forward to seeing *Poultry*.* (How else will I know what I sent there?) Aside from the fine and useful check, Galvin won my heart by saying nice things about *Lives of X*. . . .

Ever
John

*A journal of poetic parody and satire.

TO JOHN FREDERICK NIMS

Metuchen
*June 24, 1979**
[IU]

Dear John:

I am pleased to hear things go well with you and with *Ye Po Biz Gazette*. I shall look for Shapiro's *Creative Glut*. Karl always has a warp, and some of it always distorts into a truth.

I'll try to find something to proseate for you, and some poems for the fall. Right now I can't promise. I have become an obsessive wordnapper, lost in felonious footnotery as to secret drinking. I suppose a binge of that sort of thing is all right, but this may be on the way to becoming not only a ruling but a blinding passion. Vol. I is at Harper & Row being done to whatever gets it into process, and instead of letting up, I am something like a third of the way into Vol. II. It's beautiful stuff, but I keep telling myself I need to moderate—and don't.

I haven't even worked on a number of poems that stand by being snubbed. I don't mean to snub them. I get up, gamble my life on a cup of coffee and the *Times*, a word pops up, I start hunting it to the ground, and the next thing I know Judith is asking if I mean to slop through supper still in pajamas.

Well, I guess it's better than oppressing the poor.

Or is it? I started out poor and oppressed, slaving away at every 10¢ an hour cockroach job but telling myself I'd get mine when the time came. Well the time came; I'm rich by every former standard I lived by—and THERE ARE NO GODDAMN POOR LEFT TO OPPRESS: they're all insured and underwritten. What the hell ever happened to feudalism! I want to revise Emma Lazarus and recarve it: WHERE ARE YR GD POOR, WORLD?

I'm off to Alabam, briefly, then the Chautauqua longly. As we say on Eternal City CB:

c-i-v bonus amicus
or do you prefer *centum quattuor*
anyhow 10-4 good buddy.

[John]

*It's my birthday. Loving family has just sung
Happy Birthday to thee
Now you're 63
We're rehearsing the cho-ir
To sing R.I.P.

TO MILLER WILLIAMS

Metuchen
October ?, 1979
[MW]

Dear Miller:

. . . . I have become some sort of immoderate recluse. No matter what else I should be doing, I find myself starting every day with etymologizing, then looking up to find the day is gone. I am well on to vol. 2 of *The Browser's Dictionary* (it is scheduled for Aug. 1980 by Harper and Row). I love the work obsessively and am at the same time afraid it is consuming me. Sanity says I should ration my hours more wisely, but obsession wins.

E.g.: Indo-European *ni-*, down (nether); IE *sed,* sit (sedan, sedentary) later IE compound root *nizde-, sit-down* (place), with ref. to birds (place where the bird sits). [This became] L. *nidus,* H. *nido,* Fr. *nide,* nest, and Eng. *nide,* a brood of pheasants (the hatch from one nest). But where the bird sits it shits, whereby the rites of spring leave a beshat and stinking summer artifact. This birdy fact [was] noted by the Teutons as *nist-ak* (prob. form) [which became] Du. *nestich* and Old English, *nastig,* befouled and stinking, [which became our word] *nasty.* —Ah beautiful language: how am I to stop panning when the nuggets keep popping up?

And yet I must limit it. I am about decided to leave all the etymology stuff at home when I go to Fla. and give my time to a rigidly edited Selected Poems. Since I can't be moderate, let me chase one obsession at a time.

The new house proceeds slowly but well. And it has a guest room. What hope of luring you and Jordan for a visit to the sun, and some gorging on the world's best shrimp? . . . . .

A while ago Benn said of one of his friends (he could have said it of them all) *he's out of his furrow.* Without knowing it, he had recoined the exact root sense of L. *delirare,* to rant and rave (delirious), which is at root *lira,* furrow; prefixed *de-,* out of. It never ends. And never grows dull.

In some de-liration, but with love, and to Jordan

John

TO GEORGE GARRETT

Metuchen

November 1, 1979

[GG]

Dear George:

What a pleasure it is to launch my new Excalibur pen with a letter to you. It fits the hand generously and the ink flows onto the paper—

how shall I say?—affably. Which will do for describing George Garrett, affably generous of mind (which is also to say thanks for the list of reviewers which I shall transmit at once to Norton).

I have just returned from Toronto and a generalized fiasco. There is an arts organization there called Harbor Front, that proposed a great Canadian book launching for *For Instance.* Moved by the thought of selling millions of books to thousands of Canadians, I agreed to go for $200 U.S. + expenses. I must say I was put up in an excellent hotel, wined and dined choicely, squired around to radio, TV, and magazine interviews. Then came the reading and 26 people showed up. That's known as fit audience though few. Yet the book is officially launched, and I am assured it has already sold more than 3 copies in Canada alone. The mole hill labored and produced a mite. But I must say my ghost trod a real red carpet up to no throne.

There was more exciting news as I finished reading your letter and practiced curlicues with this great pen. The phone rang and some gent from U. Minn-Duluth asked if I would go there for the next fall quarter. He had phoned earlier to ask if I was willing to be considered, and called back to say the committee wanted me. The offer is generous ($15,000 for 10 weeks) and I said yes if any sort of decent housing was available. I'm to teach a course in Dante, piddle with some writing students, and give a few public prattles. But I'm damned if I'm going to put in 10 weeks in a Holiday Inn or some other closet (or among Pakistani D.P.s). I'm too old and crotchety for roughing it in the northland. I'm hoping I may find someone who is off on sabbatical and wants to rent his place. I thought at once of Joe Maiolo but can't find his address. Do you happen to have it? I suppose I can reach him c/o the university, and I will as soon as I get the promised letter from whoever it was that called. It sounds good. . . .

Coterminously,
yr worshipful and spensible* servant
John Ciardi, A.K.A., S.O.B. S.W.A.K.
and also, ever fondly
John

*The humorous opposite of indispensable.

TO MILLER WILLIAMS

Metuchen
December 21, 1979
[MW]

Dear Miller:

A happy honky honakah to you. Merry yr happies while ye may, the New Year's still a-coming. Are you going to Wash. D.C. for the poetry reception at the White House Jan 3? I think it is going to be a ludicrous brawl but Judith has insisted upon me, so while we're in DC, I am arranging to tape about 50 little word programs for National Public Radio on account of I will generally be on the run; and getting that many ready has, of course, generally screwed up my time. And ho-ho-ho. But if you're at this White House thing—which I don't recommend—that should go far to redeem the occasion.

Once in Key West I shall be swamped by galleys of *A Browser's Dictionary.* So vol. I. By now I have enough in the notebooks for vol. II and prob. III, but let it wait. Harper and Row is talking about it as if it actually means to sell a lot of copies. Hmm!

What's a good day for my visit to U Ark? My plot is to have Judith drop me in Atlanta and drive home while I fly. Suggest some days in early April and let me plot my best. . . .

A couple of reviews of *For Instance*—one in *LA Times* one in *Chi. Trib.* Favorable enough but generally pointless. Reed Whittemore says I'm the Edward G. Robinson of poetry, a tough guy who talks out of the side of his mouth. What the hell does that mean?

Kiss Jordan for me. Will hope to see you both for White House cookies.

Love
John

TO OSVALDO RAMOUS

Metuchen
December 24, 1979
[Mrs. Nevenka Ramous]

My dear Ramo[u]s:

Your letter brightened my breakfast table this morning. We have a little house in Florida and will be leaving for it soon. My typewriter is packed away, but let me confess that it makes me uneasy. It comes between me and the page. I hope my handwriting will not come between you and my friendliest good wishes and admiration.

Do you know the great California painter Rico Le Brun, now dead alas? He has a silvery black-and-white painting of two hands partly clasped in prayer and partly clenching one another in pain. Across the painting, several times repeated, is the legend "Non si puo sapere per niente."

The effect is powerful (he was dying of cancer). I respond to the painting, but I lack his sense of despair. I used up most of my desperation, still in my teens, fighting my way out of Catholicism and God. I think I used up the rest when I was in the Air Corps with what seemed to be a mathematical certainty that I could not survive. —So one eats bad food and goes out to burn to death. There is nothing to it when everyone else is doing the same thing. We always pretended we were sorry for those who died, but in some bent, secret way, we were glad. It was a sort of insane lottery, and every loser seemed to increase one's own chances.

The war over, everything began to go well. A happy marriage, children, work that gave me pleasure, and even enough money to live on well, doing only what I chose to do. At 63 my physical energies begin to fade but my mind stays eager. I do not ask it to explain itself. I count myself among the lucky ones. All I fear is a slow, lingering death. I watched my mother take six painful years to die. I wished her dead, in love and mercy. In self mercy I refuse such a death. But I still feel no sense of despair. If I am diagnosed for a terminal cancer, I shall write a letter of thanks to the universe, and kill myself. Everything must end—but why in agony?

I don't know how to make a philosophy of that. I write this letter because it gives me pleasure to speak to your mind in which I feel so much sensibility and responsiveness. I am not even sure that I am thinking. This letter is for itself and because writing it gives pleasure to my day. As one listens to music for its own sake.

As Yeats wrote:

Oh body swayed to music, o brightening glance,
How shall I tell the dancer from the dance?

There is an engagement. I am happiest when engaged. Therefore I engage. It need not come to anything—I think I have survived even ambition. It need not come to anything, because it is itself something: not much, but all there is, and therefore everything.

Let me wish you a happiest engagement in 1980.

Con affetto
John

TO OSVALDO RAMOUS

Key West
February 13, 1980
[Mrs. Nevenka Ramous]

Dear Osvaldo:

I, too, have the happy sense of having made a friend, and in that good name, let us be John and Osvaldo. There is so much on which our minds touch across this distance. Like you, I have survived religion. Sometimes I even dare think I understand why man invented God. I don't see how any creature evolving into our self-confusing species could have made it without that invention. The stone-age son who buried his father and then saw him again in his dreams KNEW he still lived, that there was a SOMEWHERE ELSE, that he, too, would go there in his turn, and therefore that he was a special deathless entity with reservations made for that SOMEWHERE ELSE.

He was further urged to his mistake by the great illusion of his senses, for they told him he was at the center of everything. Did not all of the universe form around him with himself as the center?

I tend to refer our sense of THE MYSTERY to the power of that illusion. My friend Stanley Burnshaw wrote a marvelous book on the esthetic experience. He conceives a human being as a puddle of sea with a skin around it, the salinity of that puddle being exactly equal to the sea's salinity when the first land creatures emerged from it. Everything in our physical organisms works to preserve the stated condition of that puddle. We shiver or sweat to control the temperature. We manufacture intricate chemicals and antibodies to fight off invading bodies. We are a system intricately honed to survival. These bodily responses are set off by hair-trigger mechanisms *that change our chemistry at need.* Emotion as well as bacterial invasion touches off these hair-triggers. Good art is one such emotion—or series of emotions. It, too, touches off those chemical responses. We are physiochemically changed by the experience of art. Emily Dickinson called it "the desirable goose flesh." "It is poetry," she said, "when it takes the top of my head off."

That *feels* mysterious—no question about it. But is there such a thing as a natural mystery? Not that I scorn the power and good of this *sense of the mysterious,* just as I don't have to believe Greek myth to be moved by it. I think I know what sort of psychodrama those gods and godlings were. They still express me, and I am pleased to be so expressed, but what I feel most is: "What a creature man is to have invented such stuff out of his own self-confused and self-illuminating net of nerves!"

That leaves me with two modes of speaking: the scientific mode, which is *is,* and the poetic, which is *as-if.* (The German *als ob.*) I write my poems in the mode of *as-if.* To a considerable extent, however, my mind is set to *is,* and I permit the *as-if* as my way of exploring the whole zoo and pantheon of shapes that keep emerging from my skin-bound puddle of awareness.

Does that make sense? Perhaps the ultimate madness is the act of trying to make sense of the human race. I think mother's milk is hallucinogenic. We suck love and nonsense together at our start, and then can't ever again tell which is which.

I have been called a cynic for saying such things. I am not. I think we are all almost absolutely unimportant. But we are still somehow one another. The little we come to is all there is—and therefore everything. In the world of *is* there is our sun. In predictable time it will flare up as a nova, as every star goes through its known evolution. When that happens the solar system will be converted to gas and what will be left to think about the mystery? or about anything?

But in *as-if* we feel, we answer to one another, we love, hate, make, destroy. I don't know what it comes to. Or I do know—it comes to nothing. But meanwhile it is a lovely *as-if.* Being able to sit here and mull these thoughts with a friend never seen yet deeply felt is at least a small miracle of feeling. It is something only this species can do, and I take pleasure in it, for I am of this species and its ways are mine.

Evil ways sometimes. In 1944–1945 I was an aerial gunner on a B-29 bomber in the business of destroying Japanese cities. Unlike my friends I thought a great deal about what our bombs were doing when they burst. It was our evil time, and that too had to be lived. I shot down Japanese pilots then: now I meet Japanese visiting professors and we are supposed to be friends, and almost are. I don't understand it emotionally: it happens. When my time comes I have my epitaph chosen: "Thank you for the experience which I lovingly did not understand." Let it be addressed: To whom it may concern.

And enough of this maunder. I am in Florida in a green paradise. The sun is bright, the day tropical, and a sea breeze blows in from Cuba, which is only 90 miles away. I think this piece of the world is beautiful. I sit in my newly built house and relish it. I like what I feel and see and I have a friend to tell about it. I think I am happy.

And now I must dig out a pile of papers and start to prepare my miserable income taxes, soon due—a misery to be survived annually. I hate bookkeeping and am bad at it and end up being fined for my mistakes. I would rather pay the fine than be serious about getting my figures right. It doesn't come to much one way or another. I have come to a good day for being alive and I wish you the same and many of them.

With all happy wishes,

Cordially,
John

TO JOHN WILLIAMS

Key West

c. February 20, 1980

[JW]

Dear John:

I set out—about four cards ago—to write something so riotously funny that the wit-isotopes would irradiate the cockles and produce restorative auntibawdies. So what's funny about being at the mercy of nurses?

I had one once whose formula was "Would you take this for me now?" "Would you roll over for me now?" When I insisted on doing it only for myself and only under protest, I got, "Now I want you to behave yourself for me now."

Now I want you to do as the nice nurse says now. Would you do that for me, now? Later the doctor will issue you a license for goosing officious bitches. If I could get to Denver I'd smuggle in a brown jug for you. Trouble is the airlines can't get me out for six months. They say all flights on all carriers out of Denver have been overbooked by nurses in panic flight. I think it's time you stopped giving the bitches stitches. Come back to Key West and be surly to Judith. I'll join in with you, and Nancy [Mrs. Williams] can keep score. I suppose a trade-off would be for me to be surly to Nancy while you are being surly to Judith. But I can't be surly to Nancy. How about being surly to one another? You will have had more practice but I have more talent. It should make a fucking fair grouse-out.

When? You escaped a ten-day rainy season (with interim sun patches), but it's all bright solar vitamins again. All is forgiven. Come home and let's go fishing.

Love
John

TO GEORGE GARRETT

Metuchen
May 14, 1980
[GG]

Dear George:

We have been marching different roads to the beat of the same drummer. Judith and I got back from S.F. just yesterday. Nice people, lousy weather, too much work, too little money. That Woodrow Wilson visiting fellowship thing is not for me. I did 2 weeks of that, then piddle lectures to cover expenses (and not much more) for a week in the Bay Area. I guess we had part of a good time. . . . .

Our great dog Dippy died in his sleep while we were away. He was 13½—ancient for a German Shepherd—and he had been limp and tired of late. But he went painlessly, from a good life and foreseen. Yet the house aches with his absence.

I'm just delighted that Harper & Row sent you the page proofs. My editor there is Frances Lindley, a great old gal. I have some hope invested in it [*A Browser's Dictionary*]. Even the hope of making some money. Yet, as with poetry, word-tracking has become obsessive upon me. The doing is its own pleasure, as *your* approval is.

We have achieved not only illiteracy but *emotional* illiteracy. Someone named Dorothy Kelso, reviewing *For Instance* in the *Patriot-Ledger* dismisses the poems as "tired and out of sorts . . . the writing stale, flat." Ferlinghetti, on the other hand, is a master of deep feeling.

I feel a dirty exultation at learning that *S.R.* is in deep trouble and likely to go under. I was fired from *S.R.* twice and it pleasures my most evil nature to know that both of the guys who fired me went under—for exactly the reasons I foresaw and could have warned them of.

It's like feeling over-cheerful. When that mood comes on me I feel inane until I read the *Times* and see that everything is just as bad as I always knew it was—whereupon I grow serene again in the knowledge that

I have not lost my mind.
I recognize our disastrous humankind
and am in command of my own wits again
to live and die in accurately. Amen.

That's the end of a poem I'm still working on. Will send it to you when I think I have it in place.

I'd love to see the Hanrahans and any of your friends. Will settle dates soonest. Jack is a sweet man. He just sent me a complete Shakespeare concordance—a blessing: I have been trying to make do with a partial. If you know of anyone with concordances to Chaucer, Spenser, and Milton I would pay a good price for them.

Is Susan into busy days? (That sounds like Marin County mellow-speak. Which isn't really my space, but lets me know where a lot of non-people come from and where they—and it—are at. —All this from 15 minutes in the mystical Jacuzzi. And this:

Said a specialty hooker named Jean
Who made the Jacuzzi her scene,
"A rub-a-dub-dub
Three men in a tub
Not only come close; they come clean."

Please assure Susan she's not where all this comes from but like the pure idiom, vibes that turned it on, which you know how I dig. But we dig her, too. And you.

Peace, man. The All
is everywhere
Love
John

TO JOHN STONE

Metuchen
July 14, 1980
[JS]

Dear John:

It's Bastille Day. More to the point, it is the day on which I received my first senior citizen discount. I have just returned from my optometrist who fitted me out with 2 new pairs of glasses at what I thought was the horrendous price of 192 bucks (!), but his nurse asked my age and when I said 64, she gave me a 20 buck discount. *Incipit vita nuova.* But let's face it, 20 bucks is 20 bucks.

In publishing, delay is the name of the game. The *Browser's Dictionary* was to have been physically in my hands by now with a pub. date in early August, but the last word is late August, and I would [not] be surprised to hear that the next word is September.

Them is good pieces you have writ, my son. I admire and honor your pleasure in doing well what would be empty without the pleasure and commitment of the doing.

I have just returned from Chautauqua. I think you would love that place. It's expensive and hard to get to, but it has everything: a lake, lectures, its own symphony under Sergiu Commissione, its own opera company, dance company, resident theater, etc. etc.

When I got back Miller had phoned to say he and Becky-Jordan had just escaped somehow from what might easily have been a killing auto-accident. I understood neither is harmed. I will phone him tonight when the rates are low. I am strongly in favor of keeping both of them.

Early in Aug. I go to DC to receive from the International Platform Association an engraved bowl designating me Poet of the Year and People's poet in the high tradition of Carl Sandburg! I am sure you have noticed that tendency in me. And there's more: the first recipient (2 years ago) was Rod McKuen. I have never been prone to follow in great footsteps. But damn Harper & Row thought it would be good publicity. And I'm anyway due in DC to do some taping for

NPR. So what the hell: a silver bowl is a silver bowl even when it's not silver.

Shine on.
John
Egregious Professor of
Applied Irrationality
(Theoretical) Ipsy Wipsy Institute.*

*So reads my certificate of appointment as attested by Fletcher Pratt, I.W.'s chancellor.

TO GEORGE GARRETT

Metuchen
August 14, 1980
[GG]

Dear George and Susan:

I hope, and by now half-expect, that Harper & Row has sent you *A Browser's Dictionary.* I hope it will pleasure your browse, for it has forced us to default on our heart's intention to visit you. There is some remote hope that the book may actually sell, and H & R has sent me a schedule of interviews and yak-shows for which I must be on call. I wind up in Chicago and Detroit Aug. 27–Sept. 5. Then Judith and I proceed n.w. for a visiting poopery at U.M.-Duluth till ± Nov. 22. We get back just in time for the kids to pluck us bare in the name of the little Christ-child, and then go off to Key West from New Year's to April.

Is there any chance that you two might fly down for a winter vacation? We have cramped sleeping quarters but vast lounging space. I held the 2 bedrooms down to closets and made the whole house a large living room opening out to patios. Come lounge if you can.

The U.M.-D. [University of Minnesota-Duluth] deal is a good one. $15,000 for the fall quarter. Would you be interested? If so, I could at least plant the suggestion and urge Joe Maiolo to cultivate it. Not all seeds sprout, but little sprouts without them. . . . .

Did I give you my ultimate note on literature in our time? A royalty statement from WW Norton reads for the 6 mos.

Divine Comedy	258 copies
Limericks, Too Gross	12,548 "

Fit proportion! *Metron ariston!*

So encouraged, Norton asked for a sequel, so I typed out another 144 limericks, and when Isaac Asimov sends in his we will have *A Grossery of Limericks, Too Gross* meanwhile going into paperback. And damned if this nonsense is not likely to *gross* (carefully chosen word) ± $40,000 for Isaac and me to split (for the 2 books). Fantastritch!

How goes your novel? Singingly, I hope. My advice is from the shelves of the *grossery:*

A writer has got to be deft
When he finds he has no money left.
    To hell with ideals.
    Can one live without meals?
Learn to toss off a *roman à cleft.*

We are desolate at the way this summer has turned out—mostly a madness, and too notably Garrettless. . . . Joy to you blessed two on your rock-bound coast. And do consider a winter loll in Key West. The lobster ain't much there but the shrimp is a joy. I am tentatively scheduled to do a week at Hollins for the Woodrow Wilson Fndtn starting Jan 18, but will be free else.

Con affetto
John

TO JOHN STONE

Metuchen
August 26, 1980
[JS]

Dear John:

I've been reading Lewis Thomas's *Lives of a Cell* & *The Medusa and the Snail* and thinking of you. You've prob. read Thomas, but if not, you must. I find he becomes a bit curt in being incisive, but also that he is impressive, and also that his writing interest has much in common with yours.*. . . .

I have been wallowing in etymology but plan to give it a rest. I have a stack of poems to work on, and I think I should go seriously to work on a *Selected Poems.*

It goes well. My knees get creakier, alas, and I just can't seem to lose weight. (How do I remove the calories from whiskey, doctor?) But I like working, at which I am forever messy, and it comes reasonably well.

I have sent off a new limerick book to Norton—a re-collaboration with Asimov to be called *A Grossery of Limericks.* I've had fun.

There once was a girl who intended
To keep herself morally splendid
    And ascend unto Glory.
    Which is not a bad story,
Except that that's not how it ended.

Or how about a personal tribute?—

A rascally doctor named Stone
Worked his dingus clear down to the bone
    Every day of his life
    Over someone's hot wife,
Leaving little or none for his own.

Well.

Joys in all and to all from all
John

*Dr. John Stone, cardiologist and poet at Emory University School of Medicine, has since taken his position alongside Lewis Thomas as a distinguished essayist. A collection of Stone's essays, *In the Country of Hearts: Journeys in the Art of Medicine,* was published by Delacorte Press in 1990.

TO JOHN STONE

Duluth

October 13, 1980

[JS]

Dear John:

I wrote to John Blades at *Chi. Tribune* asking to review your book [of poems, *In All This Rain*] in his "Book World." Saturday I got back a letter saying he had no room but would I review a crappy collection of "writings for children not for children." (Really!)

I was so pissed off I decided I wouldn't answer. The least acceptable answer is the refusal to say no when nothing else will do. Damn.

But stay you serene and assured. It is a good book, a rich one, lived, equaled, and said. The reward is in the doing. It would be nice to be mentioned in the review media, but they, alas, have been taken over by non-books and celebrity capers. I didn't much care when the *Times* did not mention *For Instance:* it broke my heart when it turned out that *Poetry* would not review it, though at least six of the poems had appeared there. *Poetry* is, somehow, home; from which it hurts to be excluded.

Could you be talked into a series of mass murders, public rapes, bombings, hijackings? Alternatively, could you sue the AMA for 46 million, and win, and set a precedent that forces all doctors to cut their fees to $2.43 plus tax for an office visit, thereby winning an appointment to the office of Surgeon General with the constitutionally directed right to castrate any son-of-a-bitch I decide should be castrated, and do it weekly on a coast-to-coast TV show that tops all other ratings? Take one or another of these courses, and I promise that your book will be widely reviewed and will become a book-of-the-clubbed-month feature between Anne Morrow Schmeerkäse and Jim Fixx. . . .

It's cold in Duluth. When it was 91 in Omaha, it was 52 here at 3:00 P.M. and 25 at 4:00 A.M. And I am overworked: I have a class every Tues. and Thurs. from 12:00 to 2:00. And I only get a lousy $750 every time I go to class. I bear up and think of being in Florida. Man was born to gum his bread in the sweat of his browse.

Do you know of a good psychiatric center? Son Benn is about to blow the business (in which we invested thousands and many of them) because he is in a black mood. . . . Ah, well. I may just have to put him on a weekly allowance for the rest of his (my) life—it would be cheaper.

Toward a happier audit, Judith is here (I flew to NJ and drove her out 2 weekends ago) and well recovered [from a car accident]. At least that clavicle is healing just as it is supposed to, and she has been able for these 2 weeks to remove the under-arm and lace-in-back neck-corset she was wearing. Even despite her periodic insubordination, she is pleasant company.

Be of good cheer. I am sorry about the *Chi-Trib.* I begin to suspect that the book will not accumulate a prominent press. For what solace there may be in the fact, it moves me to that admiration that produces Emily's desirable gooseflesh. Nor can I fail to believe that it will so move others. *Ave poeta!*

Love,
John

TO JOHN STONE

Duluth
November 2, 1980
[JS]

Dear John:

I'm grateful for your letter. I have been slow in answering it only partly because I have been racing off into Wisconsin to pick up some lecture checks. (Judith, besides, has recovered marvelously, and it gives us a chance to tour the countryscape very pleasantly.)

The real reason for delaying is that I kept pestering John Blades at *Chi. Trib.* He sent me a lousy book to review under an emergency deadline. I told him no book editor had the right to give an anthology called *Wonders* (and better titled *Blunders*) and then say he didn't have room for a notice of *In All This Rain.* So scolded, he allowed me 300 words (enclosed), which I single-spaced in the hope he wouldn't notice I had run in a few more. What can I tell you?—it's a mention. The book deserves more—including some minor scolding—but affadavit is better than none.

Just now and then you allow a few words that are not needed. You need as a coach a known sonofabitch who won't let you get away with anything, and I appoint me to the job. From time to time—whenever you have a poem you think you really want to go with (and always remembering that most poems belong in the waste basket for the simple reason that not every start arrives to its own end), you are to send the poem to me for any surplus words to be sneered at. Sneering is the essence. Friends can't do you any damn good unless they are known and certified sob's, and you know my talents. . . .

We'll be here until about Nov. 23–24, then home, then to Fla as soon after Xmas as Judith will let me go. I am sending the review to *Chi.* and John Blades with this letter, but I have no control as to when it will be printed. When Blades sends me a tear-sheet, I will fwd it. . . .

Did you know that Anton Chekhov went to medical school, though I don't think he ever practiced? For your quote file, this from a letter dtd Oct. 11, 1899:

> I firmly believe that my medical studies had a vital influence on my literary activity; they significantly widened the sphere of my observation, enriched me with knowledge whose true value to me as a writer can only be appreciated by someone who is himself a doctor. They also had a guiding role and I was probably able to avoid many mistakes through my concern with medicine.

He goes on. If you are interested in the whole passage you can find it on pp. 267–68 of Anton *Chekhov's Short Stories* edited by Ralph E. Matlaw, a WW Norton Critical Edition (paperback).

It is probably not worth much tracking down. I don't find Chekhov's reason entirely persuasive. If only another doctor can see the good of it, I doubt it's of much use to art. I think (as per enclosed) that your poems have found a far better use of medicine—or that your medicine has found a far better use of the arts in letting you feel from your own life sense that that bundle of guts bleeding into your hands is you and I. But I give you the biblio ref. in case you are keeping a scrap book on comments of this sort. Wm. Carlos Williams must have dropped many such along the way though I can't remember them—I wasn't looking for them. Besides, "He's dead, the old bastard./The dog won't have to sleep on his potatoes/to keep them from freezing."

May your dog ever tend your spuds.

Love,
John

TO JOHN STONE

Metuchen
December 13, 1980
[JS]

Dear John:

Herewith the *Chi. Trib* "Book World" offering to the shunted muse. . . . A too-little but maybe .001 better than nothing.

I write from the bottom of the well. I caught a cold driving home from Duluth. It hung on for 10 days. I then surfaced for 3 days and came down with a real viral lulu now in its 10th day. What the hell is *Amoxicillin*? If I know my local M.D., it must be the puniest of the antibiotics. Is medicine practiced outside of Atlanta? It seems to take all my energies just to manufacture the antibodies the infection feeds on. I am a festering exploded diagram of a no-output machine. Thank God for those sleeping pills you prescribed. I hadn't used any until this hit. They at least knock me out for a night's sleep, my one source of comfort, if any.

Mortality aside, I await only time and strength enough to head for Key West and the sun. Everything is reassuringly lousy, which is at least a proof of recognition.

Somewhere in the messy notebooks I have a poem about waking uneasily and inanely happy. Alarmed and insecure, I read the morning paper until I am reassured that everything is just as bad as it always was, and I grow serene again:

I have not lost my mind
I recognize our disastrous humankind
and am in control of my own wits again
to live and die in accurately. Amen.

(I said that to an interviewer from the Minneapolis *Star* and the last line came out "to live and die inaccurately." The proof is in the piddling.)

Let's start a new world with the Stones, the Williamses, and the Ciardis. The object is to vote others in only with the greatest care—and to see how long *that* takes to turn lousy.

But meanwhile,
all love from our house to your house,
John

TO GEORGE GARRETT

Metuchen
December 30, 1980
[GG]

Dear George:

Your letter is a brightness in a slow season. Whether this siege has worn me down or I am beginning to fail of my accumulated vices, my physical energy is low, my lungs pump too hard, and my joints howl hatefully. Yet there come sweet hours to every day, and now and then a poem, or part of a poem, and I feel re-realized. Praise to the end.

You shame me by knowing so much more than I do about today's poets. I am as guilty as Helen Vendler of knowing only what falls through my mail slot—which seems mostly dismal and over-acclaimed. We need a new general anthology from a perceptive editor. Miller Williams was the last to sing to me, really to sing. But who is there to read it, pay for it, buy it? What is it to honor language in a time of slurred tongues, tub thumpers, and void personages? The fact that I am a solitary drinker arms me. Poetry, like good bourbon, is an inner process.

Many thanks for the *Texas Review* and for the article on Dillard. To re-confess my guilt, he has been to me only a name I have been vaguely aware of. I look forward to meeting him.

Christmas, praise be, is down to last litter. Judith's sister flew in from Chicago and flew back today. We gasp and recover, spend tomorrow packing, and leave Dec. 31, doing New Year's Eve in Annapolis, then wheeling on.

I have been plugging away at etymologies but I am putting them by to work on a *Selected Poems* with slow reading time in Fla. At least to start. I think I was offered too many chances to publish when I lacked the character to say no. I have therefore let into print too many poems I wish could be made to disappear. I must go to work with a heavy duty pruner. . . .

Joys to the world. We failed ourselves in failing to get to see you in 1980. Let us permit no such violence to 1981.

Bless,
John

TO LEWIS TURCO

Key West
February 7, 1981
[LT]

Dear Lew:

. . . . I'm glad you will be doing Nemerov, Wilbur, and Eberhart for *Collier's*. Skirt Eberhart carefully. He can't tell his best from his worst, and in his maniacal ego he scorns anything but the Congressional Medal as an insult. A foible. His best is holy and entitles him. Shoe horn him gently into the encyclopedia. The entry will matter to him more than it would to most others, and now that he's pushing 80, anything could be a tombstone inscription. Give him your used mercies. —And I'll be happy to accept any you have left over.

Seasons of the Blood must be in NJ. The PO fwds only first class mail. I'll be looking for it when I get home.

Best in all
John

TO GEORGE GARRETT
Key West
March 14, 1981
[GG]

Dear George:

I wrote you in Maine—a letter you should be receiving by forwarding—and the next day your letter and *Luck's Shining Child* arrived. I am drowning in tax figures I *must* send to my tax man and have only had time to taste the first 15 pages. Yes, of course, it is a beautiful book, but more so the poems.

My first reaction, if I may say so, is a feeling of kinship, a way in common of joking oneself to death seriously. You have your idiom, I have mine, but it is astonishing how much our mood and feeling have in common.

In the same mail I got photostats of two poems I had given to a magazine called *Harpoon,* in far Alaska. I send them along. They feel to me very like being able to repair only one shoe at a time. Did you happen to see two poems of mine in *Poetry* for, I think, last November? And [an] earlier one called "Aprehendee Then Exited Vee-hicle?" There is, I feel, a commonality of feeling that I must certainly relish.

I had the same feeling years ago when I read some poems by Jarrell in a New Directions thing called *Three* (or *Six,* or *Some*) *New Poets.* John Holmes was with me, and I looked up after a few poems and said, "Hey, this guy is something. He feels like me!" Later we both changed and I lost my first response to his poems, but that kinship made a marvelous chime then. And so this, except that we are grooved into ourselves and won't change apart so much. Let there be always a gentle, comic spirit. . . . .

Tutte belle cose,
John

TO EDWARD KRICKEL
Metuchen
March 30, 1981
[EK]

Dear Prof. Krickel:

I have just returned from Florida to find awaiting me in the unforwarded 4th class mail your book on me. G. K. Hall mailed it on Jan. 31. It has been sitting here for two months and you may well have thought by now that my silence has been sullen. The fact is that I simply did not know the book was out. I read it at once and found myself grateful for the attention you had given the reading. Your judgments have been sympathetic and your strictures have been fair and even kindly.

I spent my (alas, interrupted) 3 mos. in Florida re-reading toward putting together a *Selected Poems.* I see I was offered too many chances to publish when I still lacked the character to say no. I have obviously published too many bad poems. I have been reading back as if to wave a wand and say, "Poof! You no longer exist." In almost every case I had already poofed most of the poems you mentioned as unsuccessful—those and many more.

The two cases I still have unsettled in my mind are "Gulls Land and Cease to Be" and the homecoming piece about "song, song, so-ong." I think of the first as a rhythmic capture I am happy about, the rhythm of the gulls and of the poem—to my ear, at least—coinciding in a way that pleases me. I must read the homecoming poem over and over to make sure. I hadn't thought of it being heavily indebted to Stevens. I thought I had echoed the sounds I heard, rendering them as I heard them. There is an easy danger there, I know. It is useful to me to have you raise the question. I must now run it through my own ear again and again until I feel sure one way or the other.

I have respected and respect your reluctance to intrude and I am grateful for it. I wish now you had checked with me on a few biographical details I might have set straight without interfering with your critical evaluations.

Johnny Holmes, son of John's first marriage to Sally, and Doris (his second wife) and Evan and Margaret (children of that second marriage) as well as John's own sister and brother (an FBI man) survive him and may be as embarrassed as I am at the suggestion that I was involved in a triangle with John. Since he was then married to Sally, one may even infer that I was bedding with her.

An unlucky misreading, alas. There was a girl and I was stunned when I lost her to an undergraduate friend, the same man (bless-damn him) who got his summa while I was out raking leaves for 25¢ an hour and had to settle for magna. But John was never involved, and certainly not Sally.

Done is done, and I can live with it, but I devoutly hope Doris Holmes never happens on the book, for she will cry in anguish, and I will be left with a possibly long (and always tiresome) job of anguish-soothing. Aside from that, any dog who chooses to gnaw on that bone will find no meat on it, and let him have it.

I think I could have been factually useful, too, in ordering the details of the HISC business and Hon. Ichord. Not only did the secretary of the committee remove eight names from the list but Rep. Patton prompted the removal by entering into the *Congressional Record* a piece titled "Apology to John Ciardi." I think that makes me the first red-smear victim to be apologized to in the *Congressional Record,* and I like to think of that fact as tombstone of Dies and McCarthy. Patton also had a piece of mine ("An American Declaration") inserted into the *Record* along with his "Apology."

These are, of course, details. A few others could have been set straight in the simplest way, but I am distressed only by the John Holmes love-triangle error. Well.

For the rest I am in your debt for a courteous and perceptive reading. It is curious that I should be scouring over the poems at the same time. I assure you that you have been more kindly than I have been in poofing so many of the poems.

Yours gratefully,
John Ciardi

TO MILLER WILLIAMS

Metuchen
April 6, 1981
[MW]

Dear Miller:

Tidings of good cheer. Yesterday Judith and I drove to NYC to have lunch with Isaac Asimov and his wife Janet-the-shrink. Quite elegant—at the Tavern on the Green—and Isaac picked up the fine, fat check. Later, downtown to visit Gil Gallagher, a grand baritone and restaurant manager, nibbling paté as we sipped champagne, and then off to dinner with opera singing (mostly poor) at splendiferous *Asti's* where Vienna Maniani, the owner, took care of the check in deference to Gil.

Dare I say *incipit vita nuova*? "Philately" is a XIX coinage on Gk. roots *philos* and *ateilein,* not taxed. I am lovingly disposed to being untaxed.

Then as a note on how we all live: I tipped the waiter $10, the musicians $5, hat check $2 and parking in 2 different places cost me $12. So my problem now is "how do I deduct $29.00 with no receipts to show for it?" Oh, my fathers, what a world thy son has come to!

In [the mail], the check for *How Does,* hardly a magnificence, was well received. And with it, from Harper and Row, for the royalty period Sept.-Dec. '80, a whopping $19,000 + (and that after deducting $7500 advance and a reserve for 1000 possibly-to-be-returned copies. Michener wouldn't be dazzled, but I like it much. Thar's unexpected gold in them thar roots.

Item: I am going to be in Little Rock Oct. 17 and on to Reno to arrive Oct. 21. The occasion is, alas, the Ark. Poetry Society and I'm being paid by Lily Peter, yr revered poet laureate. I accepted only on the absolute assumption that I could come to Fayetteville Oct. 18-19-20 to reconsecrate my soul in drunkenness. Do you have any? For a kiss from Jordan, I will promise to cook dinner. (I hope there is no truth to the rumor that she has become a chocolate liqueur junkie. I'll have to work on it further by turning up some cherry-chocolate liqueur. If that fails, there is Irish Cream liqueur, a mildly alcoholic, mildly chocolate cream-shake that has to be kept refrigerated.)

Item: I got various papers from U. Ark. but no check. Is I was forgotten by the little man in the computer? . . . .

Joys in all,
John

I would of had seen you in Chi. this weekend but for the elseness of things. I can't imagine, damn it, why John Nims dropped us from his anthol, especially considering them as he kept in. Time goes by odd counters. Or are we out of sync? Probably both.

TO VINCE CLEMENTE

Metuchen

September 2, 1981

[VC]

Dear Vince:

I have just returned from a stay on Nantucket, and a long happy summer at Chautauqua (2 weeks lecture), western Mass. (visits with Richard Wilbur and MacLeish), Maine (visit with George Garrett), Boston (to see my 3 sisters there), and so to 10 days of bad golf on Nantucket with one of my roommates of 1898.

I am more sorry than I can say that you called and I wasn't here. Even more sorry that a (serious[ly] misplaced) sense of shyness caused you to hang up. As they say in Brooklyn, "What's to be shy?" I want very much to meet you.

On Nov. 1 I start for Key West until May. Between now and then I shall be in and out on lecture trips, but I will be home part of the time. Please do not again drive through on your way to New Hope without phoning. If my luck holds, I'll be home. And in that case I beg you to stop by, at least for booze, potluck, and an overnight stay.

What can I tell you about "this Italian question"? It has never meant as much to me as it seems to have meant to others. I was born in the North End of Boston but taken to Medford as a baby. I grew up "in the country" (seven miles out). I did, of course, visit relatives in the North End frequently, but was early aware of it as a self-insulating non-America. The Italian community, as I felt from my earliest perception, was afraid of breaking out of its shell and strongly disapproved of children who gave up the ghetto patterns. I loved many of the people I visited and forgave them their narrowness, but I also knew from the start they were foolishly turned in on themselves. Are you possibly reacting to some guilty sense of breaking out of this sometimes sweet but always foolish self-enclosure?

I have experienced prejudice now and then, but my reaction was scorn of the prejudice, my ego secure in the fact that I was smarter and more able than such people. It's everyone's universe to live in, and any fool who feels superior to a person with a foreign name is sick.

I don't feel an "Italian question." *Lives of X* was not written as a confessional but as if an evolutionist wrote about single cells, blastopods, fishes, early mammalian forms, etc. Recognitions of what one has outlived. Having outlived a religion, combat, social do-gooding, politics, and even (I think) ambitions, I clutch my medicare card, estimate that I have ± 10 years to live (assuming I make it to 75) (if boozy chain-smokers do) and am left with the small and simple question, "What do I do day by day for about 10 more years?"

I hope one of the things I do is open my door and welcome you in.

Yours,
John

TO JEFFRY LOVILL

Key West
January 25, 1982
[JL]

Dear Jeff Lovill:

I am moved that you should want to and I will help as I can.* The immediate problem may be in setting up time for a visit. . . .

I do not have a volume of complete poems and don't want one. I was offered too many chances to publish before I had enough character to let me say no. That is luck of a sort, I suppose, yet it led me to publish too many poems I now wish had never seen print. Once I have *Browser's II* out of the way, I mean to sit tight and do a rigorously *Selected Poems,* more or less on the model of a painter doing a major retrospective show, assembling only those things I care to have represent me.

Krickel did me the honor of a careful reading [and] appraising. I think, justly and justly censorious. I only wish he had been willing to check the early biographical facts with me, for he guessed, sometimes to conclusions I find embarrassing. . . .

I am now a resident of Key West. I return to NJ during the summer and part of early autumn, but I often prowl the lecture circuit during those months. November 1 into May is delicious in Key West, and it is where I now live, but I should be happy to meet with you in NJ as time makes possible. Most of my books and all my papers are there. The only problem I see is to arrange time, but with some variables, there is time.

May your enthusiasm not sour in your throat.

Sympathetically,
John Ciardi

*Lovill was then beginning a Ph.D. dissertation on Ciardi and had written to introduce himself.

TO MILLER WILLIAMS

Key West
February 8, 1982
[MW]

Dear Miller:

I have initialed accordingly & herewith. It is a good affirmation to be contracted to you.*

My days are a madness. I have been typing, literally 10–12 hours a day, racing toward my deadline for *Browser's II,* always in fear that I can't make it. I should never have undertaken a second volume in 2 years. In future I shall insist on at least a 4–5 year interval, thus permitting myself the obsession but not at the damned cost of everything else—including, to my great guilt, poetry.

Speaking of poetry, I looked over my typescript of "Mutterings" and found I had mistyped the last line—of all things. Please make read:

the questions come, and one of them is the answer.

That's how I meant it, but the typewriter is an evil fiend.

Kiss Jordan for me—and for yourself, of course.

Love,
John

*In the publication by the University of Arkansas Press of the *Selected Poems.*

TO VINCE CLEMENTE

Key West
April 23, 1982
[VC]

Dear Vince:

Fifty—since you ask—is like doing the 100 in 18.9 seconds and knowing your next time will be slower. Throw away the stop watch and be glad you can still get one foot at a time off the ground. I'm lucky. My loves stay in place. . . .

MacLeish's death is a sadness. I really thought he was good for years more. Even for a hundred. He seemed so firm and full when I visited last summer. Archie was determined to tend Ada to her rest before he let go. I doubt she can survive long without him. It ends like shit. But then we always knew that. The joy is in being and loving.

I won't make it to 90. I doubt I'll make it to 80. That leaves me, maybe, 14 years to live in homage to good bourbon. That's enough for a party—if it's not rained out.

I'm glad you find in *Lives of X* what I thought I was putting into [it]. It was my most ignored book and now out of print. I plan to reprint it entire when I do my *Selected.*

I wish I could plan a visit. I'll be home for June. Off to Minn. in July. To Sarasota and Chautauqua in Aug. And to Kentucky Aug 30–Nov. 4. I'll be busy in June catching up with all I have neglected in order to finish *Browser's II.* Doubt I can make it to L.I. but I'd love you to come visit. We have lots of room.

John

TO JOHN FREDERICK NIMS

Metuchen

May 27, 1982

[IU]

Dear John:

I am delighted that you took those poems. I would especially like to have a poem in the anniversary issue, perhaps "Mutterings," of which I am especially fond, but you know what is possible and I am happy to go along.

Let's save one letter by letting me say now that I don't need to be paid. Let whatever the check would have been be a donation to *Poetry.*

I have finished and sent to Harper and Row the ms. of *A Second Browser's Dict.* It was a mistake to put it together in 2 years. I mean to take at least a leisurely five for *Browser's III,* if I live that long. But I have also written a lot of poems in that time, often because words beget words.

I also have enough poems for at least two books of children's poems. I dislike most of what the professionals write for children, but I am serious about my amateurishness. The National Council of Teachers of English has given me its 1982 award for children's poetry—a career award rather than an award for one book—and I like that. I also like running into mothers who were raised on my poems and who are now raising their children on them. Makes me feel grandfatherly (which is a Helluva sex, alas).

I'm having trouble with my goddamn legs and am going into the horsepistal for a battery of tests; flying to Atlanta on the 29th to have John Stone supervise the batteries. Never trust an M.D. that isn't a good poet. I never thought I would find myself unsteady on my stumps, but I'll hope there is some simple solution that will turn me into a long distance runner (retired).

John Stone tells me that the possum actually has an *os penis!* I am applying for a transplant and have people in Atlanta trapping the beasties for me. Hope you are the same—I mean ossified.

Excelsior,
John
Oswald P. Innis

TO JOHN STONE

Metuchen
June 4, 1982
[JS]

Dear John:

Thank you—all—for so much. I'll go to [Dr.] Cannamela about that blood sugar next week. If it is alcohol related it won't be a problem, for I haven't had a drink since that last jug you brought me and don't crave it. I *like* the stuff, but I am not addicted and have always been able to go dry with[out?] withdrawal symptoms. Cutting out about 1500 daily calories of bourbon also amounts to a diet and I should shed a lot of weight, which is all to the good.

Can one have a good time in the hospital? I think I did and I am, of course, pleased by the results. And it is always so good to visit with you and lovely Lu and your stout lads—this time with the special bonus of meeting your great mother.

It was a long day home. All the flights seemed to be headed for Kennedy or La Guardia, which is another country. But I made it and all is well. I even went to the country club and won $35.00 at gin rummy. I'm rich!

Damn! I forgot to fill that prescription for sleeping tablets. Is it legal to fill the prescription in Atlanta and mail it to me? If so, would you do so and let me send you a check for it plus postage?

I must get to work on the intro to *Browser's II,* and that should use up June. Perhaps I can even amuse myself between whiles in putting together a book of children's poems. They are all written: it is a question of deciding what to put in, in what order. . . .

Come winter, you and Lu must fly down to Key West for a good visit. I think you will find it is an experience. Everyone should visit once the most corrupt city in the U.S. But we will protect you by establishing a high moral tone.

It's a raw day and I don't think I'll go for a walk, but I got out of bed this morning (at 1:45) and jogged in place. Bit by bit I'll build up the count.

I obviously can't thank you enough for your love and tending, but let me at least say I thank you and cherish you. Now, doctor, heal thyself. If I can kick bourbon, you can kick peanut butter.

With love and thanks,
John

TO MILLER WILLIAMS

Metuchen
June 8, 1982
[MW]

Dear Miller:

That is a handsome broadside with two heavy yet graceful poems, right up to your best. Thanks and bless.

I must spend June on writing an intro to *A Second Browser's* and will be traveling until Nov. thereafter. But come Dec. and Fla. I shall have no etymology with me and all my time will go to poems.

I just returned from a 2nd visit to Atlanta. John put me through the hospital paces and the results were better than I deserve. John took me off alcohol because of a blood sugar problem. To my surprise, I don't even mind. With one thing and another I have shed almost fifty pounds. I estimate that without my normal bourbon ration [of] 9600 ± calories a week, I should slim down about 2½ lbs. a week! At the rate of 10 lbs. a month I should be a real skinny by the time we meet again in Ky.

And the lung doctor wrote: "Despite a lifetime of heavy smoking Mr. Giardi's (sic) pulmonary functions are normal with no signs of bronchial carcinoma. No treatment indicated." Plus 100% heart function. —What it is to have peasant ancestors! If cutting out alcohol brings down the blood sugar (as John Stone thinks), I may just live forever—I never did intend to go without taking it with me.

Benn's August marriage is off. I think he is well out of it, though he is, alas, depressed. So at least once to all men.

See you in KY.

Auguri d'oro
Giovanni

Tell Becky we have a date for my 100th birthday.

TO JOHN STONE

Highland Heights, Kentucky
September 8, 1982
[JS]

Dear John:

I returned from hell (so to speak)—it is scheduled from 4:00 to 6:00 P.M.—to find your letter, and welcome.* NKU is doing these lectures on videotape with intent to peddle them to Educ. TV. That's their notion, and at first I shied from it, but this is prob. the last time I will give this quickie (40 hr.) course in the *Divine Comedy*, and why not tape it? I haven't seen the tapes and don't know how they will turn out, but so far it feels medium +.

Many thanks for the prescription, which I will have filled tomorrow. I don't know why this neuralgic nuisance decided to visit after staying away for something like two years, but it seems to have packed in to stay. It used to come once in a while spoiling a night's sleep for an hour or two and feeling like a hot wire from my upper right gum, past the eye, and into the temple. Now I seem to be able to count on it every damn night, but in becoming a regular boarder, it seems to have become less intense. It also seems to linger on, at a bearable level. I am mildly aware of it right now, but can ignore it and go on. If it decides to settle into being a regular low-level nuisance, I think I can live with that without serious agonizing. Once I get the prescription filled, I will save the medication for such times as intensity stalks.

John, I'd love to keep the poem as my own signed copy, and maybe you will send me one later, but I want even more to nit-pick you about it. I don't, for example, need to be told that Sisyphus had a rock. I also feel that some of your details are better than others. And I feel that it softens out in the end. I refuse to believe either that the sea repents, or that it makes excuses. The sea is, in essence, garrulous, redundant, and palindromic (though don't you say that, because I mean to say it sometime in a poem).

Anyhow, scrub it through your attention again, if only to decide I am a damn fool.

The same mail brought from *Poetry* the galleys of 3 poems of mine that will be appearing soon. A sweet surprise: I had forgotten the poems and find, on reading them, that I like them. I don't mean I had lost them—they are in my messy pile of mss., but it was good to find them, and all set up in galleys.

Love to you (-all), Judith me-tooing,
John

*Ciardi was teaching the *Inferno* to students at Northern Kentucky University.

TO JOHN STONE

Highland Heights, Kentucky
September 19, 1982
[JS]

Dear John:

. . . . Have you had any thoughts on my dumb comments anent the poem? There are great nuggets in it, but I think you can make it solid gold.

George Garrett and Miller Williams were here at NKU for 3 days, and in addition to beating Miller at cribbage (for which I take small credit since he got drunk) we had a great 4 days. Arkie U. has invited me to do a semester there, and I have said no to $22,500, but told Miller I would do it for $25,000 (to compensate for what Ark. holds out in state taxes) plus $5000 in expenses to be free of tax deductions. He seems to think he might talk his dean into going along with that and if so I will go to Fayetteville for a fall (*not* a winter) semester. It should make for good times, but I doubt the dean will buy it. As a class, they cannot understand paying faculty more than *they* get.

My nightly head-splitter continues to visit. I can't pretend to be an expert on pain. When this is most intense it comes close to being unbearable. I guess I can manage to live with it if it comes to no more than a bad half hour to an hour nightly, with an occasional abeyance. But if anything can be done, I am prepared to go to considerable lengths to get it done. I know I would foresee a happier life without it.

Has Jimmy made the Olympic soccer team yet? He has my cheers and best wishes.

I enclose a poem for you. Love to Lu.

Love in fact from my house to your house,

John

TO MICHAEL CAPOBIANCO

Highland Heights, Kentucky
October 2, 1982
[Michael Capobianco]

Dear Prof. Capobianco:

. . . . I am deeply grateful for your comments on my Englishment of Dante. I am at NKU teaching a 40 hour TV-taped course on "How to Read Dante." Every time I rework my way through the text, my sins of translation re-glare from the page. The more comfort I find, therefore, in your commendation. Thank you.

I have given informal permission to a man in Texas who thinks he wants to make a movie of the *Divine Comedy* using my text. The permission is, in principle, a go ahead, but remains informal because I am not sure he realizes what is involved in preparing a scenario and in working out the necessary special effects. He thinks he has budget for it. I think a major studio might gulp at the possible cost. At any rate, I have given him permission to go ahead with the understanding that we will get to commercial arrangements if there should ever be a likely sign that it could be a commercial prospect. I also agreed to advise passingly, but insisted I did not have time to make a project of it. I simply do not have the energy of my younger years, and I am determined to conserve what is left to me for my poetry, for books for children that entice me, and for my obsession with etymology.

I am afraid, for the same reasons, that I could not undertake to collaborate on a dramatization. I know of nothing to keep you from attempting one on your own. I have long since had to conclude that I lack a true sense of the theatre, and would in any case not be much help on such a project. In spirit, of course, I would take pleasure in anything that might bring the master to a wider audience.

I can only suggest that you go ahead on to the really hard parts. To the bolgia of the grafters with its flying fiends (Cantos XXI–XXII), to the pageant in the Terrestrial Paradise. And to the *Paradiso* itself—can it be made visible to cameras? Special effects men can do incredible things, but this is a text to strain their resources.

Good luck. And, again, many thanks for lifting my spirits.

Sincerely,
John Ciardi

TO DAN JAFFE

Cincinnati
October 20, 1982
[DJ]

Dear Dan:

Forgive informal means. I write from the U. of Cincinnati General Hospital where I am confined for what seems to have been a mild stroke. Very mild I am happy to say and I have recovered to the point of wanting to go home. The M.D. agrees in general but wants me to stay for another day or two of his boredom—"just to be sure." Ridiculous, really. Yesterday I started to get up from a chair and my left side wasn't working. Not since hopscotch have I tried to walk with one side only.

But it was soon over. Yesterday I couldn't walk and today I can. It all comes, I suspect, from being (mildly) diabetic and from smoking too much. I have stopped drinking, alas. Must I also stop smoking, damn it? So far I haven't. But I suppose I must think about it.

Well.

George Garrett and Miller Williams were here for 4 days and they were great. Either would make a star for the Long Boat [Writers] Conference. Miller is at U. of Ark. George is currently at V.M.I. but joining the faculty at U. Michigan. He has in process a historical novel, *Elizabeth & James*. It will be out by next August. It could be a rave success. He is about to hit a big one. From what I have read of it, this book has everything.

I finish up here Nov. 5. On Oct 31 I fly to Chi. for a lecture. Almost as soon as I get home (about Nov 7–8) I must turn around and go to Chi. for *Poetry* night. Then back to N.J. and to Boston—to D.C. for the NCTE Convention (they are giving me an award for children's poetry),—to Phila. for a reading, home for Thanksgiving, then to Key West via a lecture or two *en route*. I don't see that this stroke or [?] as the M.D. calls it need slow me down seriously.

I cite all this to make it clear that I have no time before the first week in Dec. when I arrive in Key West for the blessed sun. Yes I could come up from there, preferably in the spring, and more preferably in late spring. And I'd love to return to KC. It seems reasonable to slow down; unreasonable to pull into a shell. But the publishing requirement is a stopper. I am already committed for the publication of everything I write. And damn it, I *don't want* to write another essay, nor do I want to deliver one. I'm a poet, damn it. Or I dream of being one.

And just between us, your dean notwithstanding, $1500 + expenses isn't much for 2 days *and* a piece of writing (which might well take several weeks). Which is too much time, unless I find myself caught up in it.

I'd love to, but I don't see how it can be made to work.

What can I tell you about the Conf., or any Conf.? People are drawn by *names,* even spurious names, so long as they are known. Last year NKU turned out 1,100 people to hear Alex Haley; less than 100 for William Stafford. . . .

I will come, of course. But you don't really compete with other conferences. Most pay at least $1500 + expenses, and you can guess what X, a person who doesn't know you, will think of the relative bidding, when he/she is offered more by someone else. I don't make the market. I think I report it fairly.

Best to your Dad. I like him, too. And your great family.

John

TO DEAN ELDON PARIZEK

Key West
February 18, 1983
[Dan Jaffe]

Dear Dean Parizek:

Please forgive this hand-painted field expedient. My typewriter is in the electric hospital and I am left with nostalgias for the old graceless Underwood upright that once plowed my half-acre for thirty years without a breakdown.

I am happy to confirm the terms of your letter. It will be a special occasion for me to be in Kansas City October 18, 19, and 20. My wife, née M. Judith Hostetter, taught journalism at KCU in 1946. It was there we met and married (at the Country Club Christian Church. The marriage that is. Whereby I became a certified country club Christian). She joins me in looking forward to old scenes.

As a matter of fact, KCU students were busy plotting our marriage. Many of her J students were in my writing class. Whenever there was a school affair Miss Hostetter and I were the chaperones. I saw their campaign plan, but I was conspiring toward the same end. Happy memories and a long happy thereafter.

We look forward to October for many good reasons, including the pleasure of meeting you, and of seeing Dan Jaffe again.

Yours faithfully,
John Ciardi

TO STUART WRIGHT

Metuchen
May 3, 1983
[SW]

Dear Stuart:

Judith and I pulled in last night from Key West, a weary 1400 mile drive and a long way to go to end up nowhere but in NJ. We had to push harder than happy on account of tomorrow I have to go to Rhode Island. . . .

May is a lost month. As soon as I get back from R.I., Judith and I go to KY for—of all things—a reunion of the 73rd Bomb Wing. I never thought I'd find myself backslapping the rubbed elbows of a bunch of overage killers, but this is special. My former pilot, co-pilot, and I are the three survivors of our original crew of eleven. Judith and I have met them and their lovely wives separately and cherished our visits, but we six have never been together, and probably never will again in this world. So we're going really for our own convention of six. Then back here and on to Medford, Mass., for the 45th re-union of my Tufts class. Forty-damn-five! There's no future in associating with people that old, but I have 3 sisters in Boston and haven't seen them for a year, which is part of most of the reason. And so ends May, but then home for an uninterrupted June and July, except for maybe a week in Nantucket.

It's time I got seriously to work on my *Selected Poems.* I've told my self to get at it for 3 years and keep running into a block about going over old stuff, but I must delay no longer. . . . .

Rejoicefully,
John

TO FLORENCE ORENSTEIN

Metuchen
May 20, 1983
[Peggy (Orenstein) Young]

Dear Floss:

I didn't let you know in Lexington that I was scanning Bud with micro-psycho-ladar, a new form of laser-beam EKG radar scan, but we stopped in D.C. and I took my prodspondar tapes to Central Intelligence for a symbolic profile read-out, and I'm sorry to say C.I. took a dim view. I tried to insert such categories as "mildly arrested adolescence," and "nice guy all the same," and "he really is not dangerous except to rational sequence." They would have none of that.

They were fixed on "chromatic retrogression of the palindromic epiphysts with non compos of the sequitur and concurrent syncresis of the transverse kinesthesia." I have to agree with the gist of their tergiversation, but I see no signs of danger. My suggestion is that you take anti-revulsion vitamins, grit your teeth, and keep him. If he shows signs of aberrant behavior, grit your teeth on him, and he will calm.

But not too calm, please. Without him the world might turn too rational to be bearable. And besides, we love him. And you, too. And could you really be happy if he decided to grow up?

Those were beautiful days in Lexington. Those were wonderful dorm parties. I apologize for being so pooped and early to bed. I just saw my M.D. who says my bedraggledness may be due to potassium deficiency induced by medication I have been on. May he be right! He put me on potassium tablets. If it works, I may yet turn out to be as adolescent as one who shall/should/must remain nameless.

Hope you had great visits in the East. No pictures yet, but if anything turns out will send you copies.

We love you both,
John (and Judith says "me too!")

P.S. He didn't really disgrace himself. Everyone understood and was prepared to be kind. It could happen to anyone with the same deficiency.

TO JEFFRY LOVILL

Metuchen
June 5, 1983
[JL]

Dear Jeff:

Congratulations. As Hopkins put it, "Sheer plod makes plough down sillion shine." You have polished your plow bright down the hard furrow. I hope I'm not too meagre a seed for your crop.

I wish, to begin with, I could recommend an academic connection. I resigned from Rutgers in 1961 and have had no academic connection since. It is, I gather, a buyer's market in education. I'm afraid you have taken vows of poverty.

I shall be happy, of course, to supply you with what books I can. Trouble is, there are many of them, mostly out of print. I have thought that I should put together 3 complete collections, one for each of my children, and I haven't entirely managed to do so. My first sad volume of juvenilia was *Homeward to America,* Henry Holt, 1940, and when I advertised for copies I had to pay $100 apiece. Only for the sake of completeness: I am working on a *Selected Poems* and have decided to use nothing from that first book. Which is enough said, I submit. If you really insist on planting tares, I could lend you a copy. Or perhaps I could photo-copy the pages and send those. Or perhaps you can get it on inter-library loan long enough to photo-copy. There is nothing in the book I value.

I have scattered all sorts of stuff, mostly bad and long-forgotten, in all sorts of little mags and I have kept no systematic records. One drowns in paper. Memory is the one most accessible file, though often hazy. I do not, for example, have a complete file of my columns for *SR.* I do have the file as my secretaries kept it from 1956–72, but not for the stuff I did for *World, World-SR,* and the later *SR,* the reason being that as a contributing editor I had no secretary. It is fugitive stuff in any case. I should like to imagine that I have written a handful of poems I need not blush for: that is no reason for amassing a library of incidental scribblings.

In any case, I will do what I can to turn up books for you.

That, in answer to Ques. 1. I don't quite know what to say to Ques. 2. If I knew of a major influence, I would labor to escape from it. I have never been a systematic reader but rather a ranger, skipper, and looter. I have sometimes thought I would like to sit down and read all of a given man's works, but I never have. Not even of John Donne. The poems, yes, but of the sermons, only passim. There's a law of diminishing returns.

Ques. 3. I don't think of myself as a critic. What little I have done is *descriptive criticism,* really teacher's work, to read (or so I hope) more closely than the student/reader and point out what I find on such reading. I would not think to tell poets what they do, nor to explain to them why they do it.

In answer to the second part of Ques. 3, I have too often let myself be distracted from poetry [by] side interests. I get caught up in something good enough in itself and wander off. I am confessing that my attention is not a hard gem-like flame. Most recently, I have been obsessed by etymology. I love it, but working on *Browser's I* and *Browser's II* (just published), I have sometimes felt the work takes me away from poetry. Or maybe I am only saying I have been in a slump recently and can't seem to find a poem. But that could also be because my mind is turned to other things, good in themselves, but, one must ask, are they good enough? Or am I?

Ques. 5. I have no quarrel with Merton, but he is religious in a way I am not. I am no mathematician but real math, though beyond me, glows with idea. (See Kasner and Newman, *Mathematics and the Imagination.*) Push Merton to an instance of his "living truth" and he'll kneel to the confession cup. I strained as an aerial navigator once and found something like a poem in the way stars dance down sight-lines. Once, by their light, I could have taken off from any point on earth (except for the polar regions) and found my way to any other point. That's a truth I can live by, and it glows brighter than Merton's church candles in my mind.

If you really mean to sow this crop of weeds, you will do well to realize that I am a-religious. I was born and brought up a Catholic, but by pagans who came disguised in a Catholic vocabulary. I think God and speech were the two primary inventions of my tilling ancestors, and that the inventions exist as testimonies to the nature of their inventors. By their works shall ye know them. . . . .

Enough for now. But ask away.

All best,
John

TO JOHN STONE

Metuchen
June 20, 1983
[JS]

Dear John:

. . . . . I'm told U.S. has stopped manufacture of non-electric typewriters. The age of universal illiteracy, already ascendant, becomes official at the next power black out. I have instructed my children to join whatever stone age clan takes over the telephone building: it has no windows, dead computers will make good barricades at the sally ports, and telephones fastened to cables make good maces for raiding parties. Also easy to carry through the cable tunnels.

I saw that Joyce program. A bit imposed upon by the TV-artsy but solid. Sometimes the right madman finds the right friends. How happy we are to inherit another man's destroying compulsion. We have all had a luxurious cry because Keats, for example, died young. We are, of course, delighted that he did—it saves us the trouble of doing so and allows us the emotion of it. I can't read *Finnegans Wake* and give up on it, but have otherwise been duly grateful to Joyce for the brilliance of the misery he endured for my generalized complacence.

Writing, like religion, is something to do because there is nothing to be done about who we are.

I hate culling poems for the *Selected.* No, it doesn't cost me much to X out a poem. I want a fairly tight retrospective show. Anything over 100 pages is egomania and I'll be well over that, alas. I just don't like exhumation.

I think I am feeling fair unto spryer now that Doc Cannamela has built up my K-balance. It would be too ridiculously easy to defend myself against charges of multiple aggravated rape, alas, but I am prepared to be mentally abusive.

Immediately after his last gasp Mozart was dead forever.

I don't go to Kansas City until October. The ukulele arrived in Hawaii in the mid 19th-C as trade goods and became the island passion, there named "the jumping flea" from *uku,* flea and *lele* jumping. (For your moozical edakashun.). . . .

Love to all
John

TO JOHN FREDERICK NIMS

Metuchen
June 23, 1983
[IU]

Dear John:

Beethoven festered in his locked room working on the *pastoral* [*Sinfonia pastorale?*] with trays of food mouldering untouched, his clothes filthy, his chamber pot unemptied, the score looking like the mud of a chicken run, snarling when the woman knocked. I'm not quite that messy. And would that I had such a score at the center of my wallow. But I have sunk into a doodlesome and compulsive rhythm of nothing and a table piled like a dumpster. Your earlier letter, gratefully received, is somewhere on it, which is to say lost forever. I have a typewriter but loathe it. I scrawl and throw away, scrawl and throw away, and snarl at Judith when she asks if I mean to stay in pajamas all day. What the hell's wrong with pajamas?

It is in fact a lousy mood cycle. I tried to break it by going off one night to play gin rummy. At high stakes I ended up winning $2.00, and it was even duller than this horse I seem to be riding. Nowhere. The best I seem able to do on this day is a few children's poems.

"I am home," said the turtle, as he pulled in his head,
And his feet, and his tail. "I am home and in bed."

Which doesn't quite make it.

There was a strong swimmer named Jack
Who swam ten miles out—and nine back.

So I miss by a mile. But these moods are something to ride out. It will end. This to explain and apologize. I am grateful for your letter, and one known to decency would have thanked you long since. . . .

I can see why you might want to shake the mss. of *Poetry,* but it's sad. I hate to think of strangers in the house. Ah, well, house angels in your head. I enclose some poems. I'd love to be in *Poetry* again, before a stranger slams the door forever.

As ever
John the Indecent

TO GIL GALLAGHER

Metuchen
June 27, 1983
[GG]

Dear Gil:

I have, alas, birthdayed! I, dashing dancer, dandy man, golden boy gunner, promising young poet, and Mother's darling cuddle woke to find myself trapped in this crapped-out old man's body! What am I doing here? Help! Someone get me out! It's no way to be a playboy, damn it!

I am even Chrissake sober. Haven't had a drink since half way to forever. Curiously, I don't even miss it! Never thought I'd see the day. But I've lost some weight—almost 50 lbs., and the forecast seems to be that if I stay off bourbon I won't need insulin but can make do with one villainous blue tablet a day.

And there's a bonus. I ran into the gent from the liquor store who gave me the big hello and why hadn't he seen me! When I told him I had stopped drinking, he said, "Jesus, I might as well close the store!" What I save per week will just about keep . . . Benn in walk-around money and car payments. These days it's drive-around money.

When do you(se) Pennsylvate? Nearer is more betterer. Fuck Canada.

'Ere's to flags of all nyetions!
John

TO ISAAC ASIMOV

Metuchen

July 17, 1983

[Eric Swenson]

Dear Isaac:

The infra structure of my various notebooks seems to be variously silted with limericks—at least enough for another *Grossness*—and my first thought is to hope that you are the same, as my second is fear that you have become all fire and air and hard, gem-like rays, as my third is "He should live so long."

And so may he. Are you in the mood for another lime-rickey go? I can't think of a title aside from *An Engrossment of Limericks,* which I have already used as a sub-title, but why not?

It has been long. I hope it has been well and good and that you and Janet shine on. I had about the most minor stroke one could suffer, and over it in a matter of hours, otherwise mortality proceeds with no unseemly incidents. Will you be in town in September? We'd love to see yez.

Tutti bestorum,
John

TO MILLER WILLIAMS

Metuchen

c. July 19, 1983

[MW]

Dear Miller:

I am mailing to you under separate cover a copy of *Lives of X.* I am assuming, I hope correctly, that you will have no problem in having it set from the book copy. The two "frame poems"—"The Evil Eye" and "Talking Myself to Sleep at one More Hilton"—are already in the text of the main volume and should be cut here. My thought is to place it at the back of the book.

I have tried a note or two but came up with nothing to which silence was not to be preferred. Perhaps the jacket copy might say that the poems are not strictly chronological and that *Lives of X* is reproduced entire for some reason I am not able to phrase.

I have as a possible item for the jacket a charcoal sketch by Larry Rivers that I think might be rather handsome. Trouble is that the gent who photographed the original—which is much larger—got the reduced photo too dark. I have that photo I could send to you, which could probably be lightened by whatever the process is. Or I could get some local photographer to do a new photo. What do you think?

Item: I have a contract for the book of poems I will send you once this is out of the way. I don't believe I have one for the *Selected Poems.* I could easily be very wrong: keeping track of such items is my chosen area of incompetence.

Sub item: my various contracts with Rutgers U. left all reprint rights to me. Bill Sloane did that with all his poets, as John Stone knows. I naturally like that arrangement but if it runs counter to your Press policy, I won't argue too hard, except that all of these poems are previously copyrighted and for whatever nothing that may be worth, I'd like to leave Judith and the kids free access to such driblets of reprint fees as there may be when I am down with John Brown's moldered body.

Speaking of which, Irv Klompus, that beautiful man, has undergone very tricky heart-valve god-knows-what by-pass surgery. I have phoned repeatedly, left messages on the answering service, sent a wire, and written, but heard nothing. My only news was in a confused phone call from Karl Klompus who, true to form, was not sure of the hospital address and gave me a phone number that doesn't work. They do do wonders with open-heart surgery these days and I continue to hope after more than two weeks of no answer that no news may be good news. I keep phoning Ruth at home and leaving messages on the telephone answer machine, but I gather Ruth has a room at the hospital and is staying there. Hope you are not the same. . . .

Item: The enclosed green sheet is for a dedication page.

I hope you and Jordan are well. I was heavily drag-ass for some time, just forceless and wobbly on my legs. My local MD seems to have spotted the trouble. I have a tendency to retain water in my lower legs and the MD on Key West put me on Lasix. (I read recently that Lasix is something they give racehorses! Ha!) That seemed to take care of the swelling but Lasix leaches potassium from the system and without K the muscles cannot contract properly. My man here put me on something called K-tabs to restore the balance, and I am back to being mean, surly, and vicious. When I stopped in Gainesville, I shot 9 holes of golf (with a cart) and had to quit after 7. Last week I took on powerful, wild Benn, went the whole 18 without trouble, and managed to teach him that wise old flab can still outshoot his ignorant strength. I won't confess my score in public (100 was not broken) but I beat him by 10 strokes.

The doctor also thought it would be good for my character if I quit smoking. I told him he was confusing certification and ordination, that I meant to go right on chain smoking, that I would risk the fact it might stunt my growth, and that in any case it was too damn late for me to die young. In 3 years, alas, I am going to be 70. I guess I'll be able to stand it so long as no one is tempted to confuse me with Richard Eberhart. I hope you do not live so long that you will become known as the Robert P. Tristram Coffin of the Ozarks. I only breathe that hope to make the point that there can be fates worse than death.

In your case it is all right to be mean. Jordan's offsetting influence will make you look good in spite of yourself.

Judith has just survived her 37th anniversary of being married hard. I, on the other hand, have been much less married, and that for what seems to be only a few rapturous moments. (We old bastards learn that it is wise to store up a few such sneaky formulas.) Poor baby, she tripped on the patio this afternoon, banged her ankle and knee, and split her lip so badly she had to have seven stitches inside her mouth—with probably a tooth or two to be fixed. Now she will go around saying I beat her up. I'd have a better chance against Ali. Do you know my ode to Muhammad Ali?

You are the greatest in every way
That ever began as common Clay!

(But try to mess with this boy, Bud,
You're going to find your name is mud.)

Grrr.

Tutte belle cose,
John

TO JOHN STONE
Metuchen
July 21, 1983
[JS]

Dear Dr.:

. . . . . I finally sent Miller the ms. of *Selected Poems.* About 170 pp. but we also plan to add all of *Lives of X*—which means, alas, a fat book. I did prune, goddamn it. And have invited him to prune more. But it is 40 years. A poor excuse for being boorishly long. I was hoping for 100 pp. plus *Lives of X* but couldn't get down to it, *Mea culpa.*

John Nims is about to leave *Poetry.* He is getting a free year for cud chewing. Great grass. He just took three poems of mine as a sort of last editorial error. I am sorry to see him go. I have always had a feeling for *Poetry.* It was a sort of home till Daryl Hine took over. Then for—how long was it—16 years?—I was frozen out. When John took over again, it was like a homecoming. And now what? . . . .

I actually played golf yesterday. For the first time in forever. I shot a snappy 108. I could actually get back to about 90 if I worked at [it]. But best of all I made it through the 18 without being entirely done in—with a cart of course. Then I stayed up all night typing up children's poems for Liz Gordon at Harper and Row. It's time I did another kiddy book.

Also a new limerick book for Norton, if Isaac still wants to play.

A fake crystal gazer named Bloom
Promised girls who would come to his room

He'd look into his ball
And prophesy all,
But once they were there, he'd just scroom.

John

TO ELLA (CIARDI) RUBERO

Metuchen
July 22, 1983
[ER]

Dear Ella:

Nothing but snow and ice here in N.J. My wife—I imagine you remember her—keeps neglecting dinner to go out and feed the passing caribou. I can always tell by what I get for dinner. But she is suffering protracted marriedblissus. She is about to have another anniversary and it depresses her. I was there when it all started and it really wasn't so bad then, though I confess that it was less than 25 years before I began to feel that it was aging me, too—though I haven't been as married as she. Well, that's how it is with girls. I, of course, remain a young rake, though I dutifully suppress the impulse. In fact, it gets easier and easier to do so.

I never know what to say about articles on therapy. Being healthy is a sick idea. I'd have to be crazy to become adjusted to what passes for reality. As luck would have it, I am in fact crazy, so I can make it.

No, it's a good piece. Your friend talked a guy out of some miseries he couldn't handle. There is that to be said for bad poetry. Personally, I don't want to be adjusted. It would be too much like being elected President of the Loony Bin. I'd rather be a Ciardi and howl at the moon. If only I could carry a tune!

I have been working away. I sent the manuscript of *Selected Poems* to the University of Arkansas Press. Bless them for being willing to lose money on it. Have also finished a new book of dirty limericks. Am pounding away at the manuscript of some children's poems. And have a good bulge on *Browser's III*.

My idiot son, Benn, has become an unemployed golf nut. It was a pleasure to go out with him yesterday and show him that wise old flab could still beat ignorant muscle. Hope you are the same.

It is 7:02 P.M. and Judith has not yet told me she adores me. You see how this marriage is going. On August 8 I am flying to Sarasota for some yak at a writers' conference on Longboat Key. That's right on the Gulf, and with the sea breezes, it is probably cooler than NJ. I went last year and enjoyed it. In Sept. we'll probably go to Nantucket.

Take care of yourself. After all, you are the only kid sister I have. At times I worry about your youth and folly, but all of us age after a while. In another twenty or thirty years you'll know what I mean. Worse, if you become well-adjusted. How could we recognize you? Don't ever change.

Love,
John

TO JEFFRY LOVILL

Metuchen
August 27, 1983
[JL]

Dear Jeff:

Good to hear. I have spare copies of a lot of things—not all. When it's convenient why don't you send me a list of what you need and I'll see what duplicate copies I can send you?

Ciardi is essentially unpronounceable in English. The "i" after the "C" is there to make it a soft "ch," about as in Eng. *char.* So in working English pronunciation it is two syllables: *chár dee,* as if "charlie" with a "d." In Italian the first syllable is punched rather hard and the "r" rolled, and the "d" sounded as a hard dental. I have cousins who sound it as *Sea-yárd-i* and my lace-curtain-Irish teachers in elementary school saddled me with that sounding for years, but I took my own sound back as soon as I escaped the school system.

The name is German in origin. It came south across the alps when Alboin with his allied Saxons and [the] conquered and annexed Gepidze brought his Longbeards (i Longobardi, i Lombardi) to conquer and keep northern Italy (Lombardia). The name began as *Gehrhardt* and was progessively Italianized to *Gerhardi, Cerardi, Ciardi.* In the 9th or 10th c. some Lombard lordling was given a southern fief on the mountain behind Vesuvius and one of his train, then probably *Cerardi,* was my ancestor.

There is an (especially ugly) Ciardi coat of arms, but the southern branch is a straight line of 12th sons of 15th sons, far offbreed. I don't know much about my mother's side because Di Benedictis is a church name given to foundlings. I have cousins there and have visited them. They seem quite obviously to be the Greek-sphere-colonial and local-tribal medley that once lived in Pompeii. An Italian is a Graeco-German who has been raped by everything else—and the next army to pass through.

To your questions:

1. I still plan to put 3 book collections together for my children. It won't be quite complete. There is one art-gallery folio with 16 etchings by Gabor Peterdi and I don't have, and can't afford, 3 copies. I finally got together 3 copies of my first sad little volume—*Homeward to America,* Holt 1940, at a $100 apiece. They are not worth it, but that's the dealer's tag for anyone who thinks he wants it. ATTWB—All the traffic will bear.

2. *Selected Poems* is at U. Ark Press. Miller Williams and I decided to reprint all of *Lives of X* as a sort of appendix. (I do think it was neglected.) That makes it about 300 pp. It aside, I pruned the *Selected* back to about 170 pp. That's about 4 pp. a year, about as much, and more, as anyone has any unbloated claim to.

3. I'm not much use on religion. I think of it as an adolescent imbalance I survived. My three older sisters got somewhat (only somewhat) guilt-ified by parochial schools. By the time I came along we had moved to Medford, Mass. and the Irish-trinity, a dogmatism that filled me with distaste from the start. Childhood memories persist, of course. But they also recede. Family legend insisted that I would return to God on my death bed. Why argue? I had my dying time on Saipan in '44–'45. I think I qualified as the atheist in the (aluminum) fox hole. Nights before a mission did not turn prayerful. I knew exactly what I wanted. It was a woman, a steak, and whiskey, in

a more or less blurred order. And since the USAAF was not supplying these items, I could only say, "Fuck it," and try to get some sleep.

The simple fact is that I do nothing with reference to God or an after life. I am a member of this species. I am interested in it. God and language seem to be its principal inventions, and I am interested in the inventions as clues to the inventor. Dante and the *Browser's Dictionaries* are part of one absorption in the same curiosity. Asimov says he wants to know what universe we are living in. So do I. But I don't speak mathematics and the language of science. Still, why pass through without looking?

Browser's II was published in May. *Browser's III* is in hand—it's there in a stack of notebooks, but I must still put in a convict's term at the miserable typewriter. I hate typing, probably because I am bad at it. The damned machine gets between me and anything. And here comes the computer! No matter: with any luck I'll be dead before anything serious happens.

If you are coming to NY for MLA in Dec., plan a little time in N.J. You will want to be with Debbie for Christmas, and we'll be leaving for Key West in early Jan.—as early as I can persuade Judith to migrate. But trains from Penn Sta. get to Metuchen in about 40 mins. Try to come at least overnight. If you don't insist on an early morning flight, I'll drive you to the airport. If early, I'll see you get driven.

All joys to you and Debbie, the child, and the child to be. Ours are 30-ish now, but I like to remember the crib-years, that flower time.

Yours,
John

TO STANLEY BURNSHAW

Metuchen
September 12, 1983
[UT]

Dear Stanley:

I had forgotten that interview with Edward Cifelli. I was wrong in saying Lawrence Thompson provides the footnote.* I am afraid that in just talking along, I passed on some Bread Loaf gossip, not from Larry, but attributed to him. It was careless, sloppy, and ignorant of me, and I can only apologize for having wandered mindless at that point.

I don't have a reference to "rapture of the deep." I read the phrase in a magazine about scuba diving somewhere, sometime, and remembered it because I have vaguely sensed something like it in swimming under water, space-time enchanted. I *feel* that a scuba diver, though schooled to keep track of his dials, might be carried away—tranced—by the magic light of the world X feet down. I have never scuba'd but I used to see once how deep I could dive, and then how much deeper, and there is a magic tug to it.

I liked Thompson but never felt that I knew him well. Frost had a talent for living in a reef of tangled dendrites of the people around him. I have never understood his talent for creating intricacy. At least up to c. age 80 when he seemed to mellow considerably and to mend emotional fences around him, or not so much to mend, as to tear them down. Why should a man of such talent, and of such seeming self-control, involve himself in such bitter and petty political intrigue? I don't know, and I don't think there is any way to really know Frost until that question is answered. . . . .

Warmly, as ever,
John

*Burnshaw was at this time collecting material for *Robert Frost Himself* (NY: G. Braziller, 1986) and had written Ciardi questioning his Frost recollections printed in *Frost: Centennial Essays*. See note, p. 278.

TO WALTER NEWMAN

Metuchen
September 12, 1983
[WN]

Dear Mr. Newman:

I prize a small side remark by Owen Barfield who wrote of "that old authentic thrill that binds one for life to his library." I see you have been captured by that thrill, as I have come to be, especially here at this sill into old age (if 67 qualifies and I fear, alas, that it does)—and for at least the first few shadowy feet into it. In any case I am honored, and even feel in some sense self-justified, that such a man has read me from children's poems to Dante via my text book. I bow, gratefully. I am just finishing my last reading of the edited copy of my *Selected Poems,* which I must send off to the U Ark Press in a day or two. For me, of course, it is the center. I hope it will not seem to be so much nonsense to you.

May I smile at your obvious pleasure at being mentioned in *Browser's III* (it is well under way)? I have good reason for mentioning you often, even to the point of wondering what many readers will make of a repeated, "I am indebted to Walter Newman of Sherman Oaks, CA"—a curious formula. But I am indebted, and deeply.*

Can you recommend a good book on Romany? I will look up those *NY'er* articles and Borrov's "Romano Lavo-Lil." It is a source too little known and almost entirely ignored by lexicographers.

Thank you for *dukkerin* as a likely source, via thieves' cant, of "dukes."

I am less sure of buccaneer—Boccanera, Boccanegro. You ask for an example of a group, class, trade, etc. named for its way of preparing food. I think at once of *bacon eater* as an early English term for a tenant farmer/peasant. And of course beefeater for a Yeoman of the Guard. Boucan—boucanier—buccaneer are proximate and chronologically sequential. Simon Boccanegra was centuries before and relatively unknown until Verdi popularized his name late in XIX. Nor is there any trace of buccaneer before *boucan.* For all these reasons, I doubt him as a source.

I have had no luck in running down lobster as slang for "farmer." I can see how newsmen on that shift might think of themselves keeping "farmer's hours." But *lobster shift* and *bulldog edition* still evade me. I have one vague ref. to Hearst's morning edition and how it and other morning papers fought like bulldogs for circulation, but how curious that reporters, so garrulous about the doings and sayings of others, have so little to say about their own terms.

That's a fascinating note by Bernstein on legal redundancy, and it may have some point, but I question the examples. *OED* gives both XII and XIV citations showing that sheep was used for young animal and mutton for a grown one—in one inventory sheep are valued at 8 d. and muttons at 10 d. I won't pretend to know much about legal Latin before 1066 but I am sure, by the name and nature of lawyers and other pretentious people, that it would show much the same redundancies, as in my translated diploma's "rights, privileges, and perquisites thereunto appertaining."

C. grandi—great fruit—to grapefruit is powerfully persuasive. And thanks too for the note on Tammany Young, badger (yes! yes!) the pajama game (which I should have known by analogy to *rag game* for garment industry).

Pop-goes the weasel. Fascinating. Do you happen to know what sort of hatter's tool a *weasel* was? Why would it be particularly pawnable?

I am strongly persuaded by *badger game—bajour.* All sources seem to act as if Romany never existed, alas. I must by all means touch my ignorance to some right reading here.

I used to have a superbly pedigreed German Shepherd. He died of old age at 13½—in his sleep after a good dog's life. That was five years ago and I still miss him, even to the point of considering another pup (except that I don't have the energy to keep half even with such an animal). Then my wife showed up with a tabby alley cat, a nice enough creature, but every time I pass it in this house I wonder how it dares be at ease in these precincts once sacred to my Dippy (Serendipidity)—a foolish name for a dog that made everyone think to address him as "Sir." These thoughts come to my mind when you speak of Mel Brooks posturing through the same studios that were once the demesne of Chaplin, Buster Keaton, Laurel and Hardy—and Harold Lloyd. So, among the commuters, trainsits Gloria on Monday, Sylvia Tuesday, Cynthia Wednesday, et seq.

Always a pleasure, sir. And with many thanks.

Cordially,
John Ciardi

*In the end Ciardi dedicated *Browser's III (Good Words to You: An All-New Dictionary and Native's Guide to the Unknown American Language* [NY:

Harper & Row, 1987]) to Newman: "To Walter Newman, a man of eager learning to whom I am indebted for so many insights and suggestions that rather than thank him piecemeal in note after note, I do so here in full title of respect, gratitude, and affection. Thank you, sir."

TO NANCY WILLIAMS

Metuchen

September 27, 1983

[NW]

Dear Nancy:

If you are still married to John Williams, please accept all my sympathy and all my love. Keep the sympathy for yourself, but please pass on as much of the love as you can spare. I think of him as our Peace Corps lad. (They advertise, as you will recall, "the toughest job you'll ever love." Loving him will probably do for as tough as a job can get. Yet why is it impossible not to?)

You on the other hand—(censored, but plain to see). . . .

Judith and I just got back (last night) from Boston and my high school class's 50th reunion. We had an astonishingly good time. I hardly knew what to expect, and it was much better—except for the food, and who cared?

On Oct. 9 we start a motor trip to Mo. and home at the end of the month by way of Detroit, with lecture dates in St. Louis, Kansas City, and Chicago. A needed lucrative month for my rich wife's exchequer. I applied for a job as a male prostitute but I was turned down.

When does John wind up at D[enver] U[niversity] and head down slope for a denser atmosphere? Bob P. is on at Tampa-St. Pete. Can't he get Nancy a job as Distinguished Professor and John as Gregius Emeritus of Irrationality (Theoretical)? It would class the joint. I mean it would really impact it in depth prestigewise.

And when will you head for Key West? I'd like to go at the end of

November, but don't want to be there alone, and Judith won't budge till Jan., damn it!

We love yez,
John

TO WALTER NEWMAN

Metuchen
September 30, 1983
[WN]

Dear Mr. Newman:

If I were not so greedily grateful, I would be embarrassed by your largesse. I especially thank you for the copies of pages from the history of piracy. The skull, often above or superimposed on crossed thighbones, was an ancient memento mori on tombs and is now used as a warning on toxic substances. I am trying to date its earliest (or at least an early) tomb use and am told it was in use by the 11th century (but without attestation) and I think it must have been so used earlier. I am still looking. I am also trying to run down its first use as a toxic warning, but without much evidence to date.

The *History of Piracy,* for which many thanks, testifies to a certain whimsy in these matters. The note on little known (but very successful) Captain Roberts who whimsically stitched his own figure on his flag (I assume a black one) standing on two skulls, is such a whimsy, but not quite the traditional death's head. Later, when one of his ships was followed out to sea by the *Swallow,* the pirate ship dropped overboard "her black flag" (no mention of any superimposed figures). It was Misson's whimsy to fly a *white* flag. And John Quelch favored a rather ornate anatomy (a skeleton) "with an Hourglass in one hand, and a dart in the Heart with three drops of blood proceeding from it in the other." They were fanciful murderers. But at least these instances are enough to feed the imaginations of fiction writers. I must dip into part of that bibliography on pirates to see what I can find—a good way to spend a day at the NYC library.

I have come on a number of articles by Owen Barfield here and there. To me, his memorable book is *History in English Words,* published by William B. Eerdmans Publishing Company, Grand Rapids, Michigan. A paperback reprint of a Faber & Faber Ltd. book. I found a copy in a college bookstore about 15 years ago when it was $2.65. There is an excellent brief foreword by W. H. Auden. Eerdmans Co. will not be the easiest to find, but you should have the book. Let me see if I can run down the address in *Literary Market Place.* It would be a pleasure to send you a copy.

The note on *masher* was from a torn old word book (no publication info) that cited a few Gypsy words (or purported Gypsy words). I can't finger it at the moment, but I am sure I will come on it when I am looking for something else. Moxio was from the same source.

I had missed *500 Years of New Words* by William Sherk. Must get my local bookstore to order it for me. The page you sent is enticing.

Do you know the work of Richard Chevenix Trench, 19th C. Anglican Archbishop of Dublin? He was a moralistic old poop but a fascinating early etymologist, and also the godfather of the *OED.* In 1850 he addressed the British Philological Society on the subject of a dictionary on historic principles and moved the assembled members to the ultimate paroxysm of British enthusiasm—a committee was formed. The committee became the directorate of the *OED* and 75 years later . . . the *Dictionary* was published. Etymology has gone far ahead in the last century, leaving Trench a bit behind, but not so far as one would suppose, for he was deeply learned and competent in Hebrew, Greek, Latin, Italian, Spanish, French, and German, with a smattering of other tongues. As far as I know nothing of his remains in print, but I have dug up a number of his books from dusty book store bins. I recommend him to you. Even his clerical moralizing is less offensive than quaint.

Thank you again for much. I regret your failed career as a pinch-bottom. Is it too late to start again? Mazeltov!

May I call you Walter? I have the firm sense that I have a friend in Sherman Oaks.

With warm good wishes,
John

TO VINCE CLEMENTE

Metuchen

October 7, 1983

[VC]

Dear Vince:

Judith and I are packing for a trip to Missouri, Chicago, & Detroit. This will have to be in haste. We'll be gone until the end of the month.

It is mostly a promotional trip for *Browser's II* with a whole chain of interviews, but I will be lecturing at Washington University, U of Mo.-Kansas City, a private school in Chi., and a couple of places in Detroit. To talk about money, that's a bit of $7,000 while doing other things. It is cash I am beginning to need. And I mention it only to explain why I insist on keeping my fees high for college and university appearances. I can't afford to constipate this golden egg goose by doing college appearances for $200 or $300. If word gets around, I am out of a market.

The main point is that the W[alt] W[hitman] birthplace is *off* the market. A small check is fine. If there is no check, that's fine, too. But if there is a college tie-in, I have to hold out for an absolute minimum of $1,000 as the cut-rate tie-in rate. As I mentioned earlier, that's nonsense, I'm not worth it, no one is worth it, but in [the] world as it is, I can get all the readings and lectures I want for considerably more than that, and if the world is willing to be silly that way, why should I argue?

This nonsense aside, and I repeat that it does not apply to the birthplace, I very much want to come—as to a shrine, for a visit with you and Ann, for pleasure in general, and much honored by the thought of the WW Birthplace Award. Thank you, friend. . . .

I think you can guess that I am not really qualified to talk about Whitman except to bow admiringly as a Byzantine might stand in awe of an Apache chief. He was an enormous SOMETHING of wholly another denomination and tradition, a voice and stance that has never been part of mine. Your people, moreover, will have paid more detailed attention to him than I have.

I have enjoyed extolling him, and noting necessary reservations, to sophomores. But who wants a sermon on total immersion by a renegade Buddhist charlatan? I mean let's bill the talk on poetry and let it be in the revered shadow of that great original. . . .

Despite my differences of personality, mind-set, and general adherence, I am thrilled by the idea of a WW Birthplace Award. (Incidentally I have scheduled for the December *Poetry* a small group of poems, including one about Walt Whitman posed with a (paper) butterfly on his finger. —Charles Feinberg bought a trunk that had belonged to WW and found the paper butterfly folded among old clothes and misc. mss. The poem is part of a reverie about breakfast on the patio with butterflies buzzing the morning glories. It could be an apt poem to read at the birthplace, though only incidentally about Walt. And an evidence that he is there—in the mind forever: which is the presence a true poet makes.)

Is this coherent? None of it should suggest any effort to gouge you for an appearance at the birthplace. A visit with you and Ann will be a great bonus.

Love,
John

TO IRV KLOMPUS

Metuchen
November 1, 1983
[IK]

Hey Doc:

I won't ask how business is. There's not a goddamn good thing to be said for growing old except that it beats the alternative. Wouldn't it be great if we could have put a few nights on ice to take out later for poker and getting drunk? I don't even ask for hell-raising and skirt-chasing: just an occasional saved interlude with the first fine careless rapture. You're an M.D. What good is all that course work in internal plumbing if you can't rig a few nostalgic flings? . . . . .

I have 2 more lectures to give this year. Otherwise I look forward to good days in my cave. I wish we could go to Key West, but Judith insists on staying for Xmas so I can have my annual flu. I could go down by myself, but I am miserable when I don't have her around to abuse.

Hope you are the same—without the flu (I haven't got it yet, but Dec. will not fail me, I'm sure). Count your days sweetly. We hope you and Ruth will have great lazy days in Sonoma—and leave the goddamn grass alone: buy a book on the local weeds and learn to be a collector.

Love,
John

TO JEFFRY LOVILL

Metuchen
November 3, 1983
[JL]

Dear Jeff:

I hope your grant comes through and that we may have the pleasure of seeing you. . . . We have a large old house with plenty of spare rooms and you are very welcome. It would be simple to pick you up at Newark if we haven't had feet and feet of snow, which is unlikely, though the unlikely is the commonest address these days. I hope you and Debbie are well. (Bring her if you can.) That first felt kick! What a moment that is! Joy of it! They grow up, alas, to become adolescent, and that must be suffered through. Worse, they grow up to be us, which is too often insufferable. But those first helpless years make a commitment that lasts through what follows. . . .

If you are in need of a grant project, let me suggest one that I suspect would persuade the givers of sums. It is my opinion that poetry and the audience for poetry has never been more divided into more and slighter splinter groups. When I was in school there was at least some general agreement about the senior poets and who they were. I find no such agreement about today's poets, senior or junior, but only 1000 groups proclaiming their own and ignoring all else.

Suggestion: get a copy of *Poets and Writers.* It lists—astonishingly—thousands of living U.S. poets. (Have there ever been 1000's at one time—or ever?) 1. Write to each asking that poet to list in numerical order those he considers to be the ten most important living poets. 2. Feed the responses into a computer and see how much (or how little) those lists have in common. 3. Suppose you were thinking of a representative anthology of the poets most respected by other poets—would your listings provide a basis for such an anthology? How many poets would appear on how many lists? If several thousand poets submit lists (I think about 5000 are listed), how many living poets could you expect to find listed as often as 100 times or even 50?—out of 5000 ballots? I would anticipate very little common agreement (how gladly would I be wrong!)—and that the results could be the basis for a possibly important article on the nature of our poetry scene and its endless divisions.

You may not be interested in that sort of stuff. I don't even know that you should be. It is, however, the sort of project made to order for grant money: postage funds, secretarial funds, funds for computer analysis. That sort of stuff seems to speak to the granters of funds. And such a project might just do good things for your reputation.

I am only tossing off a suggestion. Ignore it if it makes no sense to you. The data would gather itself and pass as indisputable. Your analysis of it could be the first stone of useful reputation. I am not much in touch with the foundations these days but I think the Ford and the Guggenheim people might go for it. They like machinery, and this project has the sort of machinery that could yield stuff for a telling analysis: straight from the poets' mouths.

I have just returned from 3 weeks of driving the Midwest with Judith. . . . It's good to be home after almost 3,000 miles.

Be well.

Yours,
John

TO MICHAEL CAPOBIANCO

Metuchen
November 5, 1983
[Michael Capobianco]

Dear Michael:

Forgive a delayed response. Just before your letter arrived I left with my wife for an almost month-long motor trip to St. Louis, Kansas City, Chicago, and Detroit with various way stations. We have just returned to find your letter waiting, along with a mountain of mail I begin to think I shall never clear away.

I am delighted by your commitment to Dante but hardly know what to think of it as a TV project. The pagination of this excerpt leaves me in some doubt, but my guess is that you may be headed for more hours than any TV program is going to make available by the time you have entirely gone to Hell. I confess that I also find myself asking what the TV camera adds to the simple reading of the poem. That's the boob tube we're talking about. Good actors could give a resonance to the lines—fine—but what is the camera doing while they talk?

I wonder if some simplifying device is not necessary and some method of condensation and economy. Sets are wildly expensive and the *Inf.* would require endless sets. I suggest instead a simple basic concept: Hell is not WHERE the damned are; it is WHAT they are. Doré made the *Inferno* a Gothic cellar: forget him. Could it be played simply on an open stage—a geometric space—in shades of light and darkness? I wonder if most of the setting and transition could not be done with a simple voice over. The VO could explain that Dante, the Christian soul in this earthly shadow, finds himself lost in the Dark Wood of error. (Dante: "Midway in our life's journey I went astray . . . etc.") But to know one is lost is the beginning of finding the way. As soon as he knows to what darkness he has fallen, he sees the first light of dawn. In Dante the Sun is always Divine Illumination: it is God leading the way. (Dante's vision of the Mount of Joy—and so on.)

The VO continues: at once he races toward that light—a foolish impulse. God cannot be reached the easy way any more than the sun can be reached by running up a hill. —And his way is blocked by Three Beasts who represent all the sins of this world. Worldliness drives him back into the dark, defeated and alone, and there a figure appears to him.

(A few lines of text)

Virgil explains why he has come and offers to lead him [through] the necessary, arduous journey, first to the recognition of what sin is, then to the renunciation of sin. Once so purified at the height of Purg., Virgil must leave him to Beatrice who will lead his purified soul to the vision of God.

And, from the text, Dante follows.

That's prob. stupid considering your longer involvement. But is there time in a TV sequence to deal with the Trojans, the *Aeneid,* Feltro & Feltro? I think he should be at the gate of Hell in three minutes and through it to the memorable encounters with the dead, the VO picking up the pieces of *essential* explanation for each but only what is essential for dramatic impact.

You realize, of course, that I am only guessing, suggesting, batting invisible ectoplasmic balls in total darkness.

Good luck,
John

TO MICHAEL CAPOBIANCO

Metuchen
November 25, 1983
[Michael Capobianco]

Dear Michael:

I know so little about stagecraft that my opinion can't count for much but I think the dramatic presentation would/will work. My first thoughts are of the commentary. Your commentary refers to the opportunists as "souls who in life were neither for good nor evil."

Dante says they are mixed with the original tenants of the vestibule, those angels who took sides neither with God nor Satan but waited on the sidelines to join the winner.

A Dante scholar, moreover, might quarrel with the statement that Hell was created for the rebellious angels. *They* created it. In a profound sense Hell is not *where* they are but *what* they are. Drop them anywhere and Hell would form around them as a projection of their inner condition of being, which is at the furthest distance from God.

In terms of Dante's universe, God is the circumference, earth the center. Hence the center of that center is the farthest distance. From his creation to his fall, Satan was in Heaven less than 20 minutes, for no imperfect thing can remain near God. (I pass a lot of subtle theological argument, but a basic Dante tenet was that all things are drawn inevitably to what they most are.) Satan fell from Heaven by his very nature. He struck the earth at a point antipodal to Jerusalem (obvious symbolism). That land that had first occupied the southern hemisphere fled north to escape him. The back-splash of his impact threw up the Mt. of Purgatory (and in the Terrestrial Paradise atop it man was created—on the back-splash of Satan). Satan plunged to the center—of darkness, of ultimate distance from God, of gravity (deformed weight), of cold. To that center drained all the waters of the earth. After Adam, flowing through the pits of the damned, they bring to that center the filthy residue of all sin.

Satan, beating his six wings to escape from this puddle, created (and creates forever) a freezing gale that locks him ever more securely into the ice he himself forms.

That's only part of it, but I gloss it to suggest my feeling that the commentary should be at a greater depth. Some, at least, of this, must be tied in with what Dante says of the damned at Charon's ferry: "They yearn for what they fear." Theirs is the condition of the addict who hates the habit but craves the dose. Hell awakes their eagerness because they are Hellish from inside themselves (all things tend to what they are most).

The commentary might say something, too, about the fact that Hell is reciprocal: as ye sinned, so are ye punished—which is to say the sinner lives forever in the act of reliving his sin. Structural-narratively, the punishment is an economical way of describing the nature of the sin. (Having made his point in this dramatic way, Dante is spared reams of sermonizing.)

I do not argue that a full commentary should gloss the TV presentation. What I have said here merely skates—which is on the surface. But even this skating, I submit, reveals some of Dante's complexity.

The punishment of the Opportunists, e.g., has as its point something like: opportunism is a moral filth that gives rise to moral filth.

At the bottom line I suggest that your commentator cannot trade in urbanity but must be a Dante scholar. Affable, but a nit-picker. For instance, you describe Beatrice as being in her early thirties. B. died at about age 16 (are we to assume that she has aged in Heaven? Yes, she has grown all-wise because she has looked upon—*entered*—the body and mind of God. But?)

Query: "that soul who, in his cowardice, made the Great Denial"—What will the viewer understand? I ask because there will be many such references, and you must decide as a working method, whether to avoid lines that clamor for a footnote or, alternatively, cut to the narrator to supply the footnote (or do it voice-over?). I have no answer. I only raise the question. . . .

I shall be leaving for Fla. after Christmas. I can take only so much with me. I doubt that I can keep sequential track of what you turn out, but will comment, perhaps worthlessly, as I can.

All best,
John

P.S. Nothing I said about the commentators is meant to suggest me: I can't do it. I was speaking from my general feeling that your commentary, as is, fails to suggest Dante's depths and his multiplicity. . . .

TO WALTER NEWMAN

Metuchen
December 31, 1983
[WN]

Dear Walter:

As I think I told you, I once (almost) qualified as a navigator at Selman Field, Monroe, Louisiana. At least I completed the course and received an honorable discharge to accept a commission but was called in and busted to pvt. because the Dies Committee found I had been in graduate school and signed some petitions in favor of the Spanish Loyalists, which made me a PAF or Premature Anti-Fascist (an official category stamped on my service record) and saved my life: I trained in a flight of 40+ guys, all of whom went to the 8th Air Force in England (then Curtis Le May's command). About a year later a former roommate in Naval Intelligence wrote me from D.C. to say he had checked the records and that everyone I had trained with was KIA or MIA and presumed dead. So happy New Year.

There was an odd provision on Saipan, the opposite of catch 22. Any flight crew member, officer or GI, could report to the CO and ground himself. The idea was crew-integrity. No one wanted to fly with a guy who had lost his nerve. I don't know what happened to officers—none turned himself in. At one time when it got really sweaty, two sgt./gunners turned themselves in to be busted to pvt. and put on permanent garbage detail within the squadron. What I remember most is that not one man (at least to my knowledge) ever ridiculed or shunned them. . . . I am not sure but what we envied them. I have them in mind because they popped up in a poem I am still working on—the ripe calories of revulsion from which yardbirds could inhale life while we still jammed ourselves into the necks of those flammable bottles, secretly wishing for the salvation of garbage.

That's a long way from Arcturus, Antares, Vega, and Denebe Kaitos. And in no time there was Loran in the Pacific and all the navigators forgot to look at the stars. Except that Loran had to be meticulously calibrated. When it got out of sync it produced instant monumental error. We were flying home, on the last leg from Oahu to San Francisco, when our Loran popped and the navigator got us a fix in the Aleutians. He also had no knowledge whatever of how to use an octant. The captain asked if I could help. I had forgotten all the fine points, but I got a quick latitude from Polaris, crossed it with that dummy navigator's dead reckoning, gave him a landfall heading that would hit the West Coast south of SF and told him to turn left when he raised it. Crude, but we came in. We also had to put out a raging fire on the way—the B-29 did that. But we put it out and came in on 3 engines. I may even have died of it: it was the worst I had seen in over 2 years of flying those incendiaries.

I also became a hero. We were taking back 13 ground people on rotation points and I was in charge of them in steerage. I had to check their assortment of belts for chute, Mae West, individual life rafts, etc. I guessed I could kick them out at need, but who would kick me? We feathered, shot CO_2 to the engine that was burning, then went into a long dive to blow out the rest.

I stood by the rear door watching the radar altimeter and talking to the pilot while those poor bastards held on to stanchions and began to puke. When we had dived over ten thousand feet, the last flame licked out—Whew!

The pilot called back to say the guys could relax and smoke but were to keep all their gear on. But they were trembling shit-scared. I sat in my gear and then (I am telling this out of order) remembered I had one more thing to do up forward. To get there through the tunnel I had to remove all my gear.

The next day at separation center one of the ground crew people took me aside and told me he had never seen such a brilliant act of leadership. That knowing how scared those guys were, I had had the presence of mind to remove all my gear and go forward, giving them back their peace of mind. Well hell, I told him, when you're a natural leader of men, you do things like that naturally. I could have added that you do them unthinkingly, but deprive a man of the heroes he invents and you leave him nothing but himself—a cruelty of which I am not capable. So happy New Year again. . . . .

I'm with you re the US army. At the end a Lt. Col. called me in and asked me to re-up, promising a warrant and a civilian-clothes appointment in D.C. I thought not.

And thanks for the clippings. Arthur Miller is an old though never an intimate friend. Always happy to be in his company. He was at UM a year before me. It's good to know the Gypsies are still at it. And yes, I suspect T-bird and Mad Dog are transient terms, but well worth a note in passing. Find something better in which to toast 1984, brace yourself for endless maudlin intellectualizing anent Orwell, and do not be the one for whom the bull toils, or at least stay out of the bull's toils.

And best in all,
John

TO MILLER WILLIAMS

Metuchen
January 1, 1984
[MW]

Dear Miller:

I had hoped to be at least on my way to Key West by now, but we have run into a series of snags—none of them mortal, all pestiferous—and still don't know when we can leave. No matter. Let me start the New Year right by starting it write.

I may have told you some of our plans. These days I sometimes confuse the intent to write with the act of having written. Senility.

Anyhow I have signed on to do the month of April at UM-Kansas City—a fine fat arrangement. I have some expectation of a few days in Oklahoma the first week in May. Then must turn around and be in Chicago for May 12. We'll be driving and must allow time but there should be time to pass through Fayetteville. I'll hope. . . .

A lovely thing came up. The Philadelphia Symphony wrote and asked permission to commission David del Tredici to do music for a children's Christmas presentation of my *John J Plenty & Fiddler Dan.* It is all tentative so far. I don't know that Del Tredici has accepted the commission, but there remains the possibility that come next December the Ciardis may be in Phila to hear ourselves being orchestrated. I'll be hoping that Del Tredici outdoes himself and that he makes *JJP & FD* something of a children's classic. What a lovely fate for a poem.

As usual we overdid Christmas. Judith just won't be held back, but I confess I grow a bit weary of watching $100 bills stream away like autumn leaves in a blow.

On the other hand (to quote Judith) what would we be saving them for? Damned if I know. And I got a sweater, shirt, and moccasins, none of which fit, along with a set of amplifiers that distort everything. It's the spirit that counts.

Love to all both you two and may the horn of plenty pour 1984 for you.

John

Let me know when you want the book of new poems. I haven't a title yet, but some good poems to work with.

TO WALTER NEWMAN

Key West
February 6, 1984
[WN]

Dear Walter:

. . . . Your letter moved me, even to patriotism. I have visited my cousins on the mountain behind Vesuvius. I found I loved them but it was like a visit in a time machine. They are essentially the people of Pompeii. When the mt. blows and the wind is right, they still get the ashes. They are beautiful people but stopped dead in their tracks by the ashes of history. I have a cousin there who is retired, having long been a straw-boss on the construction of the Autostrada. I swear he is a natural philosopher. Had his parents brought him to this country, he might have become a distinguished professor. And I blessed my grandfather for having pulled up his roots to find misery here, [because] in so doing, he gave us all chances we would never have known over there.

I don't know much about my uncle Alessio di Simone. He married my aunt and he was from the south (Avellino), having fled to escape military service. He died at 97—that gave him all of 80 years in this country without learning the language, but he was a sweet old bastard. It wasn't just in the north that Jews went native. Such common Italian names as Monelli (Salomonelli originally), Davido, Abramo, Bramonelli, Palestrino, etc. are Jewish in origin. Many of Jewish origin must have faded into the general culture and turned Catholic: there was no other way to own a piece of land.

But I have to be vague on that, too. My maternal grandfather's surname was di Benedictis, and that is one of the standard names given to foundlings left at the doors of monasteries and nunneries. Hence, origin unknown. Della Chiesa, di Deo, di Angelis, Esposito, Deodonata, della Donna, Del' Amore, etc., all pious names for foundlings. . . .

My tribe wasn't pursued by anything but poverty. Yours had the Cossacks on its tail. You and I are the lucky ones. I have tried to say something like this to my kids, but it bores them. I took them to Italy when they were in their teens and they decided it was "gross."

Those are fascinating enclosures. I have a feeling a lot of these terms are specialized and transient and that I should not use them as separate entries. But it looks like rich stuff to run into the notes. And thank you. . . .

Do you know the Wallace and Wallachinsky *People's Almanac?* Its research is lousy. It has an article on graffiti and runs 3 column-inches of stuff purportedly taken from a public wall, but in fact lifted from some stuff I made up for a column in *SR* years ago. I was half tempted to sue the bastards, but concluded the hell with it. They also messed up on Crapper. Ah, well.

My most interesting neighbor here is probably Philip Burton, the great old Englishman who adopted a Welsh kid named Richard and taught him to be an actor. I love to hear him talk about GB Shaw and the old London Theatre. . . .

Joys in all,
John

TO GIL GALLAGHER

Key West
February 12, 1984
[GG]

Dear Gil:

The old crock, having shuffled through a series of blah days, arises to the advertised green blaze that is Scriptural Florida, and propping one eye open against the glue of a generalized torpor, thinks to ask you to be his Valentine. You don't get much—St. Valentine, in fact, got martyred—but it is supposed to be the thought that counts.

Not that I have wasted the morning. I have had four cups of coffee, fed at least six of the cats of this compound, and worked at a poem I have been working on for some time for which I suspect my waste basket is greedy.

It is 11:53 and I hear lazy Judith stirring in the bedroom. Quickened to the point and purpose of life, I try to summon myself to the all-conquering fictions of my annual pass at the income tax. Isn't it bad enough to send them phlebotomizers my quarterly blood without having to retrace its annual circulation? I have work to do. . . .

That damn tax will kill me for weeks and I ain't got many. We leave Mar 15 for a quick trip home. Then to U. of Mo. Kansas City for a quite lush 5 weeks residence, followed by lectures in Mississippi, Okla., Ark., Chicago, and eventually home by about May 18. I hope then to get to work for a while.

It won't do much good. Reagan will still be president. And probably, alas, in '85. Judith and I had dinner with Joe Lash last night ("Franklin and Eleanor"). He argues that Mondale looks good—that he has the black and Spanish vote, which can be enough to swing some important states. Lash thinks that if Mondale can build up more blue-collar support, he might swing it. Maybe. Anything could be better, maybe even Mondale. Isn't anyone scared of our budget deficit? Hell, what's a few trillion? Who needs enemies so long as we have our own government to bankrupt us? . . . . .

If you can find the enclosed Valentine stir it to your heart's content: it's all attar of roses.

Joys,
John

TO VINCE CLEMENTE

Key West
February 20, 1984
[FC]

Dear Vince:

First things first [regarding arrangements for Ciardi to receive the Walt Whitman Birthplace Award]. When Gina graduates, her parents belong in the audience, so scratch May 26/27. May 19/20 cuts it a little close for our return from Chi, and Detroit. I would prefer 2/3 June therefore.

That's too late for the colleges, as you say, but if Louis Simpson sets the level for the local faculty, look for no enthusiasm. I know him only slightly but he has always been ill-disposed, probably as an act of superior recognition. Poets make up into a crappy club. . . .

I have typed up a selection of new poems, as you suggest. I will hope that one will seem right to you for a broadside. I will let you choose. If you find anything worth choosing.

Dick Wilbur has taken on a terrible chore. Wm. Shumann is doing music for a celebration of the *Statue of Liberty* and Dick has set out to write words for it. I would sooner try a sequence of sacred limericks saluting the flag to organ accompaniment. And that's how I feel about a squib on Whitman. Who could be further from me?—except that by being a master poet, he closes the distance. When I think back, I find him unbelievable. Yet in the moment before he exhausts me everything *is*. . . .

I have just placed a new book of children's poems with Harper and Row. We are still discussing the title. When I settle down after interim travels, I hope to finish off *Browser's III*. And put together a book of new poems for U Ark to do in maybe '85. . . . .

My best you you. Happy semesters, glorious commencements. I wish you serenities in these hours with your father. Love to Annie.

[John]

[Ciardi attached a short biographical sketch and ended it with the following anecdote.]

Yesterday in Key West was a rare day. A cormorant (really) turned up in the swimming pool in our compound. A pussy cat tried to stalk it. Fat chance: one knock of that beak would have sent it sprawling. My neighbor got frantic about shooing the cat away. The poor man is a poet. The cormorant knew it was safe from fluff. Not safe from everything, but certainly from fluff. Cormorants need a long take-off run and our compound is closed in by vegetation. The cormorant dipped in the pool, waddled out, waddled to the front gate past the cat, drew a sight line on the path under the bougainvillea, and made its take-off run, staying low till it passed under the bush, then soaring fast to clear the house beyond. "Like the Holy Ghost!" my neighbor said. "A visitation!" "Shit," I told him, "that bird is a bush pilot and knew exactly what it was doing in the most practical terms." Bush pilots do crash now and then, but first they line themselves up and fly. And they don't let themselves be drawn off their flight plan by imagining that pussy cats may turn into symbolic lions. Only poet-preachers do that.

TO WALTER NEWMAN

Key West
March 14, 1984
[WN]

Dear Walter:

I come to the end of my beach-combing, alas. Snows are still raging to the north but on the morning of the 17th we head that way, repack, and head for Kansas City where I am to be in residence at U. Mo.-KC in April. Lucratively, thank God: we need the money. Mar. 26–April 26 I'll be at

Twin Oaks Apts. #210 South
5000 Oak St.
Kansas City, Mo. 64111

I guess I can find Kansas City. Now if I can find Oak St. all is well.

I go to K.C. as fossil in residence. In Jan. 1940 I got my first teaching job at UKC (now UM-KC). UKC was then only a few years old. That makes me the last still-functioning member of the almost-first faculty. It's as if Reagan gave a party for Martin Van Buren: I'm not expected to do much and the principle holds that nothing gets well-paid. If Van Buren could only teach Reagan how to run for re-election, 'twould be worth it. But against what? . . . .

Do you know about circus clowns? I saw a Barnum & Bailey special on TV with a lady clown as narrator. She said there were three kinds—the Joeys (that, I know, is from Joey Grimaldi). Then, as I didn't know, she said hobo-clowns were called Charlies after Chaplin. And then she slurred the name of a third group unintelligibly—large verve, small pronunciation.

I think I have finally cracked the *piggy bank* after years of having the name elude me. The pig shape is by name-association. *Pig* in old Brit. dialect was a ceramic cup/bowl/mug—a beer mug. A common inn name was and is Pig and Whistle, whistle being a corruption of wassail (bowl), hence *wine.* Pig and Whistle finally signifies "beer and wine." And in earlier Brit. *pig-wife* = dealer in crockery. *Piggy bank,* I submit, must mean at root "crockery/ceramic" receptacle. It took the shape of a pig (as I am still guessing, but insistently) as the inn signs acquired a pig, by name-association.

I have been chasing this one for years. I have never found it so parsed, but I am persuaded that's it. As my son John L. (Jonnel, Jon'l), the new asst. D. A., would put it, I think I have a case. (He was with a law firm in Boston starting out—*o tempora, o mores*—at $38,000 but has taken a $20,000 cut to become an asst. D.A. That's not entirely altruism. He wants to work in the courtroom rather than the library and thinks that after a few years with the D.A. he can join another firm and get the job he wants. I think he would get me convicted if that would help his prospects. But blood is thicker than water—he has agreed to let his mother plea-bargain.) I think he is planning to sue us for malpractice with himself as the conclusive evidence. As with piggy-bank, I tell him he has a case but will have to broaden his charge to include the entire Indo-European genetic pool (and see if he can get some damages from it for us).

Do you know Shel Silverstein? He is going to drop by in a bit and Judith has prepared a mountain of *crudités.* The last time he was here he ate us out of carrots, cauliflower, broccoli, zucchini, turnip slices, and even the decorative red cabbage leaves. He is a beautiful kooky gent and a brilliant one. I know his stuff for children and have read glowing reviews of his recent venture into one-act plays (3 of them) off Broadway, but he has made a fortune from writing songs, about which I know nothing. I enjoy him.

I have a small collection of rare kooky friends. One ["Banana" George Blair] just flew in from Brazil where he had been water skiing on the Amazon. He took the red-eye special to Miami, drove the 160 miles from Miami, and just phoned that he will come by tonight after he finishes water skiing and has a nap. The guy is 69 and World Senior Barefoot Water Ski Champion—it comes before sleep. But everything happens in Key West, which was the most corrupt city in the U.S. before it seceded last year and proclaimed itself as the Conch (Conk) Republic. I shall be sorry to leave it. . . .

One local term. *Square grouper:* Bales of marijuana dumped overboard in shallow water when running from the Coast Guard. Local kids go out to haul it aboard and *they* get arrested when they come in—those whose fathers are not cops. The Pier House is our fanciest inn-restaurant. When a square grouper washed up on its beach, every bikini in town went home stuffed with pot.

And enough local nonsense.

International best wishes,
John

TO WALTER NEWMAN

Metuchen
May 22, 1984
[WN]

Dear Walter:

. . . . I am still on the road: I leave for S.C. day after tomorrow. On June 2-3 I am due for an honorification at the Whitman birthplace on L.I. It's a bit like braving the elements: I'm impressed, but what have I in common with Whitman's planetary circulation of wind belts? Then mid-June (forgive me) I'm going to Shangri La in Oklahoma to talk to Hallmark about poetry. My motives are pure: the money is good.

And I'm on the carpet. My son Benn has been selling carpets, quite successfully at a local (well, more than local) shlock outlet and has decided to go into business on his own with a partner, a rich kid he grew up with. Growing up with a rich kid somehow gave him the idea that he was one, and that I'm it. I'm committed to bankroll him to enormous wealth. He's right to the extent that he can't lose so long as he is crap shooting with my money. And it does look good: he even has the local mafia to take care of any labor problems. But if he is on the verge of becoming so rich, why do I feel so poor? Well, with any luck, I'll be safely dead before the foreclosure proceedings become final. And meanwhile what can I tell Hallmark about the name and nature of poetry?

I'm sad to hear your Daddy died.
May his will leave you satisfied.

or

> You're getting awful old—that's true—
> But it looks natural on you.

Do you think it will sell? . . . . .

Best,
John

TO WALTER NEWMAN

Metuchen
May 23, 1984
[WN]

Dear Walter:

. . . . . For breakfast I read a pamphlet of poems by Robert Francis, an old guy now, a marvelous nature poet with an eye to make God glad. He has been writing quiet, accurate, self-delighting nature poems for about 50 years—while remaining generally ignored. Maybe a press agent could have promoted him, but attention follows from extraneous things rather than poetic merit. Anne Morrow, a lousy poet, makes the B.O.M.* If I went in for chainsaw murders, people would start reading me and maybe discover I wrote a few pretty good things. But I'd rather not turn bloody—I tried that once and found I had no taste for it, even 6 miles up. It's like being an alcoholic: the drinking is for an inside craving—autotelic. And I have been egregiously lucky in getting paid well enough for doing things my own way. You can't make any money by selling poetry, but you can make them pay through the nose for explaining it, especially on the lecture circuit, on which I turn out to be an affable gasbag. Who's complaining?

The thing about would-be writers today is that they have been pampered into thinking any belch is an attempt at self-expression and that any attempt must be rewarded. It seems not to have occurred to them that one may try and fail, or that one need learn anything but masturbation. Among the poets the only prerequisite seems to be the excitation of one's own ignorance. Worse yet, a number of recognized poetic assholes—Robert Bly and Galway Kinnell, for example—encourage them in this view. The Republic, I say, has fallen. If the Russians won't take you (or if, as is likely, you can't take them), apply for Japanese citizenship—if you are prepared to learn the language and to live among a people who really did their homework when they went to school. I have whole sermons to thunder on this point, but what's the point? Someone said (and I damn myself for not being able to remember who it was): Mankind has never been capable of any folly it did not commit.

I find it too darkly persuasive, which leads me to think we are running out. Hitler would certainly have pushed the buttons had he had them. Are there none like him in sight with the buttons to hand? With the wife of Bath I will rejoice "that I have had the worlde as in me time."

Joys to yours,
John

*Book of the Month Club.

TO VINCE CLEMENTE

Metuchen
June 11, 1984
[VC]

Dear Vince:

It is typical of you not to have mentioned your collapse into St. Luke's. I suppose these preliminary tap-taps are mortality knocking on the door—I've had a few such knocks myself—but they have remained tentative, and so may yours. Two years ago, in fact, I had a stroke that blocked my left side. I was just consoling myself with the fact that there are wheel chairs and that I type mostly with my right index finger, when it passed—in about 18 hours—though the M.D.

kept me in the hospital for a few more days. The last one is always serious, but may yours be far in the future, and until then may all the rest be shrugable offable. Take care. You are a lovely man of great and simple first appetites, and may they long be yours to relish. . . .

By all means send your questions. I'll do what I can with them. And do come visit if you can, preferably after I have had a chance to mull the questions—in case there are any questions back. A piece in *American Poetry* sounds good. If they want, I can let them have a batch of poems.

One of my problems is lousy record keeping. Sometime ago I wrote a piece called "A Trente-sei for the Boat People." Yesterday (last Fri., I mean—this is Mon.) a guy I don't know wrote me a trente-sei, pointing out among other things that there is no such form as a trente-sei.* I must write him to say that by God there is now, and he just wrote (a not very good) one. But where did he see it? I have no record of having sent it out anywhere. But then I have no record. In fact I can't even find my copy in the stack of mss., though I'm sure it's somewhere in there.

A trente-sei is six six-line stanzas, the second of which begins with the second line of stanza one, the third with the third line, the fourth with the fourth line, etc. Them Eyetralian troubadors forgot to invent it, but I did because it is a natural form and because it just came out that way. I may even try it again.

The [Walt Whitman] birthplace is impressive. How on earth did time manage to freeze around it leaving it so substantially as it must have been in 1820 while everything else went weedy and modern around it? It must have been a more or less remote farmhouse. Did the land once stretch to L.I. Sound? I can see how it might have remained in place and unchanged through the 19th century. I can remember when Medford, Mass., in the early '20s had kept all sorts of early, even colonial, touches. Most houses still had a barn in the back yard. When did Paumonok become Far Hills? Being more remote, it would have been slower to change. But didn't there have to be some Whitman admirer and benefactor to preserve the place from the sort of post-war building that went on across the street?

I'd be happy to write a post-visit note but can't think of what to say. Let me turn it over in my mind. Send the questions and I'll see what I can come up with.

I won't tell you to stay happy—that seems to come natural to you (or a walk by the shore can do it)—but stay well. We are in your debt for a great visit. Come long enough to let us feed you. Love to Annie.

Yrs,
John

*Ciardi invented the form.

TO DAN JAFFE

Metuchen
June 30, 1984
[DJ]

Dear Dan:

I am saddened by the news of your father's surgery. When I last heard of him, he was being a vigorous golf nut. Now, alas, he is shedding parts. May he yet—as he vows—fool everyone. I feel more than an abstract sympathy for him. First because I have always liked him. Second because I can feel myself faltering and share his view—what the hell's the point of talking about it? I hope he is not in pain. He may be unhappy if you tell him I sent my warmest best (because he doesn't want his illness talked about), but I do send it.

And to you and Robin and the kids. I am grateful to you for those pieces you have written about me. You have given me all the best of it, of course, which is more than anyone deserves. But so much more reason to be grateful. Had you been merely just, I could claim a constitutional right. It's for the unearned overage that one must summon gratitude.

I am looking forward to Longboat [Writers Conference] and I think Judith will come with me if one or another emergency doesn't churn the sirens. May the news of your father be nothing but good. Love to you and to your happy house.

John

TO GIL GALLAGHER

Metuchen
July 9, 1984
[GG]

Dear Geel:

. . . . I have did my 68th birthday, trivial number. Social security refuses to pay me a nickel as yet on acct. of I earn more than 32¢ a month. Worse yet, I have to go on paying—almost $3,000 a year. For birthday #69 I have planned a ritual. The law reads that they (a) gotta start paying me at 70, and (b) I don't gotta pay no more. I shall spend #69 preparing 7,252½ papers to be on file for #70. Damned if I intend to miss a payment! (My information, probably wrong, alas, is that when the checks do start after so much delay, they will be for something over $1000. . . .)

Stay loose and profuse and to hell with stiff upper lips. I advocate the happily resigned cowardice of a genial decay.

Love from Olla Huss to Allan Hughes.

John

TO CORA (CIARDI) FENNESSEY

Metuchen
July 11, 1984
[Ella (Ciardi) Rubero]

Dear Sister in Bliss:

Thank you for your card. I see you must have bought it before the Angel of the Annunciation went on Astral TV to proclaim my canonization. Or don't you get the Celestial Channel in Boston? I can understand that there would be areas even God would not put up with. But whether or no, that's what that there Angel did. Heaven, it seems, got tired of waiting for the Vatican to catch up with the facts and had its own canonization ceremony presided over by St. Peter himself, and I am now entered in the official rolls as St. John the Doubtful. As the Angel explained to me that name signifies that I have been doubted but rise above it all. I have, of course, put in a good word for you. Over serious objections, may I say. I convinced the heavenly court nevertheless that you have a heart of gold.

It is now safe, therefore, for you to fly. With these credentials you could, in fact, manage without a plane, but it's a long flight to Key West, and if you just . . . flap your wings by yourself, the stewardesses won't feed you. But no matter: you can always pick off a migrating goose and roast it on the wing. You are granted all sorts of powers, as you will learn, once there is a saint in the family.

Judith still does not believe entirely in my sainthood. Alas, that faithless woman has never really believed. It rankles a bit to think that she, the Chosen One, should never have conquered her doubt, but I bear this slight with becoming humility, secure that you, my sister in bliss, will accept the truth with a whole heart.

Please do not write to the pope. Since he is first among the doubters, it is not fit that he be told what Heaven has decided. Leave him to Heaven, I say. He will have time to repent.

If, on the other hand, you know any guilty millionaires who would like me to lobby for them, I am prepared to listen to offers, though I owe it to myself to rebuff any insult in less than six figures—which will do as a retainer, though serious cases must, of course, be negotiated. As you might have guessed, there is more to sainthood than meets the eye. I would prefer, in fact, to keep most of it undercover.

Sorry I must go now to keep the commandments. There are several local mafiosi badly in need of saving grace, and I should be able to take those buggers for a bundle.

Yours in bliss,
St. J. the D.

TO JEFFRY LOVILL

Metuchen
July 21, 1984
[JL]

Dear Jeff:

We feel for you in these dark days, and for your grandmother. To bury a father is a numbing experience but at least in the life-order and one can go back to one's own children, loving them the more. To reach old age and then to have to bury a child leaves nothing. I hope you may find some comfort in trying to comfort her.

He does sound like a loving man, but really, how could he be proud of the fact that you were working on my writings? He was proud of *you,* sharing your enthusiasm for what you were doing. Teach his good to your own boys and they will have a legacy. I am only beginning to realize the importance of a father, for the fact is I lost mine so early that I can almost say I never had one. Now my kids are teaching me and I am appalled by what I begin to see. If only we could be born with a little previous experience in how to be a human being! Well, love and sadness may be about all we need. I am drained by the news that my old buddy, former co-pilot, and much loved friend, Bud Orenstein went to a party and died of a heart attack. Life is a bubble.

May yours catch the light and glow in it.

Fondly,
John

TO VINCE CLEMENTE

Metuchen
July 27, 1984
[VC]

Dear Vince:

You ask, "Why the hell must we give All of this up?" As a world-class giver-upper, I am required to explain that if a lot of other people had not given it up, it would by now be too miserably over-crowded to enjoy, but that is only the beginning of it, now that it is becoming over-crowded anyhow. It is because the giving up is what makes it precious. Don't be misled by those screwed up tales about Zeus swooping down to the daughters of the earth. Why bother when you live in all of eternity at once? If you could have it tomorrow or next year or next century or a millenium ago, there is no NOW to seize upon, no THEN to remember sadly. And nothing to look forward to. If time were not short, love would be pointless. As the Marine Sgt. was supposed to have shouted as he led his men over the top at Belleau Woods, "Come on, ya sons a bitches: ya wanna live forever?"

Yet when to the heart of man
Was it ever less than treason
To go with the drift of things,
To yield with a grace to reason
To bow and accept the end
Of a love or a season?

I may misquote a bit from fallible memory, but those lines slant a pretty good light. . . .

Love to Annie. Birds to your thickets.

Love,
John

Tomorrow is Judith's 38th anniversary. She says she is feeling old. I, of course, have been married only ten rapturous seconds, and am young and (balder) dashing.

TO ERIC SWENSON

Metuchen

September 3, 1984

[ES]

Mr. Eric P. Swenson
WW Norton
500 Fifth Avenue
NYC 10110

Dear Eric:

A pleasure to have your letter, nor am I hatefully displeased by the royalty check that arrived with it but separately.

I am delighted that Norton will issue a paperback of *Too Gross* in early '85. I know nothing about paperback distribution but it is my impression that Isaac sells especially well in paperback, and who am I to refuse a ride on his coat-tails? I have tried a time or two to nudge him toward a third volume, *An Engrossment of Limericks,* and the stuff for my half of the book has been in my files for almost a year now, wrapped up and ready to go, but he has heavy commitments for something like his next 100 books, whereby I doubt I can get him to play. Maybe a Nobel prize for his half of the paperback might change his mind. I estimate it is made to order for the Swedish Academy.

I hear what you say about the *Elements of Style** and have even fished my copy off the shelf to look at again, and to be surprised at how slight it is (I had forgotten). . . .

I can't say yes to the book you suggest, but I can't say no—not flatly. In October I am due at Northern Kentucky University for some lectures and a local gala to launch my newly published *Selected Poems* (U of Ark. Press). Miller Williams will be at the festivities and I want to discuss possibilities with him. If he will collaborate on it, I will think seriously about it. The drawback is that I am obsessive about my etymology and don't know whether I can manage it and a book on elements of good English usage.

The idea is certainly within my mental family, which is to say there is a kinship of ideas there. It is, however, a bit like sleeping with my brother's wife, thereby running the risk of making him jealous. Since I don't have a brother, I am spared a possible serious problem there. But granted a total lack of brother, I have to think of his taste as non-existent and doubt that I would like his stupid wife in the first place.

For textbook use I think a great deal of painful systematizing of details would be involved. Even if Miller says yes, I suspect it would take us something like five years to crank out a sound, not overly-technical, grammatical book on sound English (or rather American) usage. I am not being evasive but mulling possibilities. I may likely have to say no. No commitment, therefore, and none by you: I think I recognize the idea as a good publishing venture you might not want to delay. Feel free to approach someone else, therefore. If I finally decide to try for it (which I at least half-doubt I will), I really don't feel passionate about my damn non-existent brother's wife and won't be hurt if she takes up with the meter reader.

What I really wish is that you had taken on the *Browser's Dictionary.* Harper's did very well with the first one, but did nothing to promote (not advertise—promote) the second, and it has done only half as well (about 25,000). I expect to finish the third in '85 and I want some hard line advance discussion about promotion.

Well.

(H & R accepted a new book of children's poems but was so slow about it I demanded return of the ms. and have placed it with Houghton-Mifflin.)

And again, well.

All best,
John
Sr. Exec. Vice President in Charge
of Self Unemployment

*Swenson had written on August 24: "Strunk's *Elements of Style* has been around a very long time. What would you think of a Ciardi book on good writing? Probably it should be as opinionated as you'd like it to be."

TO VINCE CLEMENTE

Metuchen
September 5, 1984
[VC]

Dear Vince:

I am delighted that the *Selected* reached you. I hope Ark. sent you the hard cover edition. I am generally happy about the book but appalled by the price ($22.00!). I wouldn't pay that for it! Such book prices can only lead to inflationary ignorance! Ah for the days when slim books of poetry in hard cover were listed at $1.50 or $2.00. Even the paperback of this one is something like $8.95!

But maybe I will grow to afford me after all. Benn has kicked off his carpet outlet with a magnificent cash burst. I thought he was riding high on the big Labor Day week and weekend, a peak selling time, but damned if the predictedly flat day after Labor Day didn't keep on humming! He may have tapped a lode, and I am ready to think I may turn out to be a rich kid's father. I'll have to practice being nice to him just in case.

Thanks for the Pulitzer and other book awards. Do they still have a Pulitzer in poetry? or has it been dropped? I never much respected it. Nor have I ever much rated with prize judges. What is Robert Penn Warren's secret?—he has knocked off every prize in the book and a few I did not know were in any book. It's a talent to admire, and one I am not noted for, though I have no complaints. The world has paid me quite well for doing pretty much exactly as I wanted to do, and I think of that as a fortune. Lucky John, as you put it.

Do come. But plan to stay some longer than a flying visit. If you can't possibly stay overnight, come at least for the afternoon and an early dinner. (We'll make it early to give you time for the return trip to the East Pole—though if you stay till late won't you have a clear road and a fast trip back?) Our house is generally messy, but we have room for an overnight with no strain: there's Myra's room now that she has moved out. She has left her clutter in it for years now, but it is usable. (Why do moved-out kids think of their kid-rooms at home as a private storage dump?). . . .

Item: Do you know a good physicist on your faculty or locally? I have a question. Rhombus, from Greek *rhomos,* an equilateral parallelogram, is a geometer's borrowing from *rhombos* the boy's toy and noise maker called a bull-roarer, a slat on a string that whirrs and roars when twirled, in what is called a "magic circle."

My question is: what prompted that borrowing? I can find nothing on the shape of the slat Greek boys used to twirl. Is it possible that Greek boys shaped their whirligigs like diamonds fixing the string through the hole in one apex? Since history is mute, has physics a possible answer? Would such a diamond shape (a rhombus upright on one apex is roughly a diamond) cause a greater perturbation of the air than say a simple slat? I used to make bullroarers of a split shingle, boring a hole in the thick end for greater strength and they roared well enough. I never thought to give the thing a diamond shape. Would that shape roar louder? If there was no resemblance in shape between the toy and the geometric figure, why the geometer's borrowing? As I say, some physicist might have a clue. For the nonce I will only say that etymology leads to some fascinating questions, hein?

See you soon.

Love,
John

TO JEFFRY LOVILL

Metuchen
September 16, 1984
[JL]

Dear Jeff:

I mustn't call my son Benn a disaster area: he owes me too much money. He is also threatening to become rich in his new—and so far, thriving—carpet business. I must practice to know my place as the father of a rich son. I have already messed up this family because I had no experience of how to be a rich father, but they took care of that by making sure I should go broke. I was just adjusting, and now this. . . . .

Gale Research has accepted the autobiographical memo I wrote for their volume of such pieces. When they send me galleys, I'll make a photocopy and send it to you. I think you may find it relevant to the Telemachus thing, and also to my escape from the R.C.'s and their most recent Canadian missionary.* I am left in admiration to salute JP II as the greatest mind of the 7th Century, especially in his most recent call for renewed understanding between palefaces and redskins, especially with them redskins that got themselves renewed by scalped missionaries. To which he even adds a warning on the spiritual dangers of technology. It humbles me to realize how profoundly he makes a triumph of inanity. (I shouldn't say such things, I guess. If you happen to be Catholic and if I have offended you in this, I apologize to you, I really would like to believe in goodness. I certainly have convictions against offending friends gratuitously—or in any way.)

Yes, I shall be happy to look over drafts as you turn them out—for matters of fact only: any opinions you form are yours by right and not for me to persuade.

Joys to the flowering family,
John

P.S. Did U. of Ark. send you a copy of *Selected Poems*? I pruned hard in putting it together. Without making an absolute of it, the book may be useful to you toward defining the body of poems. If there was any poem about which I felt uneasy, I scratched it for this selection. . . .

If it is useful to you at any time, I'll try to say of any poem left out of the *Selected* why I left it out and why I wish it had never been published in the first place. I tried to be rigorous in this selection as a least civility to the reader[s], if any (two of whom may not be doomed to read [it] as Ph.D. candidates). . . .

*A reference to Pope John Paul's 1984 visit to Canada.

TO IRV AND RUTH KLOMPUS

Metuchen
September 26, 1984
[IK]

Dear Irv and Ruth:

I have just returned from a quick lecture-jaunt to N.C., dragging all the way. I have picked up a cold that won't quit—plus general debility. The local doc has me down as a diabetic—not on insulin but diabenese tablets. The medication (or maybe the diabetes) has been dragging me down to the point at which I can hardly walk. Crossing an airport has become an adventure. The doc thinks my weakness may be a side effect of medication, so we have switched to something else. If that doesn't work, I have problems and will plan to check in for a real working over.

Your letter and travel plans are especially heartening. I doubt I could reach to the South Seas. I was offered free (for lectures) a flight to Copenhagen and two weeks of the fjords and the North Sea, and sent regrets. I just don't damn think I could make it. Well. . . .

Thanks for preferring my limericks to Isaac's, but there will be no solo book: his is the name that sells, and I ride his coattails. What the hell: facts is facts. . . . Ah well, I have a new book of poems (*The Birds of Pompeii*) at U. Ark for publication in '85, and a new kids' book (*Doodle Soup*) for same at Houghton Mifflin. Must now get to work and finish *Browser's III.*

I enclose some stickers for your books—using a slightly larger paste-in than those you sent. How can you write L-O-V-E large enough on so small a sticker? —Them, anyway, is the sentiments. Happy travels and shine on.

Con affetto, sempre
John

TO STANLEY BURNSHAW

Metuchen
September 29, 1984
[UT]

Dear Stanley:

I was always deferential to Frost—and gladly so, as his due. I never knew Larry Thompson well. And remember that it was almost impossible to spend time with Frost apart from the Morrisons. I was deeply fond of them and remain so, but Kay—if I may say so strictly between us—had a mind that naturally spun intricate webs. It is quite possible that I came to see Frost in considerable part through her machinations. They were more intricate than evil—as I very much want to believe—but they may have influenced me more than I know in my views of Robert.

I was already aware that he was a literary politician in ways I found personally distasteful and that I will even believe were below me, though that is probably an arrogant thought. If I have been swayed to look for something like evil in Robert, it may have been Kay's hissing that I heard. I do believe he was self-centered—enough so, I believe, to have been a disastrous father. But I was never eager to rush to judgment. Greatness has its privileges, and my thoughts of him always began with an awareness of his greatness—the volcano. The side stinks—what they were and such as they were did not matter except in a gossipy way, and I have never been much of an auditor of gossip. Your letter makes me think that I fell to interpreting his motives as if he were Kay Morrison. Was it so I read that lollipop remark?* I believe she might have stewed it in witches' brew for a year before letting me know she had taken the hex off it. I am not sure—but please, this is between us: Kay and Ted were always dear friends, and I am not much good at this dark sifting of moods and motives. I'd rather be dead wrong than ingrate. As I would much rather receive your version of Robert than the one I have sometimes pondered, never to any conclusion, because the only conclusion that mattered—and matters—was/is the poems. He was always kind to me.

There was also Bill Sloane, whom I loved, though his spinnings extended even to poltergeists. In endless evenings of muttering semi-intelligibly over his pipe, Bill sang a litany of the evil in Frost. I never remembered anything specific Bill said—except that I had to plead for a pact with him in which he stopped asking me to believe in evil spirits because I could not do so.

I ponder your letter and think I may have been letting a lot of external buzzing color my view—the more readily in that it didn't matter to me. Whatever it took to be the man who wrote those poems is somehow self-justifying. From that thought I have never swayed, and all others are secondary. . . . .

Well. Between feeling lousy, I have been traveling and must leave again for NC. I haven't had time yet to read *Agenda,* only to glance at it and know I want to read carefully. And will. I tend, alas, to become illiterate (except for compulsories) until I get to Fla., when I can at last begin never to catch up. But I am only laggard (and pressed)—never sullen nor disinclined.

The sadness is that you should have to ask for help with a nomination into the Inst[itute of Arts and Letters]. Without ever understanding what it is, I have never liked the method of selection there. I sense some sort of deadhand inner-clique that works things in its image and I don't like the image. I have ignored the whole thing for years. And by way of confession, let me add that I have been a member for almost 30 years, was nominated once for the [more elite upper chamber, the American] Acad[emy] (by Archie [MacLeish]) and rejected. I confess to not having liked it. But hell.

It is in ourselves that we are, if at all—not out there. So at least I have endeavored to believe, and do.

I salute fondly the Stanley Burnshaw who is—in there, and in here.

John

*Once at Bread Loaf Ciardi sat with Frost through a sweetened documentary about Frost. When it was over, Frost wanted to know what Ciardi thought. He replied that he hadn't liked the film, "because Robert Frost is not a lollipop." Frost made no comment, but a year later he turned unexpectedly to Ciardi and said: "It's as you say, I'm not a lollipop!" See Edward Cifelli, "Ciardi on Frost: An Interview," in *Frost: Centennial Essays* (Jackson, MS: University Press of Mississippi, 1974), p. 480.

TO STANLEY BURNSHAW

Metuchen
October 29, 1984
[UT]

Dear Stanley:

. . . . . I am glad you will set the record straight on Frost. I always admired him and he was always kind to me. I never could straighten fact from buzz in the web works that surrounded him at B.L. and was generally confused by that buzz in my reading of motives. But never in my admiration of the poetry. I was more or less willing to believe he was a bastard with the saving grace of genius. I am much happier to think of him more kindly for that does fit better what I knew of him. I am particularly proud of the fact that he gave me a hard-bound copy of the JFK inaugural program and signed it "John from Robert. Americans par excellence." I'd like to join him in being that.

As a title, how about *Robert Frost After All*?

I think I am feeling better. My M.D. theorized that my blahs might be a side effect of my diabetes pills, so we switched to another medication about 3 weeks ago, and though I am not ready for the Olympics, I am feeling better, almost as if there really were energy in the world. In Ky. I took my host's dog for the longest walk I've had in about a year, and it felt good. En route to Key West I am checking into the Emory Hospital to be checked over by my dear friend John Stone, Prof. of Medicine and a damned fine poet. I relish the fact that in one week about 10 years ago he completed his qualification as a cardiovascular surgeon and signed a contract with Rutgers Press (Bill Sloane) for his first book of poems.

I have a third *Browser's Dictionary* in the notebooks but must sentence myself to months of typing (always hateful) in Fla. to get to a typescript. So be it.

Miller Williams told me *Selected* sold out in the first month and is going into a second edition (though when I asked the size of the edition, he said 1000 cloth and 2000 paper). That hardly makes me a best seller, but it ain't bad at that. All royalty checks are nice. Especially since my son Benn cleaned me out to start a rather fancy carpet outlet—which is doing stunningly well, thank you. Yesterday they grossed $42,000! The crazy bastard may get rich yet. . . .

Stay well, friend Stanley. I am about to take my nose-dive into busy trivia. And then the sunbelt.

All joys,
John

TO JEFFRY LOVILL

Metuchen
October 29, 1984
[JL]

Dear Jeff:

I flew out to Jackson to talk to the Wyoming Assoc. of Teachers of English and thought I might never get back. I missed my connection in Denver (for Cincinnati) and got re-routed via Dallas and Atlanta, arriving seven hours late—a big snowstorm in the Rockies. Northern Kentucky U. threw a big launching party for the *Selected.* Judith drove out to meet me there, Miller Williams, George Garrett, and John Stone flying in (bless them) to help the really quite lovely launch. Miller had the pleasant report that the first printing was already sold out and that he was going back to press. It wasn't, to be sure, a huge printing, but it's good to see a second one so soon. After a week at NKU we drove to Louisville for some lecturing at Bellarmine, then on to Lexington to visit Mac Cordray, my WW II pilot, and then home after almost 3 weeks.

To answer your first letter first, yes, I am the father of I.O. Scherzo (from Italian *io scherzo,* I'm joking). As a father of poets, I also gave birth to Gwendolyn Grew and Janice Appleby Succorsa. What power!

A few years later someone named, I believe, Grainger published a book called *An Encyclopedia of Poetry* (title?) and listed Grew, Scherzo, and Succorsa as American poets. I only meant to invent some examples of bad poetry I could talk about without hurting some dumb author's feelings—but as you see, out of kindness, I have become patriarchal. What do you say to a little poetry review featuring 25 or so really bad poets I invent? I.M. Bic. Anna Pest, Alex Andrine, I. Yawp, etc.

You ask for the name of what a doctor does when he misdiagnoses and then treats his misdiagnosis. Aside from *Common Practice* I don't have a label. *Iatrogenic* labels a disease or disorder brought on by medical treatment, i.e., doctor-induced, from Gk. *iatros,* healing.

I would love to visit U Ariz for a lecture ding, say, on Dante, on etymology, and a poetry reading, but, alas, my going price is high—or not "alas," for I like it that way. I don't want all the lecture dates in the USA—just the expensive ones. Technically, I am supposed to refer your inquiry to my lecture agent—Program Corp of America, where the bell goes off at $5000 plus expenses of which I would get three plus expenses. All I can suggest is that if it is called a Visiting Professorship, at least in all correspondence, I could argue that it is a sort of academic appointment and none of the agent's business, which leaves it at $3000 plus expenses. I am happy to leave it to attaché Jeff Lovill, but when the word "budget" starts the discussion, I become unlikely. I would yet love a visit out there, could it be worked for say a week in the Sun Belt. . . .

And so much for minor items. What I really want to say is that I have read the first chapter and I think you are off and running. That's not to say that I agree with everything you say about "overshooting the fulcrum."* The point is that the analyses are yours and that I would not think of arguing them. My only function will be to correct any errors of fact, if they occur, and critical analysis is not a matter of fact but of chosen interpretation, your choice being not subject to what mine might be.

I am more or less willing to go along with Miller Williams about "Preferably, I Suggest, a Self." But mostly because there are poems I care more about—I left that one out of the *Selected.* I am not convinced that it overruns or that it is a pleonasm. One could look out, for example, from a social conditioning, a habituated blindness, a creed, a sloganized activism (really the same thing, or much the same). The Self I mean is the artistic view, what the poem creates, the conditioned esthetic freedom, and I think I could argue that that is both a new element and a necessarily resolving one. In this case, it's not worth the argument.

In "Catalpa," however (and variously in the other poems you cite in this vein), "What should I keep if averages were all," satisfies me as a strong, epigrammatic, almost proverbial last line. I would even argue that [the] poem exists exactly to spring that last line in the right and final place. (And am happy to note that your prof comments too about that effect.) Is Chaucer's "He was a verray parfit gentil knight" an overshoot? Or Shakespeare's "And yet, by Heaven, I think my love as fair/ As any she belied by false compare"?

But all I am saying is (a) that I have a right to disagree, and (b) that you have—and must have—an unfettered freedom to advance your own case. You make it well. Congratulations on a good start. And good sailing ahead. I have about two weeks (or a bit less) in which to clean up 3 months' worth of trivial errands before I start south,* stopping for some lectures en route, planning to arrive in Key West on Dec. 1.

All best from Charley New York.

[John]

*The phrase refers to writing beyond the proper end of a poem.

TO WALTER NEWMAN

Key West
December 1, 1984
[WN]

Dear Walter:

I have finally settled into Key West in the hope of getting to work on the typescript of *Browser's III* only to find that I banged up my typewriter en route and must put off typing till it gets back from the hospital.

I look forward to some quiet time for I have been spinning since early Oct. First on a lecture tour to Wyo. and (mostly) Kentucky colleges. Then home to some bleak family problems. . . . Then south via visits to U. Va., Emory, U. Fla., and SFU. When I consider how my life is spent. I insist that the next months be primarily vegetable. . . .

By now you will have had your European junket and may it have been a flowering time. After many years on the road, I seem to have lost all desire to go abroad. My legs don't work well enough for tourist hiking. In the Denver airport in Oct. I finally gave up and got a skycap to wheelchair me 42 miles to my connecting gate. Time does not march on: it totters off. But I have set myself a painful daily walking schedule to strengthen my legs and have otherwise passed a series of medical tests fairly well. I'll make it yet a while.

I sent U. of Ark Press a new book of poems, *The Birds of Pompeii,* for publication in '85. And Houghton-Mifflin will do a new book of children's poems, *Doodle Soup.* It's my daughter Myra's book: I put the contract in her name and hope it will provide her with a small income for a while. She is using the $3,000 advance (this way I pay no taxes) to take a computer course. . . . .

Do you remember *Alfonse & Gaston?* (After you/no after you.) Partridge in his *Dict. of Catch Phrases* tries to give it a Canadian origin c. 1940. I would swear I remember Alfonse and Gaston as figures in a once popular U.S. comic strip of the 1920's, or just possibly of the early 1930's. The Key West library is no help. Have you any recollection of this comic strip? Or is my memory tricking me?

What are you working on? I'd love to hear from you.

Best in all,
John

TO WALTER NEWMAN

Key West
December 21, 1984
[WN]

Dear Walter:

Script reading is a new experience—and idiom—for me, but I had fun with *Sullivan Station* and can see that you did. He has the sort of likeable unreality I keep finding in TV shows (I haven't gone to a movie house for years). I can never identify what it is except that it is unreal and is somehow the essence of westerns—a kind of epic disregard. As in the fact, for instance, that in a shoot out, the hero never picks up a spare six gun or two from a fallen villain before racing after the other villains. And always throws away his expensive gun after the last shoot-out. Just once, I'd like to see a retiring hero hock his gun and belt (and buy himself a few copies of the *Browser's Dictionary*—in which case I'd be sure he had seen the light).

Well. I am half listening to the Bach Oratorio as I write, just so I can needle my house guest Peter Welt, a German-Jewish genius (half Jewish, half Prussian). He goes into shock when I say it is impossible to sing in "Cherman." Nice notes—but everything sounds the same.

Thanks for the review of Mandelbaum's *Paradiso.* I gave up reading the *NY Review of Books* after the canonization of that Vendler person became official. I find her brilliantly irrelevant.

And Mandelbaum too. It's nice of course to be cited flatteringly, but in essence M. attempts what should be poet's work, and he has no ear for it. Nor can I find a translator who has. When I read the original I know how desperately I failed, but when I read any other translation, I feel good by comparison, and not in blind ego for I have survived ambition—rather as a pitcher sizes up a batter and knows why he is about to be an easy out, because it don't mean a thing if you ain't got that swing.

Well. . . .

Your wife sounds nice. Happies and Merries to you both.

And ho-ho-ho
John

TO MILLER WILLIAMS

Key West
December 21, 1984
[MW]

Dear Miller:

Merry bahs to all humbugs and gilded happies to Jordan. You deserve no better. Such at least is the conclusion the Welts and I came to after close analysis. And you certainly deserve no better than Jordan on account of no one does.

I have been drudging daily at *Browser's III* and am making no haste slowly. If only it were possible to resign from almost everything! But let there be fertile disorder, if any. That beats a sterile tidiness. . . .

I am doing no Xmas but Elly [Welt] promises to do an Xmas turkey. The Welts are looking for a house in Key West but I doubt they will find the bargain they dream of. *Ça n'existe pas.* Not in Expensive Bone Key. And where, for that matter, does one find $130,000 houses for $50,000? They walk miles and miles daily while I sit here to scratch and peck.

Elly also threatens to do my official bio and we put in small sessions of talking into Peter's tape recorder. But everything lazily. Judith will be down right after New Year's Day.

I'm trying to get NPR [National Public Radio] to use my program more often. At least twice a week to begin. Maybe more often later. If I did it 3 times a week that would be $450 and with social security—when I start drawing it in a year and a half, I could give up the lecher circus and not starve. —If NPR doesn't go broke first. . . .

Tutte belle cose,
John

to Cora (Ciardi) Fennessey

Key West
December 30, 1984
[Ella (Ciardi) Rubero]

Dear Sister of Youth and Beauty:

Yr. visitation culminated this morning at the breakfast high mass in the Cathedral of St. Struvolli of the Banana Bread. I come from the service refreshed, restored, and I may say elevated as if into the Divine Presence. Even the Angels chorus, "Hey, Lord, damn good!"

And so we start the last day of the year in true holy observance. I hope that you too have felt the spirit of the sacred season, for I prayed like hell for yr soul and calculate that at least seven pounds of caked-on sin have been removed from it. I even consulted the local Papal delegate and he has decreed that you get three hours of plenary indulgence per struvollo, which, calculated on the pre-Gregorian calandar could get you to heaven in less than 57 centuries—*if* you make it your solemn intention to forego evil. I couldn't budge the delegate on the length of the term but have made arrangements for you to spend those 57 centuries in (at your choice) 1. A rigged Bingo game in which you win on every card. 2. The Gold Coast Clip Joint and Sporting House, in charge of the profits. 3. The Convent of St. Zoccolo della Succorsa, in the bottling department. I hope one of these assignments will make time fly for you till we meet in Heaven and get back to being piously dull.

Dec. in Fla. has been dry but otherwise perfect. But Judith will be arriving on the 3rd and that should change the weather. On the 10th or 11th we go to Miami for most of a week and thence to visit friends in Naples, Punta Gorda, and Sarasota—and there goes January. But I've been getting some work done and expect to finish, or to be very close to finishing, a third *Browser's Dict.* by the time we get back in May. Please go out and shovel some snow for me so I may have some sense of participating in how the other half lives. We hope Ella will be down in Feb. Also expect Benn to show up. Since you won't fly, would you consider coming down by Greyhound? I won't envy you four days on that land cruiser, but you'd love it once you got here and you would feel at home: all the windows need washing.

Anyhow Hoppy the New Year (munch-munch!) and happy snow removal.

Love,
John

TO JEFFRY LOVILL
Key West
January 24, 1985
[JL]

Dear Jeff:

Perspective is all. I am touched, of course, but I won't do as anyone's lodestar. You have done me the honor of paying me close attention, perhaps as close as anyone ever will. The danger is that the closeness of the look will distort the perspective. I am a [seeker?] 2nd class equipped with a 3rd class talent, and may overrate myself in saying so.

It is hard to have to think you have been chasing rainbows, but there is no pot of gold these days at the end of the Ph.D. paper chase. I hope with you that all this leads to a teaching job, for you would be good at it. But what matters most is that you are a husband, father, and competent to adjust to what comes and to support your family. The business world can be poisonous but small doses immunize. And Mithradates, as I read, died old.

At the moment, of course, the problem is just to get the thesis done, and on that you can count on me for any help I can give.

I had not known about Jeffrey Walsh's *Am. War Lit.* Did you see the *NY Review of Books* review of Mandelbaum's Dante, Dec. 20? My canonization. The review quotes more Ciardi than Mandelbaum, by way of showing him how it should be done. To the best of my knowledge it is the first time *NYRB* has mentioned me—and then they got my name through the back door. In any case, if your thesis treats the *Div. Com.*, that article should be good for a paragraph or 2.

Yes, I plan to go on with NPR. Hell, I need the money, little as it is. I'd like, in fact, to do it more often than once a week. Three times a week might almost be an income for my old age.

Just received galleys of *Doodle Soup* for publication later this year—maybe for Xmas. Tell Ryan I have reserved a copy for him. Best to Debbie, your hostages to the future, and to your mother.

Joys,
John

TO STANLEY EPSTEIN

Key West
February 6, 1985
[SE]

Dear Stan:

Glad to have your card. Let me take it as a sign that all goes well. My position report is from my son the lawyer who was down for a visit. He had a good time being touristy around the town. Every time he came in to find me scribbling or typing he gave me a lecture about living in Dullsville. Don't you ever go anywhere and do something? —And I thought I was moving right along on my new dictionary and doing some good things along the way! I guess that's where Dullsville is at. Much have I traveled in the realms of fool's gold. But iron pyrite has a nice sparkle to it. . . . .

And all best,
John

TO JEFFRY LOVILL

Key West
February 6, 1985
[JL]

Dear Jeff:

. . . . The chapter, I think, goes very well. Except for some palpable hits in Sylvia Plath, I just don't respond to the so-called Confessional poets. *Confessional,* as a matter of fact, is a misnomer. It suggests Catholicism, repentance, atonement for sins, etc. And though some of these poets have taken a stab at Catholicism, the confessional is not what they have in common, but the psychiatrist's couch; and that, I think, is the worst possible place for a writer to get his balance. Stretched out on the couch, they are encouraged to dredge up every last scrap of past experience; they are encouraged to treat it with enormous seriousness. Every solemnized kink becomes an ULTIMATE EVIDENCE. They have to be partly unbalanced to be there in the first place (though [aren't?] we all); in no time at all they are overdramatizing themselves in ways they find to be massively important though generally dull to me as the reader.

I don't doubt the reality of Anne Sexton's emotional problem—her suicide is proof enough of that—nor do I doubt that she was once a promising talent. But she went on to write bad poems and to lose her talent in the seams of that deep couch. It's as if she began telling the shrink her dreams, ran out of good ones, and began making them up to fill out her couch time. *Voulu* may be the word. That poem you cite about the falling babies is a damned good example. It's a false vision falsely felt in its concern, not about the babies (who aren't real to begin with) but about impressing her soul's resident shrink.

Sometimes I feel that these people couldn't find anything real to die of. Thank God I had agonized my way out of the Catholic Church when I was still young enough to develop a post-Trinitarian sense of humor. I'm even half-inclined to thank the army for giving me present and tangible things to die of. Having survived that, I am less inclined to choke to death on my own snarled dendrites. The Universe never promised me a meaning, I never promised it an explanation: I'm ready to call it a standoff and to let it go its way while I go mine, whatever way that turns out to be.

Which is only to say I agree with the way you have parsed my view of it. Your judgments, I cannot fail to note, are generous, even laudatory, and I thank you for that. I wish I could comment on your thesis-coach's comments but I have trouble reading them. His scrawl does seem to be in general agreement and commendation. All to the good. I have penned in a comment or two, but nothing of a great consequence. I think a potential employer, if he reads this, will be persuaded that you have sensitive things to say and that you say them well. It wouldn't hurt to give it all a *very close* stylistic scrub looking to make sure that the critical words and phrases are *exactly* put and all the prepositional turns in choice order. Precision and incisiveness are what count.

Whenever I have written something (except this letter, alas) I read it over thinking, "Let's see what this stupid jerk has done wrong this time." That's done red pencil in hand. Read the oaf hatefully and slash the red pencil through every trace of his oafishness. Never forgive him any slip: red-line it, and then don't let it into the final draft until you know what every last red line is there for. It can be a painful scrub but it's the way to a less painful last draft.

Good luck.

As ever,
John

TO MILLER WILLIAMS

Key West
February 27, 1985
[MW]

Dear Miller:

[Jim] Houtrides, Haywood Hale Broun, and a small shooting crew came down some days back & shot that interview [for Charles Kuralt's *Sunday Morning* program on CBS]. It will air Sunday morning Mar. 10.

Then off to Atlanta to talk to the local Bar Association (!) on (I think) Christian Endeavour. Something like that. It went well enough. Better. And I had a fine Stony weekend [i.e., a weekend with John and Lu Stone]. But mostly I learned with real dismay that my damned legs do not come up to modern airport minimum standards. I can't damn *walk*! You, alas, know about that, and will understand when I say *I no like*!

Love to Jordan. I heard from Elly Welt and believe it or not NKU has funded a trial Joy Conference.* I'm due there in April to talk about it. Prob. for sometime in Oct. Picket your calendar with firm tentatives, and you & George [Garrett] can carry on.

There were two consenting adults
Who agreed that they would not repulse
    One another's advances
    But just take their chances
And accept the result—as results.

Yes,
Phineas Phleabottom

*Northern Kentucky University invited Ciardi to direct a writers conference at which he could assemble some of his favorite people, and which he therefore dubbed the Joy Conference. See also letter dated November 1, 1985.

TO DAN JAFFE

Key West
March 1, 1985
[DJ]

Dear Dan:

Your father would have wanted no deep grief. As one now waiting in line I attest to that sentiment. There has to be a grief, and I share yours from my deep fondness for him. Yet you lived to share a long love and pride in one another. I think I know something about that. My father was killed in an auto accident a few days after my 3rd birthday. I am certain Herb died satisfied. May you too be happy in the good you shared.

My son Jon'l & his girl are here for a brief visit—my son the asst. d.a. Benn is in NJ and fills me with alternate spasms of fear and joy. . . .

I look fwd. to Long Boat in Aug. and hope for Judith to be along. She has decided Long Boat is too hot in August and once she has made up her mind reason will not change her, but I give myself a 50.01% chance of getting her there.

Do you ever watch Sunday morning TV? I never do but on Mar. 10 CBS will air a short interview Haywood Hale Broun did with me.

Best in all,
John

TO JEFFRY LOVILL

Key West
March 15, 1985
[JL]

Dear Jeff:

. . . . . I'm glad to have your chapter on the lost father. It is right to my reading. That is how I felt it then and up to about the time I married (at 30). It stayed with me a long time. I'd say it became history—almost someone else's history by the time we buried my mother more than 50 years later. The last poem on that was about turning back his grave covers and tucking her in.

I find myself far in the epilogue beginning to think I was lucky that he died when he did, for his death was a gift of freedom I did not recognize at the time. His death, in a sense, authorized me. My mother did not try to make up my mind for me once I had made it to my late teens. She was satisfied that I was "a good boy," she liked the fact that I read books and was good in school and had no trouble with the police, and she learned to respect me as the substitute man in her life. That left me free to choose my own way. I find myself thinking that he would have had a lot more to say—he an insurance agent with a son crazy enough to think he wanted to be a poet. —Cut the goddamn nonsense son: you gotta be practical, you know. And he would have been right enough. But might we not have disagreed to the point of bad feeling? I don't know that it would be that way (though it might). What I know is that I never had to bump heads on that point, that I was left free. . . .

Best,
John

TO JEFFRY LOVILL

Key West
April 9, 1985
[JL]

Dear Jeff:

We are getting packed to leave in about 3 days and I have to get this answer into the mail and off to you, before everything gets covered by everything else and disappears in the all-generalizing dumpster.

I'd say you've got it on (1) the madness of war and (2) the innately detestable machinery of military life. It was never my milieu. Yet there was one more thing: (3) when I was not being entirely a cog *I believed in what we were doing.* I confess to a dim view on the army's insistence on getting me killed and in showing so little concern for my private wishbook. I was not naturally inclined to take pleasure in being shot at, nor did I warm to my thoughts of what our bombs were doing when they hit the invisible people below us. Yet I would gladly have killed every man, woman, and child in Japan face-to-face, and died myself, sooner than see a Jap battleship sailed into San Francisco Bay with the surrender terms. I still have to teach myself not to hate the Japanese.

I suppose I am saying that it was a "good war"—which means one I believed in fighting. Without that belief I think I might have cracked up, as I believe I might have cracked up in Vietnam, for in that later war I would certainly have felt (as I did) that our own government was as bad as or worse than the enemy, that the dying was for nothing, that our stance was immoral.

That difference matters. In combat there is always a time when the sphincter tends to waver, when you have to give yourself a reason. WW II gave us that reason. Vietnam did not. The professional machos might have played it as a hunt and reveled in it. But the immorality of Vietnam is that our government sent boys out to die and gave them no reason for dying. I never doubted our reasons for being where we were nor the rightness of our being there.

Maybe I did not get that into the poems. Maybe because it was so basic [an] assumption that it never came up to be questioned. But it was there. Not that the army permitted me any will or choice. Yet in some crazy way I did choose what was chosen for me. I was committed to it. Why the hell else was I dying?

Well.

I'm more than ready to head north. It is beginning to get too hot here. . . .

Happy days to your house,
John

TO MILLER WILLIAMS

Metuchen
April 21, 1985
[MW]

Dear Miller:

We finally collapsed into the house last night leaving the car loaded with universal debris that Benn muscled in for us today. Everything's a mess but with small bonuses. Macmillan sent me a fairly handsome check for what must be someone else's book, and I'm waiting for them to write frantic letters of correction. I really don't see why I'm not entitled to $3460.28 for a book titled *Voices of Baseball* by someone named Chieger, but they charged off $1370.49 for book purchases I never got, subtracting that from total earnings of $4830.77, and I'm writing to complain. Whoever Chieger is, he has some nerve to charge all those books against the mistake Macmillan owes me.

And what the hell's with Ho-Miff? I found checks totaling $1555.79 for *How Does.* I assume you got the same. That comes to about $6000 a year in total royalties—so what is their damn talk of discontinuing the book? It seems to have sold 1646 copies in 6 mos. Is that pain and suffering? A back list [sale] of ± 3000 a year should carry a damn book.

Matilda Welter of Juv. books says *Doodle Soup* is rounding into shape. I sent her a collection of kids' limericks and she seems enthusiastic about it for the next kiddy book. I have a lot of poems on hand and would like to pop off one book a year for the next 5 years. If I live that long.

Clearly—as indicated by the flood of reviews of the *Selected* I am already too obsolete to be noticeable. You're clearly stupid to be publishing obsolete poets, but after the total silence with which *Lives of X* was greeted, I expect no notice. I'd be a liar if I said I am pleased by it, but I have learned to shrug it off. Because we all hoard our failures, I tell myself it's my own fault for thinking sanity may yet speak. But what's the great merit of sanity—assuming I could assume it? Yet, in a fundamental way, I insist on being obsolete. At least in the age of rock videos.

I bask in the prospect of the Joy Conf. I shall continue to hope that we can make 2 weeks of it and move it to the summer. John Nims is back from Europe and I am hoping he will make one of the company of souls if Joy carries on.

Bread Loaf is having its 60th this year and Pack asked me to drive up Aug. 14–16 to *listen* to some of the lectures and to bask in the splendor of his achievement. He even offered to provide room & board for 3 nights. I'm awed. I bear him no ill will—even like him in a way—but he's a complacent ass. I told him I would be on a cruise. I won't be, but I'd be all asea at B.L. He says he wants to invite Ted Morrison, too. Probably on the same generous terms. I doubt he'll get him. Poor Ted has Kay to tend and she, as I hear it, is far gone with Alzheimer's. Age is carrion. I've not yet recovered from MacLeish's death of rectal cancer. Having made it to spitting distance of 90, his ghost can't complain that the calendar cheated him, but it unhinges all fit proportion to think that Archie MacLeish died of a pain in the ass! Maybe none of us have anything else to die of.

Jordan will be at the Joy Conf., no? Please tell her I *insist.* And I will certainly see you, *d.v.,* in early November.

Five poems from *The Birds of Pompeii* are in the fall 1984 issue of *New Letters.* I even got a check for $37.50 for them. $7.50 per poem doesn't quite threaten Michener's take, but there are always the *Voices of Baseball* to sing to me. May they sing to you.

Love,
John

TO GIL GALLAGHER

Metuchen
April 25, 1985
[GG]

Dear Gil:

It is—will you believe it?—6:45. *A.M.,* that is. The infernal clanger buzzed me up . . . at 6:00 to do a phone interview for NPR, and now I sit here with the radio tuned to WNYC, waiting to hear my own grating growls return to me through the vapors of God. It's a first in my experience: in all my NPR prating over these last few years, I have never been up to hear myself on the air. I sit here imagining how the entire atmosphere conduces to my "om!" Not yet, of course. At the moment the air is clearing its throat with a bit of Mozart I can't identify, being a musical illiterate, but any Mozart seems a proper preamble. He does as a solid starting pitcher, good for a steady five innings, but then God knows it will be up to me to come in and win the game.

Do you see what it does to the ego to await its magnification through all of space? Though if it doesn't come on soon I may fall asleep on my own rites of canonization. Four hours' sleep is no preparation for beatitude. My halo is getting tight around my temples. (Which are so called because they in-Ark the brain, which is the temple of God.) . . . .

This side of infinity I brace myself for my 69th birthday in June and plan to consecrate the day by filling out the forms for starting to collect on social security in 1986. Damned if I will miss a single check. Because I earn more than 37¢ a month, soc. sec. wouldn't pay me at 65. Worse yet, I have to go on paying—I just had to send a check for more than $4000.00. That's adding incest to injury—an added $22,000-plus to pay from age 65 to age 70. But then there has to be a pay-off. And a fairly large one, I'm told. I should come in with about $1200 a month—or so I'm told. Not that I expect to live long enough to get back what I've paid in, but a start is a start. . . .

It's getting on to impossible 9:00 A.M. NPR told me I would be on at 8:00. But that there Mozart is still pitching a no hitter and looking as if he meant to go all the way. I think I'll be my own relief and go to bed. I was not born for the upper atmosphere. . . .

Walk with light only
John
(PIUTOSTO degli Scemi)

TO WALTER NEWMAN

Metuchen
April 29, 1985
[WN]

Dear Walter:

We arrived in NJ at the rump-stunned end of too many miles with a bunch of stops en route, all pleasantly vacuous and mentally dislocatory; arrived to a flurry of blurred family problems, all now more or less solved. Even solved triumphantly. . . .

In this churning of mixed moods I seem to have gone Sahara dry. The third *Browser's* is in the file. I still have a summer of agonizing proof-reading to do on the ms.—the most hateful part. And I must turn to [work] on the foreword but can't break the inertia.

Kay Boyle wrote to ask me about "beside oneself," usually "beside oneself with rage" (or some such). And it plays on my mind as one of those idioms I happen never to have focused on. My top-of-the-head guess is that it is a deep reference to daemonology in which the soul tends to pop out of the body at death or under great emotional stress, but how on earth do I go about checking that? I'll track it down yet. Meanwhile, it's a lovely entertaining question.

Kay Boyle also asks about *good grief,* which she finds ubiquitous in Washington, but that one is easy: from *God's grief!* and of a class with once common *'Sblood!, 'Snails! & Zwounds.* But it is another idiom I hadn't focused on.

Did you ever run into *fubar,* WW II GI for *f*ucked *u*p *b*eyond *a*ll *r*ecognition? It's another that popped into my mind after I had forgotten it.

Macmillan has just republished Eric Partridge's *Dict. of Slang and Unconventional English*—a beautiful book, and Macmillan sent me a courtesy copy. Thank God for courtesy copies. It lists at $75.00. Who can afford literacy these days?

It is a joy to be monologuing at you again after this fizzy hiatus. May spring come bursting to Sherman Oaks—and flame on.

Bestissimo,
John

TO ROBERT AND BEATRICE SNYDER

Metuchen
May 8, 1985
[RS]

Dear Bob:

In a qualified but essential way I endorse this limited species, and in that name my ignorance is happily pledged to you and to AWRF [American Wetlands Research Foundation]. I am. Attest: /s/ J.C. . . .

Benn, I think, is out of the rug business (it is seriously Mafioso in NJ), but we had a long confrontation of lawyers yesterday, and I think we are going to be bought out, not lavishly but at a fair price, and good riddance, for if we sue there might be evil discoveries. Meanwhile Benn is into tanning salons, two to start, a chain to follow (maybe), and it looks good. I feel reborn in that kid. . . .

I look fwd. to seeing you when next.

Wetlands forever,
John

Bea: There is nothing I'd like better than to discuss vice with you, necessarily nostalgically. My drunken doctor took me off booze. I was forced to abandon rape, avarice, and ambition. Now I keep running into goddamn crusaders who want me to give up cigarettes. But what have I left to live on other than nicotine and an evil mind (which is a perpetual solace). I insist that no one should give up any vice he/she has the energy to maintain. In the end one runs out of energy. Virtue, I'm afraid, will certainly triumph. But what the hell is the hurry? Stand up for sin!

P.S. A few days ago I had a letter from 93-year-old Dr. Maurice Root, an old pen-pal who retired from medicine at 80 or so. He began keeping a medical journal of his death. He has also long been a passionate and expert gardener. He writes that he now has a falling disease, and that his gardening is down to strawberries "because I haven't too far to fall from my hands and knees."

I have filed that under "mortal adjustments" and offer it, herewith, to everyone's file.

Giovanni Malefico
J. (Strawberry) Ciardi

TO JOHN FREDERICK NIMS

Metuchen
June 5, 1985
[IU]

Dear John:

. . . . I have stopped complaining about the world I never made. I grow inured to my status as an obsolete X. If Wojahn (whose name I never had heard before) is perceptive enough to think I'm as bad or worse than Karl Shapiro, I can at least go to Hell in admired company.*

The last time I looked, education seemed to be in the hands of good Joe professors who wore beads and blue jeans to the daily funeral of the English language. Have the yuppies taken over? I was in Boston last week visiting, among others, my son John (now an asst D.A. about to marry a lawyer), and I keep finding myself startled by their natural assumptions. They represent a mild case, I think, and yet I find it impossible to think along with them.

I just ran down to the local everything-store to buy this paper and the proprietor gave me a big pitch for an impressive word processor memory-storage typewriter for less than $600.00. With half my mind I think of it as a helluva buy. And with the remaining three-quarters I am terrified by it. It's like finding I have been signed up for a course in the idioms of Martians. The yuppies divide me similarly into a half and a three-quarters. They seem to be the future, but please—not until I am safely dead.

So what's wrong with stingless death? I haven't received my June *Poetry* yet, but hell it's not my pasture, I did recommend Joe Parisi highly when asked by the committee, and I have to grant him the right to run his farm in his own way. It's a bit like walking away from Bread Loaf, anent which I have nothing to say ever. May it all work out well and to one side of any dismay I might find myself feeling—were I to feel.

I do know what you are saying about Rago Napoleon. He turned very high imperial one summer at B.L. Is that a function of an insecure person clutching the little he could grab? I hope Parisi is more assured than that. I only met him that once in Chicago and liked him, though that was in another role.

I long ago decided to be stubbornly loyal to my ignorance come what might. I have also managed to offend a lot of people, though I wasn't even trying. I guess natural talent will out. But imagine what I might not have managed had I really tried! . . .

Joys in all,
John

*David Wojahn blasted Ciardi's *Selected Poems* in a *Poetry* review that also took Shapiro to task.

TO VINCE CLEMENTE

Metuchen

June 12, 1985

[VC]

Dear Vince:

You and Annie are beautiful people and you have won through to a happy flowering of your lives. May you enjoy every minute of it for many years to come, like a succession of flowering trees come into bloom.

Your sentiments touch me. What you say about me reminds me of the way I long felt, and still do, about MacLeish, my early master, my late dear friend. I have considered as a sufficient epitaph: "I didn't do everything wrong: MacLeish was my friend. . . ."

I've had some thought of creating an extended autobiography. *A Journal of Obsolescence.* There might be as many as six people in the U.S. alone who might want to read it. I wouldn't expect fervid attention. I might be moved to do it for the sake of asking myself some organizing questions.

Somehow it sounds pretentious. I don't fit into today's literary scene and its assumptions. In ego I tell myself that I uphold the good old fashioned religion, which seems to mean God loves me and I'm saved. But what good is the sermon if no one shows up for Sunday services? A retrospective or festschrift for my 70th birthday would be flattering but nowadays people (of small consequence to me) are being festschrifted on their 40th & 50th, and it turns out to be dull stuff. I am no major exhibition and I have no significant complaints. I have written as an alcoholic drinks, compulsively for its own sake, and why should I claim rewards for being in Writers Anonymous?

I can't imagine anything that would bring me critical or academic esteem in today's climate. It's a fate I share with Shapiro, Viereck, and other poets I love. And why argue? If some poems survive me, I won't know about it. I have given my body to the Rutgers Medical School for dissection: maybe I should have a poem or two tattooed on the guts. Better yet, I'd like to believe that children will continue to have fun with my poems. But will tomorrow's children be taught to read?

I'll play lucky John all the way to the anatomy lab slab *et caetera desunt.* And no complaints. I just don't feel like planning. I could have read Plato's *Republic* tonight—I've been meaning to and a publisher sent me a new good translation—but I went off to play gin rummy and came away with 90 bucks. Who's complaining?

We're off to DC next week for a meeting of the National Fndtn. for Advancement in the Arts. —To sponsor some presidential scholars, go to the White House for Reagan's inanely prepared spontaneities—and also to tape some NPR programs on Thurs. & Fri. Then home for my birthday and soon then to Detroit and Chautauqua, followed by a 3 day cruise out of Miami. Not a bad life. I expect we'll be here for the last half of August and into September. A few lecture trips then, and off to Key West by mid-November. It goes well. Somewhere in this schedule we must get to Nantucket if only briefly. And somewhere I should start proofreading the typescript of *Browser's III,* but let it happen when it does. What's the hurry? (Except that I'd like the $16,000 advance.) But I don't damn need that either if I just leave my brats to fend for themselves. Benn, I am happy to say, may be back in the carpet business and may be coming up on good fending. I'd like an affluent son. Shine on.

Love
John

to Robert and Beatrice Snyder

Metuchen

August 19, 1985

[RS]

Dear Bob & Bea:

I will miss Chris [Norton] even as I think of him warmly. Only a truly sweet, good man could try so hard to be a goddamn curmudgeon, and fail at it. I saw him at Chautauqua in July—sadly depleted, alas. My last words were, "Chris, I want you to know, despite your foul nature, that I love you." He said, "I shudder at the thought, but I have to return some of the same sentiment."

I am in that season and you two are approaching it. The death of good men is no rare and shocking news. He died in his sleep in a place he loved. There is no particular place I love, but I'll call it a good death if it's not too painful, escapes the needles-and-tubes squad, and especially if it manages not to distract my attention. When you get word of mine—sometime certainly before A.D. 2185, have a drink to the old bastard and say he had it coming. . . . .

And ever and anon,
John

to Ella (Ciardi) Rubero

Metuchen

August 23, 1985 [postmark]

[ER]

Dearest Ella:

I am fascinated by your sketch of the apartment [where Ciardi was born, 25 Sheaf St. in Boston's North End, the Italian section of town]. I remembered the stove to the left of the door and the soapstone sinks by the windows, where you have the stove. I have no memory of the bathroom and tub but the pattern of non-use of the tub is standard Italian: when Mussolini built condominiums with inside bathrooms and tubs, it was common for Romans to haul in dirt and raise tomatoes in the tubs.

I also see the nuns are still on some of your assumptions. With the exception of amputees, seminarians on a retreat, and social eunuchs, every man in his twenties is a womanizer. It works both ways. How do you keep a nice young Jewish girl from being too eager about sex? —Marry her. I can hardly, alas, remember what it was all about, but for a while it seemed to be urgent.

Oh, yes—about that map of the apartment—wasn't there a gas jet on the wall to the right of the kitchen door? (On the right as one entered.) I gather there must have been (also) electric light but I don't remember it. Your memory would, of course, be better than mine.

Ah well. The wonder to me is that we have survived it in reasonably good humor. Let's hope we all go on surviving yet a while without losing our sense of humor. Friends keep blinking out all around us. It's that season. One dear friend just died in his sleep at Chautauqua. If I can manage to die without having to pay attention to it, I'll call that good luck.

We leave for Nantucket tomorrow with a connection in Boston, but with no time for a stopover, and a huge penalty for breaking the connection, with the fare already $100 apiece each way. Flying has become gawdamighty Xpensive. But what isn't?

I'll wish you tripled dividends, old money bags.

Love,
John

TO DANIELA GIOSEFFI

Metuchen

September 5, 1985

[Sold to an unidentified collector.]

Dear Mrs. Gioseffi:

Is it gauche to address you as Mrs.? If the imperative is Ms., I must plead that I am obsolete. Ms. offends my sense of language—as if I were being made to join with activists, which ain't my club. I am so far gone along the track of the dodo that I insist language counts for more than the people who use it. Whereby I refuse to be Ms.-taken. If only in a Pickwickian sense.

I wonder, in fact, if Miss any longer connotes a junior person or an old maid. It did once of course, but my sense is that Women's Lib has triumphed to the point of making it as neutral a label as Mr. But who knows?

I have had various It.-Am. friends tell me that they have felt discriminated against. In many cases I felt that their paranoia was justified because everyone did hate them—because they were jerks. I've had a coy touch or two. Robert Lowell once wrote me a note to say a poem he had read in the *Atlantic* was the best Italo-American poem he had ever seen and I found myself thinking, "That fat head thinks he's more American than I am!" It went into my file as a quaint assumption.

Vero e che sono l'italiano deracinato—more a USAAF Tech Sgt. and more German than Italian. I've had friends in Rome tell me that I spoke the language but had the feelings of a tedesco.

I grew up in a Yankee-Irish-Italian town, and there were ethnic fistfights, but even when I lost I looked down on the slobs I had fought with. Maybe I was armored by ego. Or by self-absorption. I was listening for things in my head—for language—and always felt that what I was hearing was better, more interesting, and more absorbing than the noise around me.

The writer's ultimate sin is in thinking there is something more important than language for then one sells one's birthright for a pot of message.

Forgive me for clinging to my own fantasy. I know from what used to be the soul that the base message in sending out one's writing is "Discover me! Oh, discover me!" And what a joy it is to discover! But I am so conditioned in my old age that I tend to go numb when I hear a message. I recognize and honor the human content of your poems, but I cannot avoid the conviction that you are a messenger. That leaves me as some sort of Druid listening to the sounds from the Vatican. Which is to say, irrelevant. Except that I feel uncomfortable when a poem sets out to *say* something. I have a mortal distaste for *declaration.* I ask only for a few more years in which to woo the language in the hope of hearing what *it* wants to say. Because it is wiser, richer, and far more sensitive than I.

Does that make sense—any sense—to you? I don't know how to say it, except that I have no way to live except in my sense of this—without imagining I can know what it is. It feels as music must. Which is to say it must be self-entering, self-forming, and self-sealing. It finds itself in the course of its own going. What I cannot avoid feeling is that your poems start with ideas from *before* their beginning. Somehow that is not my way.

Which may be why I am obsolete. Having something to *say* is certainly in the mainstream of our times. Which means I am probably remote and irrelevant. Not that it matters. Except that anything I might have to say doesn't much matter. But to bless the queerness of whatever it is we seem to need. My need is of another denomination. Maybe even of a sect of one.

Except to send you warm good wishes in finding yourself as we all must, never knowing exactly what we think we have found. . . .

But

in any case,

sincerely,
John Ciardi

TO JOSEPH MAIOLO

Metuchen

September 6, 1985

[JM]

Dear Joe:

Your letter is dated June 28 and here I am opening the package [a manuscript novel] on Sept. 6. Please do not think me indifferent. I did warn you I would have trouble getting to it. But more than 2 mos. before starting is more than I had calculated. Bit by bit I have spent the whole summer avoiding the proofreading on my typescript of *Browser's III.* I have found ways of staying on the road in order to avoid the misery of proofreading. Worse yet, I shall be starting on lecture rounds before long.

In any case this is from chaos to say it's time to start a reckoning. The ms. is on my table and I look forward eagerly to beginning a reading—a bonus I will pay myself between bouts of the goddamnabilized proofreading. God knows I may have nothing to say that could be remotely useful to you, but I do look forward to [the reading], apologizing only for such long delay.

Your letter sounds good and from a happily engaged life. So be it ever. In a little over a week I am flying to Minn. but only to southernmost Luther College just north of Iowa and must get back to shuffle a few papers before I head for Ark., and then to Mich. and Northern Kentucky and Illinois before I go off to hide in Key West in Dec. It is then I will start to have some time to practice being half-thoughtfully human—half-thoughtfully because I suspect it may be better not to dwell on it too intensely.

I am delighted that you liked that autobio sketch.* And yes, I have thought of doing more with it but toyingly. That little sketch was such damned hard writing, I find myself afraid of it. The terror of being distracted from true memory by the demands of the writing, the fear of laboring to a lie. If I do let myself into it with my crazy patchwork memory it will have to be toward what really was. And does anyone dare that?

Please take this as an interim apology. I can't promise to be prompt, but maybe prompter.

Happy buzzes to all your hive.

John

*"About Being Born and Surviving It," *Contemporary Authors Autobiography Series,* v. II, ed. by Adele Sarkissian (Gale, 1985).

TO DANIELA GIOSEFFI

Metuchen
September 9, 1985
[Sold to an unidentified collector.]

Dear Daniela:

It used to be the custom for old crocks to retire to a monastery and prepare themselves for God, as Guido da Montefeltro says he did (and did in fact) in the *Inferno.* I don't have much identifiable God to prepare for, and nothing to cling to but a semi-tropistic mood, but I find myself becoming reclusive. I even tell myself I have earned the right. I have survived a theology, aerial combat, the goddamn adolescence of my children (persisting into their thirties), a warped sense of do-good decency, avarice, and even ambition. I'd like the serenity of a bookish-if-godless monastery for what time is left me. Alas, when I threw over my professorship at Rutgers almost 25 years ago, I also threw over my pension. As one consequence I must yet maunder my way around the world's lecture platforms (on wobbly legs) because I still have a living to make. Yet, given my choice, I would happily shut myself in my attic study and never come out.

I am asking you to forgive me. As I wrote once, "I have no worlds to keep and none to save." I have no faith in any decision ever made by any literary group or association or committee. As far as I know I am not a fellow of the American Academy of Poets. I am carried on the roster of the National Institute of Arts and Letters and even listed on a committee or 2 there, but I do nothing about it and avoid all meetings except for the May ceremonial—and that only because my beloved Judith insists on going to see her friends at that fluffery. I do work at being a trustee of the Nat. Fndtn. for Advancement in the Arts, but that's pure and unambitious: we give awards, recognition, and some Presidential Scholarships in the Arts to about 130 high school seniors annually, and I find it a joy to be with those bright kids here and there through the year.

I don't think, however, that I have any connection with the Academy of American Poets. Nor, as I am forced to confess, do I care whether or not anyone gets to [be] read as an Italian-American poet, male, female, or in between. There are only good poets and bad ones, and that in an age when no one seems to know the difference. Categorical poets, ethnic, by schools, programs, militance, decibel-power, mean nothing to me. I like the Wallace Stevens line: "What has there been to love that I have not loved?" Well, for one thing, categories.

You speak of being denied an audience. I don't know what that means. Audiences are not denied, as I see it: they are there to [be] captured, and the capture is finally and only accomplished in the pleasure of taking the pains to write well.

I am asking you to accept my apologies for not writing to Henri Cole (whom I do not know) because to support your desire to be given an audience to read to for ethnic reasons violates principles I have asserted and published. I do not insist on being proud of my view, but it is my view, I have asserted it repeatedly, and for better or worse it is part of me. Not that it much matters: I don't expect to be around long enough for my views to make a difference, and I doubt they would if I stayed around (perish forbid) forever.

Thanks for the poems. I respond to these much more richly than I did to the earlier ones you sent. They take the time to *be* rather than to *mean.* No matter that they are more elevated than my low mind: they are poems, captured and made, not assertions, and to that I can answer and do answer. Thank you.

I'm delighted to hear of Norman Rosten, a beautiful man. We shared good times in Key West before his Hedda died. I am hoping to find some time at home in late September to get him out here for a weekend. Judith shares my fondness for him and loves to sit and buzz-buzz with him. If you see him, please tell him he is in our thoughts and hearts.

Hors de combat, but affectionately,
John

TO ROBERT "MAC" CORDRAY

Metuchen
September 21, 1985
[RC]

Dear Mac:

We're delighted that you will be in town after that Ohio Valley Writers' Conference do, and look forward to visiting with you and Mary. . . . .

I just got back from Decorah, Iowa (Luther College), by way of Minn. and had a message from the fates on my outward connection in Chi. I went in on Eastern which pulled in at the far end of one ramp, from which I had to go into the terminal, over to the next, and out to the end of another ramp to take a No Worse Airlines flight. I managed to trek into the first terminal and my legs just plain gave out. To make it the rest of the way I had to stop and call for a wheelchair. I confess to having felt the need many times in the past, but always insisted on toughing it out. On that sad day I was finally forced to succumb, and that weighs upon me. It isn't exactly something new, but it is a message I wasn't entirely pleased to receive. The M.D.s call it a diabetic neuropathy. I call it a pain in the ass. But there is nothing to be done about either. I ain't dead yet, to be sure, but the thought of collapsing into a wheelchair doesn't exactly thrill me. It isn't the muscles. I ride an exercycle 10–20 miles a day and get only normally tired but still can't walk around the block without having my legs turn into wet noodles. I'm told the nerves keep sending the muscles the wrong messages. That, at least, feels like life itself. Whattahell. . . .

Joys in all,
John

TO VINCE CLEMENTE

Metuchen
September 24, 1985
[VC]

Dear Vince:

I keep being astonished by your diligence in this [festschrift].* Bless Eberhart! We have been good friends for a long time.

I doubt that RP Warren will feel moved to add his voice. I even doubt that he has read me. We get along fine, though distantly. My guess is that he would feel I am a peanut gallery insignificance that should at best be festschrifting *him.* (And indeed I would as a novelist, for as a poet he has never reached into my feeling.)

Sweat not if Hugh Kenner remains unheard from. We share a generalized lack of admiration. He reviewed my *Inferno* once as if he had been eating shit on a shingle. He certainly did not know what he was talking about. He made a great point of ridiculing me for writing, "Greeks. Who through a hundred thousand/Perils have reached the west." His point was that only a stupid jerk would break the line that way. Then it occurred to him to check the original and found that Dante had written *chi, per cento miglia/ Perigli.* So he added a note saying "Yea, Dante did it that way," but only in Italian, which proved I had no business doing it in English. And more of the same. I say jerk is jerk. I hope he writes ten thousand pages and that you leave it out.

Jud Jerome has sent me a copy of a long piece he has done—a good piece: he had the grace to leave some warts on my nose. But whoever said I have the skin you love to touch: I found my ego purring to it in the best ape tradition.

You mention a "pictorial essay"—is that any different from a family album from baby pictures to roly-poly confirmation to collegiate slouch to fearless young gunner to sexy young husband with dreamy eyes and set chin, to beaming daddy, to serious citizen, to old crock gone to flab? I don't think that could be anything but kitsch and irrelevant. Not that you are asking me to vote. But if I do have one, it's no. I've been looking through Gale Research's Contemptible Authors

Auto Bio series, and I find the photos frankly boring. Given a choice, I'd give you a shot of the back of my head as a frontispiece and call that enough. I'll bet Caligula was a cute baby, too.

I'll add a page about my few meetings with Sidney Bechet.

You might want to get in touch with Stanley Burnshaw. . . . I have a high regard and honest fondness of/for him as one of our best critics. His *Seamless Web* is a great book.

Judith says supper is ready. Probably hamburger.

I wish you and Annie quail and truffles,
John

*In the end the festschrift became a memorial volume, *John Ciardi: Measure of the Man* (Fayetteville, AR: The University of Arkansas Press, 1987).

TO DANIELA GIOSEFFI

Metuchen
September 26, 1985
[Sold to an unidentified collector.]

Dear Daniela:

At 44 there can seem to be reasons for ambition. I think the most mercy of my years has been in surviving ambition, that forever gnawing wish for the writer to be recognized and acclaimed. I don't mean to scorn it. It burns, or has burned, in all of us. It is part of the confusion of being of this species and of taking example from it.

I [may] even be lying to myself. Maybe no one can claim to have survived ambition. Still, insofar as one can, I think (at least I hope) I have survived it.

All right: with nothing to gain by and nothing I want to gain, I'll play Dutch uncle. If it pleases you to have Galway Kinnell call you "visionary and full of vitality," take a bow. . . . So Snodgrass says your style is "splendidly clean and straight." Snodgrass can write but he won't become famous with this opinion.

Cara mia, don't you realize that when a writer says things like that: (1) he hasn't said anything, and (2) that he's trying to be "nice" without saying anything you could quote in any way to be held against him. These are blurt-vague blurbings, not assessments. Toughen up!

I'm talking to you as I would have talked to one of my girls at Radcliffe 40+ years ago. Like you, they sat at the metaphoric piano, dreaming of going to Carnegie Hall, but playing like Liberace. And I had to keep telling them that playing pretty trills won't cut it. You either mean it hard enough to break your head on it, or you don't really mean it.

A wasted word, a fancy trill instead of a real cadence, a juicy and unexamined adjective, the itch to be beautiful (instead of real)—these are mortal sins. The point of my gruff, however, is not that they offend me but that they damn you. Get all those fancy musico-historico-artistico-high vibrato references out of your prop room. As Frost said, "The fact is the sweetest dream the labor knows." He also said, "Anything more than the truth would have seemed too weak." And what it would have seemed too weak to was, "The earnest love that laid the swales in rows." (All this from his poem, "The Mowing.") I find you guilty of overblowing your metaphoric facts. As the Bauhaus School proclaimed long since, less is more. As I will add, the pretty is never the beautiful.

If you think I am scolding you, I am. If too harshly, not nearly as harshly as you must scrub yourself: you are totally responsible for *everything* in the poem, even for the accidents (if you get lucky enough to find a good one)—every last comma, line-break, spacing, word choice, and adjective—especially the adjectives. Doubt every adjective you ever write. It is automatically guilty until it manages to prove and reprove its innocence under torture or revision (whichever comes first, and then both). I will not take it easy on you. You are already taking it too easy on yourself. You want equality, I'm giving it to you. You have every right to sweat as hard as you must to get it down, because nothing else will do it.

I grant you without reservation the pleasure of taking pains, and a damned sight more pains than you have taken to date. *Wanting to* won't do it. Only doing it does it. If I send you love you ain't got much. If I scold you, even if only to make you mad enough to dig harder to prove I'm a jerk, I'll settle for that. That's why you get no sweet blurby approval. If you are a glutton for punishment, send me some more, and maybe I'll nit-pick them. I can't promise that I will: I may be out shoveling the barn. . . .

Go and sin no more, my sweet equality,
John

TO JEFFRY LOVILL
Metuchen
September 29, 1985
[JL]

Dear Jeff:

I have just finished reading THE BLACK TOME [i.e., Lovill's doctoral dissertation], our golden names linked on the spine. I am not entirely sure what I feel, but I feel it deeply. You have done me the honor of paying attention—the closest attention anyone has ever turned on me, and what can I feel but honored that I come out so well. Thank you sir. . . .

Do you really think Miller will want to publish it? I hope so for both our sakes, but I also think it will take some careful editing for non-doctoral-tutorial reading, but I also think it can be edited. Miller has some great copyreaders on his staff. I am going to Ark. in a couple of days to read and talk about translation. I plan to whisper in Miller's ear that the book should sell more than 3 copies in the United States alone, and that he might even work up an international sale if he forces his foreign students to buy it. We can then announce to Ryan that his daddy has become an international figure.

But, hell, beyond playfulness, I am touched. We all lack depth perception when looking at ourselves, but as closely [as] I can render myself and my work in my own two dimensions, I feel you have put the right weight on the right things; or to say it more accurately, you have on things just the weight I would put on them, adding, of course (for which I thank you sir) a generous judgment not commonly found in my reviewers—and to hell with them. . . . .

I thank you, too, for keeping me wholly apart from the Couch Poets (as I prefer to call them). Plath sounds real to me, and did as an undergraduate. (Dudley Fitts and I and some others I have forgotten went to her college—was it Mt. Holyoke?—and somewhere in her letters she says kind things about what I said and did on that occasion. Christ she was a deep blue Sunday even then, but real.)

Not so Berryman—I couldn't even force my way through his Henry pieces and dream songs. Sexton was an out-and-out self-dramatizing fraud. And Lowell's *Life Studies* are rotted with dumb sentimentalism. I am always asked about them when I go off to lecture, and when I try to give these (to me) honest answers, (a) I am accused of sour grapes, and (b) I set up someone in the audience to call me a mean-minded bastard when he gets to review my next book. Fuggem awl. As cummings had his Olaf say, "There is some shit I will not eat."

Bless and thanks,
John

TO DANIELA GIOSEFFI

Metuchen
October 7, 1985
[Sold to an unidentified collector.]

Dear Daniela:

. . . . . Yes, as I said, the forties are a right time for ambition, and I wish you all the good of yours. But if I have learned anything, I think it is that poetry is an instrument. As the Sweet Singer of Michigan once wrote, "Literary is a work very difficult to do." It is a joyously difficult instrument, and the most difficult instrument forgives least. What I have been trying to say is that ambition or not is not the measure. The instrument won't respond to claims upon it. It must be wooed. One submits to it humbly and hopes it may be moved to enable one, not always. AND NOTHING ELSE MATTERS, not aspiration, not desire, not trembling sincerity, not posing oneself to be beautiful, lofty, concerned, or any damn thing else. Either what comes is memorable and sticks to memory (and even perhaps to the memory of this crazy species) or it is forgettable and gets forgotten. A bad line, a fluffed word, a wrong emotional pose, constitute damnable sins; and every reader is a Pope within himself, and wholly authorized to publish required damnations.

I wish there were some other ground rules, but I don't know what they might be. I have never known any others. . . . .

Earnest love,
John

TO WALTER NEWMAN

Metuchen
November 1, 1985
[WN]

Dear Walter:

We have just returned from two weeks on the road and a beautiful time. It centered on the Ohio Valley Writers' Conference in Northern Kentucky, just south of Cincinnati, an experiment privately called the Joy Conference.

A year ago, at a dinner Northern Kentucky Univ. gave for me, I happened to say that I knew many beautiful people but that they were scattered all over the country, and that what I'd like is an estate with many cottages on it where my friends could stay at their pleasure so we could have a Joy Conference. The next day the pres. called the provost and said, "Let's give Ciardi his Joy Conf." And so it was (minus the estate for the nonce, but maybe to come) that seven writers I admire and love came together in a big motel near NKU, and we staged a week long conference. It was a treat. As I told the people who attended, no one got on my staff unless I loved him/her. So a week among some of my favorite people. It was a first run, but a success I think. There is some experimenting to do, but I think we have the beginning of a continuing idea and that it may grow. If we ever get to a section of screen writing—it may be a few years off, I'm afraid (if ever, but who knows?)—could you be lured to Cincinnati for your room and $1700 bucks? If, that is, you ever care to try your hand at the podium. And if we turn up any screen writers, or would-be's thereof? It is at least a thought to cling to.

You write that you are starting something about disturbed kids. My dear friend Miller Williams, poet, translator, director of the U of Ark. Press (has he sent you my latest book of poems? He was supposed to, and I want to be sure you get one—so far only advance copies and only 2 of those)—in any case his lovely little demure wife has been running a clinic in Fayetteville, Ark., for schizophrenics and turns out to be a genius at it. She has 100 relatively young people who would otherwise be in state hospital beds, and has had such success at making them functional in society that clinics all over the country have been calling for her to come explain her program and its results. She has, in fact, had to refuse invitations in order to stay home and run her program, so she has been inviting people to come and see for themselves. I have visited her "shop," and I have been enormously impressed by what she has worked out in the way of therapy by assigning responsibility to kids who were never allowed any. I don't know that you want to fly to Fayetteville, Ark., for hands-on research (it's a hell of a place to get into at times—by way of Dallas would be yr direct route). But if it would be worth the trouble to see how it really works, let me know. I am sure the Williamses would be delighted to have you as a houseguest, and I'll bet 76¢ to a half-yen that you and they would become good friends. I love them. Let me know if you are at all interested and I will do phone calls accordingly. Just a thought, but I can say that I found my visit to her clinic to be an experience, and I suspect you might get some insights that might build into what you will be writing.

My late dear friend Fletcher Pratt used to love a party game in which people who bragged about their drinking discernment were blindfolded and offered seven shot glasses with various liquors in them. They could smoke, chew gum, chew bread, sip coffee, do whatever they pleased to rinse their palates between drinks. The best anyone ever got was 1. white wine, 2. bourbon, 3. scotch, 4. gin. No one ever (to my knowledge) missed gin, anywhere along the line. But, that aside, by the fifth sip they were calling beer cherry heering, and chianti bourbon. If the test was rigged by putting gin first, all of the following guesses became absurd.

The fact is that alcohol paralyzes the taste buds. Bartenders know this: if a guy orders an expensive brandy he gets it—for the first two drinks. If he goes on thereafter, he gets charged for what he ordered but he gets served whatever cheap stuff is under the bar. Try it yourself. Especially when a guy claims to *know* his liquor. I've had party fun with this taste test.

That aside, I am happy to say that though I once was a heavy drinker I was astonished at how easy it was to quit when there was reason to. Diabetes seemed to be a good reason. For thirty years I had been on a ration of at least one bottle of 100 proof bourbon (J.W. Dant) a day. The first few days were not easy. When I took Judith out for dinner on the weekend I ordered a dry Manhattan. On the next weekend I did the same, took one sip of mine, and gave the rest to Judith. And that was it: no problem. I couldn't do it with cigarettes. I'm still smoking 3 packs a day—mostly because there isn't time in a day to smoke more than that (and what the hell, it's too late for me to die young). But giving up liquor cost me nothing. If only dying turns out to be that easy, I'll settle with no complaints.

Re: "I'm not sure but I think I don't know." Go ahead and steal it. I stole it from a friend of mine who probably stole it from someone else. Take advantage of the social contract. What the hell, halitosis is better than having no breath at all. (I stole that from a priest lecturing on Alcoholics Anonymous.)

My son Benn's carpet outlet has just gone under for back taxes. He'll be lucky to come out of it without being in debt, and I'm $99,000 in the hole. (So who told me to screw around and have kids?)

May your balance ever read blacker and glossier.

Best,
John

TO JOHN FREDERICK NIMS

Key West
March 13, 1986
[IU]

Dear John:

I flew back from NJ to pick up my car and drive home but I came down with a dizzy-making cold that has me feeling like mildewed laundry. The car needs a new wheel bearing if I am to get back in one piece, and life is generally (a) dreamy & (b) insolvable except for your piece on the oeuvres of Chauncy Arty.*

I told you I had no right to improve anything but matters of fact, and of course I haven't. I wish I had been as effective and practical as you portray me for I would then be on senile velvet. I have tried a lot of things and most turned out modestly well, but my children have immodestly raided me year after year, leaving me with damn little fat on my spiritual bones. But hell, on what else shall we sooner and better go broke? Let 'er rip. I have not been the shrewd man of affairs you describe, but there are no real errors in your account. "Diversify," the old boy said, "—everyone should have some losers."

I am immensely grateful for your piece, John. You have done me the honor of paying the closest attention to my work, and you have been generous to its weaknesses; you have praised most the things that are most important to me. How shall I not be grateful? I assure you, I am.

I have never really been an innovator in the manner of Williams, Stevens, Eliot, Dizzy Pound. For me the poem has been inseparable from the thing said. Were I out for manifestos, I might claim that *Lives of X* reawakened fictional techniques in a way not common in our poetry. But I am out to found no schools. I am insistently obsolete. By whatever means, I want the poem that wakes me to my life.

Every collection is made up of the poems in it—plus one more, the total life of the poet that speaks from, through, and *uber* the total. It can be made to sound egotistical to say I have been creating my persona (not really myself) but isn't that what every poet really tries?

No one that I know of has written about my children's poems, but

I am deeply serious about them. Could my ghost return to find itself acclaimed in academic quarterlies, it would shrug. If it walked by the school yard and heard kids piping some of my poems, it would clap its hands and sing and louder sing.

Could your ghost and mine sit in some corner of the mind's eye ages hence, we wouldn't need to talk: we'd be happy to be with one another in love and good faith.

I went to bed and tossed and turned and burned with fever. I got up to write this and I feel much better. Thank you.

I don't know whether I am really failing or just feel that way with this damned virus. I'll hope to be over it in KC in about a week, and I much look forward to seeing you there. . . .

Bless and thank,
John

*Nims had written "John Ciardi: The Many Lives of Poetry," delivered as the Cockefair Chair lecture at the University of Missouri-Kansas City on March 19, 1986. The essay was subsequently published twice, in *Poetry* (August 1986) and in *John Ciardi: Measure of the Man* (1987).

TO VINCE CLEMENTE

Metuchen
March 26, 1986
[VC]

Dear Vince:

It was good of you to recommend me to Kenneth Gambone. I have just staggered home from 4 days at Sthrn Ind. U., really weakened by a long siege of flu, but surviving. I was supposed to go to Denver but had to cancel it, also canceling a talk to the Ecumenical Libraries of Kansas, in Topeka. (My agent got them a replacement, but I weep a bit for the lovely $5000 plus I won't be collecting. — What good is it to a dead man?) I have made up my mind irrevocably that *nothing* will tempt me north hereafter before April 15 (earliest date). I just don't have Sgt. Ciardi's resilience these days—nor the bastard's legs.

I explained these things to Gambone with my thanks and regrets. With Frost I find it is time to bow and accept the end of a season.

As a prized gift I found in today's mail a richly laudatory article written in Italy (in English) by Fedara Giordano, "An Archetypal World: Images of Italy in the Poetry of John Ciardi." From *Atti del Settimo Convegno Nazionale, Italy and Italians in America.* Università di Catania.

Accolades for breakfast, no less.

I suggested to Judith last night that she invite you and Annie to [Jonnel's] wedding on May 10 and she told me you were leaving for Italy. Great! Then she told me this morning (and noon) that she had spoken to you and that you would still be here May 10, and that you would come. Better! I look forward to seeing you. It will, alas, be a fractured visit with people milling everywhere, but it will be a joyous day for us, and a joy to share it with you.

In Indiana last Sunday I heard a great (to me) musical program. First a bunch of my kid-poems sung by a child-choir. Then a ballet of *John J. Plenty and Fiddler Dan,* and last a tiny but beautiful operetta of *The King Who Saved Himself from Being Saved.* I thought it was beautifully done! Among sweet rewards.

I hope your work on the festschrift will bring you sweet rewards. In addition to those that you and Annie have in one another.

Love,
John

TO MATTHEW GRAHAM

Metuchen
c. March 27, 1986
[MG]

[Matthew Graham of the English department at the University of Southern Indiana drove Ciardi to the airport late on the afternoon of Wednesday, March 26. When the plane was about to leave, Graham hesitantly slipped his first book of poems, *New World Architecture,* into Ciardi's hand.]

Dear Matthew:

I have had a lovely time with your poems last night on the plane and again this morning. I have the happily excited sense that you have found a diction and a way of connecting things (emotional syntax?) that is not only your own but that is authentic, a voice—and that it will certainly grow and develop. The point, I think, is that you have laid down a language on which everything seems possible. Impressive. Because true. Something like absolute pitch.

If you have another book ready—*when* you have one ready, I would like to see it with the thought of recommending it to Miller Williams at U. Ark. Press. I could only recommend and leave the decision to him, but I expect he would be as excited about these poems as I am. There is an idiom here and a sense that you will surely grow into it to poems that will make a difference.

All power to you. I was a bit dragged down in Ind.—still am a touch—but I'll recover. You have some lovely people there. Please give my best to them all, especially to the Blevins, but to many more.

And thanks for true poems.

Yours,
John

TO JIM CLARK

Metuchen

March 28, 1986

[JC]

[Jim Clark was on the staff of *The Denver Quarterly* and helped arrange details of a meeting to honor novelist John Williams at the University of Denver on March 29, 1986. Ciardi had been scheduled to speak on Williams' novel *Augustus.*]

Dear Jim Clark:

It is much in my mind that I expected to be on my way to Denver today. To save on air fare I had arranged a visit to Sthrn. Ind. U. and a talk in Topeka. I managed to stumble through my visit to S.I.U. but had to have my lecture agent send a replacement to Topeka and fly home for medical care. I phoned Jeff Lovill in Denver, asking him to contact you, and I am sure he will have done so.

My regrets are nevertheless real and deep. I came up from FL just in time to be laid low by the flu virus. I guess that isn't fatal, but for most of these past weeks it made death seem an easy way out. I am sorry to have failed you, and especially to have failed John Williams who is deep in my love, respect, and admiration (the rat!). I can only add to my apology that I am simply physically unable to function, though I have taken some massive injections and feel that I may become human again in a few more days.

Sincerely,
John Ciardi

Two days later, on Easter Sunday, John Ciardi suffered a heart attack and died at his home in Metuchen, New Jersey.

Correspondents

Listed in alphabetical order.

ABBE, George. Founder of a poetry book club in the mid-1950s. *Page 113.*

ARMSTRONG, James. President of Middlebury College in 1972. *Page 268.*

ASIMOV, Isaac. Writer known primarily for his science fiction; collaborated with JC on two books of limericks. *Page 366.*

BADER, Arno. Professor at the University of Michigan; arranged Hopwood lectures in 1958. *Page 164.*

BAIN, Read. Editor of American Sociological Association's *Review*, 1938–42; poetry editor of the *Humanist*, 1953–57. *Pages 107, 110, and 180.*

BENTON, Thomas Hart. The mid-century American artist. *Page 67.*

BOUCHER, Anthony. Co-editor of *Fantasy and Science Fiction* in 1952. *Page 82.*

BOWEN, Catherine Drinker. Biographer and a regular faculty member at Bread Loaf. *Page 205.*

BRINNIN, John Malcolm. Poet and biographer. *Pages 19, 21, 22, 28, 29, 31, 42, and 45.*

BROWN, Wally. Colleague of JC's at the University of Kansas City immediately after World War II. *Page 75.*

BURNSHAW, Stanley. Poet and critic. *Pages 252, 260, 289, 373, 413, and 415.*

CAPOBIANCO, Michael. Professor of mathematics; preparing a series of teleplays based on JC's translation of *The Divine Comedy. Pages 355, 384, and 385.*

CIARDI, Concetta. JC's mother. *Pages 12, 15, 186, and 188.*

CIFELLI, Edward. Professor and critic. *Page 277.*

CLARK, Grenville. Spokesman for Harvard in 1949 in the communism controversy between JC and Frank B. Ober. *Page 58.*

CLARK, Jim. Had made arrangements for JC to speak at a meeting held in honor of John Williams, March 29, 1986. *Page 459.*

CLEMENTE, Vince. Poet, professor, and critic; editor of *John Ciardi: Measure of the Man* (1987). *Pages 302, 305, 345, 348, 380, 394, 400, 406, 409, 437, 447, and 456.*

CORDRAY, Robert ("Mac"). Pilot of the B-29 on which JC served as aerial gunner on Saipan in 1944–45. *Page 446.*

COUSINS, Norman. Editor of *Saturday Review,* 1940–71 and 1973–77. *Pages 130, 140, 146, 147, 149, 154, 214, 229, 278, and 280.*

COWDEN, Roy W. JC's poetry teacher-coach at the University of Michigan; for many years director of the Hopwood competitions at University of Michigan. *Pages 69, 96, and 104.*

CUBETA, Paul. Assistant director of Bread Loaf under JC, 1956–64. *Pages 134, 136, 138, 139, 187, 189, 197, and 207.*

DECKER, Clarence. President of the University of Kansas City in the 1940s. *Pages 27, 35, 36, 38, 40, 43, 53, 83, and 103.*

DENEEN, William. An executive with *Encyclopaedia Britannica* in 1966. *Page 211.*

DE VRIES, Peter. Novelist; co-editor of *Poetry,* 1942–44. *Page 32.*

DILLON, George. Editor of *Poetry,* 1937–42 and 1946–49. *Page 17.*

DRENNER, Don V. R. Small-press publisher of poetry; former professor at the University of Kansas City where he met JC in 1940. *Page 194.*

EBERHART, Richard. Poet and winner of a Bollingen Prize, Pulitzer Prize, and National Book Award. *Pages 208, 213, and 228.*

EPSTEIN, Stanley. A student with JC at the University of Michigan, 1938–39. *Pages 316 and 424.*

FENNESSEY, Cora. JC's sister. *Pages 12, 15, 403, and 422.*

FITTS, Dudley. Classicist and translator. *Pages 105, 108, 119, 121, 123, 126, and 135.*

GALLAGHER, Gil. New York restaurant manager and member of the Chautauqua opera company. *Pages 365, 393, 403, and 432.*

GARRETT, George. Novelist and poet. *Pages 296, 297, 298, 306, 309, 316, 318, 321, 329, 332, 339, and 341.*

GIOSEFFI, Daniela. Poet who had sent her work to JC for comment and conversation. *Pages 440, 444, 448, and 451.*

GOLDBERG, Max. Professor at the University of Massachusetts and a founder of the College English Association. *Page 78.*

GRAHAM, Matthew. Poet and professor. *Page 458.*

GREGORY, Horace. Bollingen prize-winning poet (1964); also translator, critic, and professor. *Page 158.*

GROSS, Mason. President of Rutgers during JC's tenure there. *Page 183.*

HALL, Donald. Poet and professor; writing student of JC's at Harvard. *Pages 143, 144, 281, 282, and 283.*

HEBALD, Milton. Sculptor in Rome; met the Ciardis when JC was at the American Academy in Rome, 1956–57. Hebald did the illustrations for JC's *An Alphabestiary. Pages 209 and 210.*

HOLMES, Doris. Wife of John Holmes; now Doris Holmes Eyges. *Page 212.*

HOLMES, John. Poet and teacher of poets at Tufts; JC was Holmes' student and friend. *Pages 52, 57, 86, 106, 111, 116, 117, 127, 132, 162, 182, and 192.*

JAFFE, Dan. Poet and professor; writing student of JC's at Rutgers. *Pages 119, 167, 185, 190, 213, 218, 227, 244, 284, 356, 402, and 427.*

JEROME, Judson. Poet and long-time poetry columnist for *Writer's Digest. Pages 141, 154, and 170.*

KACHADOORIAN, Zubel and Irma. Artists; met the Ciardis when JC was at the American Academy in Rome, 1956–57. *Pages 161, 164, 171, 176, and 179.*

KASLE, Gertrude and Leonard. Close friends of the Ciardis. *Page 240.*

KLOMPUS, Irv and Ruth. Neighbors of the Ciardis in Metuchen. Irv had become staff physician at Bread Loaf; in 1969 he and Ruth moved to San Francisco. *Pages 233, 234, 255, 256, 261, 381, and 412.*

KRICKEL, Edward. Professor and critic; wrote *John Ciardi* (1980). *Page 342.*

LAMONT, Corliss. Member of the Emergency Civil Liberties Committee in 1962. *Page 199.*

LOVILL, Jeffry. Wrote a doctoral dissertation on JC (1985). *Pages 347, 360, 371, 382, 405, 410, 416, 423, 424, 428, 429, and 450.*

MCCOMAS, J. Francis. Coeditor of *Fantasy and Science Fiction* in 1952. *Page 81.*

MAIOLO, Joseph. Novelist and professor. *Page 442.*

MARTIN, Edward ("Sandy"). Assistant director of Bread Loaf under JC, 1965–71. *Page 206.*

MAYO, E. L. Poet and professor. Winner of American Book Award, 1982. *Page 92.*

MEREDITH, William. Poet and professor. *Page 259.*

MOORE, Merrill. Boston psychiatrist and Twayne author of *Clinical Sonnets. Pages 71, 72, 74, 79, and 80.*

MUSA, Mark. Studied Dante at Johns Hopkins and later published a translation of *The Divine Comedy. Page 174.*

NEWMAN, Walter. Etymologist who shared information with JC for the third volume of the Browser's Dictionaries, *Good Words to You*, which is dedicated to Newman. *Pages 374, 378, 388, 391, 396, 398, 399, 418, 420, 433, and 452.*

NIMS, John Frederick. Poet and professor; associate editor of *Poetry*, 1942–49, editor 1978–84; on Bread Loaf faculty for ten years. *Pages 45, 122, 159, 160, 275, 291, 301, 310, 311, 319, 349, 364, 436, and 455.*

OBER, Frank B. Baltimore attorney who claimed publicly that JC gave "aid and comfort" to communism. *Page 59.*

ODEN, Gloria. Poet and professor. *Page 165.*

ORENSTEIN, Florence. Wife of M. G. Orenstein. *Pages 184 and 359.*

ORENSTEIN, M. G. ("Bud"). Co-pilot of JC's B-29 crew on Saipan; later in the insurance business in Los Angeles. *Pages 76 and 184.*

PAQUETTE, F. Andre. Served for a short time as director of the language school at Middlebury College. *Page 245.*

PARIZEK, Dean Eldon. Geologist; Dean of the College of Arts and Sciences at University of Missouri-Kansas City 1979–84. *Page 358.*

PRATT, Fletcher. Historian and science fiction writer; regular Bread Loaf faculty member during the 1940s and '50s. *Pages 76 and 87.*

RAGO, Henry. Poet; editor of *Poetry*, 1955–69. *Pages 129 and 133.*

RAMOUS, Osvaldo. Poet of Rijeka, Yugoslavia; wrote in his native Italian and translated a group of Ciardi poems into Italian in 1979. *Pages 324 and 325.*

RANEY, William. Editor-in-chief at Bobbs-Merrill in 1963; also a regular faculty member at Bread Loaf. *Page 200.*

REXROTH, Kenneth. Poet and critic; translator of Chinese and Japanese poetry. *Page 124.*

ROETHKE, Beatrice. Wife of Theodore Roethke. *Page 201.*

ROETHKE, Theodore. Pulitzer prize-winning poet (1954); he also won a Bollingen Prize (1958). *Pages 6, 8, 9, 14, 18, 26, 54, 56, 66, 72, 84, 94, and 163.*

ROSENTHAL, M. L. Poet and critic. *Pages 137, 153, 173, and 178.*

ROSI, Edith. JC's sister. *Pages 12 and 15.*

RUBERO, Ella. JC's sister. *Pages 5, 12, 15, 24, 25, 370, and 439.*

RUKEYSER, Muriel. Mid-century American poet. *Page 55.*

SERGEIEV, Andrei. Translator of modern English and American poetry into Russian. *Page 287.*

SHAPIRO, Karl. Pulitzer prize-winning poet (1945); winner of a Bollingen prize; editor of *Poetry,* 1950–56. *Pages 55, 64, 87, 88, and 95.*

SHEA, Vernon. One of Twayne's authors, working on science fiction anthology projects. *Pages 93 and 94.*

SIMPSON, Louis. Pulitzer prize-winning poet (1964); also novelist, professor, and critic. *Page 124.*

SLOANE, William. Responsible for the publication of several of JC's books of poetry, first at Henry Holt, later at Rutgers University Press; regular on the Bread Loaf faculty from the late 1930s. *Pages 83, 139, 187, and 204.*

SNYDER, Robert and Beatrice. Friends of the Ciardis in Florida. Robert was an oceanographer. *Pages 434 and 439.*

STEINBERG, Jacob. Managing editor of Twayne Publishers in the early 1950s. *Page 79.*

STONE, John. Cardiologist, poet, and essayist; succeeded Irv Klompus as staff physician at Bread Loaf. *Pages 267, 280, 331, 333, 335, 336, 338, 350, 353, 354, 363, and 369.*

STROBEL, Marion. An associate editor of *Poetry,* 1942–49. *Pages 34, 36, 43, 47, 49, and 50.*

SWALLOW, Alan. From 1940–42 he was an instructor at the University of New Mexico; later he became director of the University of Denver Press and then publisher of Swallow Press, which featured the work of contemporary poets. *Page 30.*

SWENSON, Eric. Vice-chairman and senior editor of W.W. Norton. *Pages 294 and 407.*

THOMPSON, Lovell. An executive at Houghton Mifflin in 1958. *Page 168.*

TURCO, Lewis. Poet, professor, and critic. *Pages 314, 315, 317, and 340.*

VIERECK, Peter. Pulitzer prize-winning poet (1949) and professor of history. *Pages 51, 63, and 70.*

WEEKS, Edward. For many years poetry editor of *The Atlantic Monthly. Pages 41 and 44.*

WILBUR, Richard. Pulitzer prize-winning poet (1957 and 1988), translator, and former United States poet laureate; winner of a Bollingen prize and the National Book Award. *Pages 50, 85, 86, 88, 90, 91, 103, and 172.*

WILLIAMS, John. Novelist and poet; National Book Award, 1973; also a regular faculty member at Bread Loaf in the 1960s. *Pages 279 and 328.*

WILLIAMS, Lucy. First wife of Miller Williams. *Page 196.*

WILLIAMS, Miller. Poet, translator, and critic; Bread Loaf faculty member, 1967–72; author of *The Achievement of John Ciardi* (1968). *Pages 191, 193, 195, 202, 203, 220, 221, 222, 223, 224, 226, 228, 230, 231, 232, 233, 236, 238, 239, 242, 243, 244, 247, 249, 250, 251, 252, 253, 257, 262, 263, 265, 266, 267, 276, 284, 285, 291, 293, 294, 300, 307, 308, 313, 320, 323, 344, 348, 352, 366, 390, 421, 426, and 430.*

WILLIAMS, Nancy. Renaissance scholar; married to John Williams. *Page 377.*

WRIGHT, Stuart. Professor, publisher, and book dealer. *Page 358.*

Index